D1394640

The
Classic 1000
Vegetarian
Recipes

The Classic 1000 Vegetarian Recipes

by
Carolyn Humphries

With contributions from:
Jean Conil • Maggie Black
Carole Clement • Sarah Sanderson

foulsham
LONDON • NEW YORK • TORONTO • SYDNEY

foulsham

The Publishing House, Bennetts Close,
Cippenham, Slough, Berks SL1 5AP

ISBN 978-0-572-02808-4

Photographs by Peter Howard Smith

Printed in Great Britain by St Edmundsbury Press Ltd, Bury St Edmunds, Suffolk

Contents

Introduction

Whether you are new to vegetarian cooking or simply fed up with the same old repertoire, *The Classic 1000 Vegetarian Recipes* will fire your enthusiasm. From simple everyday fare to gourmet creations for the most sophisticated of dinner parties, there are recipes for every occasion. You'll find international old favourites such as Ratatouille and Tabbouleh, classic vegetarian like nut roasts and veggie burgers, and many exciting new dishes like Sweet Potato and Walnut Soufflé Pie or Leek and Corn Choux Ring to tempt your taste buds.

There is a range of exciting starters, snacks, soups, desserts, breads, cakes and biscuits and even some extra-special drinks and nibbles to cater for your every need, plus useful tips on making sure you eat a healthy, balanced diet.

With *The Classic 1000 Vegetarian Recipes* in your kitchen, you will never again be at a loss for what to cook and you'll know that everything you DO cook will be tasty, nutritious and simply sensational!

A Healthy Balance

Everyone needs to eat foods from the four main groups every day.

Protein for growth, skin and bone repair. Meat and fish are only two of the main sources: others are pulses (dried peas, beans and lentils), cheese, milk, yoghurt, eggs, nuts and vegetable proteins like quorn and tofu. Eat at least two portions a day. Use soya alternatives to dairy products if you are vegan.

Carbohydrates for energy and as fillers. These are found in cereals, bread, potatoes, pasta and rice. Eat lots every day. They are not fattening – it is only the fat or sugar you put on them that makes you put on weight.

Fats for body warmth and energy. If you do not eat meat and fish you can get most of what you need from milk, cheese, eggs and nuts. Also from vegetable or nut margarines and oils (but eat these sparingly).

Vitamins and Minerals for general health and well-being. Eat lots of fruit and vegetables in any form, even frozen or canned (but preferably without added sugar or salt). Vegans often suffer from a lack of vitamin B_{12}; yeast extract is an excellent source.

Notes on the Recipes

- Many of the recipes use dairy products. Vegans should either omit them or use vegan alternatives such as soya milk products. Make sure cheeses, margarine and yoghurt used are suitable for vegetarians; they are usually clearly marked on the labels.
- Some recipes use processed foods such as bread, canned soup, biscuits, baked beans, crisps, frozen pastry (paste) and stuffing mix. You should check the product labels to be certain of their suitability for vegetarians.
- A number of recipes use Worcestershire sauce, which traditionally includes anchovies, so buy a vegetarian variety from a health food shop.
- Quorn is a relatively new vegetable protein which is not approved by the Vegetarian Society because egg albumin from battery hens is used in its manufacture. You can substitute soya mince or chunks instead, if you prefer.
- Some recipes call for vegetarian gelatine. A powdered form called *Vege Gel* is available from supermarkets. Some other types may need to be dissolved differently from in the recipes. Check the packet directions.
- When following a recipe, use either metric, imperial or American measures, never a combination.
- All spoon measures are level: 1 tsp = 5 ml; 1 tbsp = 15 ml.
- Eggs are medium unless otherwise stated.
- Use your favourite good-quality light oil, like sunflower or groundnut (peanut) oil, unless otherwise stated.
- All preparation and cooking times are approximate and should be used as a guide only.
- Always wash and peel, if necessary, fresh produce before use.

- Where fresh herbs are used, they are specified in the ingredients. You can substitute dried herbs as long as they have time to cook; never use them for sprinkling on finished dishes. If you use dried rather than fresh herbs, use only half the stated quantity as they are very pungent. Packets of frozen chopped herbs such as parsley and mint are much better than the dried varieties.
- Always preheat the oven and cook on the centre shelf unless otherwise stated.
- Many recipes call for dried beans or pulses (see page 10 for cooking hints). Alternatively substitute a 425–430 g/15–15½ oz large can for every 100 g/4 oz/⅔ cup dried beans.

Cooking Pulses

- It is important to soak all pulses, except red lentils, for several hours or preferably overnight before cooking. To speed up this process, use boiling water and leave for two hours.

- When soaked, drain and place in a large saucepan of cold water. Do not add salt as this will toughen the skins. Bring the water to the boil and boil rapidly for 10 minutes. This is essential to destroy any toxins in the beans. Then reduce the heat and simmer until tender (this can be anything from 1 to 3 hours depending on the variety). Drain and use as required.

- To save fuel, cook more than you require for a recipe, then cool and store the remainder in the fridge for several days, or freeze for future use.

Soups

Some of the following are light enough for starters before a not-too-substantial main course. But many are hearty, and nutritious enough for a complete meal if served with lots of crusty bread.

Soup is a great way to get all the family – especially fussy children – to eat lots of vegetables. Purée the whole thing in a blender or food processor if lumps are not popular in your household.

Another wonderful thing about soup is that no quantities are set in stone; sling in the odd extra root vegetable if you have it, or omit the onion if you'd rather. Always taste the soup and add more seasoning if necessary before serving.

Cheese and Vegetable Soup

50 g/2 oz/¼ cup butter or margarine
1 onion, chopped
30 ml/2 tbsp finely chopped celery
25 g/1 oz/¼ cup wholemeal flour
5 ml/1 tsp made mustard
600 ml/1 pt/2½ cups milk
150 ml/¼ pt/⅔ cup vegetable stock
Salt and freshly ground black pepper
100 g/4 oz/1 cup Cheddar cheese,
  grated
100 g/4 oz finely chopped raw
  mushrooms (optional)
A little cooked sweetcorn (corn),
  peas, etc. (optional)
Chopped parsley

Melt the butter or margarine in a pan. Add the onion and celery and fry (sauté) for 3 minutes, stirring. Add the flour and mustard and cook for 1 minute. Gradually blend in the milk and vegetable stock and bring to the boil, stirring. Reduce the heat, cover and continue cooking for 10 minutes, stirring occasionally. Season and add the cheese and any other ingredients you wish at this point. Cover and simmer for a further 5 minutes. Pour into warmed bowls and garnish with parsley.

Note: To turn this into a fun main meal for the family, serve each bowl of soup with a side plate containing a selection of crudités to dip and dunk in, e.g. carrot sticks, celery sticks, tomato quarters, raw mushrooms, cauliflower florets, cheese sticks, chunks of fresh bread, etc.

Stilton and Vegetable Soup

Prepare as for Cheese and Vegetable Soup but use crumbled Stilton in place of the Cheddar cheese.

Cheese and Barley Soup

1 onion, coarsely grated
3 carrots, coarsely grated
1 parsnip, coarsely grated
4 celery sticks, grated
40 g/1½ oz/3 tbsp butter or margarine
1.2 litres/2 pts/5 cups vegetable stock
100 g/4 oz/good ½ cup pearl barley
5 ml/1 tsp dried oregano
Salt and freshly ground black pepper
175 g/6 oz/1½ cups Cheddar cheese,
  grated
300 ml/½ pt/1¼ cups milk
Snipped chives

In a large saucepan, fry (sauté) the prepared vegetables in the butter or margarine, stirring for 2 minutes. Add the stock, barley, oregano and a little salt and pepper. Bring to the boil, reduce the heat, part cover and simmer gently for 1 hour or until the barley is tender. Stir in the cheese and milk and reheat but do not boil. Taste and add more seasoning if necessary. Ladle into warm bowls and garnish with a few snipped chives.

Peasant Cabbage Soup

40 g/1½ oz/3 tbsp butter or margarine
1 large onion, finely chopped
1 large carrot, finely chopped
1 large potato, finely chopped
¼ green cabbage, finely shredded
1 red (bell) pepper, finely chopped
4 tomatoes, chopped
425 g/15 oz/1 large can haricot
  (navy) beans, drained
1 litre/1¾ pts/4¼ cups vegetable stock
1 bay leaf
Salt and freshly ground black pepper

Melt the butter or margarine in a large saucepan. Add the onion, carrot and potato and fry (sauté), stirring, for 2 minutes. Add the remaining ingredients, bring to the boil, reduce the heat and cover. Simmer gently for 30 minutes. Discard the bay leaf and serve.

French Onion Soup with Garlic and Herb Toasts

40 g/1½ oz/3 tbsp butter or margarine
4 large onions, roughly chopped
10 ml/2 tsp light brown sugar
1 litre/1¾ pts/4¼ cups vegetable stock
15 ml/1 tbsp cornflour (cornstarch)
15 ml/1 tbsp water
Salt and freshly ground black pepper
4 slices French bread
50 g/2 oz/¼ cup soft cheese with
  garlic and herbs

Heat the butter or margarine in a large saucepan. Add the onions and fry (sauté), stirring, for 5 minutes. Sprinkle on the sugar and continue frying, stirring all the time, for a further 10 minutes until a rich golden brown. Add the stock, bring to the boil, reduce the heat, cover and simmer for 15 minutes. Blend the cornflour with the water and stir into the soup. Simmer for 2 minutes, stirring. Season to taste. Meanwhile, toast the French bread and spread one side of each slice with the garlic and herb cheese. Grill (broil) until melting and bubbling. Ladle the soup into warm bowls. Float a slice of cheesy bread on top of each and serve straight away.

Ribsticker

450 g/1 lb/2⅔ cups split peas, soaked
  for several hours and drained
1 large onion, chopped
1 carrot, chopped
2 celery sticks, chopped
1 large potato, diced
¼ small swede (rutabaga), diced
1 bouquet garni sachet
2.25 litres/4 pts/10 cups water
2 vegetable stock cubes
Salt and freshly ground black pepper
150 ml/¼ pt/⅔ cup milk or single
  (light) cream

Put the peas in a large heavy-based
saucepan with the prepared vegetables, the bouquet garni and the water.
Bring to the boil, reduce the heat, part
cover and simmer gently for about 30
minutes or until all the vegetables are
tender. Discard the bouquet garni, then
purée the soup in a blender or food
processor, adding the stock cubes.
Return to the saucepan and season to
taste. Stir in the milk or cream and heat
through before serving.

Austrian Red Pepper Soup

2 onions, thinly sliced
2 red (bell) peppers, thinly sliced
30 ml/2 tbsp sunflower oil
400 g/14 oz/1 large can chopped
  tomatoes
100 g/4 oz/1 cup sauerkraut, drained
450 ml/¾ pt/2 cups vegetable stock
10 ml/2 tsp paprika
Salt and freshly ground black pepper
60 ml/4 tbsp soured (dairy sour)
  cream
Snipped chives

Fry (sauté) the onions and peppers in
the oil for 3 minutes, stirring until
softened but not browned. Add the
remaining ingredients except the cream
and chives. Bring to the boil, reduce the
heat and simmer gently for about 15 minutes until the vegetables are tender.
Taste and re-season if necessary. Ladle
into warm bowls and garnish each with a
spoonful of soured cream and a sprinkling
of chives.

Welsh Soup

100 g/4 oz/⅔ cup red lentils
1.2 litres/2 pts/5 cups water
2 leeks, chopped
4 potatoes, chopped
3 carrots, chopped
1 parsnip, chopped
2 small turnips, chopped
1 small swede (rutabaga), chopped
1 vegetable stock cube
Salt and freshly ground black pepper

Place the lentils in a pan with the water. Bring to the boil, then skim off any scum. Add the prepared vegetables and stock cube, return to the boil, then simmer for about 20 minutes until the soup is thick and the vegetables are soft. Season to taste. Leave chunky or purée in a blender or food processor.

Note: The quantities of the ingredients are totally negotiable. The amounts given are just to give you a rough idea; put in as little or as much as you like.

Kettle Broth

2 onions, finely chopped
1 leek, chopped
25 g/1 oz/2 tbsp butter or margarine
2 slices wholemeal bread, crusts
*   removed*
15 ml/1 tbsp snipped chives
900 ml/1½ pts/3¾ cups vegetable
*   stock*
Salt and freshly ground black pepper
Milk
4 marigold or chive flowers

In a saucepan, fry (sauté) the onions and leek gently in the butter or margarine for about 5 minutes until soft but not brown, stirring all the time. Tear the bread into pieces and add to the pan with the chives and stock. Season lightly, cover and simmer gently for 30 minutes. Purée in a blender or food processor, then return to the rinsed-out pan. Add enough milk to form a creamy consistency. Taste and re-season if necessary. Ladle into bowls and float a marigold or chive flower on each.

Noodle Soup

1.75 litres/3 pts/7½ cups vegetable
  stock
Salt
5 ml/1 tsp lemon grass, chopped
5 ml/1 tsp soy sauce
175 g/6 oz vermicelli

Bring the stock to the boil with the salt, lemon grass and soy sauce. Break the vermicelli into small pieces and add to the pan. Simmer for 5 minutes until just tender. Check and adjust the seasoning if necessary.

Chinese Vegetable Soup

SERVES 4

15 ml/1 tbsp oil
2 spring onions (scallions),
  diagonally sliced
50 g/2 oz French (green) beans, cut
  into short lengths
1 carrot, cut into short matchsticks
8 baby corn cobs, cut into 2 or 3
  pieces
25 g/1 oz button mushrooms, sliced
½ green chilli, seeded and chopped
  (optional)
750 ml/1¼ pts/3 cups vegetable stock
10 ml/2 tsp light soy sauce
10 ml/2 tsp sherry

Heat the oil in a wok or large saucepan. Add the prepared vegetables and stir-fry for 3 minutes. Add the remaining ingredients and simmer for 2 minutes. Serve straight away.

Spiced Carrot Soup

SERVES 4

750 g/1½ lb carrots, sliced
750 ml/1¼ pts/3 cups vegetable stock
2.5 ml/½ tsp ground cumin
2.5 ml/½ tsp ground coriander
  (cilantro)
Salt and freshly ground black pepper
A little milk
Chopped coriander

Cook the carrots in the stock for about 15 minutes until soft. Drain, reserving the stock, and mash, then return to the stock and add the seasonings; alternatively, liquidize in a blender or food processor and return to the pan. Bring to the boil, then simmer gently for 2 minutes. Thin with a little milk if necessary. Ladle into warm bowls and sprinkle with chopped coriander.

Spiced Parsnip Soup

SERVES 4

Prepare as for Spiced Carrot Soup but substitute parsnips for the carrots and add a good pinch of curry powder in addition to the other spices.

Bean and Parsnip Soup

SERVES 4

25 g/1 oz/2 tbsp butter or margarine
450 g/1 lb green beans, chopped
2 large onions, chopped
2 parsnips, chopped
900 ml/1½ pts/3¾ cups vegetable
  stock
½ bay leaf
Salt and freshly ground black pepper
Croûtons (see Milk Soup with
  Croûtons, page 22)

Melt the butter or margarine in a saucepan. Add the prepared vegetables and fry (sauté), stirring, for 2 minutes. Stir in the stock and bay leaf. Bring to the boil, reduce the heat, cover and simmer gently for about 30 minutes until the vegetables are really tender. Discard the bay leaf. Purée the soup in a blender or food processor, then pass through a sieve (strainer) to remove any 'strings' from the beans. Return to the saucepan and season to taste. Reheat, ladle into warm bowls and garnish with croûtons.

Chestnut and Carrot Soup

SERVES 4

15 ml/1 tbsp sunflower oil
1 onion, chopped
225 g/8 oz carrots, chopped
350 g/12 oz/1 large can unsweetened
  chestnut purée
450 ml/¾ pt/2 cups vegetable stock
5 ml/1 tsp ground bay leaves (or 1
  whole one)
400 g/14 oz/1 large can tomatoes
30 ml/2 tbsp tomato purée (paste)
Salt and freshly ground black pepper
5 ml/1 tsp Worcestershire sauce
Chopped parsley

Heat the oil and fry (sauté) the onion and carrot in a large pan for 3 minutes, stirring. Add the remaining ingredients except the parsley, cover and simmer for 10–15 minutes until the vegetables are soft. Remove the bay leaf, if whole, and purée the soup in a blender or food processor, or pass through a sieve (strainer). Reheat if necessary. Garnish with chopped parsley and serve.

Hallowe'en Special

SERVES 4

25 g/1 oz/2 tbsp butter or margarine
750 g/1½ lb pumpkin, diced
600 ml/1 pt/2½ cups vegetable stock
600 ml/1 pt/2½ cups milk
Salt and freshly ground black pepper
15 ml/1 tbsp granulated sugar
Grated nutmeg
30 ml/2 tbsp snipped chives

Melt the butter or margarine in a saucepan. Add the pumpkin and cook gently, stirring, for 2 minutes. Add the stock, bring to the boil, reduce the heat and simmer for 15–20 minutes or until the pumpkin is tender. Purée in a blender or food processor. Return to the saucepan. Stir in the milk, a little salt and pepper, the sugar and nutmeg to taste. Reheat but do not boil. Ladle into warm bowls and serve garnished with the chives.

Peanut and Pumpkin Soup

SERVES 4

45 ml/3 tbsp peanut (groundnut) oil
1 onion, chopped
1 carrot, diced
1 small green chilli, seeded and
   chopped
1 celery stick, diced
225 g/8 oz pumpkin, cubed
100 g/4 oz/1 cup toasted peanuts
600 ml/1 pt/2½ cups water
15 ml/1 tbsp tomato purée (paste)
1 vegetable stock cube
150 ml/¼ pt/⅔ cup dry Madeira
Salt and freshly ground black pepper
Grated nutmeg

Heat the oil in a saucepan and stir-fry all the vegetables and the peanuts for 4 minutes. Add the water, tomato purée and stock cube. Boil for 8 minutes. Purée in a blender or food processor. Add the Madeira. Reheat. Season to taste. Ladle into warm soup bowls and sprinkle with grated nutmeg.

Creamy Artichoke Soup

SERVES 4–6

1 large onion, chopped
50 g/2 oz/¼ cup butter or margarine
450 g/1 lb Jerusalem artichokes,
   scraped and diced
1.2 litres/2 pts/5 cups vegetable stock
1 large parsley sprig
Salt and freshly ground white pepper
60 ml/4 tbsp double (heavy) cream
15 ml/1 tbsp toasted flaked almonds

Fry (sauté) the onion in the butter, stirring, for 2 minutes. Add the artichokes and cook, stirring, for a further 2 minutes. Add the stock, parsley sprig and a little salt and pepper and bring to the boil. Reduce the heat, cover and simmer gently for 30 minutes or until the artichokes are really soft. Discard the parsley sprig. Purée the soup in a blender or food processor. Return to the pan and stir in the cream. Taste and re-season if necessary. Reheat but do not boil. Ladle into warm bowls and sprinkle with toasted almonds before serving.

Boozey Bortsch

SERVES 4

2 celery sticks, grated
2 carrots, grated
1 small onion, grated
350 g/12 oz cooked beetroot (red
   beets), grated
750 ml/1¼ pts/3 cups vegetable stock
150 ml/¼ pt/⅔ cup red wine
Salt and freshly ground black pepper
60 ml/4 tbsp soured (dairy sour)
   cream
10 ml/2 tsp caraway seeds

Put the vegetables in a pan with the stock and wine. Season lightly. Bring to the boil, reduce the heat, cover and simmer gently for 20 minutes or until the vegetables are really tender. Taste and re-season if necessary. Ladle into warm bowls. Add a spoonful of the soured cream to each and sprinkle with the caraway seeds.

Rosy Corn Chowder

SERVES 4

1 large potato, diced
1 onion, sliced
50 g/2 oz/¼ cup butter or margarine
200 g/7 oz/1 small can chopped
  tomatoes
300 g/11 oz/1 large can creamed-style
  sweetcorn (corn)
150 ml/¼ pt/⅔ cup passata (sieved
  tomatoes)
150 ml/¼ pt/⅔ cup vegetable stock
Salt and freshly ground black pepper
2.5 ml/½ tsp dried basil
15 ml/1 tbsp chopped parsley
Grated Cheddar cheese

Fry (sauté) the potato and onion in the butter for 2 minutes, stirring. Reduce the heat, cover and cook gently for 5 minutes, stirring occasionally, until the vegetables are almost tender. Add the remaining ingredients except the parsley and cheese. Bring to the boil, reduce the heat and simmer gently for 20 minutes. Taste and re-season if necessary. Ladle into warm bowls and sprinkle with chopped parsley. Serve with grated cheese.

Potato and Corn Chowder

SERVES 4

1 bunch of spring onions (scallions)
  chopped
2 potatoes, diced
25 g/1 oz/2 tbsp butter or margarine
30 ml/2 tbsp plain (all-purpose) flour
600 ml/1 pt/2½ cups vegetable stock
60 ml/4 tbsp dried milk powder (non-
  fat dry milk)
200 g/7 oz/1 small can sweetcorn
  (corn)
100 g/4 oz/1 cup Cheddar cheese,
  grated
Salt and freshly ground black pepper
A little chopped parsley

Fry (sauté) the spring onions and potatoes gently in the butter or margarine, stirring, for 4 minutes without browning. Blend in the flour and cook for 1 minute. Gradually blend in the stock and milk powder and bring to the boil. Reduce the heat, cover and simmer for 10 minutes. Stir in the contents of the can of corn and the cheese. Heat through and season to taste. Ladle into warm bowls and sprinkle with a little parsley before serving.

Scratch 'n' Scrape Soup

SERVES 4

75 g/3 oz/¾ cup millet
750 ml/1¼ pts/3 cups vegetable stock
2 small leeks, sliced
1 large carrot, sliced
1 small parsnip, sliced
75 ml/5 tbsp single (light) cream
Grated nutmeg
Salt and freshly ground black pepper
Chopped parsley

Pour boiling water over the millet in a sieve (strainer). Drain well, then place in a saucepan with the stock and prepared vegetables. Bring to the boil, reduce the heat, cover and simmer gently for about 25 minutes or until the millet and vegetables are tender. Purée in a blender or food processor. Return to the saucepan and stir in the cream. Season with nutmeg, salt and pepper to taste. Reheat but do not boil. Ladle into warm bowls and sprinkle with chopped parsley before serving.

Simple Sweetcorn Soup

SERVES 4

5 ml/1 tsp oil
1 onion, chopped
450 g/1 lb potatoes, sliced
350 g/12 oz/1 large can sweetcorn (corn)
900 ml/1½ pts/3¾ cups vegetable stock
Salt and freshly ground black pepper

Heat the oil and fry (sauté) the onion for 3 minutes. Add the remaining ingredients. Bring to the boil, then simmer for 30 minutes. Blend, mash or leave lumpy. Reheat if necessary and serve hot.

Sweetcorn and Roots Soup

SERVES 4

Prepare as for Simple Sweetcorn Soup but use only 225 g/8 oz potatoes and add 2 sliced carrots and 1 sliced turnip.

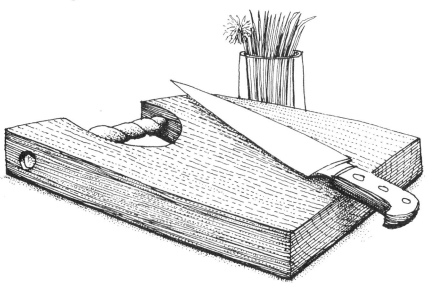

Chinese Leaf Chowder

SERVES 4

375 g/13 oz Chinese leaves (stem
lettuce)
300 ml/½ pt/1¼ cups vegetable stock
2 onions, finely chopped
3 tomatoes, finely chopped
50 g/2 oz/½ cup salted peanuts,
crushed
15 ml/1 tbsp smooth peanut butter
Freshly ground white pepper
Pinch of chilli powder

Shred the Chinese leaves very finely, especially any stems. Put the stock in a large saucepan and pack in the leaves. Cover tightly. Bring to the boil and cook for 3 minutes. Remove from the heat, uncover the pan and stir in the remaining ingredients except the pepper and chilli powder. Cover and cook over a gentle heat for 5 minutes or until the onions are tender. Season with pepper and chilli powder to taste. Serve very hot.

Spinach Chowder

SERVES 4

Prepare as for Chinese Leaf Chowder but substitute young spinach leaves for the Chinese leaves.

Spring Green Chowder

SERVES 4

Prepare as for Chinese Leaf Chowder but substitute spring greens (spring cabbage) for the Chinese leaves.

Worzel Flower Soup

SERVES 4

1 cauliflower, cut into florets
1 swede (rutabaga), diced
1 onion, sliced
1.2 litres/2 pts/5 cups vegetable stock
Salt and freshly ground black pepper
15 ml/1 tbsp tomato purée (paste)
15 ml/1 tbsp chopped thyme

Place the vegetables and stock in a saucepan, bring to the boil then simmer for at least 1 hour until the vegetables are really soft. Season with salt and pepper. Add the tomato purée and thyme. Leave lumpy or purée in a blender or food processor.

Creamy Worzel Flower Soup

SERVES 4

Prepare as for Worzel Flower Soup but add 1 large diced potato with the vegetables. When cooked, stir in 150 ml/¼ pt/⅔ cup double (heavy) cream.

Beer Soup with Sweet Onion

SERVES 4

15 ml/1 tbsp walnut oil
1 large red onion, chopped
300 ml/½ pt/1¼ cups flat brown beer
300 ml/½ pt/1¼ cups water
Salt and freshly ground black pepper
5 ml/1 tsp sugar
Pinch of grated nutmeg
4 French bread sippets
60 ml/4 tbsp Cheddar cheese, grated

Heat the oil in a saucepan and gently fry (sauté) the onion until golden. Add the beer and water, then boil for 10 minutes. Season to taste and add the sugar and nutmeg. Place in four flameproof bowls and top with the bread sippets and grated cheese. Brown under the grill (broiler) until the cheese has melted.
Note: Sippets are slices of French bread baked in the oven.

Milk Soup with Croûtons

SERVES 4

1 slice wholemeal bread, cubed
Butter or margarine, for frying
300 ml/½ pt/1¼ cups milk
Salt
1 egg, beaten
5 ml/1 tsp curry powder
Freshly ground white pepper
Pinch of dried basil

Fry (sauté) the bread in a little butter or margarine until crisp to make the croûtons. Heat the milk with a pinch of salt. Slowly add the egg and curry powder. Stir and heat until thickened, without allowing the soup to boil. Season with salt, pepper and basil. Ladle into warm bowls. Serve sprinkled with croûtons.

Garlic Soup of Provence

SERVES 4

45 ml/3 tbsp olive oil
12 garlic cloves, peeled
225 g/8 oz potatoes, diced
600 ml/1 pt/2½ cups water
2 egg yolks
15 ml/1 tbsp cornflour (cornstarch)
150 ml/¼ pt/⅔ cup milk
Salt and freshly ground black pepper
Coriander (cilantro) leaves

Heat the oil in a saucepan and stir-fry the garlic without browning for 30 seconds. Add the potatoes and water. Boil for 8 minutes until the potatoes are tender. Pass through a sieve (strainer) or purée in a blender or food processor. Reheat the purée. In a bowl, whisk the egg yolks and cornflour blended with the cold milk. Pour in a cup of the warm soup and stir well. Add this mixture to the remaining soup. Simmer for 4 minutes, stirring continually. Season to taste. Ladle into warm bowls and sprinkle with coriander leaves.

Verdant Watercress Soup

25 g/1 oz/2 tbsp butter or margarine
2 bunches of watercress, roughly
chopped
1 onion, chopped
1 potato, chopped
2.5 ml/½ tsp celery seeds
450 ml/¾ pt/2 cups milk
300 ml/½ pt/1¼ cups vegetable stock
Salt and freshly ground black pepper
Crème fraîche, to garnish

Melt the butter or margarine in a large saucepan. Add the watercress, onion, potato and celery seeds and fry (sauté) gently, stirring, for 5 minutes. Add the milk and stock and season to taste. Bring to the boil, reduce the heat and simmer for 10–15 minutes, until the vegetables are soft. Cool slightly, then purée in a food processor or blender or pass through a sieve (strainer). Reheat. Taste and re-season if necessary. Ladle into bowls. Add a swirl of crème fraîche to garnish.

Cream of Watercress Soup

Prepare as for Verdant Watercress Soup but use only 300 ml/½ pt/ 1¼ cups milk. Add 150 ml/¼ pt/⅔ cup double (heavy) cream after puréeing.

Cream of Parsley Soup

1 onion, finely chopped
25 g/1 oz/2 tbsp butter or margarine
1 large bunch of parsley, finely
chopped
25 g/1 oz/¼ cup plain (all-purpose)
flour
750 ml/1¼ pts/3 cups vegetable stock
150 ml/¼ pt/⅔ cup milk
150 ml/¼ pt/⅔ cup single (light)
cream
Salt and freshly ground black pepper

Fry (sauté) the onion in the butter or margarine for 2 minutes, stirring, until soft but not brown. Add the parsley and flour and cook, stirring, for 1 minute. Remove from the heat and blend in the stock and milk. Bring to the boil, reduce the heat and simmer for 15 minutes, stirring occasionally. Stir in the cream and season to taste. Reheat but do not boil. Serve straight away.

Note: For a smooth soup, roughly chop the onion and parsley. Cook as above, then purée in a blender or food processor. Return to the saucepan and add the cream and seasoning.

Avocado Smoothie

1 large onion, finely chopped
1 garlic clove, crushed
50 g/2 oz/¼ cup unsalted (sweet)
  butter
40 g/1½ oz/⅓ cup plain (all-purpose)
  flour
900 ml/1½ pts/3¾ cups vegetable
  stock
2 ripe avocados
Grated rind and juice of 1 small
  lemon
5 ml/1 tsp chopped coriander
  (cilantro)
1.5 ml/¼ tsp ground cumin
150 ml/¼ pt/⅔ cup single (light)
  cream
Salt and freshly ground black pepper

Fry (sauté) the onion and garlic in the butter for 4 minutes until golden and soft. Stir in the flour and cook for 2 minutes, stirring. Add the stock, bring to the boil and simmer for 2 minutes, stirring all the time. Halve and stone (pit) the avocados. Scoop the flesh into a blender or food processor. Add the lemon rind and juice, the coriander and cumin. Run the machine until smooth, then gradually add the thickened stock mixture, running the machine all the time. (If your processor won't take all the mixture, pour some into a clean sauce-pan, then purée the remainder and add to the saucepan.) Stir in most of the cream and season to taste. Heat through but do not boil. Serve immediately, ladled into soup bowls with a swirl of the remaining cream on top of each.

Mushroom and Basil Soup

25 g/1 oz/2 tbsp butter or margarine
1 onion, chopped
225 g/8 oz button mushrooms,
  quartered
15 ml/1 tbsp wholemeal flour
2.5 ml/½ tsp ground mace
600 ml/1 pt/2½ cups vegetable stock
150 ml/¼ pt/⅔ cup milk
Salt and freshly ground black pepper
2.5 ml/½ tsp dried basil
Chopped parsley
A few sliced raw mushrooms
  (optional)
6 ml/4 tbsp crème fraîche (optional)

Melt the margarine in a pan and fry (sauté) the onion for 3 minutes, stirring. Add the mushrooms and continue cooking for 1 minute, stirring. Add the flour and mace and cook for a further minute. Gradually stir in the stock and milk and bring to the boil, stirring. Cover, reduce the heat and simmer for 10 minutes, stirring occasionally. Season to taste and stir in the basil. Purée in a blender or food processor if liked. Reheat and serve in warmed bowls sprinkled with chopped parsley. Add a few sliced raw mushrooms or a spoonful of crème fraîche with the parsley, if liked.

All-year Tomato Soup

SERVES 4

25 g/1 oz/2 tbsp butter or margarine
1 onion, chopped
1 celery stick, finely chopped
400 g/14 oz/1 large can tomatoes
30 ml/2 tbsp wholemeal flour
600 ml/1 pt/2½ cups vegetable stock
5 ml/1 tsp chopped basil
Salt and freshly ground black pepper
20 ml/4 tsp tomato purée (paste)
5 ml/1 tsp Worcestershire sauce
150 ml/¼ pt/⅔ cup milk
Chopped parsley

Melt the butter or margarine in a large pan. Add the onion and fry (sauté) for 3 minutes, stirring. Add the celery and cook for 2 minutes, stirring. Add the remaining ingredients except the parsley and cover. Bring to the boil, reduce the heat and simmer for 10 minutes or until the vegetables are soft. Cool slightly, then purée in a food processor or blender or pass through a sieve (strainer). Reheat, taste and re-season if necessary. Ladle into warm soup bowls and sprinkle with chopped parsley before serving.

Curried Apple and Sultana Soup

SERVES 4

25 g/1 oz/2 tbsp butter or margarine
1 onion, finely chopped
40 g/1½ oz/⅓ cup plain (all-purpose)
flour
15 ml/1 tbsp curry paste
900 ml/1½ pts/3¾ cups vegetable
stock
750 g/1½ lb cooking (tart) apples,
sliced
15 ml/1 tbsp lemon juice
50 g/2 oz/⅓ cup sultanas (golden
raisins)
Salt and freshly ground black pepper
60 ml/4 tbsp crème fraîche

Melt the butter or margarine in a saucepan. Add the onion and fry (sauté) for 3 minutes, stirring. Add the flour and curry paste and cook, stirring, for 1 minute. Stir in the stock, apples and lemon juice. Bring to the boil, stirring all the time. Reduce the heat, cover and simmer gently for 10 minutes until the apples are really tender. Purée in a blender or food processor. Return to the saucepan and stir in the sultanas. Simmer for a further 4–5 minutes. Season to taste. Ladle into warm bowls and top each with a swirl of crème fraîche.

Apple and Cider Soup

600 ml/1 pt/2½ cups water
75 g/3 oz/⅓ cup granulated sugar
Good pinch of salt
1.5 kg/3 lb cooking (tart) apples,
*   chopped*
50 g/2 oz/1 cup white breadcrumbs
5 cm/2 in piece cinnamon stick
Thinly pared rind and juice of 1
*   large lemon*
450 ml/¾ pt/2 cups strong, dry cider
45 ml/3 tbsp apple jelly (clear
*   conserve)*
Plain yoghurt

Put the water in a saucepan with the sugar and salt. Heat until the sugar has dissolved. Add the apples, breadcrumbs, cinnamon, lemon rind and juice. Bring to the boil, reduce the heat and simmer gently for 10 minutes or until the apples are really tender. Discard the cinnamon stick and lemon rind. Purée in a blender or food processor and return to the pan. Stir in the cider and apple jelly and heat, stirring, until the jelly dissolves. Ladle into warm bowls and garnish each with a swirl of plain yoghurt before serving.

Apple and Beetroot Wine Soup

45 ml/3 tbsp walnut or sunflower oil
1 small onion, chopped
1 small carrot, chopped
2 small cooked beetroot (red beets),
*   chopped*
1 fennel stalk, chopped
600 ml/1 pt/2½ cups vegetable stock
1 cooked beetroot, cut into
*   matchsticks*
2 apples, cut into matchsticks
150 ml/¼ pt/⅔ cup red wine
Salt and freshly ground black pepper
5 ml/1 tsp sugar (optional)
Hard-boiled (hard-cooked) eggs
Brown bread

Heat the oil in a saucepan and stir-fry the chopped vegetables until lightly browned. Pour in the stock. Boil for 8 minutes. Meanwhile, marinate the beetroot and apple strips in the wine for 8 minutes. When the soup is ready, add the beetroot and wine mixture to the hot soup. Simmer for 4 minutes. Season to taste, adding a little sugar if liked. Serve with hard-boiled eggs, cut into wedges, and brown bread.

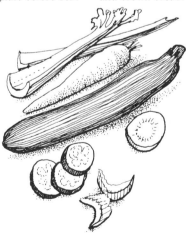

Raisin Soup with Yoghurt

SERVES 4

100 g/4 oz seedless (pitless) grapes
50 g/2 oz/⅓ cup raisins
300 ml/½ pt/1¼ cups water
150 ml/¼ pt/⅔ cup dry white wine
1 small carton plain yoghurt
5 ml/1 tsp sugar
1.5 ml/¼ tsp ground cinnamon
Cream crackers, to serve

Combine all the ingredients in a blender or food processor and purée. Serve chilled with cream crackers.

Soft Fruit Soup

SERVES 4

450 g/1 lb soft fruit such as raspberries, strawberries, blackcurrants
100 g/4 oz/⅓ cup sugar
900 ml/1½ pts/3¾ cups milk

Put the fruit in a pan and heat gently until soft. Mash, then whisk in the sugar. Rub through a sieve (strainer) to remove any pips, if you wish. Bring the milk to the boil, then allow it to cool before slowly stirring into the fruit. Chill before serving.

Lemon and Egg Soup

SERVES 4

30 ml/2 tbsp olive oil
1 small onion, chopped
1 carrot, chopped
1 celery stick, chopped
600 ml/1 pt/2½ cups vegetable stock
15 ml/1 tbsp cornflour (cornstarch)
45 ml/3 tbsp water
Grated rind and juice of 2 lemons
3 egg yolks
Salt, freshly ground black pepper and sugar
15 ml/1 tbsp lemon grass or coriander (cilantro), chopped

Heat the oil in a saucepan and stir-fry the vegetables without browning for 3 minutes. Add the stock and boil for 8 minutes. Purée in a blender or food processor. Reheat the soup to boiling point. Blend the cornflour with the water in a bowl, then whisk in the lemon rind and juice and the egg yolks. Pour approximately 2 ladlefuls of the hot soup into this mixture, stirring gently, then add the blended lemon mixture to the remaining soup. Bring to the boil and simmer for 4 minutes. Season to taste, ladle into warm bowls and sprinkle with lemon grass or coriander.

Chilled Tomato Soup

400 g/14 oz/1 large can chopped
*   tomatoes*
15 ml/1 tbsp red wine vinegar
15 ml/1 tbsp olive oil
45 ml/3 tbsp crème fraîche
2.5 ml/½ tsp made mustard
5 ml/1 tsp dried basil
Salt and freshly ground black pepper

Rub the tomatoes through a sieve (strainer). Add all the remaining ingredients and mix well. Season to taste and chill before serving.

Avocado and Tomato Soup

1 ripe avocado
2 tomatoes, skinned, seeded and
*   chopped*
15 ml/1 tbsp clear honey
Juice of 1 orange
Juice of 1 lemon
300 ml/½ pt/1¼ cups water or dry
*   white wine*

Halve and stone (pit) the avocado and scoop out the pulp. Place in a blender or food processor with the tomato pulp, honey, orange juice, lemon juice and water or wine. Blend the mixture to a purée. Serve chilled.

Guacamole Soup

Prepare as for Avocado and Tomato Soup but add a chopped red (bell) pepper when blending, a good pinch of chilli powder, ½ crushed garlic clove and a dash of Worcestershire sauce.

Mexican Gazpacho with Chilli

1 red (bell) pepper, seeded and
*   chopped*
2 tomatoes, skinned, seeded and
*   chopped*
½ cucumber, sliced but unpeeled
1 garlic clove
1 small red onion, chopped
1 green chilli, seeded and chopped
4 slices stale bread
300 ml/½ pt/1¼ cups water
45 ml/3 tbsp wine vinegar
30 ml/2 tbsp olive oil
5 ml/1 tsp sugar
10 ml/2 tsp salt
Croûtons

Place all the ingredients except the croûtons in a 2 litre/3½ pt/8½ cup earthenware container with a lid. Leave to marinate for two days in the fridge. During this time the mixture will ferment slightly and mature. The soup can be kept in the fridge for one week. Blend to a purée and chill. Serve cold with a garnish of fried croûtons.

Spanish Gazpacho

Prepare as for Mexican Gazpacho but omit the chilli and use only half an onion.

Starters

All the recipes in this section make delicious first courses for just about any occasion. Many make mouthwatering light lunches or suppers too – served in slightly larger portions.

When choosing a suitable appetiser, make sure it will complement the rest of the meal. For instance, choose something light and refreshing before a hot, heavy main course. Or serve a more substantial starter before a light main meal. Avoid fruit in the starter if there is fruit in the main course. Don't serve a salad starter followed by salad instead of vegetables in the main course. Avoid similar ingredients in both, such as cheese soup followed by lasagne topped with cheese sauce.

Colour plays an important role too. Imagine your meal is an oil painting: there should be lots of colours offsetting each other, not clashing or boringly similar.

About Fast Formal Starters

- When planning a three-course meal, go for a starter with few ingredients, if possible ones you keep on the shelf or have ready prepared. For instance, if you eat eggs, hard-boiled (hard-cooked) eggs keep well for a week or more in the fridge, and dress up any cold dish beautifully.

- Make sure that the same fruit or salad vegetable does not feature in the rest of your meal. For instance, tomato-sauced noodles after tomato salad would be a bad idea.

- A 50 g/2 oz/¼ cup dollop of cottage cheese mixed with a few capers or chopped stuffed olives makes a presentable starter served on a lettuce leaf with an attractive salad garnish.

- Quartered hard-boiled eggs themselves make a good starter if 'bound' with Mayonnaise (see page 305) and garnished with a sprinkling of vivid red paprika on top.

- An almost instant starter is a wedge of melon per person, served with a small bowl of ground ginger and a grinding of black pepper.

- A small portion of a simple salad such as sliced tomatoes sprinkled with French Dressing (see page 303) is also a good choice.

Tomato or Cucumber Cups

Cut medium-large tomatoes in half across, or cut unpeeled thick cucumbers into 6 cm/2½ in lengths, discarding the ends. Make sure that they will stand on end level. With a teaspoon, scoop out the tomato seeds and juice or take out the cucumber seeds and some of the flesh from one end without piercing the other. You will then have hollow cups. Turn them upside-down to drain for a few minutes, then season the insides with a few drops of soy sauce. Fill with a savoury spread, mounding it high; if possible, choose a contrast-coloured spread such as Green Pea Spread (see page 302) in Tomato Cups or Red Lentil Spread (see page 302) in Cucumber Cups. Garnish each cup (if you have time) with a parsley sprig or with a dab of quark. To serve as a starter, place 2 or 3 cups on each of 4 small plates. Serve with small knives and forks.

Tomato and Avocado Salad

SERVES 4

4 lettuce leaves
400 g/14 oz/1 large can tomatoes
Freshly ground black pepper
90 ml/6 tbsp French Dressing (see
*   page 303) or use bottled*
30 ml/2 tbsp lemon juice
2 firm ripe avocados

Tear up the lettuce and divide between four small bowls. Drain the tomatoes over a jug (keep the juice to drink). Divide the tomatoes between the bowls, halving them if large. Sprinkle with pepper. Mix the well shaken dressing and lemon juice in a bowl. Halve the avocados, take out the stones (pits) and scoop out the flesh in pieces with a spoon. Toss the pieces at once in the dressing and spoon the fruit and dressing over the tomatoes.

Grilled Italian Avocados

SERVES 4

2 ripe avocados, sliced
120 ml/4 fl oz/½ cup passata (sieved
*   tomatoes)*
5 ml/1 tsp dried basil
Salt and freshly ground black pepper
100 g/4 oz Mozzarella cheese, sliced

Put the avocado slices in four shallow individual ovenproof dishes. Spoon the passata over. Sprinkle with basil, salt and pepper. Top with the cheese. Grill (broil) under a moderate grill (broiler) until the cheese melts and bubbles and the avocados are warm. Do not overcook or the cheese will become rubbery and the avocados bitter. Serve straight away.

Cheesy Avocados

SERVES 4

30 ml/2 tbsp Mayonnaise (see page 305)
5 ml/1 tsp tomato purée (paste)
2 drops of Tabasco sauce
Salt and freshly ground black pepper
2 ripe avocados, halved and stoned
*   (pitted)*
4 Cheddar cheese slices
Brown Garlic Bread (see page 325)

Mix together the mayonnaise, tomato purée, Tabasco sauce, salt and pepper. Fill the cavities in the avocados with the mixture. Place slices of cheese over the top. Grill (broil) gently for about 3 minutes until the cheese melts. Serve with Brown Garlic Bread.

Normandy Tomatoes

SERVES 4

4 large tomatoes, halved
225 g/8 oz Camembert cheese, rinded
*   and chopped*
50 g/2 oz/1 cup breadcrumbs
A little chopped parsley
Watercress

Remove the seeds from the tomatoes and place the 'shells' on a flameproof dish. Mix the cheese with the breadcrumbs and fill the tomato halves. Sprinkle with parsley. Place under a moderately hot grill (broiler) for 2 minutes or until the cheese melts, taking care that the breadcrumbs do not burn. Serve in a ring of watercress.

Somerset Tomatoes

SERVES 4

Prepare as for Normandy Tomatoes but substitute grated Cheddar cheese for the Camembert and sprinkle with snipped chives instead of parsley.

Tomato and Goat's Cheese Platter

SERVES 4

6 tomatoes, sliced
100 g/4 oz goat's cheese, sliced
8 black olives, halved and stoned
    (pitted)
30 ml/2 tbsp oil
15 ml/1 tbsp vinegar
Pinch of mustard powder
Salt and freshly ground black pepper
A few snipped chives

Interleaf slices of tomatoes with slices of goat's cheese on individual plates. Sprinkle with the olives. Shake the remaining ingredients, except the chives, together in a screw-topped jar. Drizzle over the salad and garnish with snipped chives just before serving.

Tomato and Mozzarella Platter

SERVES 4

Prepare as for Tomato and Goat's Cheese Platter but substitute Mozzarella for the goat's cheese and garnish with chopped basil instead of chives.

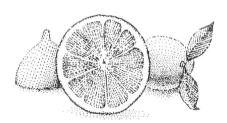

Pawpaw Pecan Cocktail

SERVES 4

2 ripe pawpaws
1 fresh sweet grapefruit
Juice of 1 lemon
30 ml/2 tbsp Kirsch, gin or Cointreau
4 cos (romaine) or Chinese (stem
    lettuce) leaves
60 ml/4 tbsp chopped pecan nuts
Mint leaves
4 cocktail cherries

Peel the pawpaw and cut into slices, removing and discarding the black seeds. Cut the grapefruit into segments. In a bowl, combine the pawpaw with the grapefruit segments. Sprinkle with the lemon juice and liqueur of your choice. Serve on lettuce leaves and top with the pecan nuts. Garnish with mint leaves and cocktail cherries.

African Queen Peanut Dip

SERVES 4

225 g/8 oz/2 cups raw peanuts
120 ml/4 fl oz/½ cup hot water
45 ml/3 tbsp clear honey
150 g/5 oz creamed coconut
Pinch of chilli powder
Salt
Mixed fruit pieces

Place the peanuts on a baking sheet and toast for 3 minutes. Place in a blender or food processor and purée with the hot water. Add the honey, coconut cream, chilli and salt to taste and blend to a purée. Serve with wedges of apple, pear, banana, peach or pineapple chunks.

Crisp and Fruity Firsts

1 small head of radicchio
1 head chicory (Belgian endive)
2 oranges
75 g/3 oz/¾ cup raspberries
Freshly ground black pepper
Olive oil
Raspberry vinegar

Separate the radicchio into leaves and tear into small pieces. Place in a bowl. Cut a cone-shaped core out of the base of the chicory, then cut into chunky pieces and separate the layers. Remove all the skin and pith from the oranges, cut into slices, then quarter each slice. Mix with the salad leaves, then spoon on to four individual plates. Dot the raspberries around. Add a good grinding of pepper over each, then drizzle with the oil and vinegar and serve.

Strawberry and Cucumber Platter

225 g/8 oz strawberries, sliced
1 cucumber, peeled and sliced
Salt and freshly ground black pepper
45 ml/3 tbsp olive oil
15 ml/1 tbsp lemon juice
15 ml/1 tbsp chopped mint
5 ml/1 tsp caster (superfine) sugar
Mint sprigs

Arrange the strawberry and cucumber slices attractively on four individual plates. Add a good grinding of pepper over each. Whisk the oil, lemon juice, chopped mint and sugar together with a little salt and pepper and drizzle over. Garnish with mint sprigs and serve.

A Peach of a Starter

Lollo Rosso leaves, shredded
4 ripe peaches, halved and stoned
  (pitted)
225 g/8 oz/1 cup cream cheese
30 ml/2 tbsp single (light) cream
75 g/3 oz/¾ cup walnut halves
Salt and freshly ground black pepper
2 stuffed green olives

Put some shredded lettuce on four individual plates and top with two peach halves, cut sides up. Beat the cheese with the cream. Reserve four walnut halves for garnish and chop the remainder. Beat into the cheese and season to taste. Pile on to the peaches and garnish each with half a stuffed olive and a walnut half.

Pears with Walnut Whip Dressing

6 ripe dessert pears
Lettuce leaves
75 g/3 oz/½ cup walnut halves
150 ml/¼ pt/⅔ cup whipping cream
10 ml/2 tsp lemon juice
5 ml/1 tsp caster (superfine) sugar
30 ml/2 tbsp Mayonnaise (see page 305)
5 ml/1 tsp dried tarragon
Salt and freshly ground black pepper
Small parsley sprigs

Peel, halve and core the pears and arrange on a bed of lettuce on six individual plates. Reserve six walnut halves for garnish and finely chop the remainder. Whip the cream with the lemon juice and sugar. Fold in the mayonnaise, chopped nuts and tarragon. Season to taste. Spoon over the pears and garnish with the reserved walnuts and small parsley sprigs.

Tropical Salad

SERVES 4

2 ripe avocados
15 ml/1 tbsp lemon juice
1 small, ripe mango, diced
2 kiwi fruit, sliced
4 spring onions (scallions), chopped
100 g/4 oz seedless (pitless) black
   grapes
100 g/4 oz/1 cup white hard cheese,
   diced
45 ml/3 tbsp cider vinegar
5 ml/1 tsp clear honey
30 ml/2 tbsp sesame oil
Freshly ground black pepper
15 ml/1 tbsp sesame seeds

Halve the avocados, discard the stones (pits) and scoop out the flesh, leaving the shells intact. Place the shells in small dishes. Cut the flesh into neat pieces and place in a bowl. Toss in the lemon juice. Add the mango, kiwi fruit, spring onions, grapes and cheese. Blend together the vinegar, honey, oil and a little pepper, pour over the salad and toss gently. Pile back into the avocado shells and sprinkle with a few sesame seeds before serving.

Exotic Fruit Cocktail

SERVES 4

1 mango
1 pawpaw
2 kiwi fruit
2 small bananas
Mint leaves
A few cranberries, fresh or frozen
Juice of 1 lime

Using a sharp knife, peel the mango and pawpaw. Remove the stone (pit) and seeds and cut into thin slices. Peel and slice the kiwi fruit and bananas. Combine the fruits and arrange in individual serving bowls or glasses. Decorate with mint leaves and cranberries. Chill until required and, just before serving, squeeze lime juice over each portion.

Fruity Melon Starter

SERVES 4

1 ripe honeydew melon, quartered,
   seeded (pitted) and skinned
225 g/8 oz/1 cup cottage cheese
15 ml/1 tbsp milk
100 g/4 oz mixed black and green
   grapes, halved and seeded (pitted)
Toasted flaked almonds

Cut the melon into thin slices and arrange attractively on serving plates. Beat the cottage cheese and milk together and fold in the grapes. Just before serving, spoon over or beside the melon slices and garnish with a few toasted flaked almonds.

Pineapple Honolulu

4 lettuce leaves
4 radicchio leaves
5 pineapple slices, cored
30 ml/2 tbsp Worcestershire sauce
1 small onion, chopped
5 ml/1 tsp grated fresh root ginger
30 ml/2 tbsp sunflower oil
150 g/5 oz mushrooms, sliced
175 g/6 oz/¾ cup cottage cheese

Arrange the lettuce and radicchio leaves on four plates and top each with a pineapple slice. Place the Worcestershire sauce, onion, ginger, remaining pineapple slice and the oil in a blender or food processor and blend together. Pour over the mushrooms and toss for a few minutes. Place a spoonful of cottage cheese on top of each pineapple slice and spoon the mushrooms all around.

Melon and Mandarin Cocktail

2 small Galia or other round melons
2 × 300 g/2 × 11 oz/2 small cans mandarin oranges, drained
60 ml/4 tbsp ginger wine

Halve the melons and scoop out the seeds (pits). Place in dishes. Spoon the fruit in the centre and drizzle the ginger wine over.

Grapefruit Cocktail

3 × 285 g/3 × 10½ oz/3 large cans grapefruit segments in natural juice
30 ml/2 tbsp sherry
Ground ginger

Drain the fruit (keep the juice to drink). Divide the segments between four stemmed dessert glasses. Sprinkle with sherry. Serve with a small bowl of ground ginger.

Avocado and Grapefruit Cocktail

Halve two ripe avocados lengthways, remove the stones (pits) and brush with sherry on the cut sides. Fill with drained canned grapefruit segments and dust with ground ginger.

Happy Apple Starter

1 red-skinned eating (dessert) apple
50 g/2 oz piece unpeeled cucumber, diced
30 ml/2 tbsp dry white wine
100 g/4 oz/1 cup cooked fresh or thawed frozen (uncooked) small green peas
5 ml/1 tsp dried savory
Salt and freshly ground black pepper
Wholewheat crackers

Core and dice the apple and mix with the diced cucumber. Toss well in the wine to coat all the apple. Mix in the peas and savory. Season if you wish. Pile in a salad bowl. Spoon into small bowls or dessert glasses at the table and serve with wholewheat crackers.

Walnut Skordalia

SERVES 4

250 ml/8 fl oz/1 cup Mayonnaise (see page 305)
2 garlic cloves, chopped
25 g/1 oz/¼ cup walnuts, chopped
25 g/1 oz/½ cup breadcrumbs
Juice of ½ lemon
30 ml/2 tbsp plain yoghurt
15 ml/1 tbsp sesame seeds, toasted
10 ml/2 tsp chopped basil
A mixture of the following 'dippers':
small cauliflower florets, button
mushrooms, celery sticks cut into
strips, carrots cut into strips,
fennel bulbs cut into strips, mouli
(Japanese white radish), thickly
sliced, mangetout (snow peas),
French (green) beans, apple or
pear slices

Put the mayonnaise, garlic, walnuts, breadcrumbs, lemon juice, yoghurt, sesame seeds and basil in a blender or food processor and purée until smooth. Pour into one large or two small bowls to serve. Arrange the vegetable dippers decoratively on a serving plate and serve with the dip.

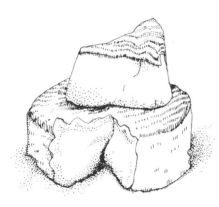

Deep-fried Brie with Coconut

SERVES 6

450 g/1 lb Brie or Camembert cheese
30 ml/2 tbsp plain (all-purpose) flour
5 ml/1 tsp celery salt or plain salt
2 eggs, beaten
50 g/2 oz/½ cup desiccated (shredded) coconut
Oil, for deep-frying
Celery sticks

Cut the cheese into 12 small triangles. Season the flour with the celery or plain salt. Coat the cheese triangles with seasoned flour, then dip in beaten egg and roll in the desiccated coconut. Heat the oil and deep-fry the cheese triangles for 1 minute until golden brown. Drain well on kitchen paper. Arrange on serving plates with celery sticks. Serve immediately.

Welsh Baked Eggs

SERVES 4

50 g/2 oz/¼ cup butter or margarine
4 small leeks, thinly sliced
Salt and freshly ground black pepper
4 eggs
60 ml/4 tbsp single (light) cream
4 parsley sprigs

Melt the butter in a saucepan. Add the leeks and cook, stirring, for 1 minute. Cover with a lid, reduce the heat and cook for a further 5 minutes until softened. Season lightly. Spoon into four ramekin dishes (custard cups). Break an egg over each and add a spoonful of cream. Sprinkle with salt and pepper and bake in a preheated oven at 200ºC/ 400ºF/gas mark 6 for 8–10 minutes or until the eggs are cooked to your liking.

Courgette and Onion Baked Eggs

Prepare as for Welsh Baked Eggs but substitute 2 thinly sliced courgettes (zucchini) and a finely chopped onion for the leeks.

Woodland Baked Eggs

SERVES 4

Prepare as for Welsh Baked Eggs but substitute 175 g/6 oz sliced oyster mushrooms for the leeks.

Asparagus Baked Eggs

SERVES 4

Prepare as for Welsh Baked Eggs but use only half the amount of butter. Use this to grease the ramekin dishes (custard cups). Use 298 g/10½ oz/1 small can cut asparagus spears instead of leeks. Drain and place in the greased dishes. Continue as before.

Jellied Eggs with Olives

SERVES 4

4 eggs
450 ml/¾ pt/2 cups vegetable stock
1 large bay leaf
15 g/½ oz vegetarian gelatine
Oil, for greasing
4 stuffed olives
4 cocktail gherkins (cornichons)
Shredded lettuce
4 cucumber slices
Parsley sprigs

Boil the eggs for 5 minutes, then plunge immediately in cold water to prevent further cooking. Meanwhile, put the stock, bay leaf and gelatine in a pan. Stir until the gelatine dissolves, then bring just to the boil. Remove from the heat and leave to infuse for 15 minutes. Discard the bay leaf. Pour a thin layer of the stock into four lightly oiled ramekin dishes (custard cups). Chill until set. Cut each olive into four slices and arrange around the edge of the jelly in each dish. Make several slices in the gherkins, cutting from the tip but not right through the stalk end, and open out to form a fan. Lay this in the centre of each dish. Shell the eggs and lay one in each dish. Pour the remaining stock over and chill until set. Turn each one out on to a bed of shredded lettuce and garnish each with a twist of cucumber and a small parsley sprig.

Curried Egg Puffs

SERVES 6

*65 g/2½ oz/good ½ cup plain (all-
 purpose) flour*
Salt and freshly ground black pepper
150 ml/¼ pt/⅔ cup water
50 g/2 oz/¼ cup butter or margarine
30 ml/2 tbsp grated Pecorino cheese
2 eggs, beaten
50 g/2 oz/¼ cup low-fat soft cheese
*60 ml/4 tbsp Mayonnaise (see page
 305)*
5 ml/1 tsp curry paste
*2 large hard-boiled (hard-cooked)
 eggs, chopped*
*1 spring onion (scallion), finely
 chopped*
15 ml/1 tbsp chopped parsley
A little cold milk
Parsley sprigs

Sift the flour and a pinch of salt on to a
sheet of greaseproof (waxed) paper.
Heat the water and butter or margarine in
a saucepan until the fat melts. Remove
from the heat and add the flour all in one
go. Beat well until smooth and the mixture leaves the sides of the pan clean. Add
the Pecorino cheese and gradually beat in
the eggs until smooth and glossy but the
mixture still holds its shape. Either put
the mixture in a piping bag fitted with a
large plain tube (tip) or use a teaspoon to
make small balls, slightly apart, on a
greased baking sheet (the mixture should
make about 30). Bake in a preheated oven
at 200°C/400°F/gas mark 6 for about 20
minutes until puffy and golden brown.
Cool on a wire rack. Mash the soft cheese
with half the mayonnaise and the curry
paste. Stir in the chopped egg and onion.
Season lightly. Make a slit in the side of
each choux ball and fill with this mixture.

Pile on to six small plates. Mix the
remaining mayonnaise with the parsley
and thin to a coating sauce with milk.
Spoon over the choux balls and garnish
each with a parsley sprig.

Crunchy Egg Starter

SERVES 4

½ iceberg lettuce, shredded
*4 hard-boiled (hard-cooked) eggs,
 sliced*
4 tomatoes, sliced
1 celery stick, finely chopped
25 g/1 oz/¼ cup chopped mixed nuts
150 ml/¼ pt/⅔ cup mayonnaise
*150 ml/¼ pt/⅔ cup soured (dairy sour)
 cream*
15 ml/1 tbsp chopped parsley
Salt and freshly ground black pepper
Paprika

Divide the lettuce among four individual plates. Arrange the eggs and
tomatoes overlapping in a circle on top.
Blend together the remaining ingredients
except the paprika and spoon into the
centre. Dust with paprika before serving.

Curried Egg Mayonnaise

SERVES 4

*4 hard-boiled (hard-cooked) eggs,
 chopped*
*15 ml/1 tbsp Chutney (see page 321)
 or use bought*
45 ml/3 tbsp Mayonnaise (see page 305)
Salt and freshly ground black pepper
5 ml/1 tsp curry powder
Watercress

Mix together all the ingredients except
the watercress. Chill until ready to
serve, spooned on a bed of watercress.

Eggs in Curry 'Cream' Sauce

4 large lettuce or Chinese (stem lettuce) leaves
10 ml/2 tsp capers, drained
6 hard-boiled (hard-cooked) eggs
50 ml/2 fl oz/3½ tbsp mayonnaise
75 ml/5 tbsp silken tofu
1.5–2.5 ml/¼–½ tsp curry powder
Lemon juice
Pumpernickel

Place the leaves flat on 4 small plates. Sprinkle with a few capers. Shell the eggs, cut them in half across, and arrange 3 egg halves in the centre of each lettuce leaf. For the Curry 'Cream' Sauce, whisk together the mayonnaise, tofu, curry powder and a few drops of lemon juice until smooth. Taste, and add extra curry powder or lemon juice if you wish. Spoon some of the mixture over each egg half. Serve with pumpernickel.

Poached Egg Florentine

300 ml/½ pt/1¼ cups Bechamel Sauce (see page 311)
1 egg yolk
50 g/2 oz/½ cup Emmental (Swiss) cheese, grated
Salt and freshly ground black pepper
225 g/8 oz leaf spinach
50 g/2 oz/¼ cup butter or margarine
4 eggs
30 ml/2 tbsp grated Pecorino cheese
5 ml/1 tsp paprika

Reheat the sauce with the egg yolk and grated Emmental cheese. Season to taste. Keep warm. Cook the spinach gently with a little of the butter for 5 minutes and season to taste. Fill four small earthenware dishes with the spinach. Meanwhile, melt a knob of the remaining butter in each of four egg poaching cups. Drop an egg into each one. Cover and poach for about 5 minutes until the whites are firm but the yolks remain soft (or poach in water with a little lemon juice added). Slip each egg on top of the spinach. Coat with a little cheese sauce. Sprinkle over the grated cheese and paprika. Flash under the grill (broiler) for 30 seconds to brown the cheese.

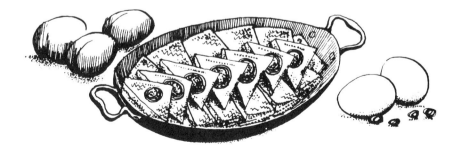

Broad Beans and Carrot Custard Pie

*225 g/8 oz/2 cups shelled broad
  (lima) beans*
*225 g/8 oz baby carrots, washed and
  diced*
*1 small piece of fresh root ginger,
  peeled and chopped*
45 ml/3 tbsp clear honey
45 ml/3 tbsp chopped parsley
*600 ml/1 pt/2½ cups single (light)
  cream*
3 eggs, beaten
Salt and freshly ground black pepper
2.5 ml/½ tsp ground aniseed or cloves
Butter or margarine, for greasing

Boil the broad beans for 5 minutes.
Drain, rinse in cold water, drain again
and remove the outer skin from each
bean. Blanch the carrots for 5 minutes in
salted water. Drain. Purée the ginger with
the honey and 75 ml/5 tbsp hot water. In
a bowl, combine the parsley, cream, eggs
and honey mixture. Season to taste,
adding aniseed powder to taste. Grease a
1.2 litre/2 pt/5 cup shallow baking dish
and half fill it with carrots and skinned
broad beans. Top up with the egg and
cream mixture. Place in a baking tin (pan)
half-filled with hot water. Bake in a preheated oven at 200°C/400°F/gas mark 6
for 45 minutes.

Leek and Almond Cream

Butter or margarine
*450 g/1 lb leeks, white parts only,
  sliced*
175 g/6 oz/1¼ cups blanched almonds
*150 ml/¼ pt/⅔ cup single (light)
  cream*
4 eggs, beaten
1.5 ml/¼ tsp salt
*1.5 ml/¼ tsp freshly ground black
  pepper*
1.5 ml/¼ tsp grated nutmeg
1 slice bread, cubed
*50 g/2 oz/½ cup Emmental (Swiss)
  cheese, grated*

Heat a little butter in a shallow pan and
stir-fry the leeks for 2 minutes, without browning. Add the almonds and cook
for a further minute. Remove from the
heat. In a bowl, blend the cream, eggs,
salt, pepper and nutmeg and soak the
bread cubes in this mixture. Add the
cooked leeks and almonds. Leave to
absorb the flavours for 20 minutes. Fill
four individual 150 ml/¼ pt/⅔ cup well
buttered ramekin dishes (custard cups)
with the leek mixture. Sprinkle with grated cheese. Stand in a baking tin (pan)
half-filled with water and bake in a preheated oven at 190°C/375°F/gas mark 5
for 20 minutes.

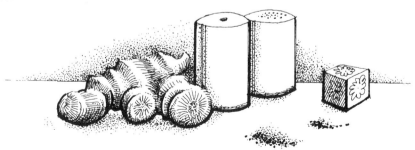

Moreish Onions

*450 g/1 lb small onions, weighing
   about 25 g/1 oz each*
60 ml/4 tbsp sunflower oil
45 ml/3 tbsp clear honey
60 ml/4 tbsp wine vinegar
300 ml/½ pt/1¼ cups sweet white wine
15 ml/1 tbsp tomato purée (paste)
1 celery stick, thinly sliced
1 fennel stalk, thinly sliced
Salt and freshly ground black pepper
*Assorted hard cheeses (e.g. Cheddar,
   Emmental), sliced*

Peel the onions. Heat the oil in a saucepan and stir-fry the onions until lightly coloured. Add the honey and caramelize a little for 30 seconds, then pour in the vinegar, wine and tomato purée. Add the celery and fennel and boil for 6 minutes. Season and cool in its own liquor. Serve cold with the liquid. Use to accompany slices of assorted hard cheeses.

Pepperonelli

3 (bell) peppers of different colours
1 potato, sliced and cut in thin strips
Oil, for shallow-frying
1 red onion, cut into strips
2 fennel stalks, cut into thin strips
45 ml/3 tbsp olive oil
15 ml/1 tbsp wine vinegar
1 garlic clove, crushed
Salt and freshly ground black pepper
Hard-boiled (hard-cooked) eggs
Lettuce leaves

Cut the peppers into halves and discard the seeds. Grill (broil) the peppers, exposing the shiny side. When it begins to blister, remove and peel off the skin. Cut the peeled peppers into thin strips. Fry (sauté) the potato strips in oil for 1–3 minutes, without browning. Drain well. In a bowl, combine all the potato, onion and fennel strips with the peppers. Mix the remaining ingredients except the eggs and lettuce, seasoning to taste. Pour over the salad and toss. Serve with hard-boiled eggs cut into wedges and lettuce leaves.

Pistou

225 g/8 oz/2 cups pine nuts
6 basil leaves
2 garlic cloves
60 ml/4 tbsp walnut or olive oil
50 g/2 oz/1 cup white breadcrumbs
50 g/2 oz/¼ cup fromage frais
30 ml/2 tbsp boiling water (optional)
Toasted French bread slices

In a mortar, pound all the ingredients except the French bread to a fine paste. Add 30 ml/2 tbsp boiling water for a smoother mixture, or purée in a blender or food processor. Serve on toasted French bread slices.

Green Bean Medley

225 g/8 oz thin French (green)
*   beans, trimmed*
100 g/4 oz/1 cup flageolet beans,
*   cooked (see page 10)*
2 hard-boiled (hard-cooked) eggs
45 ml/3 tbsp walnut oil
15 ml/1 tbsp lemon juice
2.5 ml/½ tsp made English mustard
Salt and freshly ground black pepper
4 spring onions (scallions), chopped

Boil the French beans in salted water for 7 minutes. Drain and rinse with cold water. Drain again and pat dry. Drain and rinse the flageolets, if using canned. Mix the two beans together. For the egg dressing, separate the yolks from the whites of the eggs. Pass the yolks through a sieve (strainer) and mix with the oil and lemon juice. Add the mustard. Season to taste. Toss the beans in the dressing. Chop the egg white and sprinkle on top of the salad with the chopped spring onions.

Carrot and Yoghurt Pâté

30 ml/2 tbsp walnut or sunflower oil
1 small onion, sliced
225 g/8 oz young carrots, sliced
250 ml/8 fl oz/1 cup water
30 ml/2 tbsp clear honey
1 small carton plain yoghurt
Salt and freshly ground black pepper
Juice and rind of 1 lemon
4 Chinese (stem lettuce) or cos
*   (romaine) lettuce leaves*
30 ml/2 tbsp toasted almonds
1 orange, divided into segments

Heat the oil in a shallow pan or wok and stir-fry the onion and carrots for 4 minutes. Add the water and the honey. Boil for 5 minutes until the carrots are soft. Drain and mash the mixture coarsely. Cool, then blend in the yoghurt. Season to taste and add the lemon juice and rind. Serve on salad leaves sprinkled with the toasted almonds. Garnish with orange segments just before serving.

Aubergine Caviare

SERVES 4

1 aubergine (eggplant)
Salt and freshly ground black pepper
30 ml/2 tbsp plain (all-purpose) flour
45 ml/3 tbsp sunflower oil
1 garlic clove, chopped
75 g/3 oz/⅓ cup cream cheese
Toast

Slice the aubergine. Sprinkle with salt and leave for 30 minutes to allow the removal of the bitter juices. Wash, drain and pat dry. Sprinkle with flour and shake off any surplus. Heat the oil in a shallow pan and fry (sauté) the aubergine slices for 5 minutes. Drain. Purée the aubergine with the garlic and what remains of the oil in a blender or food processor. In a bowl, blend the aubergine purée with the cream cheese. Season to taste. Serve in individual ramekin dishes (custard cups) with toast.

Baked Aubergine Custards

SERVES 4

1 aubergine (eggplant)
Salt and freshly ground black pepper
Plain (all-purpose) flour
90 ml/6 tbsp oil
3 eggs
150 ml/¼ pt/⅔ cup single (light)
*   cream*
1 garlic clove, chopped
4 tomatoes, seeded, skinned and
*   finely chopped*
½ small red chilli, seeded and
*   chopped*
5 ml/1 tsp cornflour (cornstarch)
45 ml/3 tbsp water
2.5 ml/½ tsp sugar
8 mint leaves

Peel and cube the aubergine. Sprinkle with salt and leave for 30 minutes to release the bitter juices. Rinse and pat dry. Coat the cubes in flour seasoned with a little salt and pepper. Heat the oil and fry (sauté) the aubergine for 1 minute. Drain on kitchen paper. In a bowl, beat the eggs and cream together. Add the chopped garlic and seasoning. Half-fill four 250 ml/8 fl oz/1 cup ramekin dishes (custard cups) with the cream mixture and top up with cooked aubergine. Place the ramekins in a roasting tin (pan) half-filled with hot water. Bake in a preheated oven at 180°C/350°F/gas mark 4 for 15–20 minutes. Meanwhile, prepare the tomato coulis. Heat the tomato pulp and chopped chilli in a saucepan. Mix the cornflour and water in a cup and add to the tomato coulis. Cook for 4 minutes. Season with salt and sugar only. To serve, pour a pool of the sauce on to four plates and turn out a custard on to each of them. Garnish with mint leaves.

Broccoli Beignets

SERVES 4

Juice of 1 lemon
90 ml/6 tbsp olive oil
1 garlic clove
5 ml/1 tsp each coarsely crushed
*   black peppercorns and mustard*
*   seeds*
450 g/1 lb broccoli, divided into 8
*   small sprigs*
60 ml/4 tbsp seasoned flour
3 eggs
30 ml/2 tbsp breadcrumbs
30 ml/2 tbsp cornmeal
30 ml/2 tbsp chopped parsley
Oil, for deep-frying
Pink Dressing (see page 306) or
*   Curried Fruit Mayonnaise (see*
*   page 308)*

Purée the lemon juice, olive oil, garlic, peppercorns and mustard seeds in a blender and place in an earthenware dish. Add the broccoli, turn to coat and marinate for 15 minutes, turning from time to time. Have ready three soup plates, one with seasoned flour, one with beaten eggs and one with the crumbs, cornmeal and chopped parsley well mixed together. Dip the broccoli sprigs in seasoned flour, then in beaten egg and finally well coat in the crumb mixture. Deep-fry in hot oil for 2–3 minutes. It is not necessary to cook the broccoli sprigs through as it is better to have them crunchy. Drain well on kitchen paper and serve hot with Pink Dressing or Curried Fruit Mayonnaise.

Cauliflower Beignets

SERVES 4

Prepare as for Broccoli Beignets but use cauliflower instead of broccoli and serve with Blue Cheese Dressing (see page 307).

Chinese Cocktail Rolls

SERVES 4

225 g/8 oz/2 cups plain (all-purpose)
*   flour*
Salt
Cayenne
4 eggs
30 ml/2 tbsp sunflower oil
25 g/1 oz/¼ cup blue cheese,
*   crumbled*
100 g/4 oz/½ cup cream cheese
30 ml/2 tbsp chopped parsley
30 ml/2 tbsp snipped chives
Salt and freshly ground black pepper
100 g/4 oz field mushrooms, chopped
30 ml/2 tbsp breadcrumbs
30 ml/2 tbsp peanuts, chopped
5 ml/1 tsp celery seeds
30 ml/2 tbsp seasoned flour
30 ml/2 tbsp sesame seeds
Oil, for deep-frying
Tomato ketchup (catsup) or any spicy
*   sauce*

In a bowl, combine the flour with a good pinch of salt and cayenne. Blend with 1 beaten egg and the oil to form a dough. Knead well, then leave to rest for 20 minutes, covered with clingfilm (plastic wrap). Mix the cheeses, herbs, a little salt and pepper, the mushrooms, one of the remaining beaten eggs, the breadcrumbs, nuts and celery seeds to a paste. Divide into balls, then roll into 'sausages' 6 cm/ 2½ in long. On a floured surface, roll out the pastry thinly. Cut the pastry into rectangles 7.5 × 2.5 cm/3 × 1 in. Place a cheese roll inside each rectangle of pastry. Moisten the edges and tightly roll up. Tuck the ends under and roll each piece in seasoned flour. Dip in the remaining beaten eggs, then coat with sesame seeds. Heat the oil and deep-fry for 2 minutes until golden. Drain on kitchen paper and serve hot with tomato ketchup or any spicy sauce.

Jerusalem Artichoke Sauté

SERVES 4

*450 g/1 lb Jerusalem artichokes,
  scrubbed and sliced*
90 ml/6 tbsp butter and oil, mixed
*2 bananas, not too ripe, peeled and
  diagonally sliced*
1 onion, chopped
100 g/4 oz/1 cup unsalted peanuts
Grated rind and juice of 1 lime
Salt and freshly ground black pepper
Lettuce leaves
Mustard and cress
30 ml/2 tbsp chopped parsley

Boil the artichokes in water for 3 minutes. Drain and dry on kitchen paper.
Heat the butter and oil in a shallow pan
and fry (sauté) the artichokes and
bananas for 2–3 minutes, then add the
onion, peanuts, lime rind and juice. Toss
for 1 minute more. Season to taste. Serve
on a bed of lettuce leaves and mustard
and cress. Garnish with parsley.

Deep-fried Dwarf Beans

SERVES 4

450 g/1 lb dwarf beans, trimmed
100 g/4 oz/1 cup seasoned flour
2 eggs, beaten
Oil, for deep-frying
Celery salt
Chilli powder
*Flavoured mayonnaise (see pages
  306–9)*

Boil the beans in salted water for 7
minutes. Drain. Rinse in cold water,
drain again and dry on kitchen paper. Tie
up the beans in four small bundles with
string. Dip the bunches in seasoned flour,
then in beaten egg, then again in seasoned flour. Heat the oil to 190ºC/375ºF
and deep-fry for 3 minutes. Drain well on
kitchen paper. Sprinkle the beans with
celery salt and chilli powder. Remove the
strings. Serve with any flavoured mayonnaise.

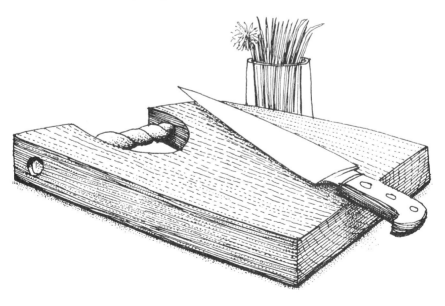

Spicy Sweet and Sour French Beans

450 g/1 lb thin French (green)
  beans, topped and tailed but left
  whole
40 g/1½ oz/3 tbsp butter or margarine
3 spring onions (scallions), chopped
100 g/4 oz button mushrooms, sliced
1 green chilli, seeded and chopped
30 ml/2 tbsp Worcestershire sauce
15 ml/1 tbsp dark soy sauce
30 ml/2 tbsp light brown sugar
30 ml/2 tbsp red wine vinegar

Cook the beans in boiling, salted water for 4–5 minutes until just tender. Drain and return to the saucepan. Meanwhile, melt the butter or margarine in a frying pan (skillet). Add the spring onions, mushrooms and chilli and fry (sauté) until lightly golden, then add to the beans. Put the remaining ingredients in the frying pan. Heat, stirring, until the sugar dissolves. Bring to the boil, pour over the beans and toss over a gentle heat until piping hot. Spoon on to warm plates and serve straight away.

Warm Flageolet-stuffed Marrow

900 g/2 lb marrow (squash)
225 g/8 oz dwarf French (green)
  beans, trimmed and cut into small
  pieces
425 g/15½ oz/1 large can flageolet
  beans
Juice of 1 lemon
1 small onion, chopped
5 ml/1 tsp made English mustard
45 ml/3 tbsp olive oil
5 ml/1 tsp white pickling vinegar
Salt and freshly ground black pepper
45 ml/3 tbsp chopped parsley
1 bunch of chives, snipped

Peel the marrow and halve lengthways, then halve again crosswise. Remove the seeds to hollow the cavities. Boil the pieces in salted water for 8–10 minutes (do not overcook or the pieces will lose their shape). Drain and pat dry on kitchen paper. Boil the green beans for 7 minutes. Drain. Heat the flageolets in a saucepan. Drain, rinse with boiling water and drain again. Combine the two beans in a bowl. Blend the remaining ingredients except the parsley and chives in a bowl and toss the beans in it. To serve, fill each marrow cavity with the beans. Place on plates and sprinkle over chopped parsley and fresh snipped chives.

Fragrant Marrow with Almonds

450 g/1 lb marrow (squash)
50 g/2 oz/½ cup seasoned flour
3 eggs, beaten
15 ml/1 tbsp chopped tarragon
15 ml/1 tbsp chopped basil
Grated rind of 1 lemon
1 green chilli, seeded and chopped
Salt and freshly ground black pepper
90 ml/6 tbsp butter and oil mixed
60 ml/4 tbsp flaked almonds
Tomatoes, cut into wedges
Mayonnaise (see page 305)

Peel the marrow and cut in half. Scoop out the seeds. Cut the pulp into 5 cm/ 2 in squares. Coat each piece in seasoned flour. Mix the beaten egg with the herbs, lemon rind, chopped chilli and seasoning. It is best to cook the marrow in two batches using a large 23 cm/9 in frying pan (skillet). Heat the butter and oil until foaming. Dip half the marrow in the egg mixture and shallow-fry on both sides for 3–4 minutes, turning over from time to time. Repeat with the remaining marrow. Place in a shallow dish. Toast the flaked almonds and sprinkle on top of the fried marrow. Serve with wedges of tomatoes and use the Mayonnaise as a dip.

Fragrant Courgettes with Hazelnuts

Prepare as for Fragrant Marrow with Almonds but substitute courgettes (zucchini), cut into chunky slices, for the marrow and hazelnuts for the almonds.

Fragrant Pumpkin with Coconut

Prepare as for Fragrant Marrow with Almonds but substitute pumpkin for the marrow and flaked coconut for the almonds.

Pea Soufflés

50 g/2 oz/¼ cup butter or margarine
1 small onion, chopped
225 g/8 oz/2 cups frozen peas,
thawed
20 ml/4 tsp chopped mint
40 g/1½ oz/⅓ cup plain (all-purpose)
flour
300 ml/½ pt/1¼ cups milk
Salt and freshly ground black pepper
3 eggs, separated
15 ml/1 tbsp finely grated Cheddar
cheese

Melt the butter or margarine in a saucepan. Add the onion and peas, stir well, then cover and cook over a gentle heat for 5 minutes, stirring occasionally. Purée in a blender or food processor, then return to the saucepan. Stir in the mint and flour and cook, stirring, for 1 minute. Blend in the milk, bring to the boil and cook for 2 minutes, stirring all the time. Season to taste. Remove from the heat and beat in the egg yolks. Whisk the egg whites until stiff and fold into the mixture with a metal spoon. Turn into four greased individual soufflé dishes (or one 1.2 litre/2 pt/5 cup dish). Bake in a preheated oven at 200 °C/ 400°F/gas mark 6 for about 25 minutes (about 35–40 minutes for a large soufflé) or until risen and golden. Serve immediately.

Cantonese-style Vegetables

SERVES 6

60 ml/4 tbsp olive oil
1 small piece of fresh root ginger,
    chopped
225 g/8 oz carrots, cut into
    matchsticks
225 g/8 oz turnips, cut into
    matchsticks
225 g/8 oz swede (rutabaga), cut into
    matchsticks
227 g/8 oz/1 small can bamboo
    shoots, drained and cut into
    matchsticks
225 g/8 oz celery sticks, cut into
    matchsticks
1 large onion, quartered and
    separated into layers
225 g/8 oz French (green) beans,
    trimmed
Salt and freshly ground black pepper
120 ml/4 fl oz/½ cup vegetable stock
Grated rind and juice of 1 lemon
2 egg yolks
30 ml/2 tbsp water
5 ml/1 tsp cornflour (cornstarch)
A little sugar
Chinese (stem lettuce) or cos
    (romaine) lettuce leaves
30 ml/2 tbsp sesame seeds, toasted

In a large wok or pan, heat the oil and ginger, then stir-fry all the vegetables for 3 minutes. Season to taste, add the stock, cover and boil for 3 minutes. Add the lemon rind and juice. Drain all the mixture through a colander into a bowl. Collect the juices and place in the pan. Blend the egg yolks and water with the cornflour. Gradually add to the pan and cook for 1 minute, stirring to thicken. Blend all the vegetables with the sauce. Season to taste with salt, pepper and sugar. Pile on to lettuce leaves and sprinkle with the sesame seeds.

Vegetable and Mozzarella Bakes

SERVES 4

1 carrot, grated
4 spring onions (scallions), thinly
    sliced
2 small courgettes (zucchini), thinly
    sliced
60 ml/4 tbsp vegetable stock or water
Salt and freshly ground black pepper
120 ml/4 fl oz/½ cup passata (sieved
    tomatoes)
5 ml/1 tsp dried basil
100 g/4 oz Mozzarella, sliced

Mix the carrot, onions and courgettes together and divide between 4 individual gratin dishes. Spoon the stock or water over and season lightly. Cover with foil and bake in a preheated oven at 180°C/350°F/gas mark 4 for 30 minutes. Remove the foil and spoon over the passata. Sprinkle with the basil and arrange the cheese on top. Re-cover with foil and return to the oven for about 10 minutes until piping hot and the cheese has melted.

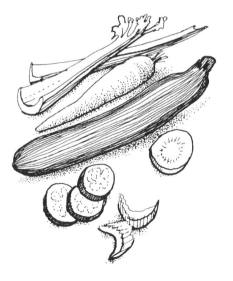

48

Fragrant Dolmas

*225 g/8 oz can vine leaves, rinsed
and dried*
*175 g/6 oz/1½ cups cooked long-grain
rice*
*½ bunch of spring onions (scallions),
finely chopped*
100 g/4 oz/⅔ cup dried figs, chopped
1 large carrot, grated
Pinch of ground cinnamon
Pinch of grated nutmeg
5 ml/1 tsp dried mint
15 ml/1 tbsp lemon juice
Salt and freshly ground black pepper
300 ml/½ pt/1¼ cups pure orange juice
150 ml/¼ pt/⅔ cup water
Plain yoghurt

Put a layer of vine leaves in the base of a large casserole dish (Dutch oven). Mix together all the remaining ingredients except the orange juice, water and yoghurt, seasoning lightly with salt and pepper. Put spoonfuls of the mixture on the remaining vine leaves and roll up to form parcels. Pack tightly into the casserole dish, if necessary making two layers with a layer of non-stick baking parchment in between. Pour over the orange juice and water. Bake in a preheated oven at 160°C/325°F/gas mark 3 for 1½ hours. Leave to stand for about 15 minutes, spoon on to serving plates and serve warm with a spoonful of plain yoghurt on each plate.

Oriental Asparagus

450 g/1 lb baby asparagus spears
15 ml/1 tbsp light soy sauce
1 garlic clove, crushed
5 ml/1 tsp grated fresh root ginger
15 ml/1 tbsp sesame oil
*150 ml/¼ pt/⅔ cup double (heavy)
cream*
Salt and freshly ground black pepper

Lay the asparagus in a flameproof casserole (Dutch oven). Mix the soy sauce with the garlic, ginger and oil and pour over the asparagus. Leave to marinate for 1 hour, turning occasionally. Bring to the boil, cover, reduce the heat and cook very gently for about 8 minutes or until the asparagus is just tender. Meanwhile, boil the cream with a little salt and pepper for about 5 minutes until thickened and reduced. Drizzle over the asparagus and serve straight away.

Asparagus with Sun-dried Tomato Butter

SERVES 4–6

750 g/1½ lb asparagus
100 g/4 oz/½ cup unsalted (sweet)
  butter
4 halves sun-dried tomatoes in oil,
  drained and finely chopped
30 ml/2 tbsp sun-dried tomato oil
30 ml/2 tbsp chopped parsley
Salt and freshly ground black pepper

Trim off about 5 cm/2 in from the base of the asparagus stalks. Tie the spears in a bundle. Stand it in a saucepan of salted water. Cover with a lid (or foil if the lid won't fit). Bring to the boil, reduce the heat and cook over a moderate heat for 10 minutes. Turn off the heat and leave undisturbed for 5 minutes. Drain. Meanwhile, melt the butter in a small saucepan. Stir in the tomatoes, oil and parsley and season to taste. Lay the asparagus on warm serving plates, spoon the tomato butter over and serve hot.

Asparagus, Bean Sprouts and Red Bean Assortment

SERVES 4–6

225 g/8 oz asparagus
225 g/8 oz spring onions (scallions)
225 g/8 oz bean sprouts
100 g/4 oz/1 cup macaroni
60 ml/4 tbsp olive oil
1 green chilli, seeded and cut into
  strips
75 ml/5 tbsp medium-dry white wine
5 ml/1 tsp chopped fresh root ginger
15 ml/1 tbsp caraway or celery seeds
225 g/8 oz red kidney beans, cooked
  (see page 10)
Salt and freshly ground black pepper
Mixed green lettuce and salad leaves
2 grapefruit, segmented
30 ml/2 tbsp wine vinegar (optional)

Scrape and trim the asparagus. Cut into small pieces, 3 cm/1¼ in long. Parboil for 2 minutes in salted water and drain. Trim the onions and cut into 3 cm/1¼ in strips with green stems. Wash and rinse the bean sprouts and pat dry on kitchen paper. Boil the macaroni for 12 minutes. Rinse and pat dry. Heat the oil in a wok or large frying pan (skillet) and quickly fry (sauté) the onion, chilli and asparagus for 2 minutes. Add the wine, ginger, caraway or celery seeds and macaroni. Toss for 1 more minute, then add the kidney beans, bean sprouts and seasoning and cook for a further minute. Serve in four bowls lined with salad leaves and garnish with grapefruit segments. Drizzle over a little wine vinegar if liked.

Asparagus Mousse with Toasted Almonds

SERVES 4

225 g/8 oz thin asparagus spears
3 spring onions (scallions), sliced
150 ml/¼ pt/⅔ cup water
10 ml/2 tsp vegetarian gelatine
150 ml/¼ pt/⅔ cup whipping cream,
  whipped
Salt and freshly ground white pepper
Celery salt
Grated nutmeg
Oil, for greasing
75 g/3 oz/¾ cup toasted flaked
  almonds
Toast fingers

Scrape the asparagus lightly and cut into small pieces. Boil the asparagus and spring onions in the water for 6 minutes. Dissolve the gelatine in the hot liquid and bring almost to the boil again. Purée the mixture in a blender or food processor or pass it through a sieve (strainer) with the liquid. Cool. When completely cold, fold in the whipped cream and season with salt, pepper, celery salt and nutmeg. Divide the mixture between four lightly oiled individual moulds. Chill to set the mixture. Turn out the mousses on to plates and sprinkle with toasted flaked almonds just before serving. Serve with toast fingers.

Pan-fried Asparagus and Egg Cutlets

SERVES 4

50 g/2 oz/¼ cup butter or margarine
50 g/2 oz/½ cup plain (all-purpose)
  flour
600 ml/1 pt/2½ cups milk
4 eggs, beaten
Salt and freshly ground white pepper
Grated nutmeg
8 asparagus tips
4 hard-boiled (hard-cooked) eggs,
  sliced
50 g/2 oz/½ cup flaked almonds
50 g/2 oz/2 cups cornflakes, crushed
60 ml/4 tbsp seasoned flour
Oil, for shallow-frying
Watercress or curly endive (frisée
  lettuce)

Heat the butter or margarine, add the flour and cook until smooth, without colouring. Gradually stir in the milk. When thick, remove from the heat and blend in half the beaten egg. Season with salt, white pepper and a pinch of nutmeg. Boil the asparagus for 5 minutes. Drain and cut into small pieces. Add them with the hard-boiled eggs to the sauce while still hot. Pour this mixture into a well-oiled shallow tin (pan) 2.5 cm/1 in deep. Chill until very cold. Mix together the nuts and cornflakes. Turn out the asparagus mixture on to a clean board and cut into squares. Coat each square with seasoned flour, dip in the remaining beaten egg, then coat on both sides with the nuts and cornflakes. Heat the oil until very hot and shallow-fry the squares, four at a time, for 1 minute on each side until golden. Drain on kitchen paper. Garnish with watercress or curly endive.

Courgette Fritters with Yoghurt Sauce

SERVES 4

100 g/4 oz cucumber, roughly
* chopped*
2 garlic cloves, crushed
120 ml/4 fl oz/½ cup plain yoghurt
Salt and freshly ground black pepper
4 small courgettes (zucchini)
60 ml/4 tbsp plain (all-purpose) flour
50 g/2 oz/1 cup wholemeal
* breadcrumbs*
50 g/2 oz/½ cup chopped almonds
2 eggs, beaten
Oil, for shallow-frying

First make the sauce. Put the cucumber, one of the crushed garlic cloves, the yoghurt and a little salt and pepper in a blender or food processor and blend well. Transfer to a small serving bowl. Trim the courgettes and cut into batons about 5 cm/2 in long and 5 mm/¼ in wide. Season the flour with salt and pepper. Mix the breadcrumbs and nuts on a plate. Beat the remaining crushed garlic into the eggs. Coat the courgette batons with seasoned flour, then dip in beaten egg and roll in breadcrumbs and nuts. Heat the oil in a frying pan (skillet) and quickly fry (sauté) the coated courgette batons for 1 minute. Remove from the pan and drain well on kitchen paper. Serve immediately with the yoghurt sauce.

Mushroom and Pepper Moulds

SERVES 8

100 g/4 oz/½ cup butter or margarine
25 g/1 oz/¼ cup plain (all-purpose)
* flour*
600 ml/1 pt/2½ cups milk, heated
25 g/1 oz vegetarian gelatine
Salt and freshly ground white pepper
4 eggs, beaten
1 red (bell) pepper, diced
100 g/4 oz/1 cup frozen peas
50 g/2 oz onion, chopped
225 g/8 oz white mushrooms, sliced
Extra butter, for greasing

In a pan, melt half the butter or margarine, add the flour and cook for 1 minute, stirring. Stir in the milk gradually to avoid lumps. Dissolve the gelatine in the hot sauce and bring almost to the boil again. Season to taste. Remove from the heat and cool. When cold, blend in the beaten eggs. Blanch the red pepper and peas for 3 minutes, then drain. Heat the remaining butter in a pan and stir-fry the onion and mushrooms for 2 minutes. Add the peas and peppers and gradually blend in the sauce away from the heat. Fill individual 150 ml/¼ pt/⅔ cup well-buttered moulds (molds) and bake in a preheated oven at 180°C/350°F/gas mark 4 for 20 minutes until set like a custard. Serve hot or cold.

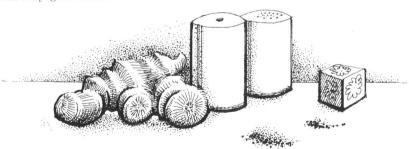

Potted Mushrooms with Tarragon and Brandy

SERVES 4

175 g/6 oz/¾ cup butter
275 g/10 oz button mushrooms,
* sliced*
15 ml/1 tbsp chopped tarragon
15 ml/1 tbsp brandy
Salt and freshly ground black pepper
Good pinch of grated nutmeg
Lettuce leaves
Thin rye crispbreads

Melt 100 g/4 oz/½ cup of the butter in a saucepan. Add the mushrooms and cook, stirring, until well coated in the butter. Add the tarragon, brandy, a little salt and pepper and the nutmeg. Cover and simmer gently for 5 minutes until the mushrooms are tender. Spoon with their juices into 4–6 ramekin dishes (custard cups). Press down. Leave until cold then chill until set. Melt the remaining butter and pour over. Chill again until set. Loosen the edges of the pots and turn the mushrooms out on to a bed of lettuce. Serve with crispbreads.

Gingered Mushroom and Courgette Kebabs

SERVES 4

50 g/2 oz/¼ cup butter
5 ml/1 tsp grated fresh root ginger
2 garlic cloves, crushed
3 even-sized courgettes (zucchini)
24 button mushrooms
15 ml/1 tbsp chopped parsley
Crusty bread

Melt the butter in a saucepan and add the ginger and garlic. Leave to stand for 5 minutes. Meanwhile, trim each courgette then cut into eight pieces. Thread alternately with the mushrooms on eight soaked wooden skewers. Lay in single line in a baking tin (pan) and brush with the butter mixture. Grill (broil), turning and brushing with more butter, for about 6 minutes or until the mushrooms and courgettes are golden and just cooked. Add the chopped parsley to the remaining flavoured butter and heat through. Lay two kebabs on each of four warmed serving plates and spoon the remaining butter over. Serve hot with crusty bread.

53

Mushrooms with Chilli Yoghurt

450 g/1 lb button mushrooms
300 ml/½ pt/1¼ cups vegetable stock
60 ml/4 tbsp cider vinegar
1 garlic clove, crushed
5 ml/1 tsp dried mint
2.5 ml/½ tsp caster (superfine) sugar
45 ml/3 tbsp plain yoghurt
2 spring onions (scallions), finely
  chopped
1 fresh green chilli, seeded and
  chopped
Salt and freshly ground black pepper

Put the mushrooms in a saucepan with the stock. Bring to the boil, cover, reduce the heat and simmer for 10 minutes. Put the vinegar, garlic, mint and sugar in a saucepan with 60 ml/4 tbsp of the mushroom cooking liquid. Bring to the boil. Add the drained mushrooms and simmer, stirring occasionally, for 10 minutes. Leave to cool. Drain off any remaining liquid and discard. Stir in the yoghurt, most of the spring onions (reserving a little for garnish) and the chilli and season to taste with salt and pepper. Spoon into small dishes and sprinkle with the remaining spring onions before serving.

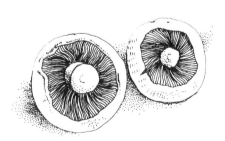

Pickled Mushrooms with Mozzarella

225 g/8 oz button mushrooms
300 ml/½ pt/1¼ cups ginger wine
20 ml/4 tsp light brown sugar
225 g/8 oz Mozzarella cheese, sliced
Freshly ground black pepper
Green olives
Ciabatta bread

Put the mushrooms in a pan with the wine and sugar. Bring to the boil, reduce the heat, cover and simmer gently for 10 minutes until syrupy. Spoon into a clean, warm jar and loosely cover. When cold, screw down the lid and store in a cool place for up to a week until ready to use. Spoon on to individual plates. Surround with slices of Mozzarella and add a good grinding of pepper. Scatter a few green olives over and serve with ciabatta bread.

Breaded Mushrooms

450 g/1 lb button mushrooms
30 ml/2 tbsp plain (all-purpose) flour
Salt and freshly ground black pepper
1–2 eggs, beaten
50 g/2 oz/1 cup wholemeal
  breadcrumbs
Oil, for deep-frying
Tartare Sauce (see page 306)

Dust the mushrooms in seasoned flour and shake off the surplus. Dip in beaten egg, then breadcrumbs. Deep-fry in hot oil for about 4 minutes until golden. Drain on kitchen paper. Serve hot with Tartare Sauce.

Mushroom and Peanut Cocktail

225 g/8 oz button mushrooms, halved
or quartered
50 g/2 oz/½ cup Dry Roasted
Peanuts, (see page 350)
100 g/4 oz mixed black and green
grapes, halved and seeded (pitted)
60 ml/4 tbsp mayonnaise
5 ml/1 tsp tomato purée (paste)
A few drops of Worcestershire sauce
Salt and freshly ground black pepper
Sunflower seeds
Shredded lettuce

Blanch the mushrooms if preferred or leave raw. Mix with the peanuts and grapes. Blend together the mayonnaise, tomato purée, Worcestershire sauce and a little salt and pepper. Fold in the mushroom mixture. Sprinkle with sunflower seeds. Serve on a bed of shredded lettuce.

Spicy Mushroom and Cashew Nut Cocktail

Prepare as for Mushroom and Peanut Cocktail but substitute cashew nuts for the peanuts and add a few drops of Tabasco sauce to the dressing.

Savoury Stuffed Mushrooms

85 g/3½ oz/1 packet stuffing mix (any
flavour)
4 large flat mushrooms
175 g/6 oz/1½ cups Cheddar cheese,
grated

Make up the stuffing as directed on the packet. Remove the mushroom stalks, chop the stalks and mix them into the stuffing. Peel the mushroom caps and lay in a shallow ovenproof dish, gills facing upwards. Spoon the stuffing into the mushroom caps and sprinkle with cheese. Bake in a preheated oven at 190°C/375°F/gas mark 5 for 15–20 minutes.

Mushrooms in Champagne Sauce with Quails' Eggs

SERVES 4

4 quails' eggs
20 ml/4 tsp oil
2 small shallots, chopped
225 g/8 oz button mushrooms
150 ml/¼ pt/⅔ cup champagne or
    sparkling wine
2.5 ml/½ tsp cornflour (cornstarch)
75 ml/5 tbsp soured (dairy sour)
    cream
15 ml/1 tbsp mixed chopped chervil,
    coriander (cilantro) and mint
Salt and freshly ground black pepper
¼ cucumber, cut into 5 mm/¼ in
    cubes
1 head chicory (Belgian endive),
    leaves separated
Ground turmeric and paprika

Cook the quails' eggs in boiling water for 6 minutes. Shell, place in a bowl and cover with warm water. To make the sauce, heat the oil in a small saucepan, add the shallots and stir-fry for 1 minute, without browning. Add the mushrooms and toss for 2 minutes, then remove with a draining spoon and keep warm. Add the champagne or sparkling wine and boil rapidly for 10 minutes to reduce by half. Stir the cornflour into the soured cream and add to the pan with the herbs. Boil for 4 minutes, stirring, until thickened. Season to taste and add the mushrooms and cucumber. Simmer for 2 minutes only. Spoon into the centre of four serving plates and arrange the chicory leaves all around in a petal pattern. Cut the quails' eggs in half and arrange two in the centre of each plate. Sprinkle with a mixture of turmeric and paprika.

Mushroom and Herb Pâté

SERVES 6

30 ml/2 tbsp oil
1 small onion, chopped
2 garlic cloves, chopped
225 g/8 oz mushrooms, sliced
5 ml/1 tsp tomato purée (paste)
15 ml/1 tbsp mixed chopped herbs,
    e.g. coriander (cilantro), basil,
    mint, tarragon, parsley, majoram
2 eggs, beaten
Salt and freshly ground black pepper
30 ml/2 tbsp breadcrumbs
Lettuce leaves
Coriander leaves
Brown Garlic Bread (see page 325)

Heat the oil in a frying pan (skillet) and stir-fry the onion and garlic for 2 minutes until soft but not brown. Add the mushrooms and cook for 4 minutes, then blend in the tomato purée and herbs. Season the beaten eggs with salt and pepper, pour into the pan and cook gently, stirring, until lightly scrambled. Stir in the breadcrumbs. Transfer the mixture to a blender or food processor and blend to a smooth purée. If a coarser texture is preferred, blend for only a few seconds, or put the mixture through a mincer (grinder). Arrange the lettuce leaves on six serving plates and place spoonfuls of the pâté in the centre of each. Garnish with coriander leaves and serve with garlic bread.

Baked Blue Cheese Mushrooms

225 g/8 oz large flat mushrooms,
*   peeled*
50 g/2 oz/¼ cup butter or margarine
2 shallots, finely chopped
175 g/6 oz/1½ cups blue cheese,
*   crumbled*
25 g/1 oz/½ cup breadcrumbs
Salt and freshly ground black pepper

Remove and chop the mushroom stalks. Melt the butter or margarine in a pan, add the stalks and shallots and cook for 2 minutes, stirring. Leave to cool for 5 minutes, then add the cheese and breadcrumbs. Season and mix well. Divide between the mushroom caps. Grease a large shallow dish and place the mushroom caps in it. Add 30 ml/2 tbsp water. Cover with foil and bake in a pre-heated oven for 12 minutes at 200°C/400°F/gas mark 6 until the mushrooms are cooked and the topping is bubbling.

Triple Cheese Pâté

225 g/8 oz/2 cups red Leicester
*   cheese, grated*
50 g/2 oz/¼ cup butter, softened
45 ml/3 tbsp single (light) cream
A few drops of Tabasco sauce
15 ml/1 tbsp chopped parsley
200 g/7 oz/1 small carton low-fat soft
*   cheese*
25 g/1 oz/¼ cup walnuts, chopped
Salt and freshly ground black pepper
100 g/4 oz/½ cup soft cheese with
*   garlic and herbs*
Walnut halves
Parsley sprigs

Mash the red Leicester with the butter, half the cream, the Tabasco and parsley until well blended. Mix the low fat soft cheese with the chopped walnuts and a little seasoning. Blend the garlic and herb cheese with the remaining cream until smooth. Press half the red Leicester mixture into the base of a 450 g/1 lb loaf tin (pan), lined with non-stick baking parchment. Spread half the walnut cheese over. Then spread all the garlic and herb mixture over that, then the remaining walnut cheese and, finally, the remaining red Leicester mixture. Press down firmly, cover and chill for several hours until fairly firm. Turn out on to a serving dish, remove the paper and serve, garnished with extra walnuts and parsley sprigs.

Cheddar Cheese Pâté

225 g/8 oz/2 cups Cheddar cheese,
* grated*
25 g/1 oz/2 tbsp butter or margarine
45 ml/3 tbsp white wine or vegetable
* stock*
Salt and freshly ground black pepper

Mix together all the ingredients to make a smooth paste. Press into a dish and cover with foil. Chill before serving with warm toast or crackers.

Brandy Walnut Cheese Pâté

Prepare as for Cheddar Cheese Pâté but substitute brandy for the wine or stock and add 50 g/2 oz/½ cup chopped walnuts.

Blue Cheese Pâté

Prepare as for Cheddar Cheese Pâté but substitute Stilton or Danish blue for half the Cheddar and moisten with red wine instead of white.

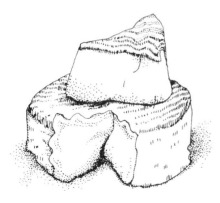

Golden Potted Cheese

100 g/4 oz/½ cup butter or margarine
Pinch of ground mace
Salt and freshly ground black pepper
225 g/8 oz/2 cups Cheddar cheese,
* grated*
15 ml/1 tbsp milk
15 ml/1 tbsp sherry
Crisp toast and fresh vegetable sticks

Mix together all the ingredients except the toast and vegetables. Pack into one large or four small pots. Cover and chill. Serve with toast and vegetable sticks.

Cauliflower Cheese Pots

½ small cauliflower, cut into small
* florets*
A little butter or margarine, for
* greasing*
Good pinch of grated nutmeg
Salt and freshly ground black pepper
75 g/3 oz/¾ cup Cheddar cheese,
* grated*
2 eggs
150 ml/¼ pt/⅔ cup single (light)
* cream*
15 ml/1 tbsp grated Pecorino cheese

Steam the cauliflower or cook in boiling, lightly salted water until just tender. Do not overcook. Drain, if necessary and arrange in four buttered ramekin dishes (custard cups). Sprinkle with nutmeg, a little salt and pepper and the Cheddar cheese. Beat the eggs and cream together and pour over. Bake in a preheated oven at 180°C/350°F/gas mark 4 for about 20 minutes or until set and lightly golden. Dust with grated Pecorino before serving.

Broccoli Blue Cheese Bakes

SERVES 4

Prepare as for Cauliflower Cheese Pots, but substitute 100–175 g/4–6 oz broccoli for the cauliflower and use 50 g/ 2 oz/½ cup crumbled Danish blue cheese in place of the Cheddar.

Hot Cheese and Potato Pâté with Herbs

SERVES 4

225 g/8 oz potatoes, peeled and thinly
*   sliced*
30 ml/2 tbsp olive oil
150 g/5 oz/⅔ cup fromage frais
Salt and freshly ground black pepper
60 ml/4 tbsp chopped herbs (e.g.
*   parsley, chives, basil, thyme)*
Juice of ½ lemon
Salted wholemeal crackers

Boil the potatoes for 6 minutes, drain and mash to a purée. Combine with the remaining ingredients except the crackers, seasoning to taste. Serve hot with salted wholemeal crackers.

Scrumptious Samosas

MAKES 30

1 small onion, finely chopped
30 ml/2 tbsp oil
2.5 ml/½ tsp ground cumin
5 ml/1 tsp ground coriander
*   (cilantro)*
5 ml/1 tsp garam masala
1 fresh green chilli, seeded and
*   chopped*
150 g/5 oz/1 small can garden peas
175 g/6 oz/¾ cup mashed potato
15 ml/1 tbsp chopped coriander
Salt and freshly ground black pepper
225 g//8 oz/2 cups plain (all-purpose)
*   flour*
150 ml/¼ pt/⅔ cup water
A little beaten egg
Oil, for deep-frying

Fry (sauté) the onion in 15 ml/1 tbsp of the oil for 2 minutes. Add the spices and fry for a further 1 minute. Remove from the heat and stir in the peas with their liquid, the potato and coriander. Season with a little salt and pepper. Sift the flour with a good pinch of salt into a bowl. Add the remaining 15 ml/1 tbsp of oil and the water and mix to form a firm dough. Knead gently on a lightly floured surface. Divide into 15 equal pieces and roll each in a ball. Flatten to rounds about 12.5 cm/5 in across. Cut each round in half and brush all round with beaten egg. Put a spoonful of the potato mixture in the centre of each semicircle. Fold one corner in to the centre of the rounded side. Fold the other one over to cover the first completely, forming a filled triangle. Press the edges well together to seal. Repeat until all the samosas are made. Deep-fry in hot oil, a few at a time, until crisp and golden. Drain on kitchen paper and serve hot.

59

Cream Cheese and Leek Dip

3 leeks, white part only, sliced
25 g/1 oz/2 tbsp butter or margarine
30 ml/2 tbsp plain (all-purpose) flour
150 ml/¼ pt/⅔ cup milk
100 g/4 oz/½ cup fromage frais
Salt and freshly ground black pepper
Toast or crackers

Wash the leeks in plenty of water. Drain and pat dry on kitchen paper. Heat the butter or margarine in a saucepan and stir-fry the leeks without browning. Sprinkle over the flour to absorb the butter and stir the milk into this mixture. Bring to the boil and simmer for 5 minutes. Cool, then blend in the fromage frais and season to taste. Serve cold with toast or crackers.

Creamy Cheese Tartlets

225 g/8 oz frozen puff pastry (paste),
  thawed
50 g/2 oz/½ cup Cheddar cheese,
  grated
1.5 ml/¼ tsp chilli powder
150 g/5 oz/1¼ cups shelled fresh or
  frozen peas
75 g/3 oz/⅓ cup curd (smooth
  cottage) cheese, well drained
1 shallot, chopped
1 egg, beaten
Salt and freshly ground black pepper
5 ml/1 tsp clear honey
Apple wedges

On a floured board, roll out the pastry thinly. Sprinkle over the grated cheese and chilli powder and roll again to incorporate the cheese into the pastry. Prick the pastry with a fork to prevent rising. Cut out eight rounds of pastry with a 6 cm/2½ in pastry cutter. Grease the tins and line them with the pastry rounds. Prick the bottom of the pastry again. Rest for 20 minutes at room temperature. Meanwhile, cook the peas until tender, then drain, place in a blender or food processor and purée. Add the curd cheese, shallot and beaten egg. Season with salt, pepper and honey. Run the machine briefly to blend. Spoon the mixture into each tartlet. Smooth the top with a palette knife. Bake in a preheated oven at 200°C/400°F/gas mark 6 for 15–20 minutes. Unmould on to a plate garnished with apple wedges.

Green Olive Pâté

*150 g/5 oz/scant 1 cup large green
olives, stoned (pitted)*
1 green chilli, seeded and chopped
2 spring onions (scallions), chopped
2 dill pickles, chopped
15 ml/1 tbsp capers, chopped
*30 ml/2 tbsp chopped parsley or
coriander (cilantro) leaves*
2 garlic cloves, chopped
30 ml/2 tbsp olive oil
100 g/4 oz/½ cup fromage frais
Toasted French bread slices

Pound all the ingredients except the bread in a mortar to a paste. Alternatively, mince them or purée using 45 ml/ 3 tbsp boiling water in a blender or food processor. Serve on toasted French bread slices.

Red Devilled Pâté

*425 g/15 oz/1 large can red kidney
beans, drained*
15 ml/1 tbsp tomato purée (paste)
5 ml/1 tsp soy sauce
5 ml/1 tsp lemon juice
A few drops of Tabasco sauce
Salt and freshly ground black pepper
Paprika
Wholemeal toast or rye bread

Put all the ingredients except the paprika and toast or bread into a blender or food processor. Purée for 2–3 minutes until the mixture is smooth. Moisten with a little vegetable stock if necessary. Turn into a bowl and chill. Garnish with paprika and serve with wholemeal toast or rye bread.

Lentil and Olive Dip

175 g/6 oz/1 cup red lentils
*45 ml/3 tbsp tahini (sesame seed
paste)*
30 ml/2 tbsp lemon juice
75 ml/5 tbsp thick plain yoghurt
1 large garlic clove, crushed
*15 ml/1 tbsp chopped stoned (pitted)
black olives*
Salt and freshly ground black pepper
A few whole black olives
15 ml/1 tbsp chopped parsley
Pitta bread

Put the lentils in a saucepan with enough water to cover them. Bring to the boil, reduce the heat, cover and simmer for about 25 minutes until pulpy. Drain if necessary. Turn into a bowl and beat in the tahini and lemon juice. Leave to cool, then stir in the yoghurt, garlic and chopped olives. Season to taste. Spoon on to individual plates, garnish with a few whole olives and a little chopped parsley and serve with fingers of warm pitta bread.

Spicy Red Lentil Pâté

100 g/4 oz/⅔ cup red lentils
450 g/¾ pt/2 cups boiling water
50 g/2 oz/½ cup desiccated (shredded)
*   coconut*
10 ml/2 tsp lemon juice
4 drops of Tabasco sauce
Salt and freshly ground black pepper
Pinch of ground nutmeg
Tortilla chips

Put the lentils and water into a large pan. Bring to the boil and reduce the heat. Cover and simmer for 12 minutes or until soft. Drain and reserve the liquid. Stir in the coconut, lemon juice, Tabasco sauce, salt, pepper and nutmeg to taste. Put in a food processor or blender and purée until smooth, adding a little reserved stock if necessary. Chill thoroughly before serving with Tortilla chips.

Baked Bean Pâté

400 g/14 oz/1 large can baked beans
100 g/4 oz/1 cup Cheddar cheese,
*   grated*
50 g/2 oz/1 cup breadcrumbs
5 ml/1 tsp yeast extract
5 ml/1 tsp dried mixed herbs
Salt and freshly ground black pepper
Fresh vegetables cut into matchsticks
*   or small florets*

Place all ingredients except the vegetables in a food processor or blender and purée for 1½ minutes. Turn into a container. Chill until ready to serve with vegetable 'dippers'.

Chick Pea Caviare

45 ml/3 tbsp walnut or olive oil
1 small onion, chopped
225 g/8 oz/2 cups fresh cooked or
*   canned chick peas (garbanzos)*
120 ml/4 fl oz/½ cup water
90 ml/6 tbsp plain yoghurt
Salt and freshly ground black pepper
30 ml/2 tbsp tahini paste
Cheese crackers or vegetable sticks

Heat the oil in pan and stir-fry the onion until golden. Add the cooked chick peas and water. Boil for 5 minutes. Pass the mixture through a sieve (strainer) or purée in a blender or food processor. Blend in the yoghurt and season to taste. Add the tahini paste. Serve with cheese crackers or vegetable sticks.

Oriental Tofu Bites

275 g/10 oz block firm tofu, drained
and cubed
60 ml/4 tbsp sunflower oil
150 ml/¼ pt/⅔ cup soy sauce
30 ml/2 tbsp white wine vinegar
30 ml/2 tbsp light brown sugar
15 ml/1 tbsp tomato purée (paste)
15 ml/1 tbsp grated fresh root ginger
1 garlic clove, crushed
2.5 ml/½ tsp Chinese five spice
powder
½ cucumber, cubed
Rice wine (optional)

Put the tofu in a bowl. Whisk together the remaining ingredients except the cucumber and rice wine and pour over the tofu. Toss gently, then leave to marinate overnight, turning occasionally. Spear on cocktail sticks (toothpicks) with the cucumber cubes and serve, preferably with a glass of rice wine.

Main Meals

All these recipes are packed with goodness. Some are simple, everyday affairs, others are elegant enough for even the most sophisticated dinner party.

Many of them have serving suggestions to make perfectly complemented main courses. However, these are just ideas. Some warm, fresh rolls and a crisp green salad are an excellent accompaniment to just about any of these dishes, or choose one of the salads or side dishes from the next chapter.

Vegetable-based Main Courses

Hungarian Vegetable Goulash

SERVES 4

60 ml/4 tbsp sunflower oil
2 red onions, coarsely chopped
2 garlic cloves, chopped
15 ml/1 tbsp paprika
2 celery sticks, sliced
2 carrots, sliced
2 parsnips, sliced
2 turnips, cut into 2.5 cm/1 in cubes
1 red (bell) pepper, diced
*225 g/8 oz potatoes, cut into 2.5 cm/
    1 in cubes*
600 ml/1 pt/2½ cups vegetable stock
30 ml/2 tbsp tomato purée (paste)
Thyme or sage sprig
*75 g/3 oz/¾ cup baked beans or
    cooked peas*
10 ml/2 tsp cornflour (cornstarch)
150 ml/¼ pt/⅔ cup plain yoghurt
Salt and freshly ground black pepper
Chopped parsley
*225 g/8 oz/2 cups self-raising (self-
    rising) flour*
100 g/4 oz/½ cup butter or margarine
5 ml/1 tsp caraway seeds
1.5 ml/¼ tsp salt
1 egg
30 ml/2 tbsp warm water
Chopped parsley

Heat the oil in a large heavy-based saucepan and stir-fry the onions and garlic for 3 minutes until soft but not brown. Sprinkle in the paprika and add all the other vegetables except the baked beans or cooked peas. Cover with the stock and bring to the boil. Stir in the tomato purée and add the thyme or sage, cover and simmer gently for 15 minutes. Stir in the beans or peas. In a cup, blend the cornflour (cornstarch) with the yoghurt (dilute with 60 ml/4 tbsp water if too firm) and stir into the vegetable mixture. Simmer for 5 minutes until thickened. Check the seasoning. Meanwhile, place the flour and butter or margarine in a bowl and rub in with the fingertips. Add the caraway seeds and salt and bind with egg and water. Roll the dough into 12 balls the size of walnuts. Cook in boiling salted water in a shallow pan for 6–8 minutes. Remove with a draining spoon. Transfer the vegetable casserole to a large heated serving dish or serve straight into heated soup plates. Top with caraway dumplings and sprinkle with chopped parsley.

Brussels Sprout and Chestnut Colcannon

SERVES 4

75 ml/5 tbsp sunflower oil
2 onions, chopped
*225 g/8 oz small fresh or frozen
    Brussels sprouts, cooked and cooled*
*225 g/8 oz chestnuts, cooked, peeled
    and cooled, or canned chestnuts,
    drained*
1 eating (dessert) apple, sliced
50 g/2 oz/½ cup peanuts
Salt and freshly ground black pepper
Pinch of mace or nutmeg
Plain yoghurt (optional)

Heat the oil in a large frying pan (skillet) and stir-fry the onions for 2 minutes until soft but not brown. Add the Brussels sprouts, chestnuts, apple and peanuts. Toss together and fry (sauté) for 5 minutes until golden. Season to taste with salt, pepper and mace or nutmeg and serve immediately on individual plates. Drizzle a little yoghurt over each portion, if liked, before serving.

Leek and Sprout Hotpot

SERVES 4

450 g/1 lb potatoes, scrubbed and
thinly sliced
1 leek
450 g/1 lb Brussels sprouts, trimmed
and bases slit
150 ml/¼ pt/⅔ cup vegetable stock
5 ml/1 tsp made English mustard
5 ml/1 tsp chopped tarragon
50 g/2 oz/½ cup Cheddar cheese,
grated

Cook the potato slices in boiling, lightly salted water for 4 minutes. Drain. Slice the leek lengthways and cut it into 2.5 cm/1 in lengths. Put the sprouts and leek in a flameproof casserole (Dutch oven). Add the stock, bring to the boil and simmer gently for 3 minutes. Stir in the mustard and tarragon. Lay the potato slices on top. Cover with cheese. Bake in a preheated oven at 190°C/375°F/gas mark 5 for about 45 minutes until golden and just cooked through. Serve hot.

Corn and Tomato Cups

SERVES 4

1 onion, thinly sliced
2 large tomatoes, skinned and sliced
1 avocado, stoned (pitted), peeled and
sliced
50 g/2 oz/½ cup sweetcorn (corn)
4 slices wholemeal bread
50 g/2 oz/¼ cup butter or margarine
3 eggs, beaten
300 ml/½ pt/1¼ cups milk
Salt and freshly ground black pepper
Grated nutmeg
100 g/4 oz/1 cup Emmental (Swiss)
cheese, grated
Toasted sesame seeds
Salad
Jacket potatoes

Grease the bases of four individual ovenproof dishes. Arrange the onion, tomatoes, avocado and corn in them. Cut the bread slices in small triangles and brush with melted butter or margarine. Arrange, overlapping, on top of the vegetables in each dish. Beat together the eggs and milk and season with salt, pepper and nutmeg. Pour over the contents of each dish and leave to soak for 20 minutes. Bake the puddings in a preheated oven at 190°C/375°F/gas mark 5 for 40 minutes, then remove and sprinkle with grated cheese. Place under a hot grill (broiler) for 3 minutes until golden. Sprinkle with toasted sesame seeds and serve at once with salad and jacket potatoes.

Gougère Niçoise

50 g/2 oz/¼ cup butter or margarine
120 ml/4 fl oz/½ cup water
Pinch of salt
150 g/5 oz/1¼ cups plain (all-
*   purpose) flour, sifted*
2 eggs, beaten
100 g/4 oz/1 cup Emmental (Swiss)
*   cheese, grated*
50 g/2 oz/½ cup French (green) beans
50 ml/2 fl oz/3½ tbsp oil
1 small onion, chopped or sliced
2 courgettes (zucchini), sliced
2 tomatoes, skinned, seeded and
*   chopped*
50 g/2 oz/½ cup peanuts
Salt and freshly ground black pepper
15 ml/1 tbsp chopped parsley
45 ml/3 tbsp grated Cheddar cheese

Make up the pastry. Place the butter or margarine and water in a saucepan, heat gently until the fat has melted, then bring to the boil. Remove the pan from the heat and add the salt and all the flour. Beat thoroughly, then return to the heat. Heat gently, beating all the time, for about 3 minutes until the mixture is smooth and leaves the sides of the pan clean. Leave to cool for 1–2 minutes. Beat the eggs into the dough, adding a little at a time, until the dough is soft enough to pipe. When all the egg has been absorbed, stir in the Emmental cheese. Lightly oil a round 25 cm/10 in cake tin (pan). Start piping the choux in the centre of the tin and pipe in a spiral until the bottom of the tin is covered (or spread some of the dough over the base). Next, pipe little buns of choux around the outside edge of the tin as if to make a crown of choux (or add small spoonfuls round the edge). Bake in a preheated oven at 200°C/400°F/gas mark 6 for 30 minutes until risen, golden brown and just firm to the touch. Meanwhile, make the filling. Cook the French beans in boiling water for 5 minutes, then cut into small pieces. Heat the oil in a frying pan (skillet) and stir-fry the onion for 2 minutes. Add the courgettes and tomatoes and cook for 3 minutes until the vegetables are tender but still crunchy. Combine with the peanuts and beans and season with salt and pepper. When cooked, carefully turn the gougère out of the tin and transfer to a larger 30 cm/12 in serving plate. Fill with the vegetable mixture, sprinkle with chopped parsley and grated cheese and serve at once.

Vegetable Grill

15 g/½ oz/1 tbsp butter or margarine
30 ml/2 tbsp sunflower oil
3 × 300 g/3 × 11 oz/3 small cans
*   new potatoes, drained*
3 celery sticks, chopped
4 small carrots, chopped
150 ml/¼ pt/⅔ cup plain yoghurt
15 ml/1 tbsp mayonnaise
Salt and freshly ground black pepper
75 g/3 oz/¾ cup Cheddar cheese, grated
2 tomatoes, sliced

Put the fat and oil in a deep frying pan (skillet) and toss the potatoes in it for 2 minutes over a moderate heat. Add the chopped vegetables and stir-fry for 3 minutes. Reduce the heat to as low as possible. Mix together the yoghurt, mayonnaise and a little seasoning, and stir them into the vegetables. Leave to stand over the very low heat, well below the boil, for 3 minutes. Turn the yoghurt-coated vegetables into a flameproof serving dish, and cover with the cheese. Place under the grill (broiler) for 3–4 minutes to melt the cheese. Serve garnished with tomato.

Caponata

1 aubergine (eggplant), cubed
Salt and freshly grated black pepper
1 red (bell) pepper, halved
45 ml/3 tbsp olive oil
1 courgette (zucchini), cubed
6 okra pods (ladies' fingers),
   trimmed, stems removed
1 onion, chopped
1 large tomato, skinned, seeded and
   chopped
150 ml/¼ pt/⅔ cup sherry
2 garlic cloves, chopped
30 ml/2 tbsp chopped basil
60 ml/4 tbsp breadcrumbs
60 ml/4 tbsp grated Cheddar cheese

Sprinkle the aubergine with salt and leave for 30 minutes to extract the bitter juices. Wash, drain and pat dry. Lay the pepper halves on a grill (broiler) rack, skin sides up, and grill (broil) until they blister. Peel off the grilled skin. Cut the flesh into small cubes. Heat the oil in a pan and stir-fry the vegetables, except the tomato, for 3 minutes. Add the tomato pulp, sherry, garlic and basil. Stew for 15 minutes only. Season to taste. Divide the mixture between six individual earthenware dishes, 250 ml/8 fl oz/1 cup capacity. Sprinkle over the breadcrumbs and grated cheese. Bake in a preheated oven at 200°C/400°F/gas mark 6 for 15 minutes to brown the top. Serve piping hot.

Tomato and Green Bean French Tart

225 g/8 oz puff pastry (paste)
50 g/2 oz/½ cup Cheddar cheese,
   grated
5 ml/1 tsp paprika
30 ml/2 tbsp olive oil
1 onion, chopped
1 garlic clove, chopped
4 tomatoes, skinned, seeded and
   coarsely chopped
50 g/2 oz/⅓ cup black olives, stoned
   (pitted)
75 g/3 oz French (green) beans,
   lightly cooked and diced
Salt and freshly ground black pepper
Ground mace
15 ml/1 tbsp chopped basil
3 eggs, beaten
120 ml/4 fl oz/½ cup single (light)
   cream
Green salad

Roll out the puff pastry thinly. Dust it with the grated cheese and paprika, then flour and roll again to press the ingredients well into the pastry. Prick the pastry with a fork all over. Line a well oiled 23 cm/9 in flan tin (pie pan) with the pastry, trimming the edges. (The leftovers can be used for other dishes.) In a wok or frying pan (skillet), heat the oil and stir-fry the onion and garlic for 1 minute. Add the tomato pulp, olives and French beans. Cook for 1 minute. Season to taste with salt, pepper and mace and add the basil. Leave to cool. Blend the eggs and cream together and add to the vegetables. Fill the pastry case with the egg and vegetable mixture. Bake in a preheated oven at 220°C/425°F/gas mark 7 for 25 minutes. Serve hot or cold with green salad.

Bean and Potato Boxties

225 g/8 oz potato, coarsely grated
150 g/5 oz French (green) beans,
   boiled and cut into strips
2 eggs, beaten
30 ml/2 tbsp flour
Oil, for shallow-frying
Salt
Tomato ketchup (catsup)

Put the grated potato in a cloth or kitchen paper and press out the liquid. In a bowl, mix the grated potato with the beans, egg and flour. Shallow-fry (sauté) spoonfuls of the mixture in hot oil, four at a time, on both sides for 2½ minutes. Drain on kitchen paper and season with salt. Serve hot with ketchup.

Vegetable Terrine

1 small carrot, finely diced
1 small turnip, finely diced
50 g/2 oz French (green) beans,
   finely diced
50 g/2 oz/¼ cup butter or margarine
30 ml/2 tbsp clear honey
50 g/2 oz/½ cup peas
50 g/2 oz/½ cup sweetcorn (corn)
100 g/4 oz button mushrooms, sliced
5 ml/1 tsp celery seeds
Pinch of dried thyme
15 ml/1 tbsp flour
300 ml/½ pt/1¼ cups milk
1 onion, chopped
15 g/½ oz/1 tbsp vegetarian gelatine
150 g/5 oz/⅔ cup cream cheese
5 ml/1 tsp salt
1.5 ml/¼ tsp white pepper
1.5 ml/¼ tsp grated nutmeg
Lettuce leaves

Blanch the diced vegetables in boiling salted water for 3 minutes. Drain and rinse with cold water. Drain again. In a wok, heat 40 g/1½ oz/3 tbsp of the butter or margarine and the honey and stir-fry all the vegetables for 2 minutes. Add the celery seeds and thyme. Remove from the heat. Heat the remaining butter or margarine with the flour for 1 minute. Blend in the milk and chopped onion. Bring to the boil and simmer for 5 minutes until the sauce is thick, stirring all the time. Dissolve the gelatine in 45 ml/3 tbsp hot water. Stir into the sauce and bring almost to the boil. Blend in the cream cheese. Season with salt, white pepper and grated nutmeg. Mix in the cooked vegetables. Spoon the mixture into six individual oiled ramekin dishes (custard cups) or a 450 g/1 lb loaf tin (pan). Leave to cool, then chill until set. Turn out on to lettuce leaves.

French Creamy Pea Flan

SERVES 4

125 g/5 oz/1¼ cups fresh or frozen
petits pois
8 spring onions (scallions), chopped
30 ml/2 tbsp clear honey
Salt and freshly ground black pepper
15 g/½ oz/1 tbsp butter or margarine
15 ml/1 tbsp flour
120 ml/4 fl oz/½ cup double (heavy)
cream
2 eggs, beaten
75 g/3 oz/¾ cup shredded lettuce
leaves
2.5 ml/½ tsp chopped tarragon
15 ml/1 tbsp chopped mint
20 cm/8 in unbaked pastry (paste)
flan case (pie shell)

Boil the peas and spring onions in 300 ml/½ pt/1¼ cups of salted water for 5 minutes. Stir in the honey. Season to taste. Cream the butter or margarine and flour to a paste. Gently whisk this paste into the hot pea liquid mixture. Boil for 4 minutes, then remove from the heat and allow to cool. Blend the cream and beaten eggs and add to the cold pea mixture with the lettuce, tarragon and mint. Season to taste. Fill the flan case with the mixture. Bake in a preheated oven at 200°C/400°F/gas mark 6 for 20 minutes. When set, serve hot or cold.

Oriental Vegetable Casserole

SERVES 6

45 ml/3 tbsp sunflower oil
1 onion, chopped
2 garlic cloves, chopped
30 ml/2 tbsp curry powder
1 red (bell) pepper, cut into 2.5 cm/
1 in squares
1 green chilli, seeded and sliced
1 celery stick, cut into chunks
100 g/4 oz French (green) beans,
trimmed and cut into small pieces
100 g/4 oz/1 cup peas
1 carrot, diced
1 turnip, diced
100 g/4 oz/1 cup sweetcorn (corn)
450 g/1 lb small new potatoes,
scraped
12 button (pearl) onions
6 cauliflower florets
Salt
30 ml/2 tbsp tomato purée (paste)
100 g/4 oz/1 cup haricot beans,
cooked (see page 10)
45 ml/3 tbsp chopped parsley

In a large, heavy-based pan, heat the oil and stir-fry the onion and garlic for 30 seconds. Add the curry powder, red pepper, chilli and all the other vegetables. Cover with about 1 litre/1¾ pts/3¾ cups water and boil gently for 20–30 minutes. Season with salt, then add the tomato purée and cooked beans. Reheat for 5 minutes. Serve in soup plates with some of the liquid. Sprinkle with chopped parsley.

Steamed Vegetable Fruits

30 ml/2 tbsp olive oil
3 shallots, sliced
2 courgettes (zucchini), sliced
1 aubergine (eggplant), sliced
3 tomatoes, sliced
1 large garlic clove, crushed
60 ml/4 tbsp water
A few drops of soy sauce
Salt
2 large square slices wholemeal
  bread
Mixed Pulse Salad (see page 227)

Heat the oil in a deep frying pan (skillet) with a lid. Add the shallots, courgettes and aubergine and fry (sauté) for 5 minutes, turning constantly. Add the tomatoes and the garlic to the pan. Pour in the water and soy sauce. Cover tightly, reduce the heat and simmer gently for 10 minutes or until the vegetables are soft; season after cooking if you wish. While cooking, toast the bread on both sides, and cut into eight triangles. Arrange the vegetables in a shallow dish with the bread triangles around them. Serve with Mixed Pulse Salad.

Potato and Onion Goulash

60 ml/4 tbsp butter and oil
225 g/8 oz pickling onions
1 red (bell) pepper, diced
450 g/1 lb new potatoes of even size,
  scrubbed
15 ml/1 tbsp paprika
600 ml/1 pt/2½ cups water
30 ml/2 tbsp tomato purée (paste)
Salt and freshly ground black pepper
5 ml/1 tsp caraway seeds
150 ml/¼ pt/⅔ cup soured (dairy sour)
  cream
75 g/3 oz/¾ cup toasted hazelnuts
45 ml/3 tbsp coarsely chopped
  coriander (cilantro)

In a large heavy-based pan, heat the butter and oil and stir-fry the onions for 3 minutes until lightly brown. Add the red pepper and cook for 1 minute. Put in the potatoes and paprika and toss well. Cover the vegetables with the water. Add the tomato purée, seasoning and caraway seeds. Boil gently for 18–20 minutes. Remove from the heat and blend the soured cream into the liquid. Sprinkle with toasted hazelnuts and chopped coriander just before serving.

Artichoke, Cucumber and Potato Flash

SERVES 4

45 ml/3 tbsp olive oil
40 g/1½ oz/3 tbsp butter
225 g/8 oz potatoes, cut into 1 cm/
  ½ in cubes
400 g/14 oz/1 large can artichoke
  bottoms
1 small cucumber, peeled and cut
  into thick chunks
75 g/3 oz/¾ cup cashew nuts,
  coarsely chopped
Salt and freshly ground black pepper
45 ml/3 tbsp chopped parsley

Heat the oil and butter in a frying pan (skillet) and fry (sauté) the potatoes for 5 minutes over a low heat, tossing from time to time. Add the artichoke bottoms and stir. Then add the cucumber chunks and cook for 1 minute only. Add the cashew nuts. Season with salt and pepper. During the cooking, the sautéeing and stirring process must be continuous to avoid over-browning. Drain and serve on plates, sprinkled with parsley.

Chinese Rainbow of Peppers

SERVES 4

225 g/8 oz/2 cups short-cut macaroni
60 ml/4 tbsp olive or walnut oil
1 onion, cut into thin strips
2 garlic cloves, chopped
225 g/8 oz mangetout (snow peas)
1 each large yellow, red and green
  (bell) peppers, cut into thin strips
120 ml/4 fl oz/½ cup vegetable stock
5 ml/1 tsp cornflour (cornstarch)
45 ml/3 tbsp water
Salt and freshly ground black pepper
5 ml/1 tsp sugar
2.5 ml/½ tsp Chinese five spice
  powder
100 g/4 oz/1 cup Cheddar cheese,
  grated (optional)

Boil the macaroni for 12 minutes in lightly salted water. Drain, rinse with cold water and drain again. Heat the oil in a wok or large frying pan (skillet) and stir-fry the onion, garlic, mangetout and peppers for 2–3 minutes. Add the stock. Boil for 3 minutes. Blend the cornflour with the water and stir in. Boil for a further minute. Season with salt, pepper, sugar and Chinese spices. Serve in individual Chinese bowls with grated Cheddar cheese handed separately, if liked.

Stir-fry Special

½ cucumber, diced
1 bunch of watercress, chopped
1 carrot, cut into matchsticks
1 onion, sliced
100 g/4 oz mushrooms, sliced
100 g/4 oz/1 cup flageolet beans,
  cooked (see page 10)
30 ml/2 tbsp sunflower oil
30 ml/2 tbsp soy sauce
15 ml/1 tbsp medium-dry sherry
1.5 ml/¼ tsp ground ginger
Good pinch of chilli powder
10 ml/2 tsp light brown sugar
Chinese egg noodles, cooked

Fry (sauté) all the prepared vegetables in the oil in a large frying pan (skillet) or wok for 3 minutes, stirring. Add the remaining ingredients except the noodles, and continue frying for 5 minutes, tossing all the time. Serve hot on a bed of Chinese egg noodles.

Vegetable Crumble

450 g/1 lb courgettes (zucchini),
  sliced
15 ml/1 tbsp olive oil
1 red (bell) pepper, sliced
100 g/4 oz mushrooms, sliced
200 g/7 oz/1 small can tomatoes
2 garlic cloves, crushed
1 onion, chopped
Salt and freshly ground black pepper
5 ml/1 tsp dried marjoram
175 g/6 oz/1½ cups Cheddar cheese,
  grated
100 g/4 oz/2 cups wholemeal
  breadcrumbs

Cook the courgettes in boiling salted water for 5 minutes. Drain. Heat the oil and fry (sauté) the remaining vegetables and seasoning for about 10 minutes until softened. Stir in the courgettes. Spoon the vegetables into a shallow, ovenproof dish. Mix together the cheese and breadcrumbs and sprinkle over the top. Bake in a preheated oven at 200°C/400°F/gas mark 6 for about 25 minutes until heated through and lightly browned.

Memory Stew

275 g/10 oz French (green) beans,
  topped and tailed, or frozen sliced
  green beans
300 ml/½ pt/1¼ cups vegetable stock
200 g/7 oz/1 small can sweetcorn
  (corn)
4 spring onions (scallions), sliced
3 tomatoes, quartered
1 eating (dessert) apple, chopped
50 g/2 oz/½ cup walnut pieces, finely
  chopped
Salt and freshly ground black pepper

Cook the beans in the stock in a covered pan for 7 minutes. Add the contents of the can of corn and all the remaining ingredients. Mix well, cover and cook until the vegetables are tender, stirring once or twice.

Surprise Potato Bake

SERVES 4

*900 g/2 lb potatoes, peeled and cut
  into small pieces*
1 egg, beaten
50 g/2 oz/¼ cup butter or margarine
45 ml/3 tbsp milk
Salt and freshly ground black pepper
1 onion, chopped
50 g/2 oz/½ cup chopped hazelnuts
5 ml/1 tsp ground cumin
2.5 ml/½ tsp ground turmeric
1 celery stick, chopped
2 tomatoes, chopped
15 ml/1 tbsp tomato purée (paste)
5 ml/1 tsp lemon juice
*75 g/3 oz/¾ cup desiccated (shredded)
  coconut*

Cook the potatoes in boiling, salted water for about 10–15 minutes until tender. Drain the potatoes and beat in the egg, half the butter or margarine and the milk. Season to taste. Meanwhile, melt the remaining butter or margarine in a pan. Add the onion and fry (sauté) for 3 minutes, stirring. Add the hazelnuts, cumin, turmeric, celery, tomatoes, tomato purée and lemon juice and continue cooking for 5 minutes, stirring all the time. In a greased casserole dish (Dutch oven), put a layer of half the potato mixture, followed by the tomato mixture then the remaining potatoes. Sprinkle with coconut and bake in a preheated oven at 190°C/375°F/gas mark 5 for 40 minutes.

Potato and Pistachio Venetian Cakes

SERVES 4

*3 large baking potatoes, 200 g/7 oz
  each, scrubbed*
90 ml/6 tbsp seasoned flour
75 g/3 oz/¾ cup fine cornmeal
*75 g/3 oz amaretti biscuits (cookies),
  crushed*
1 egg, beaten
45 ml/3 tbsp water
2 egg yolks
25 g/1 oz/2 tbsp butter
Salt and freshly ground black pepper
*75 g/3 oz/¾ cup pistachio nuts,
  skinned and roughly chopped*
*75 g/3 oz/½ cup sultanas (golden
  raisins)*
120 ml/4 fl oz/½ cup oil
Lettuce leaves
Vinaigrette Dressing (see page 303)

Prick the potatoes, wrap in foil and bake in a preheated oven at 200°C/400°F/gas mark 6 for 1 hour. Prepare three plates, one with seasoned flour, one with cornmeal mixed with the amaretti biscuits and one with beaten egg and water. When the baked potatoes are cooked, unwrap and cut in half. Scoop out the pulp and sieve (strain) it to remove lumps. In a bowl, blend the potato purée with the egg yolks and butter. Season. Add the pistachio nuts and sultanas. Cool the potato mixture. When cold, divide into 12–16 balls. Roll them in the seasoned flour and shape into patties using a palette knife. Heat the oil in a shallow pan. Coat the potato cakes in beaten egg, then in the cornmeal mixture. Shallow-fry on both sides for 2 minutes until golden brown. Drain and serve with lettuce leaves tossed in Vinaigrette Dressing.

Potato and Cabbage Casserole

750 g/1½ lb potatoes, peeled and cut into chunks
A little milk
A knob of butter or margarine
450 g/1 lb green cabbage, shredded
1 small onion, finely chopped
Salt and freshly ground black pepper
75 g/3 oz/¾ cup Cheddar cheese, grated
10 ml/2 tsp sunflower seeds
Mixed Bean Salad (see page 227)

Cook the potatoes in boiling salted water until just tender. Drain, then mash with a little milk and butter or margarine. Cook the cabbage in a little boiling salted water until just tender. Drain. Combine the cabbage, onion, potatoes and seasoning. Put into a greased casserole dish (Dutch oven). Sprinkle the grated cheese and sunflower seeds on top and cook in a preheated oven at 200ºC/400ºF/gas mark 6 for 30 minutes until browned. Serve hot with Mixed Bean Salad.

Savoy Casserole

1 large onion, chopped
2 carrots, chopped
45 ml/3 tbsp oil
750 g/1½ lb Savoy cabbage, shredded
1 leek, chopped
150 ml/¼ pt/⅔ cup water
50 g/2 oz/⅓ cup raisins
2.5 ml/½ tsp caraway seeds
45 ml/3 tbsp wholemeal breadcrumbs
45 ml/3 tbsp cider vinegar
10 ml/2 tsp clear honey
Salt and freshly ground black pepper

In a large pan, sauté the onion and carrots in 30 ml/2 tbsp of the oil until the onion softens. Mix in the remaining oil and the cabbage and leek, stirring well. Add 30 ml/2 tbsp of the water and cover the pan, reduce the heat and simmer for 4 minutes. Stir in the raisins, seeds and breadcrumbs, and the remaining water with the vinegar and honey. Cover again, and simmer for 10–12 minutes, stirring once or twice. The dish is ready when the vegetables are soft and the liquids absorbed. Season to taste before serving.

Root Vegetable Satay

*1 large turnip, cut into bite-sized
    pieces*
*2 large carrots, cut into bite-sized
    pieces*
*1 large parsnip, cut into bite-sized
    pieces*
15 g/½ oz/1 tbsp butter or margarine
15 ml/1 tbsp clear honey
Salt and freshly ground black pepper
150 ml/¼ pt/⅔ cup milk
75 ml/5 tbsp crunchy peanut butter
1.5 ml/¼ tsp chilli powder
50 g/2 oz/½ cup chopped mixed nuts

Cook the vegetables in boiling slightly
salted water until just tender. Drain.
When cool enough to handle, thread on
soaked wooden skewers. Melt the butter
or margarine and honey together. Lay the
skewers on foil on a grill (broiler) rack.
Brush with the honey mixture and season.
Grill (broil), turning occasionally and
brushing with the honey mixture until
lightly golden. Meanwhile, warm the milk
and peanut butter together in a small pan
with the chilli powder, stirring. Pour into
four small bowls and sprinkle with nuts.
Arrange the vegetable skewers on warm
serving plates with the bowls of sauce.
Serve hot.

Italian Bean Sprouts

400 g/14 oz/1 large can tomatoes
15 ml/1 tbsp oil
1 onion, chopped
1 celery stick, chopped
*Good pinch of dried minced (ground)
    garlic*
75 g/3 oz button mushrooms, sliced
2.5 ml/½ tsp dried basil or marjoram
175 g/6 oz/1½ cups bean sprouts
30 ml/2 tbsp white wine
Salt and freshly ground black pepper

Drain the can of tomatoes, reserving
the juice. Heat the oil in a large frying
pan (skillet) with a lid, and stir-fry the
onion, celery and garlic for 4 minutes.
Add the tomatoes, 45 ml/3 tbsp of the
juice, the mushrooms and herbs. Cover,
reduce the heat and simmer for 12–13
minutes. Stir in the bean sprouts with the
wine after 10 minutes, then continue simmering, covered, for the remaining 3–4
minutes or until the bean sprouts are just
tender but still with a little 'bite'. Season
to taste.

Potato Bake

750 g/1½ lb potatoes, thinly sliced
1 large onion, chopped
175 g/6 oz/1½ cups Cheddar cheese,
*   grated*
5 ml/1 tsp chopped thyme
5 ml/1 tsp chopped sage
Salt and freshly grated black pepper
1.5 ml/¼ tsp grated nutmeg
150 ml/¼ pt/⅔ cup milk
Classic Tomato, Onion and Chive
*   Salad (see page 228)*

Layer the potatoes, onion, cheese, herbs and seasonings in a greased dish and pour over the milk. Cover and cook in a preheated oven at 190°C/ 375°F/gas mark 5 for 45 minutes to 1 hour or until the potatoes are cooked through. Remove the cover after 30 minutes to allow the top to brown. Serve with Classic Tomato, Onion and Chive Salad.

North-of-the-border Marrow

750 g/1½ lb marrow (squash)
400 g/14 oz/1 large can tomatoes
75 g/3 oz/¾ cup rolled oats
1 onion, finely chopped (or 15 ml/
*   1 tbsp snipped chives if you prefer)*
5 ml/1 tsp chopped mint
Salt and freshly ground black pepper
175 g/6 oz/1½ cups Cheddar cheese,
*   grated*
Snipped chives, for garnishing
4 poached eggs

Peel and seed the marrow and cut into 2.5 cm/1 in pieces. Place all the ingredients, except the cheese, chives for garnishing and eggs, in a large pan and simmer, stirring occasionally, for 15–20 minutes or until the marrow is tender. Stir in the cheese until melted. Turn into a serving dish, top with the poached eggs and garnish with chives.

Melting Marrow

SERVES 4

900 g/2 lb marrow (squash)
30 ml/2 tbsp sunflower oil
50 g/2 oz/¼ cup butter or margarine
*2.5 ml/½ tsp ground coriander
(cilantro)*
2.5 ml/½ tsp ground cumin
2.5 ml/½ tsp dried sage
Salt and freshly ground black pepper
*175 g/6 oz/1½ cups Cheddar cheese,
grated*
Chopped parsley

Peel and seed the marrow and cut into 2.5 cm/1 in pieces. Put all the ingredients except the cheese and parsley in a large pan and cook gently, stirring occasionally, for 15 minutes until the marrow is cooked. Remove from the heat and stir in the cheese. A lovely sauce is formed by the cheese and marrow juices. Serve the marrow with all the cheesy juices spooned over, garnished with chopped parsley.

Country Garden Pie

SERVES 4

*450 g/1 lb potatoes, cut into small
chunks*
25 g/1 oz/2 tbsp butter or margarine
15 ml/1 tbsp milk
*350 g/12 oz/3 cups chopped leftover
cooked vegetables (e.g. cabbage,
swede [rutabaga], carrots, peas)*
400 g/14 oz/1 large can baked beans
2 slices wholemeal bread, chopped
10 ml/2 tsp yeast extract
30 ml/2 tbsp boiling water
Salt and freshly ground black pepper
*75 g/3 oz/¾ cup Cheddar cheese,
grated*
A leafy green vegetable

Cook the potatoes in boiling, lightly-salted water until tender. Drain and mash with the butter and milk. Meanwhile, mix the vegetables with the beans and bread. Dissolve the yeast extract in the water and stir into the mixture. Season to taste. Turn into an oven-proof dish and cover with the potato. Sprinkle with the cheese. Bake in a pre-heated oven at 220°C/420°F/gas mark 7 for 35 minutes or until piping hot and golden brown on top. Serve with a leafy green vegetable.

Creamed Cauliflower Supper

SERVES 4

1 vegetable stock cube
Pinch of dried minced (ground)
*   garlic*
350 g/12 oz thin-skinned potatoes,
*   thinly sliced*
450 g/1 lb cauliflower florets
297 g/10½ oz/1 small carton silken
*   tofu*
20 ml/4 tsp white wine vinegar
Good pinch of dry mustard
A few drops of Tabasco sauce
Good pinch of salt
Dill (dill weed) seeds

Put two saucepans of water to heat. Add the vegetable stock cube to one, and sprinkle the dried garlic into the other. Add the potatoes to the pan with the stock cube as soon as the water boils. Bring back to the boil and cook for 6 minutes or until the slices are just tender. Drain and spread in an even layer in a shallow 20 cm/8 in pie plate or baking dish. Keep warm. Tip the cauliflower florets into the pan with the garlic when on the boil, bring back to boiling and cook for 8–10 minutes until tender. While cooking, drain the tofu, and whisk it in a bowl with the vinegar, mustard, Tabasco and salt until creamy. Drain the cauliflower when ready, and mash it into the tofu mixture. Taste and adjust the seasoning. Spread the creamed cauliflower over the potatoes and sprinkle with dill seeds.

Crumble-topped Spinach

SERVES 4

900 g/2 lb fresh or frozen spinach
45 ml/3 tbsp sunflower oil
1 onion, chopped
Salt and freshly ground black pepper
2.5 ml/½ tsp grated nutmeg
150 ml/¼ pt/⅔ cup plain yoghurt
100 g/4 oz/2 cups wholemeal
*   breadcrumbs*
50 g/2 oz/½ cup any chopped nuts
Poached eggs

Wash and drain the spinach, then cook in a covered pan without any extra water for 5 minutes until soft – or according to the packet directions if frozen. Drain well in a colander. Heat 15 ml/1 tbsp of the oil in a pan and fry (sauté) the onion for 3 minutes, stirring. Return the spinach to the pan, add a little salt, pepper and the nutmeg and continue cooking for 5 minutes, stirring once. Stir in the yoghurt. Put into a greased casserole (Dutch oven). Mix together the breadcrumbs, chopped nuts and the remainder of the oil and sprinkle over the spinach. Bake in a preheated oven at 190°C/375°F/gas mark 5 for 20 minutes. Serve hot with poached eggs.

Chestnut Bake

SERVES 4

1 onion, chopped
15 ml/1 tbsp sunflower oil
225 g/8 oz mushrooms, sliced
100 g/4 oz carrots, finely chopped
2 celery sticks, finely chopped
5 ml/1 tsp chopped rosemary
5 ml/1 tsp chopped thyme
5 ml/1 tsp chopped sage
15 ml/1 tbsp soy sauce
Salt and freshly ground black pepper
320 g/12 oz/1 large can unsweetened chestnut purée
450 ml/³⁄₄ pt/2 cups vegetable stock
Pasta shapes
A mixed salad

Fry (sauté) the onion in the oil for 3 minutes, stirring. Add the mushrooms, carrots and celery and cook for a further 5 minutes, stirring occasionally. Add all the seasonings, chestnut purée and stock and mix well. Put into a greased casserole (Dutch oven) and bake in a preheated oven at 180°C/350°F/gas mark 4 for 40 minutes. Serve with pasta and a mixed salad.

Celery, Cheese and Yoghurt Flan

SERVES 4

175 g/6 oz shortcrust pastry (basic pie crust)
4 celery sticks, chopped
100 g/4 oz Cheddar cheese, thinly sliced
2 eggs
45 ml/3 tbsp plain yoghurt
5 ml/1 tsp made mustard
Salt and freshly ground black pepper
Sesame seeds

Roll out the pastry and use to line a 20 cm/8 in flan dish (pie pan). Place the dish on a baking sheet. Arrange the celery over the bottom of the pastry case and cover with sliced cheese. Beat together the eggs, yoghurt, mustard and seasoning. Pour over the cheese. Sprinkle with sesame seeds. Bake in a preheated oven at 190°C/375°F/gas mark 5 for 35 minutes until the filling is set and the pastry golden brown.

Corn, Cheese and Yoghurt Flan

SERVES 4

Prepare as for Celery, Cheese and Yoghurt Flan but substitute 350 g/12 oz/1 large can of drained sweetcorn (corn) for the celery and red Leicester for the Cheddar cheese. Sprinkle with fennel seeds instead of sesame before baking.

Creamed Mushroom Tart with Brandy

*225 g/8 oz shortcrust pastry (basic
    pie crust)*
*50 g/2 oz/¼ cup butter or margarine,
    melted*
*50 g/1 lb button mushrooms,
    trimmed*
2 shallots, chopped
Salt and freshly ground black pepper
Grated nutmeg
60 ml/4 tbsp brandy
*150 ml/¼ pt/⅔ cup single (light)
    cream*
2 eggs, beaten
*50 g/2 oz/½ cup Cheddar cheese,
    grated*

Roll out the pastry on a floured board. Cut out a round to fit a 23 cm/9 in flan tin (pie pan). Oil the tin and line it with the pastry. Brush with butter or margarine. Add crumpled foil and bake blind in a pre-heated oven at 200°C/400°F/gas mark 6 for 15 minutes. For the filling, heat the butter in a wok or frying pan (skillet) and stir-fry the mushrooms and shallots for 2 minutes. Season with salt, pepper and nutmeg. Add the brandy and remove from the heat. In a cup, blend the cream and eggs. Sprinkle the bottom of the pastry case with grated cheese and add the mushrooms. Cover with the egg mixture. Bake in the oven for 15 minutes or until the custard is set. Serve hot or cold.

Creamy Leek Pancakes

2 leeks, thinly sliced
50 g/2 oz/¼ cup butter or margarine
*100 g/4 oz/1 cup self-raising (self-
    rising) flour*
2 eggs, beaten
*600 ml/1 pt/2½ cups beer and water
    in equal proportions*
Salt and freshly ground black pepper
75 ml/5 tbsp oil
75 g/3 oz/⅓ cup cream cheese
75 g/3 oz/¾ cup creamy blue cheese
1 egg, beaten
45 ml/3 tbsp grated Cheddar cheese

Fry (sauté) the leeks in the butter in a frying pan (skillet) over a low heat for 2 minutes without browning until soft and cooked. Transfer the butter and leeks to a large bowl. Blend in the flour, beaten eggs, beer and water to form a thin pancake batter. Season with a pinch of salt. Heat a little of the oil in a small pancake pan and pour in 45 ml/3 tbsp of the batter. Cook on both sides for 1 minute until golden. Turn on to a flat tray to cool. Make eight thin pancakes. For the filling, beat the cream cheese and blue cheese in a bowl until smooth, then beat in the beaten egg. Season to taste. Spread a quarter of this mixture on one pancake and sand-wich it with another. Repeat to produce four portions. Place the double pancakes on a large baking sheet. Sprinkle with the grated cheese and glaze under the grill (broiler). Serve flat on a plate, cut into quarters.

No Hassle Vegetable Pie

225 g/8 oz/2 cups plain (all-purpose)
  flour
Pinch of salt
100 g/4 oz/½ cup butter or margarine
60 ml/4 tbsp water
175 g/6 oz frozen mixed vegetables
400 g/14 oz/1 large can mushroom
  soup
5 ml/1 tsp dried mixed herbs
Milk

Mix together the flour and salt. Rub in the butter or margarine until the mixture resembles breadcrumbs. Stir in enough of the water to form a firm dough. Knead gently on a lightly floured surface. Roll out two-thirds of the dough and use to line a 20 cm/8 in pie dish. Heat the vegetables in a pan of water for a few minutes, then drain. Mix with the soup and herbs and pour into the pastry-lined dish. Roll out the remaining pastry and lay over the top, sealing the edges together with a little water. Brush the top with milk. Make a small slit in the centre to allow steam to escape. Place on a baking sheet and bake in a preheated oven at 200°C/400°F/gas mark 6 for 20–30 minutes until golden brown on top.

Broccoli and Tomato Flan

100 g/4 oz shortcrust pastry (basic
  pie crust)
100 g/4 oz small broccoli florets
2 eggs
150 ml/¼ pt/⅔ cup milk
Salt and freshly ground black pepper
225 g/8 oz/1 small can chopped
  tomatoes, drained
100 g/4 oz/1 cup Cheddar cheese,
  grated
Salad

Roll out the pastry and use to line an 18 cm/7 in flan dish (pie pan). Cook the broccoli in boiling water for 2 minutes, then drain. Place in the flan dish. Beat the eggs and milk with a little salt and pepper and pour into the pastry case (pie shell). Top with the tomatoes, then sprinkle with the cheese. Bake in a preheated oven at 180°C/350°F/gas mark 4 for about 30 minutes until the filling is set. Serve hot or cold with salad.

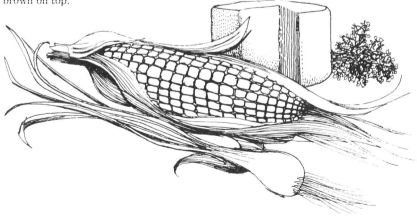

Spring Vegetable Flan

SERVES 4

225 g/8 oz mixture of diced carrots,
  turnips, peas, beans, sweetcorn
  (corn), chopped onions
1 baked flan case (pie shell) 23 cm/9
  in diameter
A little melted butter or margarine
Salt and freshly ground black pepper
50 g/2 oz/½ cup Cheddar cheese,
  grated
30 ml/2 tbsp chopped parsley
150 ml/¼ pt/⅔ cup single (light)
  cream
5 ml/1 tsp made English mustard
2 eggs, beaten
4 hard-boiled (hard-cooked) eggs,
  halved
Lettuce leaves

Boil the vegetable mixture for 3 minutes only and drain well. Place in a bowl. Brush the bottom of the pastry case with butter or margarine and sprinkle with salt and pepper. Mix together the remaining ingredients except the hard-boiled eggs. Blend this mixture with the vegetables. Pour into the flan case. Bake in a preheated oven at 200°C/400°F/gas mark 6 for 25 minutes. Cool. When cold, divide into eight portions. Top each portion with half an egg. Serve with lettuce leaves.

Onions Stuffed with Mushrooms and Olives

SERVES 4

4 large onions, 100g/4 oz each
50 g/2 oz/¼ cup butter or margarine
12 black olives, stoned (pitted)
4 mushrooms, trimmed and chopped
6 peanuts, chopped
1 hard-boiled (hard-cooked) egg,
  chopped
45 ml/3 tbsp breadcrumbs
2 garlic cloves, chopped
30 ml/2 tbsp chopped basil
Salt and freshly ground black pepper
1 egg, beaten
120 ml/4 fl oz/½ cup vegetable stock
30 ml/2 tbsp grated Cheddar cheese

Peel the onions and cut a slice off the top near the stem. Boil for 15 minutes. Squeeze out most of the inside, leaving a shell of 1 cm/½ in thick. Chop the centre part of the onion, leaving the four shells as cases for the filling. For the stuffing, heat the butter or margarine and stir-fry all the remaining ingredients except the egg, stock and cheese. Purée in a blender or food processor with the egg. Season to taste. Spoon the mixture into the onion cavities. Set them in individual 225 ml/8 fl oz/1 cup ramekin dishes (custard cups). Pour a little stock around, cover with lids or foil and braise in a preheated oven at 190°C/375°F/gas mark 5 for 15 minutes. When nearly cooked, sprinkle with grated cheese and glaze under the grill (broiler).

French Pea Baguette Slice

1 long French stick
50 g/2 oz/¼ cup butter or margarine
2 garlic cloves, chopped
30 ml/2 tbsp chopped parsley
5 ml/1 tsp dried thyme
100 g/4 oz/1 cup fresh, frozen or
*   processed peas*
1 egg, beaten
45 ml/3 tbsp double (heavy) cream
25 g/1 oz/2 tbsp chopped spring
*   onion (scallion)*
100 g/4 oz/1 cup Cheddar cheese,
*   grated*

Halve the French bread lengthways, then halve each crossways. Toast the four pieces. Prepare a garlic paste by creaming the butter with the garlic, parsley and thyme. Spread this mixture on to the bread. Boil the peas for 10 minutes, then mash to a purée. In a bowl, combine the pea purée with the beaten egg, cream and chopped onion. Spread the mixture thickly over the bread, sprinkle with grated cheese and glaze under the grill (broiler) until golden.

Prime Pumpkin Pie

350 g/12 oz wholemeal or plain
*   shortcrust pastry (basic pie crust)*
225 g/8 oz pumpkin, cut into 2.5 cm/
*   1 in cubes*
2 egg whites
175 g/6 oz/¾ cup cream cheese
100 g/4 oz/1 cup cooked rice
Salt and freshly ground black pepper
1.5 ml/¼ tsp ground ginger
15 ml/1 tbsp tomato purée (paste)
25 g/1 oz/¼ cup flour
25 g/1 oz/¼ cup salted peanuts
Tomato salad

Line a 20 cm/8 in deep flan tin (pie pan) with the pastry. Boil the pumpkin cubes in salted water for 10 minutes. Drain, then cool. Whisk the egg whites until stiff. In a large bowl, blend the cream cheese, rice, seasoning, ginger, tomato purée and flour. Fold in the egg whites. Add the pumpkin cubes and stir well. Fill the pastry shell to the top. Sprinkle over the peanuts. Bake in a preheated oven at 200°C/400°F/gas mark 6 for 30 minutes. Cool and serve cold with a tomato salad.

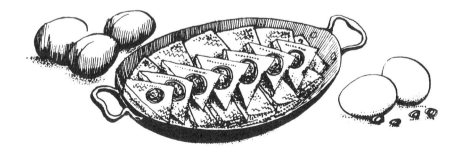

Mushroom Stroganoff

SERVES 4

75 g/3 oz/⅓ cup butter or margarine
1 onion, chopped
2 garlic cloves, crushed
1.6 kg/3½ lb mushrooms, quartered
150 ml/¼ pt/⅔ cup white wine
15 ml/1 tbsp cornflour (cornstarch)
300 ml/½ pt/1¼ cups single (light)
   cream
15 ml/1 tbsp lemon juice
Salt and freshly ground black pepper
Boiled rice or pasta

Melt the butter or margarine and fry (sauté) the onion and garlic for a few minutes until softened. Add the mushrooms and simmer for up to 30 minutes until the liquid has evaporated. Add the wine and simmer for 5 minutes. Mix the cornflour with a little water, then stir it into the pan with the cream. Bring to the boil, then simmer for 5 minutes until thickened, stirring continuously. Add the lemon juice and seasoning. Serve hot with rice or pasta.

Sweet and Sour Stir-fry

SERVES 4

15 ml/1 tbsp oil
1 onion, sliced
1 red or green (bell) pepper, sliced
175 g/6 oz mushrooms, sliced
430 g/15½ oz/1 large can pineapple
   chunks in juice
30 ml/2 tbsp tomato ketchup (catsup)
30 ml/2 tbsp soy sauce
30 ml/2 tbsp vinegar
15 ml/1 tbsp clear honey
60 ml/4 tbsp vegetable stock
15 ml/1 tbsp cornflour (cornstarch)
Freshly ground black pepper
175 g/6 oz bean sprouts
Rice or noodles

Heat the oil in a wok or large frying pan (skillet) until almost smoking. Add the onion, pepper and mushrooms and stir-fry for 3–4 minutes. Meanwhile, mix together all the remaining ingredients except the bean sprouts and rice or noodles. Add to the pan and heat through, stirring. Add the bean sprouts and stir-fry for 2 minutes until hot. Serve at once with rice or noodles.

Spectrum Stir-fry

1 leek, sliced
200 g/7 oz/1 small can Mexican
  sweetcorn (corn with bell peppers)
100 g/4 oz/1 cup cooked red kidney
  beans (see page 10)
1 carrot, chopped
4 spring onions (scallions), chopped
2 celery sticks, chopped
15 ml/1 tbsp sherry
15 ml/1 tbsp soy sauce
15 ml/1 tbsp tomato purée (paste)
15 ml/1 tbsp water
45 ml/3 tbsp oil
Plain boiled rice or Chinese egg
  noodles

Cook the leek in boiling water for 5 minutes. Meanwhile, drain the corn and beans if necessary. Put in a bowl, drain and add the cooked leek. In a separate bowl, mix together the carrot, spring onions and celery. Blend together the remaining ingredients except the oil, rice or noodles. Heat the oil in a deep frying pan (skillet) or wok. Add the carrot, onions and celery and stir over a moderate heat for 2 minutes. Add the leek, sweetcorn and beans, and continue stirring for 3 minutes. Add the blended ingredients, cover the pan and simmer for 2 minutes or until it is all absorbed. Serve hot with plain boiled rice or Chinese egg noodles.

Cheesy Stuffed Courgettes

4 large courgettes (zucchini)
1 packet savoury rice, any flavour
Oil
120 ml/4 fl oz/½ cup water
75 g/3 oz/¾ cup Cheddar cheese,
  grated

Trim the courgettes, halve lengthways and scoop out the seeds. Cook in boiling water for 3 minutes, then drain. Cook the rice as directed on the packet. Stuff the rice into the courgettes and add a drop of oil to each one. Lay in a baking tin (pan). Pour the water around. Sprinkle the cheese over each courgette. Bake in a preheated oven at 200°C/400°F/gas mark 6 for 20 minutes or until tender.

Workaday Spud and Swede Pie

450 g/1 lb potatoes, sliced
450 g/1 lb swede (rutabaga), sliced
45 ml/3 tbsp milk
Salt and freshly ground black pepper
100 g/4 oz/1 cup Cheddar cheese,
  grated
50 g/2 oz/2 small packets ready salted
  crisps (chips), lightly crushed
Baked beans

Cook the vegetables in boiling salted water for about 15 minutes until soft. Drain well then mash together. Stir in the milk and season to taste. Spoon into an ovenproof dish. Mix together the cheese and crisps and sprinkle over the top. Bake in a preheated oven at 200°C/400°F/gas mark 6 for 15 minutes until crisp. Serve with baked beans.

Mediterranean Summer Pudding

This is delicious served on its own or with some slices of fresh Mozzarella and a green side salad. You can spoon a little extra passata over the turned-out pudding, if you like.

30 ml/2 tbsp olive oil, plus a little for greasing
1 leek, sliced
1 onion, chopped
1 garlic clove, crushed
1 red (bell) pepper, cut into chunks
450 ml/3/4 pt/2 cups passata (sieved tomatoes)
90 ml/6 tbsp dry white wine
4 sun-dried tomatoes in olive oil, cut into chunks
15 ml/1 tbsp chopped fresh basil
50 g/2 oz stoned (pitted) black olives
1 x 440 g/15 1/2 oz/ large can of artichoke hearts, drained and quartered
Salt and freshly ground black pepper
A good pinch of caster (superfine) sugar
7–8 slices of white bread from a large sliced loaf, crusts removed
A sprig of fresh basil for garnishing

Heat the oil in a saucepan, add the leek, onion, garlic and pepper and cook gently, stirring frequently, for 5 minutes to soften. Add the passata, wine and sun-dried tomatoes, bring to the boil, reduce the heat and simmer for about 5 minutes, stirring frequently, until everything is tender but there is still plenty of tomato sauce. Stir in the basil, olives, artichoke hearts, salt, pepper and sugar to taste.

Meanwhile, lightly oil a 1.2 litre/2 pt/ 5 cup pudding basin. Cut one slice of bread into a large circle. Lay it on top of the vegetable mixture so it is coated on one side in tomato sauce. Put it in the base of the prepared pudding basin, tomato-side down. Cut five more slices in halves and dip, one at a time, in the same way and use as many as necessary to line the sides of the basin, tomato-sides down, overlapping the circle in the base and making sure there are no gaps round the sides at the top of the basin. Place the basin on a plate (to catch any drips). Dip the last slices of bread in the same way (but if you have half a slice of bread left over from lining the sides, you will only need to dip one more slice) and reserve. Spoon the vegetable mixture into the bread-lined basin. Lay one of the remaining slices of bread on top, tomato-side up then cut the remaining one to fill in the gaps round the edge. Cover with a circle of non-stick baking parchment, then put a saucer, rounded-side down, on top and weigh down with heavy weights or cans of food. Leave to cool, then chill overnight.

When ready to serve, loosen the edge carefully with a round-bladed knife. Place a serving plate on top, hold firmly, invert and give a good shake, so the pudding turns out on to the plate. Spoon any tomato sauce drips from the plate over, if liked. Garnish with a sprig of basil and serve cut in wedges.

Conil's Stuffed Cabbage

150 g/5 oz dried apricots or peaches
4 large cabbage leaves
150 g/5 oz/⅔ cup cottage cheese
1 egg, beaten
50 g/2 oz/1 cup wholemeal
breadcrumbs
150 g/5 oz/1¼ cups mixed walnuts
and hazelnuts, chopped
Pinch of ground mixed (apple pie)
spice
Salt and freshly ground black pepper
30 ml/2 tbsp olive oil
1 small onion, chopped
2 large tomatoes, peeled and chopped
Pinch of dried oregano
Salt and freshly ground black pepper
5 ml/1 tsp cornflour (cornstarch)
45 ml/3 tbsp water
Creamed potatoes

Place the dried apricots or peaches in a bowl, cover with water and leave to soak for 2 hours. Drain well and put through a mincer (grinder) or chop finely in a food processor. Trim the centre cores from the cabbage leaves and blanch the leaves in boiling water for 30 seconds. Spread the leaves out on a board ready to be filled. To make the stuffing, place the cottage cheese in a bowl and blend it with the egg and breadcrumbs. Add the apricots or peaches, nuts and spice, season with salt and pepper and mix well. Divide the stuffing mixture into four portions and place one on each cabbage leaf. Wrap the leaves round the stuffing to make neat parcels. Arrange in an ovenproof dish. Heat the oil in a frying pan (skillet) and stir-fry the onion for 2 minutes until soft but not brown. Add the tomatoes and oregano and season to taste with salt and pepper. Blend the cornflour and water and add to the sauce mixture. Cook for a fur-

ther 3 minutes, stirring, until thickened. Check the seasoning, then pour the sauce around the cabbage parcels. Bake in a preheated oven at 200°C/400°F/gas mark 6 for 15 minutes and serve very hot with creamed potatoes.

Veggie-stuffed Leaves

4 large cabbage leaves
175–250 ml/6–8 fl oz/¾–1 cup
vegetable stock
100 g/4 oz vegetarian burger or
meatball mix
45 ml/3 tbsp oil
1 small onion, chopped
1 small tomato, chopped

Lay the cabbage leaves flat in a frying pan (skillet) and pour about 2 cm/¾ in stock over them. Cover the pan and simmer the leaves for 2–3 minutes until soft. Remove the leaves and lay them flat, side by side, leaving the stock in the pan. Reconstitute the mix according to the packet directions and leave to stand. Heat 30 ml/2 tbsp of the oil in a separate, fairly large frying pan and fry (sauté) the chopped vegetables for 2 minutes. Add the mix and the remaining oil and stir for another 2 minutes. Cool for 1 minute, then divide the mix between the cabbage leaves, laying it in a line down the centre rib of each leaf. Roll the leaf round it like a tube. Return the rolls to the pan containing the stock, placing them folded sides down. Pour in more stock if needed to prevent drying out while cooking. Cover and simmer for about 5 minutes to heat the rolls well through. Place them on a warmed serving dish and spoon a little hot stock over them. Serve with mashed potato (instant if you are short of time) or Rose-red Potatoes (see page 198).

Doddle Dolmas

SERVES 4–6

12 large cabbage leaves
350 g/12 oz/3 cups chopped cooked
mixed vegetables
Spicy Tomato Sauce (see page 315)
or 300 ml/½ pt/1¼ cups passata
(sieved tomatoes)

Cook the leaves in boiling salted water for about 5 minutes until just soft. Drain. Place a spoonful or two of the vegetables on each leaf at one end and roll over to make a parcel, turning in the edges as you go. Arrange in a single layer in an ovenproof dish. Pour over the Spicy Tomato Sauce or passata. Bake in a preheated oven at 180°C/350°F/gas mark 4 for 15–20 minutes until heated through.

Pane Agro Dolce

SERVES 4

225 g/8 oz/2 cups strong plain
(bread) flour
2.5 ml/½ tsp salt
150 ml/¼ pt/⅔ cup milk
1 sachet dried yeast
1 egg, beaten
60 ml/4 tbsp oil
1 large onion, chopped
2 garlic cloves, chopped
2 tomatoes, skinned, seeded and
chopped
1 courgette (zucchini), sliced
Salt and freshly ground black pepper
5 ml/1 tsp chopped mint or tarragon
5 ml/1 tsp chopped oregano
Milk or beaten egg, to glaze
30 ml/2 tbsp sesame seeds

Sift the flour and salt together in a bowl and make a well in the centre. Heat the milk to no hotter than blood heat, sprinkle with the yeast and stir. Pour into the well in the flour, cover with a clean cloth and leave to stand for 15 minutes until the yeast starts foaming. Add the egg and 15 ml/1 tbsp of the oil to the yeast mixture and beat to a dough. Knead well, shape into a ball, cover again and leave to rise for 45 minutes. Meanwhile, prepare the filling. Heat the remaining oil in a frying pan (skillet) and stir-fry the onion for 2 minutes until lightly golden. Add the garlic and tomatoes and simmer for 12 minutes. Add the courgette and cook for a further 3 minutes. Season to taste with salt and pepper and the herbs and leave to cool. Grease a round 18 cm/7 in cake tin (pan) with a little oil. Turn the dough on to a lightly floured surface and knock back (punch down). Divide into two and roll one piece into an 18 cm/7 in round. Roll the other into a larger round and use to line the base and sides of the cake tin. Prick the base all over with a fork. Fill with the courgette and tomato mixture and cover with the second round of dough. Brush with milk or beaten egg and sprinkle with sesame seeds. Leave to rest for 25 minutes, then bake in a preheated oven at 200°C/400°F/gas mark 6 for 20–25 minutes until golden. Serve cut into wedges.

Onion and Apple Crumble

SERVES 2

3–4 eating (dessert) apples, sliced
2 onions, sliced
5 ml/1 tsp dried sage
Pinch of grated nutmeg
Salt and freshly ground black pepper
50 g/2 oz/½ cup plain (all-purpose)
  flour
50 g/2 oz/¼ cup butter or margarine
50 g/2 oz/1 cup breadcrumbs

Grease an ovenproof dish. Arrange alternating layers of apple and onion in the dish, seasoning with sage, nutmeg, salt and pepper as you go. Rub the flour and butter or margarine together until the mixture resembles breadcrumbs. Stir in the breadcrumbs and sprinkle over the dish. Bake in a preheated oven at 200°C/400°F/gas mark 6 for about 30 minutes until the filling is soft and the topping golden.

Cheesy Onion and Apple Crumble

SERVES 2

Prepare as for Onion and Apple Crumble but add layers of grated Cheddar cheese (about 100 g/4 oz/1 cup in all) with the onion and apple.

Record-quick Ratatouille

SERVES 4

30 ml/2 tbsp olive oil
2 large onions, chopped
1 red (bell) pepper, sliced
1 yellow or green (bell) pepper, sliced
450 g/1 lb courgettes (zucchini), sliced
400 g/14 oz/1 large can chopped
  tomatoes
Salt and freshly ground black pepper
225 g/8 oz quick-cook wholewheat
  noodles, cooked

Heat the oil in a large, deep frying pan (skillet) with a lid or a wok. Add the onions and stir over a moderate heat for 2 minutes. Add the remaining fresh vegetables and stir, turning them over for another 3 minutes. Add the tomatoes and their juice, season to taste, cover the pan and cook gently for 5 minutes. Serve spooned over the noodles.

Corncrust Tart

SERVES 4

225 g/8 oz/2 cups fine cornmeal
1.5 ml/¼ tsp salt
45 ml/3 tbsp oil
Cold vegetable stock
175 g/6 oz/1¼ cups cooked flageolet
  beans (see page 10)
1 onion
1 carrot
50 g/2 oz celery sticks
½ green (bell) pepper, seeded
½ garlic clove
5 ml/1 tsp ground cumin
3 drops of Tabasco sauce

Mix together the cornmeal, salt, 15 ml/1 tbsp of the oil and enough stock to make a firm dough. Press the pastry (paste) all over the base and sides of a well-oiled 23 cm/ 9 in pie plate. Bake in a preheated oven at 180ºC/350ºF/gas mark 4 for 10–15 minutes. Drain the beans if necessary. Chop finely together in a food processor, if possible, the onion, carrot, celery, pepper and garlic. Fry (sauté) the chopped vegetables in the remaining oil for 4 minutes. Stir in the beans, cumin and Tabasco. Put the mixture into the hot pastry case (shell) and return to a preheated oven for 10–15 minutes until the case is firm and the filling well heated.

Cheese and Tomato Corncrust Tart

SERVES 4

Prepare as for Corncrust Tart but spoon 227 g/8 oz/1 small can chopped tomatoes over the filling and sprinkle with 75 g/3 oz/¾ cup grated Cheddar cheese before baking.

Parsley Dumpling Supper

SERVES 2–4

1 quantity Parsley Dumplings (see
  page 174)
2 onions, sliced
15 g/½ oz/1 tbsp butter or margarine
100 g/4 oz/1 cup Cheddar cheese,
  grated
Salad

Prepare and cook the Parsley Dumplings. Drain and arrange in a single layer in a flameproof dish. Meanwhile fry (sauté) the onions in the butter or margarine until soft and golden. Scatter over the dumplings. Top with the cheese and place under a hot grill (broiler) until golden and bubbling. Serve with salad.

Pacific Chop Suey

SERVES 4

175 g/6 oz onion, chopped
175 g/6 oz celery sticks, chopped
75 g/3 oz white cabbage, shredded
45 ml/3 tbsp oil
45 ml/3 tbsp vegetable stock
225 g/8 oz/1 small can pineapple in
  natural juice, drained and
  chopped
100 g/4 oz bean sprouts
25 g/1 oz/¼ cup flaked almonds or
  Brazil nuts, chopped
30 ml/2 tbsp soy sauce
Brown rice, cooked

Stir-fry the onion, celery and cabbage in the oil in a large frying pan (skillet) or wok for 3 minutes. Add the stock, cover and cook for 5 minutes. Stir in the pineapple, bean sprouts, nuts and soy sauce. Cover and cook for a further 4 minutes, stirring occasionally. Serve on a bed of cooked brown rice.

Chinese Leaf 'Bake'

SERVES 4

Oil
60 ml/4 tbsp medium oatmeal
1 leek, sliced
450 g/1 lb Chinese leaves (stem lettuce), shredded
150–175 g/5–6 oz/1¼–1½ cups Cheddar cheese, grated
100 g/4 oz/½ cup cottage cheese with chives
5 ml/1 tsp cumin seeds
2.5 ml/½ tsp ground cumin
4 eggs
Salt and freshly ground black pepper

Oil the inside of a 20 cm/8 in shallow baking dish suitable for serving. Sprinkle the oatmeal over the base. Blanch the leek and Chinese leaves for 30 seconds in boiling water. Drain and return to the pan. Beat the Cheddar into the cottage cheese and add the cumin seeds, ground cumin and eggs. Beat well. Combine the cheese and egg mixture with the vegetables and season well. Spread the mixture evenly over the oatmeal in the baking dish and bake in a preheated oven for 15 minutes at 190°C/375°F/gas mark 5 until set.

Leeks with Turnip and Apple Sauce

SERVES 4

4 leeks, sliced
600 ml/1 pt/2½ cups vegetable stock
450 g/1 lb young turnips, cut into small chunks
2 sharp eating (dessert) apples, chopped
15 g/½ oz/1 tbsp butter or margarine
Pinch of ground cinnamon
Small pinch of freshly ground black pepper
A few drops of soy sauce
Oat cakes or bran crispbreads

Cook the leeks in the boiling stock in a covered pan for 5 minutes or until tender. Remove the leeks and keep warm in a covered dish. Add the turnip to the stock, bring back to the boil and cook for 7 minutes. Add the apples and cook for a further 3–4 minutes, until both the turnips and apples are soft. Drain. Purée in a food processor or blender if possible, with the fat and flavourings. Coat the leeks with the sauce. Serve in bowls with oat cakes or bran crispbreads.

Curried Potato Garland

150 g/5 oz/1 large packet instant potato powder or granules
1.5 ml/¼ tsp curry powder
Pinch of cayenne
450 g/1 lb/1 large packet frozen mixed vegetables
Salt and freshly ground black pepper
5 ml/1 tsp tomato purée (paste)
300 ml/½ pt/1¼ cups water
175 ml/6 fl oz/¾ cup milk
40 g/1½ oz/3 tbsp butter or margarine

Mix the dried potato, curry powder and cayenne in a bowl. Cook the frozen mixed vegetables according to the packet directions. When ready, drain and season if you wish. Keep warm. While cooking, blend the tomato purée into the water in a saucepan. Add the milk and 25 g/1 oz/2 tbsp of the butter or margarine and heat to boiling point. Reconstitute the potato with this liquid, and leave to stand while you pile the vegetables in the middle of a warmed serving platter. Spoon the curried potato into a ring around them. Dot the vegetables with the remaining butter or margarine and serve at once.

Speedy Stuffed Peppers

2 large sweet red (bell) peppers, halved
227 g/8 oz/1 small packet frozen mixed vegetables
1 spring onion (scallion), chopped
25 g/1 oz/½ cup wholemeal breadcrumbs
50 g/2 oz/½ cup Cheddar cheese, grated
15 ml/1 tbsp soy sauce
1 small egg

Cook the pepper halves in boiling water for 8 minutes. Drain. Cook the frozen vegetables according to the packet directions. Drain the hot vegetables and mix with the onion, breadcrumbs and grated cheese. Beat the soy sauce into the egg, and stir into the stuffing mixture. Use to fill the pepper halves. Put the filled peppers, cut side up, on a baking sheet and bake in a preheated oven at 190°C/375°F/gas mark 5 for 12–15 minutes.

Vegetarian Shropshire Fidget Pie

SERVES 4

150 g/5 oz/1¼ cups self-raising (self-rising) flour
2.5 ml/½ tsp salt
100 g/4 oz/½ cup butter or margarine, cut into small pieces
75 g/3 oz/⅓ cup mashed potatoes
450 g/1 lb potatoes, thinly sliced
2 cooking (tart) apples, sliced
225 g/8 oz vegetarian sausages, diced
Salt and freshly ground black pepper
5 ml/1 tsp light brown sugar
150 ml/¼ pt/⅔ cup vegetable stock
Beaten egg or milk, to glaze

Sift the flour and salt into a bowl. Add the butter or margarine and rub in with the fingertips. Work in the mashed potato to form a firm dough. Chill while preparing the filling. Layer the potatoes, apples and sausages in a pie dish, seasoning with salt, pepper and the sugar between the layers. Pour on the stock. Roll out the pastry to just larger than the top of the pie dish and trim. Dampen the edge of the dish with water and lay the pastry trimming strips on it. Brush with water. Lay the pastry lid on top and press down around the edge to seal. Knock up and flute with the back of a knife. Make a slit to allow steam to escape. Brush with beaten egg or milk and bake in a pre-heated oven at 200°C/400°F/gas mark 6 for 15 minutes, then reduce the heat to 180°C/350°F/gas mark 4 and continue cooking for about 45 minutes or until the filling is cooked through. Cover the top with foil if over-browning.

Spinach, Carrot and Mustard Cutlets

SERVES 4

450 g/1 lb frozen chopped spinach, thawed
2 carrots, grated
25 g/1 oz/2 tbsp butter or margarine
30 ml/2 tbsp black mustard seeds
2 egg yolks, beaten
225 g/8 oz/2 cups Cheddar cheese, grated
Salt and freshly ground black pepper
Pinch of grated nutmeg
1 egg, beaten
100 g/4 oz/2 cups wholemeal breadcrumbs
Oil, for shallow-frying

Put the spinach in a saucepan with the carrots. Cook gently for 5 minutes, stirring. Drain off any liquid. Stir in half the butter or margarine and leave to cool. Meanwhile, melt the remaining butter and fry (sauté) the mustard seeds until they start to pop. Add to the spinach mixture. Mix in the egg yolks, cheese, a little salt and pepper and the nutmeg. Chill for 30 minutes. With floured hands, shape into eight wedge-shaped cakes ('cutlets'). Dip in beaten egg, then breadcrumbs to coat completely. Shallow-fry in hot oil until golden brown on both sides. Drain on kitchen paper and serve hot.

Hearty Mushroom Curry

l large onion, chopped
1 garlic clove, crushed
30 ml/2 tbsp olive oil
30 ml/2 tbsp mild curry paste
900 ml/1½ pts/3 cups vegetable stock
225 g/8 oz/1⅓ cups whole brown
   lentils
100 g/4 oz mushrooms, quartered
100 g/4 oz oyster mushrooms,
   quartered
150 ml/¼ pt/⅔ cup plain yoghurt
15 ml/1 tbsp curried fruit chutney
Salt and freshly ground black pepper
Plain boiled rice
15 ml/1 tbsp chopped coriander
   (cilantro)
Popadoms

Fry (sauté) the onion and garlic in the oil for 2 minutes, stirring. Add the curry paste and cook for 1 minute. Stir in the stock and bring to the boil. Stir in the lentils, cover, reduce the heat and simmer gently for 1½ hours. Add the mushrooms and continue cooking for 30 minutes, stirring occasionally, until the lentils and mushrooms are tender and nearly all the liquid has been absorbed. Stir in the yoghurt and chutney and season to taste. Pile on to a bed of boiled rice, garnish with the coriander and serve with popadoms.

Photograph opposite: **Chinese Vegetable Soup (page 16)**

Leek and Corn Choux Ring

65 g/2½ oz/⅔ cup plain (all-purpose)
   flour
Pinch of salt
50 g/2 oz/¼ cup butter or margarine
150 ml/¼ pt/⅔ cup water
2 eggs, beaten
50 g/2 oz/½ cup Cheddar cheese,
   grated
3 leeks, sliced
200 g/7 oz/1 small can sweetcorn
   (corn), drained
5 ml/1 tsp dried oregano
4 large, ripe tomatoes, skinned,
   seeded and chopped
Salt and freshly ground black pepper

Sift the flour and salt on to a sheet of greaseproof (waxed) paper. Put half the butter or margarine in a saucepan with the water. Heat gently until the fat melts, then bring to the boil. Remove from the heat. Add all the flour in one go and beat with a wooden spoon until the mixture leaves the sides of the pan clean. Cool slightly, then beat in the eggs a little at a time, beating well after each addition until the mixture is smooth and glossy but still holds its shape. Spoon round the edge of a greased 23 cm/9 in shallow round baking dish. Sprinkle with the cheese. Heat the remaining butter in a saucepan. Add the leeks, cover and cook gently for 5 minutes. Add the remaining ingredients and simmer uncovered, fairly rapidly, for about 5 minutes until the leeks are bathed in sauce. Taste and re-season if necessary. Turn into the choux ring. Bake in a preheated oven at 220°C/425°F/gas mark 7 for about 30 minutes until the pastry (paste) is puffy and golden brown.

Monday Pie

350 g/12 oz/3 cups cooked leftover
  vegetables, chopped
400 g/14 oz/1 large can baked beans
75 g/3 oz/1½ cups wholemeal
  breadcrumbs
5 ml/1 tsp onion powder
10 ml/2 tsp yeast extract
30 ml/2 tbsp hot water
2.5 ml/½ tsp dried mixed herbs
Salt and freshly ground black pepper
450 g/1 lb/2 cups mashed potato
50 g/2 oz/½ cup Cheddar cheese,
  grated

Mix the vegetables with the beans, breadcrumbs and onion powder in a 1.2 litre/2 pt/5 cup ovenproof dish. Blend the yeast extract with the water and stir in with the herbs. Season with salt and pepper. Spread the mashed potato over the top to cover completely and sprinkle with the cheese. Bake in a preheated oven at 220°C/425°F/gas mark 7 for 35 minutes until golden brown and piping hot.

Monday Special Pie

Prepare as for Monday Pie but put a layer of 225 g/8 oz/2 cups thawed, frozen leaf spinach on top of the bean mixture and dust with grated nutmeg before adding the potato topping. Garnish with sliced tomatoes on top of the cheese before baking.

Photograph opposite: **Walnut Skordalia (page 36)**

Aubergine Moussaka

2 aubergines (eggplant), sliced
30 ml/2 tbsp tomato purée (paste)
75 ml/5 tbsp water
100 g/4 oz/2 cups wholemeal
  breadcrumbs
1 garlic clove, crushed
75 ml/5 tbsp red wine
30 ml/2 tbsp olive oil
5 ml/1 tsp dried oregano
5 ml/1 tsp ground cinnamon
175 g/6 oz/1½ cups chopped mixed
  nuts
50 g/2 oz/½ cup sunflower seeds
Salt and freshly ground black pepper
75 g/3 oz/¾ cup Feta cheese,
  crumbled
150 ml/¼ pt/⅔ cup plain Greek-style
  yoghurt
1 egg
50 g/2 oz/½ cup Cheddar cheese,
  grated

Cook the aubergines in boiling, salted water for 4–5 minutes or until tender. Drain, rinse with cold water and drain again. Mix the tomato purée with the water, then stir in the breadcrumbs, garlic, wine, oil, oregano, cinnamon, nuts and sunflower seeds. Season to taste. Put a layer of aubergine in the base of a greased 1.5 litre/2½ pt/6 cup ovenproof dish. Cover with half the nut mixture. Add a layer of half the remaining aubergine, then the Feta cheese. Top with the remaining nut mixture, then a final layer of aubergine. Beat together the yoghurt and egg with the grated cheese and a little salt and pepper. Spoon over the aubergines and bake in a preheated oven at 190°C/375°F/gas mark 5 for about 30–35 minutes until golden brown and the topping is set.

Potato Moussaka

Prepare as for Aubergine Moussaka (see page 97) but substitute 450g/1 lb sliced potatoes for the aubergines.

Baked Bean and Mushroom Pancakes

1 quantity Basic Pancake Mix (see page 343)
1 onion, finely chopped
50 g/2 oz/¼ cup butter or margarine
100 g/4 oz button mushrooms, sliced
400 g/14 oz/1 large can baked beans
10 ml/2 tsp brown table sauce
50 g/2 oz/½ cup Cheddar cheese, grated

Make up the pancakes and keep warm while preparing the filling. Fry (sauté) the onion in half the butter or margarine for 3 minutes, stirring. Add the mushrooms and cook, stirring, for a further 3 minutes. Stir in the beans and sauce and heat through. Divide the mixture among the pancakes, roll up and place in a shallow, flameproof dish. Melt the remaining butter and drizzle over then sprinkle with the cheese. Place under a hot grill (broiler) until the cheese melts and bubbles. Serve hot.

Chilli Bean Pancakes

1 quantity Basic Pancake Mix (see page 343)
1 small onion, chopped
15 ml/1 tbsp olive oil
2.5 ml/½ tsp chilli powder
5 ml/1 tsp ground cumin
5 ml/1 tsp dried oregano
200 g/7 oz/1 small can chopped tomatoes
15 ml/1 tbsp tomato purée (paste)
430 g/15½ oz/1 large can mixed pulses, drained
Salt and freshly ground black pepper
50 g/2 oz/½ cup Cheddar cheese, grated

Make up the pancakes and keep warm while preparing the filling. Fry (sauté) the onion in the oil for 3 minutes until softened but not browned. Stir in chilli powder to taste and the cumin and cook for 1 minute, stirring. Add the oregano, tomatoes and tomato purée and simmer for 5 minutes, stirring. Stir in the pulses and heat through. Season to taste. Divide the filling among the pancakes, roll up and place in a shallow flameproof dish. Sprinkle with the cheese and place under a hot grill (broiler) until the cheese melts and bubbles.

Far-Eastern Croquettes

3 spring onions (scallions), finely
chopped
1 carrot, grated
1 parsnip, grated
5 cm/2 in piece cucumber, finely
chopped
3 outside Chinese leaves (stem
lettuce), finely shredded
15 ml/1 tbsp sunflower oil
15 ml/1 tbsp soy sauce
5 ml/1 tsp grated fresh root ginger
15 ml/1 tbsp medium-dry sherry
5 ml/1 tsp light brown sugar
10 ml/2 tsp cornflour (cornstarch)
Salt and freshly ground black pepper
750 g/1½ lb/3 cups mashed potato
30 ml/2 tbsp plain (all-purpose) flour
2 eggs, beaten
2 × 85 g/2 × 3½ oz/2 small packets
sage and onion stuffing mix
Oil, for deep-frying

Fry (sauté) the spring onions, carrot,
parsnip, cucumber and Chinese leaves
in the sunflower oil in a pan for 4 minutes,
stirring. Blend together the soy sauce,
ginger, sherry, sugar and cornflour. Stir
into the pan and cook until thickened.
Season to taste and leave to cool. Mix the
mashed potato with the flour so it holds
its shape. Divide into 8 portions. With
floured hands, flatten a portion on one
hand. Put an eighth of the filling in the
centre and roll up to form a croquette.
Repeat with the remaining potato and filling. Dip in beaten egg then stuffing mix.
Deep-fry in hot oil for 4–5 minutes until
piping hot, golden brown and crisp. Drain
on kitchen paper.

Instant Ratatouille Supper

4 servings instant mashed potato
Knob of butter
2 × 430 g/2 × 15½ oz/2 large cans
ratatouille
50 g/2 oz/½ cup Cheddar cheese,
grated

Make up the potato according to the
packet directions. Spoon round the
edge of a large, shallow, flameproof dish.
Dot with butter and place under a hot grill
(broiler) to brown. Meanwhile, heat the
ratatouille in a saucepan. Spoon into the
dish, sprinkle with the cheese and return
to the grill for a few minutes until the
cheese melts.

Curried Parsnip Flan

175 g/6 oz/1½ cups wholemeal flour
Salt and freshly ground black pepper
75 g/3 oz/⅓ cup butter or margarine
5 ml/1 tsp ground cumin
450 g/1 lb parsnips, sliced
300 ml/½ pt/1¼ cups single (light)
  cream
30 ml/2 tbsp curry paste
50 g/2 oz/½ cup chopped mixed nuts
3 eggs, beaten
45 ml/3 tbsp plain yoghurt
50 g/2 oz/½ cup flaked almonds

Mix the flour with a pinch of salt in a bowl. Rub in the fat, then stir in the cumin. Mix with enough cold water to form a firm dough. Knead gently on a lightly floured surface, then roll out and use to line a 23 cm/9 in flan tin (pie pan). Fill with crumpled foil, then bake in a preheated oven at 200°C/400°F/gas mark 6 for 10 minutes. Remove the foil and cook for a further 5 minutes to dry out. Meanwhile, cook the parsnips in boiling, salted water until tender. Drain and purée in a food processor or blender with the cream and curry paste. Stir in the chopped nuts and season with salt and pepper. Beat the eggs and yoghurt together and blend in briefly. Turn the mixture into the baked flan case (pie shell) and sprinkle with the almonds. Bake in a preheated oven for about 20 minutes until golden and set.

Ratatouille Flan

175 g/6 oz/1½ cups plain (all-
  purpose) flour
Salt and freshly ground black pepper
75 g/3 oz/⅓ cup butter or margarine
30 ml/2 tbsp sesame seeds
1 onion, sliced
1 small aubergine (eggplant), sliced
1 large courgette (zucchini), sliced
1 red (bell) pepper, sliced
30 ml/2 tbsp olive oil
200 g/7 oz/1 small can chopped
  tomatoes
15 ml/1 tbsp tomato purée (paste)
5 ml/1 tsp caster (superfine) sugar
5 ml/1 tsp Herbes de Provence (or
  dried mixed herbs)
50 g/2 oz/½ cup Cheddar cheese,
  grated

Mix the flour with a pinch of salt in a bowl. Add the fat and rub in with the fingertips. Stir in the sesame seeds and mix with enough cold water to form a firm dough. Knead gently on a lightly floured surface, then roll out and use to line a 23 cm/9 in flan tin (pie pan). Prick the base with a fork then fill with crumpled foil. Bake in a preheated oven at 200°C/400°F/gas mark 6 for 10 minutes. Remove the foil and return to a preheated oven for 5 minutes to dry out. Meanwhile, put the prepared vegetables in a saucepan with the oil. Fry (sauté), stirring for 3 minutes until well coated with the oil. Add the tomatoes, tomato purée, sugar, herbs and a little salt and pepper. Bring to the boil, cover and simmer gently for 15 minutes until tender. Turn into the cooked flan, sprinkle with the cheese and return to a preheated oven for 5 minutes until the cheese melts.

Cheatin' Country Pie

50 g/2 oz/¼ cup butter or margarine
2 leeks, sliced
2 carrots, sliced
1 parsnip, sliced
2 small potatoes, sliced
2 celery sticks, sliced
250 ml/8 fl oz/1 cup vegetable stock
25 g/1 oz/¼ cup plain (all-purpose)
  flour
100 g/4 oz sliced vegetarian 'ham',
  chopped
45 ml/3 tbsp single (light) cream
5 ml/1 tsp dried mixed herbs
Salt and freshly ground black pepper
225 g/8 oz/2 cups wholemeal flour
100 g/4 oz/½ cup white vegetable fat
  (shortening)
Beaten egg, to glaze

Melt the butter or margarine in a saucepan. Add the prepared vegetables and cook, stirring, for 2 minutes. Add the stock, bring to the boil, cover, reduce the heat and simmer gently for 10 minutes. Blend the white flour with a little cold water to a smooth paste. Stir into the pan and bring to the boil, stirring all the time. Remove from the heat, stir in the 'ham', cream and herbs and season to taste. Leave to cool while making the pastry (paste). Mix the wholemeal flour with a pinch of salt. Add the fat and rub in with the fingertips. Mix with enough cold water to form a firm dough. Knead gently on a lightly floured surface. Cut in half and roll out one half. Use to line a 20 cm/8 in pie dish. Brush the edges with water. Turn the cool filling into the dish. Roll out the remaining pastry and use as a lid. Knock up the edge and crimp between finger and thumb. Make a slit in the centre to allow steam to escape and make a tassle out of any trimmings. Put in the centre and brush all over with beaten egg. Place on a baking sheet and bake in a preheated oven at 200°C/400°F/gas mark 6 for about 30 minutes until crisp and golden and the filling is really tender. Serve hot.

Winter Chestnut Pie

50 g/2 oz/¼ cup butter or margarine
1 onion, chopped
225 g/8 oz chestnut mushrooms,
  quartered
25 g/1 oz/¼ cup plain (all-purpose)
  flour
250 ml/8 fl oz/1 cup vegetable stock
30 ml/2 tbsp dried milk powder (non-
  fat dry milk)
430 g/15½ oz/1 large can whole
  chestnuts, drained and quartered
Salt and freshly ground black pepper
30 ml/2 tbsp chopped parsley
225 g/8 oz puff pastry (paste)
Beaten egg, to glaze

Melt the butter or margarine in a saucepan. Add the onion and mushrooms and fry (sauté), stirring for 3 minutes. Stir in the flour and cook for 1 minute, stirring. Gradually blend in the stock and the milk powder. Bring to the boil and cook for 2 minutes, stirring all the time. Add the chestnuts, salt and pepper to taste and the parsley. Turn into a pie dish. Roll out the pastry to just larger than the dish and trim the edge. Brush the dish edge with water and lay the pastry trimmings around it. Brush with beaten egg. Lift the pastry lid in position and press the edges together to seal. Knock up and flute with the back of a knife. Make a slit in the centre and a few leaves out of any trimmings. Lay in place and brush with beaten egg. Bake in a preheated oven at 200°C/400°F/gas mark 6 for about 30 minutes until risen, crisp and golden.

Barley Flower Pie

SERVES 4

50 g/2 oz pearl barley
450 ml/¾ pt/2 cups boiling water
1 small cauliflower, cut into florets
175 g/6 oz broccoli, cut into florets
100 g/4 oz/½ cup butter or margarine
1 bunch of spring onions (scallions),
   chopped
25 g/1 oz/¼ cup plain (all-purpose)
   flour
30 ml/2 tbsp dried milk powder (non-
   fat dry milk)
Salt and freshly ground black pepper
45 ml/3 tbsp chopped parsley
175 g/6 oz/1½ cups wholemeal flour
Beaten egg, to glaze

Put the barley in a saucepan with the boiling water. Leave to stand for 15 minutes, then bring to the boil, reduce the heat, cover and simmer gently for 1¼ hours until tender. Add the cauliflower and broccoli for the last 5 minutes cooking time. Strain the liquid into a measuring jug and make up to 300 ml/ ½ pt/1¼ cups with water if necessary. Melt 25 g/ 1 oz/2 tbsp of the butter or margarine in a pan, add the spring onions and fry (sauté), stirring, for 1 minute. Add the flour and cook for 1 minute. Blend in the barley cooking water and the milk powder. Bring to the boil and cook for 2 minutes, stirring. Add the cooked vegetables, season to taste and stir in the parsley. Turn into a large pie dish. Dampen the rim with water. Mix the wholemeal flour with a little salt. Rub in the remaining butter or margarine. Mix with enough cold water to form a firm dough. Knead gently on a lightly floured surface. Roll out to slightly larger than the pie dish. Trim the edge and lay the trimmings round the rim of the dish. Brush with more water. Lay the lid in position. Knock up the edge and flute with the back of a knife. Make a slit in the centre to allow the steam to escape. Make some leaves out of any remaining pastry trimmings and use to decorate the pie. Brush all over with beaten egg, then bake in a preheated oven at 200°C/400°F/gas mark 6 for about 30 minutes until golden brown.

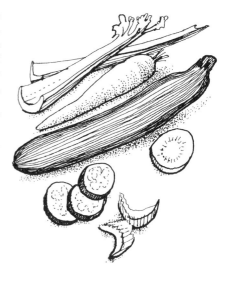

Sweet Potato and Walnut Soufflé Pie

150 g/5 oz/1¼ cups wholemeal flour
1.5 ml/¼ tsp ground cinnamon
Salt and freshly ground black pepper
100 g/4 oz/½ cup butter or margarine
75 g/3 oz/¾ cup red Leicester cheese, grated
3 eggs, separated
350 g/12 oz sweet potatoes, diced
60 ml/4 tbsp milk
75 g/3 oz/¾ cup walnut pieces, chopped

Mix the flour with the cinnamon and a pinch of salt in a bowl. Rub in half the butter or margarine, then stir in the cheese. Mix one of the egg yolks with 45 ml/3 tbsp cold water and stir into the mixture. Add a little more water, if necessary, to form a firm dough. Knead gently on a lightly floured surface. Roll out and use to line a 23 cm/9 in flan dish (pie pan). Prick the base with a fork. Line with crumpled foil and bake in a preheated oven at 200°C/400°F/gas mark 6 for 10 minutes. Remove the foil and return the flan to a preheated oven for 5 minutes to dry out. Meanwhile, cook the sweet potatoes in boiling, lightly salted water until tender. Drain and mash well with the remaining butter or margarine and the milk. Beat in the remaining two egg yolks and the nuts. Season to taste. Whisk the egg whites until stiff. Fold into the sweet potato mixture with a metal spoon. Turn into the pastry case and return to a pre-heated oven. Bake for about 25 minutes until risen, set and golden brown. Serve straight away.

Focaccia

400 g/14 oz/3½ cups plain (all-purpose) flour
Salt
15 ml/1 tbsp caster (superfine) sugar
75 ml/5 tbsp olive oil
15 g/½ oz easy-blend dried yeast
250 ml/8 fl oz/1 cup hot water
2 onions, sliced
1 garlic clove, crushed
50 g/2 oz/⅓ cup stuffed olives, sliced
50 g/2 oz/⅓ cup stoned (pitted) black olives, sliced
2 egg yolks, beaten
15 ml/1 tbsp caraway seeds
15 ml/1 tbsp coriander (cilantro) seeds
Salad

Mix the flour with 10 ml/2 tsp salt and the sugar in a bowl. Add 45 ml/3 tbsp of the oil and the yeast. Mix with the hot water to form a soft but not sticky dough. Knead gently on a lightly floured surface. Wrap in a greased plastic bag while preparing the filling. Heat the remaining oil in a saucepan. Add the onions and garlic and fry (sauté) gently, stirring, for 3 minutes until soft but not brown. Divide the dough into quarters. Roll out each to a round and place on greased baking sheets. Spread the onion mixture over, then scatter with the olives. Bake in a preheated oven at 200°C/400°C/gas mark 6 for 15 minutes. Brush with the beaten egg yolks and sprinkle with the seeds and a little salt. Return to the oven and bake for a further 5–10 minutes until golden and cooked through. Serve straight from the oven with salad.

Tofu- and Quorn-based Main Courses

Tofu Medley

1 garlic clove, chopped
5 ml/1 tsp grated fresh root ginger
60 ml/4 tbsp pineapple juice
60 ml/4 tbsp medium sherry
1 green chilli, seeded and chopped
2.5 ml/½ tsp salt
5 ml/1 tsp yeast extract
225 g/8 oz firm tofu, cut into 2.5 cm/
* 1 in cubes*
1 aubergine (eggplant), sliced
45 ml/3 tbsp seasoned flour
2 eggs, beaten
60 ml/4 tbsp sesame seeds
Oil, for shallow-frying
1 celeriac (celery root), cut into
* 2.5 cm/1 in cubes*
1 large potato, cut into 2.5 cm/1 in
* cubes*
1 large onion, quartered and
* separated into layers*
5 ml/1 tsp cornflour (cornstarch)
45 ml/3 tbsp water

Blend the first 7 ingredients in a shallow dish. Add the tofu cubes and leave to marinate for about 1 hour. Drain and keep the liquid for the sauce. Sprinkle salt over the aubergine slices and leave for 20 minutes. Rinse off the salt and pat dry. Dip the slices in the flour, then beaten egg, then coat in sesame seeds. Heat about 105 ml/8 tbsp oil to smoking point and shallow-fry (sauté) the aubergine slices for 1 minute. Drain on kitchen paper. Blanch the celeriac, potato and onion in boiling, salted water for 1 minute. Drain and pat dry. Heat a little more oil and fry the tofu for 1 minute until brown, then add the blanched vegetables and marinade. Boil for 1 minute. Blend the cornflour with the water, stir in and boil for 1 minute. Season to taste. Serve the tofu mixture on four plates. Garnish with the fried aubergines, which should be very crisp.

Sweet and Sour Tofu

225 g/8 oz firm tofu
15 g/½ oz/1 tbsp butter or margarine
15 ml/1 tbsp oil
320 g/12 oz/1 large can pineapple
* chunks*
1 carrot, cut into matchsticks
½ green (bell) pepper, diced
2.5 ml/½ tsp ground ginger
15 ml/1 tbsp light brown sugar
15 ml/1 tbsp soy sauce
15 ml/1 tbsp malt vinegar
15 ml/1 tbsp tomato purée (paste)
15 ml/1 tbsp cornflour (cornstarch)
15 ml/1 tbsp water
Plain boiled rice

Cut the tofu into bite-sized chunks. Heat the butter or margarine and oil in a large frying pan (skillet) and fry (sauté) the tofu for about 5 minutes until golden brown, stirring. Drain on kitchen paper. Drain the pineapple, reserving the juice. Make the juice up to 300 ml/½ pt/ 1¼ cups with water and pour into a saucepan. Add the pineapple, carrot, pepper, ginger, sugar, soy sauce, vinegar and tomato purée. Bring to the boil and simmer for 3 minutes. Blend the cornflour with the water and stir into the pan. Cook, stirring, for 2 minutes until thickened and clear. Mix in the tofu and heat through. Serve on a bed of rice.

Carrot and Spinach Tofu Cakes

SERVES 6

175 g/6 oz carrots, sliced
450 g/1 lb firm tofu
75 g/3 oz/¾ cup flour
275 g/10 oz spinach, cooked
5 ml/1 tsp grated nutmeg
Salt and freshly ground black pepper
Seasoned flour
2 eggs, beaten
225 g/8 oz/4 cups breadcrumbs
450 g/1 lb plum tomatoes, skinned,
*   seeded and chopped*
15 ml/1 tbsp soy sauce
15 ml/1 tbsp malt vinegar
15 ml/1 tbsp light brown sugar
Chilli powder
Oil, for deep-frying
350 g/12 oz/3 cups baby carrots,
*   lightly cooked*

Boil the sliced carrots for 12–15 minutes. Drain and mash to a purée. Blend with half the tofu and half the flour to form a stiff paste. Squeeze the cooked spinach as dry as possible, then blend with the remaining tofu and flour to form a stiff paste. Season with nutmeg, 5 ml/ 1 tsp salt and a little black pepper. Shape the two purées into balls as big as eggs. Sandwich one of each together in pairs. Press and flatten to small cakes, then freeze until firm. When hard, dip in seasoned flour, then beaten eggs and coat in breadcrumbs. Purée the tomatoes, add the soy sauce, vinegar and sugar and a little salt and chilli powder. Boil for 5 minutes and keep hot. Deep-fry the cakes four at a time for 1 minute until golden. Drain well. Serve one cake per portion with baby boiled carrots and a spoonful of the tomato sauce.

Smoked Tofu and French Bean Stir-fry

SERVES 4

30 ml/2 tbsp sesame oil
450 g/1 lb French (green) beans, cut
*   into 2 or 3 pieces*
1 red (bell) pepper, cut into thin
*   strips*
225 g/8 oz block smoked tofu, cubed
15 ml/1 tbsp light brown sugar
15 ml/1 tbsp white wine vinegar
15 ml/1 tbsp soy sauce
1.5 ml/¼ tsp cayenne
150 ml/¼ pt/⅔ cup vegetable stock
10 ml/2 tsp sesame seeds

Heat the oil in a wok or large frying pan (skillet). Add the beans and pepper and stir-fry for 5 minutes. Add the tofu and remaining ingredients, except the sesame seeds, bring to the boil, stirring and cook for 7 minutes, stirring occasionally. Sprinkle with the sesame seeds and serve straight away.

Tofu Kedgeree

SERVES 4

225 g/8 oz/1 cup long-grain rice
5 ml/1 tsp turmeric
1 onion, chopped
25 g/1 oz/2 tbsp butter or margarine
225 g/8 oz/1 block smoked tofu,
    cubed
100 g/4 oz/1 cup frozen peas
Pinch of grated nutmeg
Salt and freshly ground black pepper
2 hard-boiled (hard-cooked) eggs,
    quartered
15 ml/1 tbsp chopped parsley

Cook the rice according to the packet directions adding the turmeric to the water. Drain, rinse with boiling water, drain again and return to the saucepan. Meanwhile, fry (sauté) the onion in the butter or margarine for 3 minutes until soft but not brown. Add the tofu and peas and cook, stirring gently, for 5 minutes. Add to the rice and season with nutmeg and a little salt and pepper. Toss gently, then add the eggs and toss again. Heat through for a minute or two, then serve, garnished with chopped parsley.

Swedish Quorn

SERVES 4

1 onion, thinly sliced
100 g/4 oz mushrooms, quartered
175 g/6 oz quorn chunks
450 ml/¾ pt/2 cups vegetable stock
2.5 ml/½ tsp soy sauce
7.5 ml/1½ tsp yeast extract
2.5 ml/½ tsp dried basil
15 ml/1 tbsp plain (all-purpose) flour
100 g/4 oz/½ cup quark
Pasta

Put the onion, mushrooms, quorn and 300 ml/½ pt/1¼ cups of the stock into

a large pan and bring to the boil. Add the seasonings, cover and simmer for about 1 hour. Mix together the remaining stock, the flour and quark to a thick paste and stir into the stew. Heat through, stirring. Serve with pasta.

Quorn Mattar

SERVES 4

15 ml/1 tbsp sunflower oil
2 onions, chopped
3 garlic cloves, crushed
350 g/12 oz/3 cups frozen peas,
    thawed
5 ml/1 tsp ground ginger
5 ml/1 tsp chilli powder
10 ml/2 tsp ground cumin
15 ml/1 tbsp ground coriander
    (cilantro)
30 ml/2 tbsp chopped mint
2.5 ml/½ tsp salt
225 g/8 oz/2 cups minced (ground)
    quorn
10 ml/2 tsp yeast extract
150 ml/¼ pt/⅔ cup vegetable stock
150 ml/¼ pt/⅔ cup plain yoghurt
45 ml/3 tbsp lemon juice
Boiled rice
Chapatis

Heat the oil and fry (sauté) the vegetables, spices and salt for a few minutes until softened. Add the quorn, yeast extract and stock, bring to the boil, cover and simmer for 30 minutes until most of the liquid has evaporated. Stir in the yoghurt and lemon juice and stir until absorbed and heated through. Serve hot with boiled rice and chapatis.

Creamy Stroganoff

SERVES 4

175 g/6 oz quorn pieces
300 ml/½ pt/1¼ cups red wine
25 g/1 oz/2 tbsp butter or margarine
2 onions, chopped
4 garlic cloves, crushed
5 ml/1 tsp dried mixed herbs
100 g/4 oz mushrooms, sliced
300 ml/½ pt/1¼ cups Bechamel Sauce
(see page 311)
5 ml/1 tsp dried tarragon
Salt and freshly ground black pepper
Pasta

Marinate the quorn in the wine for 1 hour. Melt the butter or margarine and fry (sauté) the onions, garlic and herbs for 3 minutes. Add the quorn, wine and mushrooms and simmer for 5 minutes. Add the Bechamel Sauce, tarragon and salt and pepper. Simmer for 20 minutes until the quorn is tender. Serve with pasta.

Vegetarian Spaghetti Bolognese

SERVES 3–4

15 ml/1 tbsp olive oil
1 onion, chopped
1 garlic clove, crushed
175 g/6 oz/1½ cups minced (ground)
quorn
100 g/4 oz mushrooms, sliced
400 g/14 oz/1 large can tomatoes
30 ml/2 tbsp tomato purée (paste)
120 ml/4 fl oz/½ cup red wine
15 ml/1 tbsp yeast extract
2.5 ml/½ tsp red wine vinegar
2.5 ml/½ tsp sugar
5 ml/1 tsp dried mixed herbs
Salt and freshly ground black pepper
225 g/8 oz spaghetti
Grated Pecorino cheese

Heat the oil and fry (sauté) the onion, garlic and quorn for 3 minutes. Add the remaining ingredients except the spaghetti and cheese and simmer for 30 minutes. Meanwhile, cook the spaghetti in boiling, salted water until just tender. Drain. Spoon the spaghetti on to a serving dish and pour the sauce over the top. Serve with grated Pecorino cheese.

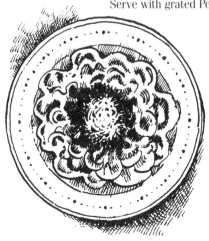

Chilli Con Quorni

SERVES 4

15 ml/1 tbsp olive oil
2 garlic cloves, crushed
1 onion, chopped
5 ml/1 tsp chilli powder
225 g/8 oz/2 cups minced (ground)
   quorn
400 g/14 oz/1 large can tomatoes
30 ml/2 tbsp tomato purée (paste)
100 g/4 oz mushrooms, sliced
425 g/15 oz/1 large can red kidney
   beans, drained
1 vegetable stock cube
15 ml/1 tbsp yeast extract
Salt and freshly ground black pepper
Boiled rice
Garlic bread

Heat the oil and fry (sauté) the garlic, onion and chilli powder for 3 minutes until soft. Add the remaining ingredients except the rice and bread with any left-over wine you may have. Bring to the boil and simmer for at least 45 minutes, adding a little water if the mixture becomes too dry. Adjust the seasoning to taste. Serve with rice and garlic bread.

Chilli Con Quorni Pie

SERVES 2

Use half the quantity of the Chilli Con Quorni recipe. Place in an ovenproof dish and top with 450 g/1 lb/2 cups mashed potato. Sprinkle with 50 g/2 oz/ ½ cup grated Cheddar cheese and bake in a preheated oven at 200°C/400°F/gas mark 6 for about 25 minutes until golden.

Quorn and Vegetable Curry

SERVES 4

30 ml/2 tbsp oil
2 bay leaves
2.5 cm/1 in piece of cinnamon stick
10 cardamom pods, split
5 cloves
15 ml/1 tbsp ground coriander
   (cilantro)
15 ml/1 tbsp ground cumin
Pinch of chilli powder
10 ml/2 tsp sweet pickle
15 ml/1 tbsp tomato purée (paste)
2 garlic cloves, crushed
1 onion, chopped
175 g/6 oz/1½ cups minced (ground)
   quorn
350 g/12 oz potatoes, diced
100 g/4 oz/1 cup frozen peas, thawed
150 ml/¼ pt/⅔ cup vegetable stock
Salt and freshly ground black pepper
50–75 g/2–3 oz creamed coconut
15 ml/1 tbsp garam masala

Heat the oil and fry (sauté) the spices, pickle and tomato purée for 1 minute. Add the garlic, onion and quorn and fry for 3 minutes. Add the vegetables, stock and seasoning, bring to the boil, then simmer for at least 1 hour, adding more water if the mixture becomes too dry. Stir in the coconut and garam masala just before serving and heat through.

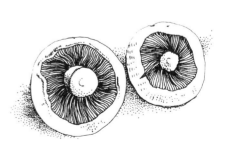

Quorn and Flageolet Hotpot

40 g/1½ oz/3 tbsp butter or margarine
1 onion, finely chopped
1 garlic clove, crushed
225 g/8 oz quorn pieces
2 × 425 g/2 × 15 oz/2 large cans
  flageolet beans, drained
300 ml/½ pt/1¼ cups vegetable stock
30 ml/2 tbsp redcurrant jelly (clear
  conserve)
5 ml/1 tsp dried rosemary
450 g/1 lb potatoes, thinly sliced
Salt and freshly ground black pepper

Melt 25 g/1 oz/2 tbsp of the butter or margarine in a flameproof casserole (Dutch oven). Add the onion and garlic and fry (sauté) for 2 minutes. Stir in the quorn and fry, stirring, for 2 minutes. Stir in the beans, stock, redcurrant jelly and rosemary. Bring to the boil and simmer for 5 minutes. Remove from the heat. Lay the potato slices over and dot with the remaining butter. Season lightly, then bake in a preheated oven at 180°C/350°F/gas mark 4 for about 45 minutes or until the potatoes are golden.

Quorn Moussaka

450 g/1 lb courgettes (zucchini)
  sliced
1 onion, finely chopped
1 garlic clove, crushed
15 ml/1 tbsp olive oil
225 g/8 oz/2 cups minced (ground)
  quorn
5 ml/1 tsp dried oregano
2.5 ml/½ tsp ground cinnamon
400 g/14 oz/1 large can chopped
  tomatoes
15 ml/1 tbsp tomato purée (paste)
150 ml/¼ pt/⅔ cup water
1 vegetable stock cube
Salt and freshly ground black pepper
150 ml/¼ pt/⅔ cup Greek-style plain
  yoghurt
1 egg
50 g/2 oz/½ cup Cheddar cheese,
  grated

Boil the courgettes in lightly salted water for 4 minutes. Drain, rinse with cold water and drain again. Fry (sauté) the onion and garlic in the oil for 3 minutes. Add the quorn and continue frying, stirring, for 3 minutes. Add the oregano, cinnamon, tomatoes, tomato purée, water and crumbled stock cube. Bring to the boil and simmer fairly rapidly for about 10 minutes until the mixture forms a rich sauce. Season to taste. Layer the courgette and quorn mixtures in a 1.5 litre/2½ pt/6 cup ovenproof dish, finishing with a layer of courgettes. Beat the yoghurt and egg together and stir in the cheese and a little salt and pepper. Spoon over the courgettes and bake in a preheated oven at 190°C/375°F/gas mark 5 for about 35 minutes or until golden brown and the topping is set.

Quorn Cottage Pie

100 g/4 oz/1 cup minced (ground)
quorn
½ onion, chopped
10 ml/2 tsp oil
150 ml/¼ pt/⅔ cup Vegetable Gravy
(see page 316)
15 ml/1 tbsp tomato purée (paste)
225 g/8 oz/2 cups any cooked
vegetables, chopped
15 ml/1 tbsp yeast extract
450 g/1 lb/2 cups mashed potato

Fry (sauté) the quorn and onion in the oil for 4 minutes until soft. Stir in the remaining ingredients except the potato and spoon into an ovenproof dish. Spread the mashed potato on the top. Bake in a preheated oven at 200°C/400°F/gas mark 6 for 30 minutes until crisp and brown.

Haberdasher

450 g/1 lb potatoes, finely diced
1 large onion, chopped
50 g/2 oz/¼ cup butter or margarine
225 g/8 oz quorn pieces
400 g/14 oz/1 large can baked beans
225 g/8 oz/2 cups leftover cooked
vegetables (e.g. cabbage, broccoli,
cauliflower, carrots), chopped
15 ml/1 tbsp Worcestershire sauce
Salt and freshly ground black pepper
Crusty bread

Fry (sauté) the potato and onion in the butter or margarine in large frying pan (skillet) for 10 minutes, stirring occasionally, until cooked through and golden. Add the remaining ingredients except the bread and season well with salt and pepper. Cook, stirring, for 5 minutes until piping hot. Serve in warm bowls with lots of crusty bread.

Pulse-based Main Courses

Bean Cassoulet Toulouse-Lautrec

SERVES 4

225 g/8 oz/2 cups haricot (navy)
  beans, soaked overnight
15 ml/1 tbsp olive oil
2 onions, thickly sliced
2 celery sticks, sliced
1 red (bell) pepper, chopped
1 fennel bulb, sliced
3 garlic cloves, chopped
1 small green chilli, seeded and
  sliced
30 ml/2 tbsp red wine
50 g/2 oz/½ cup pine nuts
Thyme sprig
Marjoram sprig
5 ml/1 tsp Dijon mustard
1 vegetable stock cube
2 large tomatoes, skinned, seeded
  and chopped
50 g/2 oz/1 cup wholemeal
  breadcrumbs
75 g/3 oz/¾ cup Cheddar cheese,
  grated

Drain the soaked beans, rinse, drain again and cook in boiling water for 30 minutes. Drain and place in a casserole (Dutch oven). Heat the oil in a frying pan (skillet) and stir-fry the onions, celery, pepper, fennel, garlic and chilli for 5 minutes. Add to the beans. Cover the contents of the casserole with water and add the wine, pine nuts, herbs and mustard. Crumble in the stock cube. Cover and bake in the oven at 150°C/300°F/gas mark 2 for 1½–2 hours or until the beans are tender. Remove the casserole from the oven and increase the heat to 220°C/425°F/gas mark 7. Spread the chopped tomato on top of the casserole and cover with breadcrumbs. Top with the cheese. Return, uncovered, to a preheated oven and cook for 12 minutes until golden. Serve straight from the casserole.

Felafel Jerusalem

SERVES 4

450 g/15½ oz/1 large can chick peas
  (garbanzos), drained
1 red onion, chopped
1 garlic clove, chopped
1 green chilli, seeded and chopped
3 mint leaves, chopped
5 ml/1 tsp ground cumin
5 ml/1 tsp caraway seeds
75 g/3 oz/¾ cup plain (all-purpose)
  flour
1 egg, beaten
Oil, for shallow-frying
4 pitta breads
1 bunch of watercress
1 avocado, sliced
2 tomatoes, sliced

Put the chick peas, onion, garlic, chilli, herbs and spices in a blender or food processor. Blend to a paste and transfer to a bowl. Divide the paste into eight portions and shape into balls. Flatten, coat with flour and dip in beaten egg. Shallow-fry the felafel in hot oil for 4 minutes until golden on both sides. Drain well on kitchen paper. To serve, make a cut into the side of each pitta bread and open up to form a pocket. Place two felafel in each pitta and add watercress and slices of avocado and tomato.

Chick Pea and Spinach Casserole

450 g/1 lb fresh spinach, stems removed, washed and drained
30 ml/2 tbsp melted butter and oil
1 garlic clove, chopped
225 g/8 oz/1 small can chick peas (garbanzos)
100 g/4 oz Feta cheese, cubed
Salt and freshly ground black pepper
120 ml/4 fl oz/½ cup soured (dairy sour) cream
Plain boiled noodles
Grated Cheddar cheese

Shred the spinach leaves. Heat the butter and oil in a saucepan and cook the spinach for 4 minutes. Add the chick peas and Feta cheese. Season to taste and stir in the soured cream just before serving. Serve with plain boiled noodles with plenty of grated cheese.

Lentil Patties

225 g/8 oz/1⅓ cups green or brown lentils
600 ml/1 pt/2½ cups water
15 ml/1 tbsp oil
1 small onion, chopped
1 green chilli, seeded and chopped
Pinch of ground cumin
Pinch of ground ginger
Pinch of curry powder
Salt
1 egg, beaten
30 ml/2 tbsp plain yoghurt
30 ml/2 tbsp plain (all-purpose) flour
100 g/4 oz/1 cup rolled oats
Salad
Oil, for shallow-frying

Place the lentils in a bowl, cover with boiling water and leave to soak for 1 hour. Drain and place in a saucepan with the measured amount of water. Boil for 20 minutes until tender, then drain and mash to a purée. Leave to cool. Heat 15 ml/1 tbsp of oil in a frying pan (skillet) and stir-fry the onion and chilli for 3 minutes. Sprinkle in the cumin, ginger and curry powder and season with salt. Blend the lentil purée with the onion and spice mixture, mix well and form into ten large balls. Flatten each to a patty shape. Beat the egg and yoghurt together. Coat the patties in flour, then dip in egg and yoghurt. Finally, dip in rolled oats. (If necessary, use a palette knife to retain the shape of the patties.) Shallow-fry in hot oil for 2–3 minutes until golden brown on both sides. Drain well on kitchen paper. Serve warm with salad.

Mexican Tacos

4 taco shells
30 ml/2 tbsp oil
1 small onion, chopped
1 green chilli, seeded and sliced
50 g/2 oz/½ cup baked beans, mashed
1 avocado, stoned (pitted), peeled and
   diced
1 tomato, skinned, seeded and diced
Salt and freshly ground black pepper
Lettuce leaves

Place the taco shells in the oven to warm while preparing the filling. Heat the oil in a frying pan (skillet) and stir-fry the onion and chilli for 2 minutes. Add the mashed beans and cook for 2 minutes more. Stir in the avocado and tomato and season with salt and pepper. Line the taco shells with lettuce leaves and spoon the bean mixture on top. Serve immediately.

Mexican Bean Fiesta

150 g/5 oz/1¼ cups haricot (navy)
   beans
1.2 litres/2 pts/5 cups water
60 ml/4 tbsp corn or sunflower oil
1 red onion, chopped
1 red (bell) pepper, diced
1 celery stick, diced
1 fennel stalk, diced
75 g/3 oz/¾ cup sweetcorn (corn),
   frozen or canned
2 garlic cloves, chopped
4 tomatoes, skinned, seeded and
   chopped
6 basil leaves, chopped
1 green chilli, seeded and chopped
15 ml/1 tbsp cornflour (cornstarch)
120 ml/4 fl oz/½ cup water
15 ml/1 tbsp yeast extract
Salt and freshly ground black pepper
15 ml/1 tbsp clear honey
50 g/2 oz/½ cup Cheddar cheese,
   grated

Soak the beans in cold water for 6 hours. Wash in plenty of fresh water. Place the beans in a flameproof casserole (Dutch oven) and cover with the measured water. Bring to the boil. Remove any scum. Cover and bake in a preheated oven at 180°C/350°F/gas mark 4 for 2 hours. In a wok, heat the oil and stir-fry the onion, pepper, celery, fennel and sweetcorn for 4 minutes. Add the garlic and cook for 30 seconds, then blend in the tomatoes, basil leaves and chilli. Simmer for 5 minutes. In a cup, mix the cornflour and cold water and add to the boiling ingredients. Cook for 4 minutes. Stir in the yeast extract and season to taste. Add the honey. Drain the beans and mix them into the sauce. Place in individual soup bowls. Sprinkle with grated cheese and brown under the grill (broiler).

Lentil Cakes with Chicory

SERVES 4

225 g/8 oz/1⅓ cups green lentils
1 carrot, diced
1 small onion, chopped
50 g/2 oz/¼ cup long-grain rice
2 eggs, beaten
2 garlic cloves, chopped
25 g/1 oz/¼ cup wholemeal flour
Salt and freshly ground black pepper
45 ml/3 tbsp seasoned flour
Oil, for shallow-frying
4 chicory (Belgian endive) heads
45 ml/3 tbsp olive oil
15 ml/1 tbsp wine vinegar
4 ml/¾ tsp made English mustard
30 ml/2 tbsp chopped parsley

Boil the lentils, carrot and onion in salted water for 25 minutes. Drain and purée in a blender or food processor. Meanwhile, boil the rice for 20 minutes. Drain and blend into the lentil purée. Add the eggs, garlic and wholemeal flour. Season to taste. Shape the mixture into four patties. Coat in seasoned flour. Shallow-fry in hot oil for 3 minutes on each side until golden. Cut the chicory into thin slices. Wash and drain. Blend the olive oil, vinegar and mustard and sprinkle over the chicory. Serve one lentil cake per portion with this salad, sprinkled with parsley.

Lentil and Baby Vegetable Platter

SERVES 4

150 g/5 oz/⅔ cup green lentils
40 g/1½ oz/3 tbsp butter or margarine
2 garlic cloves, chopped
Salt and freshly ground black pepper
30 ml/2 tbsp olive oil
15 ml/1 tbsp wine vinegar
8 pickling onions, peeled
16 baby carrots, scraped
4 baby sweetcorn (corn) cobs
30 ml/2 tbsp clear honey
16 mangetout (snow peas), topped and tailed

Soak the lentils for 25 minutes – this will help in keeping their shape – then simmer gently for 16 minutes. Drain. Add a third of the butter or margarine and half the garlic. Season to taste. Add 15 ml/ 1 tbsp of the oil and the vinegar. In a wok, heat the remaining butter or margarine and oil and stir-fry the onions, carrots and sweetcorn for 2 minutes. Add 120 ml/ 4 fl oz/1 cup water and boil for 5 minutes until the liquid has evaporated. Add the honey and mangetout and cook for a further 2 minutes. Season to taste. On four plates spoon the hot green lentils and surround with the vegetables, arranged decoratively.

Quick Bean Grill

SERVES 2

400 g/14 oz/1 large can ratatouille
200 g/7 oz/1 small can butter beans,
  drained
2.5 ml/½ tsp dried tarragon
Freshly ground black pepper
50 g/2 oz/1 cup breadcrumbs
50 g/2 oz/½ cup Cheddar cheese,
  grated

Heat together the ratatouille, butter beans, tarragon and pepper, then place in an ovenproof dish. Mix together the breadcrumbs and cheese and sprinkle over the top. Place under the grill (broiler) until the cheese has melted and browned.

Chilli White Beans

SERVES 4

1 onion, chopped
50 g/2 oz/¼ cup butter or margarine
50 g/2 oz/½ cup wholemeal flour
2.5 ml/½ tsp chilli powder
2.5 ml/½ tsp ground cumin
450 ml/¾ pt/2 cups vegetable stock
30 ml/2 tbsp tomato purée (paste)
225 g/8 oz/2 cups cannellini beans,
  cooked (see page 10)
Salt and freshly ground black pepper
5 ml/1 tsp chopped oregano
5 ml/1 tsp chopped parsley
50 g/2 oz/½ cup pumpkin seeds
Plain boiled rice
Grated Cheddar cheese
Shredded lettuce
30 ml/2 tbsp quark or soured (dairy
  sour) cream

Fry (sauté) the onion in the butter or margarine for 3 minutes, stirring. Add the flour, chilli powder and cumin. Continue cooking for 1 minute. Gradually add the stock, bring to the boil and cook for a further 3 minutes, stirring. Add the tomato purée, beans, salt and pepper to taste, the herbs and pumpkin seeds. Cover and simmer gently for 5 minutes. Spoon on to beds of boiled rice, garnish each with a spoonful of quark or soured cream and serve with shredded lettuce and cheese.

Indian Chick Pea and Fried Cheese Dumplings

450 g/1 lb/2⅔ cups chick peas
  (garbanzos)
1.75 litres/3 pts/7½ cups water
1 Ceylon tea bag
2.5 ml/½ tsp ground cinnamon
2.5 ml/½ tsp grated nutmeg
2.5 ml/½ tsp freshly ground black
  pepper
10 ml/2 tsp caraway seeds
Grated rind and juice of 1 lemon
Grated rind and juice of 1 lime
5 ml/1 tsp salt
25 g/1 oz stem ginger in syrup, cut
  into strips
150 g/6 oz/1½ cups coriander
  (cilantro) leaves, chopped
105 ml/7 tbsp sunflower oil
2 tomatoes, skinned, seeded and cut
  into wedges
225 g/8 oz/1 cup cream cheese
60 ml/4 tbsp seasoned flour
1 egg, beaten
50 g/2 oz/1 cup breadcrumbs
Oil, for deep-frying

Boil the chick peas in the water for 5 minutes, brew a tea bag in the liquid for 5 minutes, then discard. Continue simmering the chick peas for another hour or so until tender. Drain. Blend in all the spices and seeds, lemon and lime rind and juice. Add the salt, ginger strips and most of the coriander leaves. Heat the sunflower oil in the chick pea pan, add the mixture and stir to develop a good spice flavour. Add the tomatoes and chick peas and cook for a further 1 minute. Shape the cream cheese into walnut-sized balls. Coat in seasoned flour, then beaten egg, then breadcrumbs. Deep-fry in hot oil for 2 minutes until golden. Serve three cheese balls per person with a scoop of the chick pea mixture. Sprinkle over the remaining chopped coriander leaves.

Veggie Wedges

150 g/5 oz/1¼ cup haricot (navy)
  beans, cooked (see page 10)
150 g/5 oz/1¼ cups green lentils,
  cooked
150 g/5 oz/1¼ cups split green peas,
  cooked
50 g/2 oz/½ cup blue cheese, mashed
15 ml/1 tbsp celery seeds
50 g/2 oz/¼ cup butter or margarine
50 g/2 oz/½ cup peanuts, chopped
4 eggs, beaten
Salt and freshly ground black pepper
225 g/8 oz green cabbage, shredded
  and boiled or steamed
Mayonnaise (see page 305) or
  French Dressing (see page 303)

Purée all the pulses in a blender or food processor. Combine the paste in a bowl with the blue cheese, celery seeds, butter, nuts and eggs. Season to taste with about 1 level teaspoon of salt and a good grinding of pepper. Oil an oblong 750 ml/1¼ pt/3 cup baking tin (pan). Fill with the mixture to the top and cover with greased greaseproof (waxed) paper. Bake in a preheated oven at 200°C/400°F/gas mark 6 for 30 minutes. Cool and turn out on to a board. Cut into thick slices and serve with the shredded cabbage and Mayonnaise or French Dressing.

Two Bean Casserole

SERVES 4

SERVES 4

50 g/2 oz/¼ cup butter or margarine
1 onion, chopped
175 g/6 oz/1½ cups haricot (navy)
  beans, cooked (see page 10)
175 g/6 oz/1½ cups red kidney beans,
  cooked
400 g/14 oz/1 large can chopped
  tomatoes
30 ml/2 tbsp clear honey
5 ml/1 tsp wholegrain mustard
Salt and freshly ground black pepper
15 ml/1 tbsp pumpkin seeds
Green tagliatelle (verdi), cooked

Melt the butter or margarine in a pan and fry (sauté) the onion for 3 minutes, stirring. Add the remaining ingredients, except the tagliatelle, bring to the boil, cover and cook for about 8 minutes or until the beans are bathed in a rich sauce. Serve hot with green tagliatelle.

Red Kidney Bean Croustade

SERVES 4

100 g/4 oz/1 cup chopped mixed nuts
100 g/4 oz/1 cup Cheddar cheese,
  grated
6 slices wholemeal bread
5 ml/1 tsp chopped mixed herbs
45 ml/3 tbsp sunflower oil
1 onion, chopped
30 g/2 tbsp wholemeal flour
1.5 ml/¼ tsp chilli powder
300 ml/½ pt/1¼ cups vegetable stock
225 g/8 oz/2 cups red kidney beans,
  cooked (see page 10)
30 ml/2 tbsp sunflower seeds
30 ml/2 tbsp chopped parsley
Salt and freshly ground black pepper

Put the nuts, cheese, bread and herbs in a food processor and process for 1 minute. Add 30 ml/2 tbsp of the oil and continue to process for a further minute. Turn into a greased 20 cm/8 in flan dish (pie pan) and press down well. Cook in a preheated oven at 190°C/375°F/gas mark 5 for 15 minutes. Meanwhile, make the filling. Fry (sauté) the onion in the remaining oil for 2 minutes, stirring. Add the flour and chilli powder and cook for 1 minute. Stir in the stock, bring to the boil and cook for 2 minutes, stirring all the time. Add the kidney beans, sunflower seeds and parsley, stir well and season to taste. Pour the filling over the croustade base and cook in the oven for a further 15 minutes. Serve hot.

Lentil Supper

SERVES 4

350 g/12 oz/2 cups red lentils
1 onion, chopped
900 ml/1½ pts/3¾ cups vegetable stock
2.5 ml/½ tsp dried mixed herbs
Salt and freshly ground black pepper
15 ml/1 tbsp wholemeal breadcrumbs
75 g/3 oz/¾ cup Cheddar cheese,
*   grated*
Snipped chives
Tortilla chips or savoury crackers

Put the lentils, onion and stock in a large pan. Bring to the boil, reduce the heat, cover and simmer gently, stirring occasionally, for about 15 minutes or until the lentils are cooked and have absorbed all the liquid. Add all the remaining ingredients, except the chives and chips, and reheat for 3 minutes, stirring. Spoon into small bowls, garnish with chives and serve with tortilla chips or crackers to dip in.

Mixed Bean and Cheese Scramble

SERVES 4

225 g/8 oz/2 cups mixed beans or
*   pulses, cooked (see page 10)*
50 g/2 oz/¼ cup butter or margarine
2 eggs, beaten
100 g/4 oz/1 cup Cheddar cheese,
*   grated*
Salt and freshly ground black pepper
Pinch of cayenne
60 ml/4 tbsp milk
45 ml/3 tbsp chopped parsley
Hot toast

Put all the ingredients except the parsley and toast into a large saucepan, mix well and cook gently, stirring until scrambled. Pile on to hot toast and sprinkle with parsley before serving.

Dhal with Cheese

275 g/10 oz/1⅓ cups red lentils
600 ml/1 pt/2½ cups vegetable stock
1 bay leaf
Salt and freshly ground black pepper
25 g/1 oz/2 tbsp butter or margarine
15 ml/1 tbsp oil
1 onion, chopped
2.5 ml/½ tsp ground ginger
2.5 ml/½ tsp ground coriander
  (cilantro)
2.5 ml/½ tsp ground cumin
175 g/6 oz/1½ cups Cheddar cheese,
  cubed
Naan bread

Place all the ingredients except the cheese and naan bread, in a large pan. Bring to the boil, reduce the heat, cover and simmer gently for 20 minutes or until the lentils are soft and have absorbed all the liquid. Stir from time to time to prevent sticking. Add the cheese, spoon through until just beginning to melt, then serve straight away with naan bread.

Curried Beans

50 g/2 oz/¼ cup butter or margarine
15 ml/1 tbsp oil
1 large onion, chopped
15 ml/ 1 tbsp wholemeal or plain
  (all-purpose) flour
15 ml/1 tbsp medium-hot curry
  powder
2 cloves
1.5 ml/¼ tsp ground ginger
1.5 ml/¼tsp ground cinnamon
15 ml/1 tbsp tomato purée (paste)
30 ml/2 tbsp Chutney (see page 321)
  or use bought
15 ml/1 tbsp lemon juice
600 ml/1 pt/2½ cups vegetable stock
Salt and freshly ground black pepper
350 g/12 oz/3 cups red kidney beans,
  cooked (see page 10)
Desiccated (shredded) coconut
Pat's Perfect Rice (see page 172)
Popadoms

Heat the butter or margarine and oil in a large pan. Add the onion and fry (sauté) for 3 minutes, stirring. Stir in the flour, spices, tomato purée, chutney, lemon juice and stock. Season lightly. Bring to the boil, cover, reduce the heat and simmer for 25 minutes, stirring occasionally. Add a little more stock if necessary. Add the beans and heat through. Garnish with desiccated coconut and serve with rice and popadoms.

Butter Bean Goulash

SERVES 4

50 g/2 oz/¼ cup butter or margarine
1 garlic clove, crushed
1 onion, chopped
100 g/4 oz mushrooms, sliced
400 g/14 oz/1 large can chopped
*   tomatoes*
350 g/12 oz/3 cups butter beans,
*   cooked (see page 10)*
30 ml/2 tbsp tomato purée (paste)
Salt and freshly ground black pepper
15 ml/1 tbsp paprika
2.5 ml/½ tsp ground cumin
2.5 ml/½ tsp ground coriander
*   (cilantro)*
Chopped parsley
Soured (dairy sour) cream
Crusty bread
Green salad

Melt the butter or margarine in a pan, add the garlic, onion and mushrooms and fry (sauté) for 3 minutes, stirring. Add all the remaining ingredients except the parsley, soured cream, bread and salad, cover and simmer gently for 10 minutes. Remove the lid and continue cooking for about 5 minutes until the beans are bathed in a rich sauce. Spoon into warm bowls. Garnish with chopped parsley and a swirl of soured cream. Serve with crusty bread and a green salad.

Butter Beans and Mushroom Bake

SERVES 4

30 ml/2 tbsp olive oil
225 g/8 oz mushrooms, sliced
25 ml/1½ tbsp plain (all-purpose) or
*   wholemeal flour*
300 ml/½ pt/1¼ cups milk
100 g/4 oz/1 cup Cheddar cheese,
*   grated*
225 g/8 oz/1⅓ cups butter beans,
*   cooked (see page 10)*
Salt and freshly ground black pepper
Pinch of grated nutmeg
45 ml/3 tbsp breadcrumbs
45 ml/3 tbsp sesame seeds
25 g/1 oz/2 tbsp butter or margarine

Heat the oil in a pan. Add the mushrooms and fry (sauté) for 2 minutes, stirring. Add the flour and cook for 1 minute. Stir in the milk, bring to the boil and cook for 2 minutes, stirring all the time. Add 75 g/3 oz/¾ cup of the cheese, the butter beans, seasoning and nutmeg and stir well. Turn into a greased ovenproof dish and sprinkle with the breadcrumbs, sesame seeds and the remaining grated cheese. Dot with butter or margarine. Bake in a preheated oven at 190°C/375°F/gas mark 5 for 30 minutes.

Spicy Pinto Stew

SERVES 4

15 ml/1 tbsp olive oil
1 garlic clove, crushed
2.5 ml/½ tsp grated fresh root ginger
175 g/6 oz/1 cup pinto beans, soaked
  and boiled (see page 10)
200 g/7 oz/1 small can chopped
  tomatoes
1 onion, chopped
30 ml/2 tbsp soy sauce
5 ml/1 tsp Chinese five spice powder
150 ml/¼ pt/⅔ cup vegetable stock
1 red (bell) pepper, chopped
225 g/8 oz mushrooms, sliced
4 courgettes (zucchini), sliced
Salt and freshly ground black pepper
Crusty bread

Heat the oil and fry (sauté) the garlic and ginger very gently for 2 minutes. Add the beans and the remaining ingredients except the bread, bring to the boil, cover and simmer for 20 minutes. Season to taste, then serve hot with lots of crusty bread.

Baked Bean Lasagne

SERVES 4

15 ml/1 tbsp sunflower oil
1 onion, chopped
2 garlic cloves, crushed
225 g/8 oz mushrooms, sliced
400 g/14 oz/1 large can baked beans
30 ml/2 tbsp tomato ketchup (catsup)
45 ml/3 tbsp soy sauce
Pinch of chilli powder
Freshly ground black pepper
8 sheets no-need-to-precook lasagne
300 ml/½ pt/1¼ cups Bechamel Sauce
  (see page 311)
100 g/4 oz/1 cup Cheddar cheese,
  grated
Grated Pecorino cheese (optional)

Heat the oil in a large pan and fry (sauté) the onion and garlic for about 4 minutes until softened. Add the mushrooms and cook for 2 minutes. Stir in the beans, tomato ketchup, soy sauce, chilli powder and pepper. Layer the bean mixture and lasagne sheets in a shallow ovenproof dish, finishing with a layer of lasagne. Stir the Cheddar cheese into the Bechamel Sauce and pour over the top. Sprinkle with Pecorino cheese, if using. Bake in a preheated oven at 190°C/ 375°F/gas mark 5 for 40 minutes.

Mung Bean and Pumpkin Speciality

225 g/8 oz/2 cups mung beans
45 ml/3 tbsp olive oil
1 red onion, chopped
2 garlic cloves, crushed
225 g/8 oz/1 cup long-grain rice
5 ml/1 tsp ground turmeric
5 ml/1 tsp yeast extract
750 ml/1¼ pts/3 cups hot water
Salt and freshly ground black pepper
Oil for shallow-frying
15 ml/1 tbsp pumpkin seeds
150 g/5 oz/1¼ cups pumpkin flesh,
*   cut into 5 mm/¼ in cubes*
8 plums, halved and stoned (pitted)
45 ml/3 tbsp mixed chopped herbs,
*   (e.g. basil, mint, lemon balm,*
*   parsley, marjoram)*
Coriander (cilantro) sprigs

Cover the beans in boiling water, then soak for 2 hours. Drain the beans, rinse and drain again. Heat the oil in a large frying pan (skillet) and stir-fry the onion and garlic for 1 minute until soft but not brown. Stir in the beans, rice and turmeric and cook, stirring, for 2 minutes to allow the flavours to blend. Dissolve the yeast extract in the hot water and pour into the pan. Cook gently for 35–40 minutes until the rice and beans are tender and the water has been absorbed. Season to taste with salt and pepper. Meanwhile, heat a little oil in a frying pan and fry the pumpkin seeds until browned. Drain on kitchen paper. Cook the pumpkin pulp in boiling water for 6 minutes until tender and drain well. Spoon the cooked rice and bean mixture on to four heated serving plates and surround with plum halves. Sprinkle with fried pumpkin seeds. Pile the cooked pumpkin on top and sprinkle with chopped fresh herbs. Serve garnished with a coriander sprig.

Baked Bean Loaf

400 g/14 oz/1 large can baked beans
1 small onion, chopped
50 g/2 oz/1 cup breadcrumbs
30 ml/2 tbsp tomato ketchup (catsup)
1 egg, beaten
5 ml/1 tsp yeast extract
5 ml/1 tsp dried mixed herbs
Salt and freshly ground black pepper

Mix together all the ingredients. Pour into a greased loaf tin, lined with non-stick baking parchment. Bake in a preheated oven at 180°C/350°F/gas mark 4 for 30 minutes until set.

Baked Bean Savoury

25 g/1 oz/2 tbsp butter or margarine
1 onion, chopped
2 × 400 g/2 × 14 oz/2 large cans
  baked beans
4 hard-boiled (hard-cooked) eggs,
  quartered
Salt and freshly ground black pepper
5 ml/1 tsp tomato purée (paste)
A few drops of Worcestershire sauce
100 g/4 oz/1 cup Cheddar cheese,
  grated
50 g/2 oz/1 cup breadcrumbs
Pinch of dried mixed herbs
Crusty bread
Green salad

Melt the butter or margarine in a pan. Add the onion and fry (sauté) gently, stirring for 5 minutes until soft. Stir in the beans, eggs, a little salt and pepper, the tomato purée and Worcestershire sauce and heat through. Turn into a flameproof casserole (Dutch oven). Mix the cheese and breadcrumbs together and sprinkle over. Place under a hot grill (broiler) until the cheese is melted and golden. Serve with crusty bread and a green salad.

Middle-Eastern Tabbouleh

175 g/6 oz/1½ cups bulgar wheat
325 ml/11 fl oz/1⅓ cups boiling water
5 ml/1 tsp salt
45 ml/3 tbsp olive oil
45 ml/3 tbsp lemon juice
1 large garlic clove, crushed
A good handful of parsley, chopped
30 ml/2 tbsp chopped mint
10 ml/2 tsp chopped coriander
  (cilantro)
Freshly ground black pepper
4 large tomatoes, seeded and
  chopped
¼ cucumber, finely diced
1 green (bell) pepper, finely diced
Black olives

Put the wheat in a bowl. Pour on the boiling water, sprinkle with the salt and stir. Leave to stand for 20 minutes until the wheat has absorbed all the water and is soft. Drizzle over the oil and lemon juice. Add the herbs and a good grinding of black pepper. Toss well, cover and chill overnight. Just before serving add the tomatoes, cucumber and pepper and toss gently but thoroughly. Stud with olives and serve.

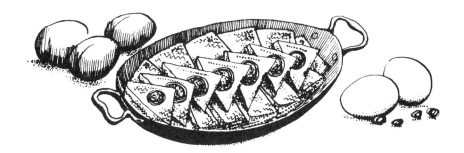

Algerian Couscous

SERVES 4

2 leeks, trimmed and cut into chunks
1 small fennel bulb, trimmed and
    sliced
2 large tomatoes, skinned, seeded
    and chopped
430 g/15½ oz/1 large can chick peas
    (garbanzos), drained
2 carrots, peeled and thinly sliced
1 celery stick, sliced
1 green chilli, seeded and sliced
Good pinch of cumin
2 garlic cloves, crushed
Mint sprig
30 ml/2 tbsp tomato purée (paste)
Salt and freshly ground black pepper
1 litre/1¾ pts/4¼ cups vegetable stock
50 g/2 oz/¼ cup butter or margarine
225 g/8 oz/1½ cups couscous
50 g/2 oz/½ cup frozen peas and
    sweetcorn (corn), cooked
50 g/2 oz/⅓ cup raisins
50 g/2 oz/½ cup split blanched
    almonds, lightly toasted
Watermelon wedges
A few fresh dates

Place the leeks, fennel, tomatoes, chick peas, carrots, celery, chilli, cumin, garlic, mint and tomato purée in a large saucepan. Season with salt, and add the stock. Bring to the boil and simmer for 25 minutes until the vegetables are tender. Drain off 300 ml/½ pt/1¼ cups of the stock and pour into a jug. To cook the couscous, heat the butter or margarine in a frying pan (skillet), add the couscous and heat gently, stirring, for 3 minutes. Gradually add the reserved stock and cook for 6 minutes. Transfer to a dish and leave to stand for 10 minutes. Stir in the cooked peas and sweetcorn, the raisins and almonds, mix well and season to taste with salt and pepper. Divide the vegetables between four soup plates and add a little vegetable cooking stock to each. Serve the couscous separately in individual dishes. To be truly authentic, serve wedges of watermelon and fresh dates with this couscous dish. The Arabs eat the watermelon seeds as well as they are very nutritious.

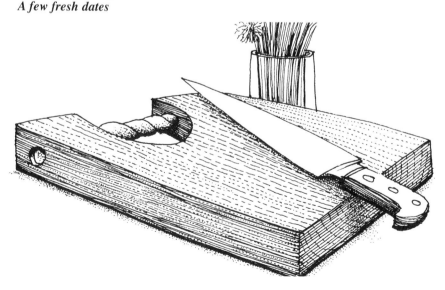

Vegetable Stew with Cheese Dumplings

65 g/2½ oz/good ¼ cup butter or
 margarine
1 onion, chopped
1 garlic, clove, crushed
2 leeks, sliced
3 carrots, sliced
2 celery sticks, chopped
1 red (bell) pepper, sliced
2 courgettes (zucchini), sliced
430 g/15½ oz/1 large can black-eyed
 beans, drained
430 g/15½ oz/1 large can butter
 beans, drained
750 ml/1¼ pts/3 cups vegetable stock
1 bay leaf
Salt and freshly ground black pepper
100 g/4 oz/1 cup self-raising (self-
 rising) flour
75 g/3 oz/¾ cup Cheddar cheese, grated
15 ml/1 tbsp chopped parsley
60 ml/4 tbsp water

Melt 40 g/1½ oz/3 tbsp of the butter or
margarine in a flameproof casserole
(Dutch oven). Add the onion and garlic and
fry (sauté) for 2 minutes. Stir in the leeks,
carrots and celery and fry for a further 2
minutes, stirring. Add the pepper and courgettes, the two types of beans, the stock, bay
leaf and a little salt and pepper. Bring to the
boil, reduce the heat, cover and simmer gently for 30 minutes. Discard the bay leaf.
Meanwhile put the flour in a bowl. Rub in the
remaining butter or margarine and stir in
50 g/2 oz/½ cup of the cheese, the parsley
and a little salt and pepper. Mix with the
water to form a soft but not sticky dough.
Shape into 6 balls. Arrange around the top of
the stew, re-cover and cook gently for 15
minutes until the dumplings are fluffy.
Sprinkle with the remaining cheese then
flash under a hot grill (broiler) to brown.

Lentil Pud

175 g/6 oz/1 cup brown or green
 lentils, soaked for 2 hours
1 garlic clove, crushed
175 g/6 oz/1½ cups Cheddar cheese,
 grated
15 ml/1 tbsp tomato ketchup (catsup)
10 ml/2 tsp sweet pickle
A dash of soy sauce
Salt and freshly ground black pepper

Drain the lentils, place in a pan of fresh
water, bring to the boil, then simmer
for about 45 minutes until tender. Drain.
Add the garlic, most of the cheese, the
ketchup, pickle, soy sauce and salt and
pepper. Pour into a greased ovenproof
dish and sprinkle with the remaining
cheese. Bake in a preheated oven at
200°C/400°F/gas mark 6 for 20 minutes
until golden.

Bortsch Crumble

100 g/4 oz/⅔ cup red lentils
1 onion, grated
1 turnip, grated
1 small swede (rutabaga), grated
2 large cooked beetroot (red beets),
* grated*
750 ml/1¼ pts/3 cups vegetable stock
15 ml/1 tbsp red wine vinegar
1 small bay leaf
Salt and freshly ground black pepper
100 g/4 oz/1 cup wholemeal flour
50 g/2 oz/½ cup rolled oats
1.5 ml/¼ tsp cayenne
75 g/3 oz/⅓ cup butter or margarine
10 ml/2 tsp caraway seeds
100 g/4 oz/1 cup Cheddar cheese,
* grated*
150 ml/¼ pt/⅔ cup quark

Put the lentils in a saucepan with the prepared vegetables. Pour on the stock, add the vinegar and the bay leaf. Sprinkle with a little salt and pepper. Bring to the boil, reduce the heat and simmer, stirring occasionally, for 30 minutes until the vegetables and lentils are tender. Taste and re-season if necessary. Turn into a 1.75 litre/3 pt/7½ cup ovenproof dish. Meanwhile, put the flour and oats in a bowl with 2.5 ml/½ tsp salt and the cayenne. Rub in the butter or margarine until the mixture resembles bread-crumbs. Stir in the caraway seeds and cheese. Spoon over the beetroot mixture and press down well. Bake in a preheated oven at 200°C/400°F/gas mark 6 for about 35 minutes until the topping is golden brown. Serve hot with the quark handed separately.

Bean and Cashew Burgers

175 g/6 oz/1½ cups aduki beans,
* soaked for several hours and*
* drained*
1 carrot, grated
1 small parsnip, grated
25 g/1 oz/¼ cup cashew nuts,
* chopped*
50 g/2 oz/1 cup granary breadcrumbs
2.5 ml/½ tsp soy sauce
2.5 ml/½ tsp yeast extract
Salt and freshly ground black pepper
1 egg, beaten
Oil, for shallow-frying

Put the beans in a pan with enough water to cover. Bring to the boil and boil rapidly for 10 minutes. Reduce the heat and simmer for a further 20–30 minutes until really tender. Drain and mash well. Mix with the remaining ingredients except the oil, adding enough of the beaten egg to bind. With lightly floured hands, shape the mixture into four burgers. Chill for 30 minutes. Shallow-fry in hot oil until golden on both sides. Drain on kitchen paper and serve hot.

Country Cassoulet

SERVES 6

450 g/1 lb/4 cups haricot (navy)
beans, soaked for several hours
and drained
3 garlic cloves, crushed
1.2 litres/2 pts/5 cups water
30 ml/2 tbsp olive oil
6 large vegetarian sausages, cut into
bite-sized pieces
100 g/4 oz smoked tofu, cubed
1 bouquet garni sachet
1.5 ml/¼ tsp ground mace
400 g/14 oz/1 large can chopped
tomatoes
30 ml/2 tbsp tomato purée (paste)
Salt and freshly ground black pepper
25 g/1 oz/2 tbsp butter or margarine,
melted
100 g/4 oz/2 cups wholemeal
breadcrumbs
15 ml/1 tbsp chopped parsley

Put the beans in a large flameproof casserole (Dutch oven). Add the garlic and water. Bring to the boil and boil rapidly for 10 minutes. Reduce the heat and simmer gently for 1 hour. Meanwhile, heat the oil in a frying pan (skillet) and fry (sauté) the sausages until golden brown. Add the tofu and toss together. Stir these into the beans with all the remaining ingredients except the butter or margarine, breadcrumbs and parsley. Season well. Bring to the boil, cover and simmer gently for 2 hours or until the beans are tender and bathed in a rich sauce. Taste and re-season if necessary. Discard the bouquet garni. Mix the melted butter with the breadcrumbs and parsley. Scatter over the surface of the cassoulet and place under a moderate grill (broiler) until the top is golden brown and crisp.

Old-fashioned Baked Beans

SERVES 4

450 g/1 lb/4 cups haricot (navy)
beans, soaked for several hours
and drained
1 large bay leaf
3 cloves
6 peppercorns
2.5 cm/1 in piece cinnamon stick
30 ml/2 tbsp black treacle (molasses)
300 ml/½ pt/1¼ cups water
15 ml/1 tbsp plain (all-purpose) flour
15 ml/1 tbsp milk
1.5 ml/¼ tsp dried basil
Salt and freshly ground black pepper
3 large tomatoes, skinned, seeded
and chopped

Put the soaked beans in a flameproof casserole (Dutch oven) and cover with cold water. Bring to the boil and boil rapidly for 10 minutes. Add the bay leaf, cloves, peppercorns and cinnamon. Simmer for 1½ hours or until the beans are tender. Drain and discard the flavourings. Blend the treacle with the water. Blend the flour with the milk until smooth. Mix together and stir into the casserole. Add the basil and a little salt and pepper and stir in the tomatoes. Cover and cook in a preheated oven at 180°C/350°F/gas mark 4 for 1 hour until the beans are bathed in a rich sauce. Taste and re-season if necessary.

Boston-style Baked Beans

SERVES 6

Prepare as for Old-fashioned Baked Beans but add a chopped onion and 225 g/8 oz/2 cups quorn pieces, both fried (sautéed) in a little olive oil for 2 minutes, to the beans before baking in the oven.

Greek-style Lentil Loaf with Hummous Sauce

SERVES 6

175 g/6 oz/1 lentils
1 bunch of spring onions (scallions), finely chopped
100 g/4 oz button mushrooms, sliced
45 ml/3 tbsp olive oil
100 g/4 oz/2 cups breadcrumbs
2.5 ml/½ tsp dried oregano
15 ml/1 tbsp chopped parsley
Salt and freshly ground black pepper
1 egg
15 ml/1 tbsp milk
15 ml/1 tbsp Worcestershire sauce
5 ml/1 tbsp yeast extract
4–6 preserved vine leaves, rinsed and dried
400 g/14 oz/1 large can red pimientos, drained
225 g/8 oz/1 cup hummous
Parsley sprigs
Lemon wedges

Put the lentils in a pan with plenty of cold water. Bring to the boil and boil for 40 minutes or until tender. Drain. Meanwhile, fry (sauté) the spring onions and mushrooms in 30 ml/2 tbsp of the oil for 3 minutes, stirring. Stir in the lentils, breadcrumbs, herbs and a little salt and pepper. Beat the egg and milk with the Worcestershire sauce. Mix with the lentils. Blend the yeast extract with 15 ml/1 tbsp of boiling water and stir into the mixture. Line a greased 900 g/2 lb loaf tin (pan) with vine leaves so they overhang the top edge all round. Press half the lentil mixture into the tin. Cover with the pimientos, then press the remaining lentil mixture on top, and fold over the vine leaves. Cover with greased foil, twisting and folding under the rim. Place in a roasting tin containing 2.5 cm/1 in boiling water. Bake in a preheated oven at 190°C/375°F/gas mark 5 for about 1 hour until firm. Cool for 10 minutes. Meanwhile, blend the hummous with the remaining oil a little at a time, then beat in enough boiling water to form a thickish pouring sauce. Slice the loaf thickly and serve with the hummous garnished with parsley and lemon.

Haricots Provençale

SERVES 4

225 g/8 oz/2 cups haricot (navy) beans, soaked for several hours and drained
2 large onions, sliced
2 garlic cloves, crushed
30 ml/2 tbsp olive oil
400 g/14 oz/1 large can chopped tomatoes
2 sun-dried tomatoes, chopped
Salt and freshly ground black pepper
Plain boiled rice
30 ml/2 tbsp chopped parsley
A few black olives

Put the beans in a saucepan and cover with cold water. Bring to the boil and boil rapidly for 10 minutes. Reduce the heat and simmer for 1½ hours until tender. Drain. Meanwhile, fry (sauté) the onions and garlic in the oil for 3 minutes, stirring until softened but not browned. Add the canned and sun-dried tomatoes. Bring to the boil, reduce the heat and simmer gently for 10 minutes. Add the beans and simmer again for 5 minutes. Season to taste. Pile on to a bed of boiled rice and sprinkle with chopped parsley. Scatter a few olives over and serve.

Photograph opposite: **Gougère Niçoise (page 68)**

Lentil Pot

*225 g/8 oz/1½ cups green or brown
   lentils*
25 g/1 oz/2 tbsp butter or margarine
2 red onions, chopped
1 large carrot, chopped
1 turnip chopped
2 celery sticks, chopped
2 courgettes (zucchini), chopped
600 ml/1 pt/2½ cups vegetable stock
Salt and freshly ground black pepper
1 bouquet garni sachet
Chopped parsley
Crusty bread

Cover the lentils in boiling water, soak for 1 hour, then drain. Melt the butter or margarine in a saucepan. Add the prepared vegetables and fry (sauté) for 5 minutes, stirring, until lightly golden. Add the lentils and stock. Season with a little salt and pepper and add the bouquet garni. Bring to the boil, reduce the heat, cover and simmer gently for about 20 minutes until the vegetables are just tender and the lentils have absorbed the liquid. If the vegetables aren't quite tender, add a little more water. The cooked dish should look quite dry. Discard the bouquet garni, taste and re-season if necessary. Serve in warm bowls, sprinkled with chopped parsley, with lots of crusty bread.

Lentil Stew with Caraway Dumplings

*225 g/8 oz/1½ cups brown or green
   lentils*
1.2 litres/2 pts/5 cups vegetable stock
175 g/6 oz button mushrooms
1 large onion, chopped
*100 g/4 oz baby sweetcorn (corn)
   cobs*
100 g/4 oz baby carrots, scraped
30 ml/2 tbsp red wine vinegar
5 ml/1 tsp light brown sugar
2.5 ml/½ tsp dried mixed herbs
Salt and freshly ground black pepper
*100 g/4 oz/1 cup self-raising (self-
   rising) flour*
*50 g/2 oz/½ cup shredded vegetable
   suet*
30 ml/2 tbsp snipped chives
10 ml/2 tsp caraway seeds

Cover the lentils in boiling water, soak for 1 hour, then drain. Put the lentils in a saucepan with half the stock, the vegetables, vinegar, sugar, herbs and a little salt and pepper. Bring to the boil, reduce the heat, part cover and simmer gently for about 45 minutes or until the lentils are mushy, adding more stock if necessary. Meanwhile, mix the flour with a little salt and pepper, the suet, half the chives and the caraway seeds. Mix with enough cold water to form a soft but not sticky dough. Shape into eight small balls. Simmer gently in the remaining stock in a covered pan for about 20 minutes until fluffy and cooked through. Arrange around the top of the lentil stew just before serving and sprinkle with the remaining chives.

Photograph opposite: **Middle-Eastern Tabbouleh (page 123)**

'Roasts' and so on ...

Vegetable Burgers

100 g/4 oz/1 cup rolled oats
75 g/3 oz/¾ cup wholemeal flour
2 celery sticks, finely chopped
3 carrots, grated
50 g/2 oz/½ cup Cheddar cheese,
  grated
½ onion, finely chopped
15 ml/1 tbsp tomato purée (paste)
15 ml/1 tbsp soy sauce
5 ml/1 tsp dried mixed herbs
Salt and freshly ground black pepper
1 egg, beaten
Oil, for shallow-frying
Baps
Ketchup (catsup)
Mustard
Salad

Mix together all the ingredients, except the oil, baps, ketchup, mustard and salad, into four burgers – not too thick. Fry (sauté) in hot oil for 5 minutes, turning once. Drain on kitchen paper and serve in baps with ketchup, mustard and salad.

Nutty Vegetable Burgers

Prepare as for Vegetable Burgers but substitute 50 g/2 oz/½ cup chopped mixed nuts for half the oats.

Vegetable Hot Dogs

Prepare as for Vegetable Burgers, but shape into sausages before cooking. Serve in finger rolls with fried (sautéed) onions, mustard and ketchup (catsup).

Flageolet Roast

15 ml/1 tbsp dried breadcrumbs
100 g/4 oz/1 cup flageolet beans,
  cooked (see page 10)
1 bunch of spring onions (scallions),
  chopped
½ small swede (rutabaga), grated
1 small potato, grated
1 carrot, grated
1 garlic clove, crushed
25 g/1 oz/2 tbsp butter or margarine
15 ml/1 tbsp tomato purée (paste)
25 g/1 oz/½ cup wholemeal
  breadcrumbs
15 ml/1 tbsp tomato relish
5 ml/1 tsp dried oregano
Salt and freshly ground black pepper
1 egg, beaten
Passata (sieved tomatoes)

Grease a 450 g/1 lb loaf tin and sprinkle with the dried breadcrumbs. Mash the flageolet beans well. Fry (sauté) the spring onions, swede, potato, carrot and garlic in the butter or margarine for 1 minute, stirring. Cover and cook gently for 10 minutes, stirring occasionally. Stir in the tomato purée, wholemeal breadcrumbs, tomato relish, oregano and the flageolet beans. Mix together and season well. Stir in the beaten egg. Turn into the prepared tin, cover with foil and bake in a preheated oven at 190°C/375°F/gas mark 5 for 1½ hours or until firm. Leave the roast to cool slightly for 10 minutes, then turn out and serve with warm passata as a sauce.

Simple Bean and Nut Roast

SERVES 4

30 ml/2 tbsp sunflower oil
1 onion, chopped
225 g/8 oz/2 cups any pulses, cooked
(see page 10)
100 g/4 oz/1 cup chopped mixed nuts
100 g/4 oz/1 cup Cheddar cheese,
grated
2 eggs, beaten
5 ml/1 tsp yeast extract
2.5 ml/½ tsp chopped marjoram
2.5 ml/½ tsp chopped sage
Salt and freshly ground black pepper
Broccoli in Tomato Sauce (see page
194)

Heat the oil and fry (sauté) the onion for 3 minutes, stirring. Mash the pulses and mix well with the onion and the remaining ingredients except the Broccoli in Tomato Sauce. Place the mixture in a greased 450 g/1 lb loaf tin (pan) and bake in a preheated oven at 190°C/375°F/gas mark 5 for 30 minutes or until set. Leave to cool slightly, then turn out and serve with Broccoli in Tomato Sauce.

Nut Roast Plait

SERVES 4

100 g/4 oz mushrooms, chopped
50 g/2 oz/¼ cup butter or margarine
1 quantity Golden Potted Cheese (see
page 58)
1 Simple Bean and Nut Roast (see
left)
225 g/8 oz frozen puff pastry (paste),
thawed
Beaten egg, to glaze
Parsley sprigs

Cook the mushrooms in the butter or margarine for 2 minutes until softened. Leave to cool. Mix in with the Potted Cheese and spread over the top of the Nut Roast. Roll out the pastry into a large rectangle and brush all over with beaten egg. Place the Nut Roast in the centre. Cut the pastry diagonally from within 2.5 cm/1 in of the loaf to the outer edge along both sides. Fold the ends up over the loaf. Plait one strip at a time from either side up and over the top of the loaf, tucking the ends in neatly. Brush with the remaining beaten egg. Cook in a preheated oven at 200°C/400°F/gas mark 6 for about 40 minutes, covering with foil half-way through to prevent the pastry over-browning. Transfer to a serving plate. Garnish with parsley sprigs and serve hot, cut into slices.

Walnut and Courgette Moussaka

SERVES 4

4 courgettes (zucchini), sliced
4 slices wholemeal bread, cubed
1 garlic clove, crushed
75 ml/5 tbsp dry white wine
50 g/2 oz/¼ cup butter or margarine,
  melted
5 ml/1 tsp dried mixed herbs
30 ml/2 tbsp tomato purée (paste)
75 ml/5 tbsp water
225 g/8 oz/2 cups walnuts, chopped
Salt and freshly ground black pepper
175 g/6 oz/1½ cups Cheddar cheese,
  grated
450 ml/¾ pt/2 cups Bechamel Sauce
  (see page 311)
Mixed salad

Cook the courgettes in boiling, salted water until tender. Drain, rinse with cold water and drain again. Put the bread in a bowl with the garlic, wine, melted butter or margarine and the herbs. Mix well. Blend the tomato purée with the water and stir in with the nuts. Season with a little salt and pepper. Put a layer of about a third of the courgettes in the base of a greased 1.5 litre/2½ pt/6 cup ovenproof dish. Cover with half the nut mixture. Repeat the layers and finish with a final layer of courgettes. Stir half the cheese into the Bechamel Sauce. Spoon over and sprinkle with the remaining cheese. Bake in a preheated oven at 200ºC/400ºF/gas mark 6 for 35 minutes until hot through and the top is golden brown. Serve hot with a mixed salad.

Spinach and Cashew Nut Loaf

SERVES 4

225 g/8 oz frozen spinach, thawed
1 large onion, quartered
1 garlic clove, crushed
175 g/6 oz/1½ cups cashew nuts
4 slices wholemeal bread
1 egg
5 ml/1 tsp yeast extract
1.5 ml/¼ tsp dried mixed herbs
Salt and freshly ground black pepper

Squeeze out any moisture from the spinach. Place in a food processor and chop with the onion, garlic, nuts and bread. Alternatively, pass through a coarse mincer (grinder). Lightly beat the egg with the yeast extract and stir into the mixture with the herbs. Season lightly. Turn into a greased 450 g/1 lb loaf tin and cover with foil. Bake in a preheated oven at 180ºC/350ºF/gas mark 4 for 1 hour or until firm to the touch. Cool slightly, then turn out of the tin and serve hot or cold.

Spinach and Peanut Loaf

SERVES 4

Prepare as for Spinach and Cashew Nut Loaf but substitute peanuts for the cashew nuts and use dried oregano instead of mixed herbs.

Basic Nut Roast

SERVES 4

150 g/5 oz/1¼ cups chopped mixed
   nuts
75 g/3 oz/1½ cups wholemeal
   breadcrumbs
½ onion, chopped
15 ml/1 tbsp soy sauce
2.5 ml/½ tsp dried thyme
5 ml/1 tsp lemon juice
25 g/1 oz/2 tbsp butter or margarine
5 ml/1 tsp oil
5 ml/1 tsp yeast extract
150 ml/¼ pt/⅔ cup water
Roast potatoes
Vegetables

Mix together the first eight ingredients in a bowl. Dissolve the yeast extract in the water, then add it to the mixture. Mix thoroughly. Press gently into a small greased loaf tin (pan) or baking dish. Bake in a preheated oven at 190°C/375°F/gas mark 5 for 30–40 minutes until crisp on top and hot in the centre. Serve sliced with roast potatoes and vegetables.

Spicy Soya Roast

SERVES 6

1 large onion, finely chopped
1 leek, thinly sliced
30 ml/2 tbsp olive oil
1 potato, grated
1 carrot, grated
1 parsnip, grated
30 ml/2 tbsp mild curry paste
50 g/2 tbsp rye breadcrumbs
30 ml/2 tbsp curried fruit chutney
2 × 425 g/2 × 15 oz/2 large cans
   soya beans, drained
Salt and freshly ground black pepper
2 eggs, beaten
1 Weetabix, crushed
Passata (sieved tomatoes)
Coriander (cilantro) leaves

Fry (sauté) the onion and leek in the oil for 3 minutes, stirring in a saucepan. Stir in the remaining prepared vegetables and fry for 1 minute. Remove from the heat and stir in the curry paste, breadcrumbs and chutney. Mash the beans thoroughly and add with a little salt and pepper. Mix well, then stir in the beaten eggs to bind. Grease a 900 g/2 lb loaf tin and dust with the crushed Weetabix. Turn the soya mixture into the tin and level the surface. Cover with greased foil and bake in a preheated oven at 190°C/375°F/gas mark 5 for about 1½ hours or until firm to the touch. Cool for 5 minutes, then turn out, slice, and serve on plates with a little warm passata spooned to one side and a garnish of coriander leaves.

Anyday Roast

5 ml/1 tsp yeast extract
30 ml/2 tbsp milk
100 g/4 oz/1 cup plain (all-purpose)
  flour
100 g/4 oz/1 cup fine oatmeal
50 g/2 oz/1 cup wholemeal
  breadcrumbs
175 g/6 oz/1½ cups shredded
  vegetable suet
2 large onions, chopped
2.5 ml/½ tsp dried thyme
2.5 ml/½ tsp dried oregano
1 egg, beaten
Salt and freshly ground black pepper
Roast potatoes
A green vegetable
Vegetable Gravy (see page 316)

Blend the yeast extract with the milk in a large bowl. Mix in the remaining ingredients except the potatoes, green vegetable and gravy, seasoning well with salt and pepper. Add a little more milk, if necessary, to form a soft but not sloppy consistency. Turn into a greased roasting tin and level the surface. Roast in a pre-heated oven at 180°C/350°F/gas mark 4 for about 1 hour or until golden and set. Serve with roast potatoes, a green vegetable and gravy.

Rice-based Main Courses

Spanish Vegetable Paella

45 ml/3 tbsp olive oil
1 onion, chopped
150 g/5 oz/⅔ cup long-grain rice
5 ml/1 tsp turmeric
5 ml/1 tsp curry powder
Salt to taste
1 green chilli, seeded and sliced
75 g/3 oz/¾ cup red and green (bell)
*   peppers, diced*
2 garlic cloves, chopped
50 g/2 oz/⅓ cup green olives, stoned
*   (pitted)*
450 ml/¾ pt/2 cups water
1 vegetable stock cube
2 tomatoes, skinned, seeded and
*   chopped*
50 g/2 oz/½ cup pine nuts
50 g/2 oz/½ cup peas

Place a 1.75 litre/3 pt/7½ cup metal paella pan or flameproof casserole (Dutch oven) on the stove and heat the oil. Stir-fry the onion for 1 minute, then add the rice, turmeric, curry powder, salt, chilli, peppers, garlic, olives, water and stock cube. Boil for 5 minutes. Add the tomatoes, pine nuts and peas. Cover and bake in a preheated oven at 200°C/ 400°F/gas mark 6 for 30–40 minutes until the rice is cooked and has absorbed all the liquid.

Leftover Stuffed Peppers

4 red (bell) peppers
2 eggs, beaten
225 g/8 oz/2 cups cold cooked
*   Spanish Vegetable Paella (see left)*

Slice the stems from the peppers and set aside. Cut a slice off the pepper tops and remove the seeds with a spoon. In a bowl, blend the eggs with the cooked paella. Spoon the mixture into the cavities of the peppers. Stand them in a deep ovenproof dish. Part fill the dish with hot water and bake in a preheated oven at 190°C/375°F/gas mark 5 for 30 minutes until tender and the filling is set. Meanwhile, blanch the pepper top stems in boiling water for 3 minutes and sit them on top of the cooked peppers before serving.

Oriental Rice with Bean Sprouts

SERVES 4

75 g/3 oz/⅓ cup butter or margarine
1 garlic clove, crushed
1 onion, chopped
2 celery sticks, chopped
1 green (bell) pepper, chopped
225 g/8 oz/1 cup long-grain brown rice
450 ml/¾ pt/2 cups vegetable stock
5 ml/1 tsp ground turmeric
2.5 ml/½ tsp ground ginger
Salt and freshly ground black pepper
100 g/4 oz/1 cup mixed pulses, cooked (see page 10)
225 g/8 oz/1 small can pineapple chunks, drained
350 g/12 oz bean sprouts
Soy sauce
Green salad

Melt 50 g/2 oz/¼ cup of the butter or margarine in a large pan. Add the garlic, onion, celery and pepper and fry (sauté) for 2 minutes, stirring. Add the rice, stock, turmeric, ginger and seasoning. Bring to the boil, reduce the heat, cover and simmer gently for 35 minutes or until the rice is just tender and has absorbed all the stock. Add the pulses, pineapple, bean sprouts and the remaining butter or margarine and heat through, stirring, for a further 3 minutes. Pile on to warm plates and serve with soy sauce and a green salad.

Busy Risotto

SERVES 4

1 onion, chopped
25 g/1 oz/2 tbsp butter or margarine
50 g/2 oz carrots, chopped
50 g/2 oz celery, chopped
100 g/4 oz/1 cup frozen peas
50 g/2 oz mushrooms, sliced
225 g/8 oz/1 cup long-grain brown rice
600 ml/1 pt/2½ cups vegetable stock
5 ml/1 tsp Worcestershire sauce
15 ml/1 tbsp tomato purée (paste)
5 ml/1 tsp dried mixed herbs
Salt and freshly ground black pepper
225 g/8 oz bean sprouts
15 ml/1 tbsp Dry Roasted Peanuts (see page 350)
200 g/7 oz/1 small can sweetcorn (corn)
30 ml/2 tbsp pumpkin seeds
225 g/8 oz/1⅓ cups any pulses, cooked (see page 10)

Fry (sauté) the onion in the butter or margarine in a large frying pan (skillet) or wok for 3 minutes, stirring. Add the carrots, celery, peas, mushrooms and rice and cook, stirring, for a further 2 minutes. Add the stock, Worcestershire sauce, tomato purée, herbs and seasoning to taste. Bring to the boil. Cover, reduce the heat and simmer gently for 35 minutes or until the rice is just tender. Add the remaining ingredients. Re-cover and heat through for 5 minutes. Serve straight from the pan.

Rice Cake

4 eggs, beaten
225 g/8 oz/2 cups cooked Pilaf with
  Saffron (see below)
Seasoned flour
50 g/2 oz/½ cup mixture of
  breadcrumbs and fine cornmeal
Oil, for shallow-frying
Green salad or mangetout (snow
  peas)

In a bowl, blend half of the beaten eggs into the cold rice pilaf. Divide the mixture into four cakes or balls. Dip in seasoned flour, then in the remaining beaten egg and finally coat in the crumb mixture. Heat the oil in a shallow pan and fry (sauté) the cakes for 2 minutes on each side until golden. Drain on kitchen paper. Serve with green salad or cooked mangetout.

Pilaf with Saffron

30 ml/2 tbsp sunflower oil
1 onion, chopped
225 g/8 oz/1 cup long-grain rice
600 ml/1 pt/2½ cups water
15 ml/1 tbsp yeast extract
Salt and freshly ground black pepper
1 sachet of saffron
5 ml/1 tsp ground turmeric
75 g/3 oz/¾ cup sweetcorn (corn)
Simple Fresh Tomato Sauce (see
  page 315)
Grated Cheddar cheese

In a shallow pan, heat the oil and stir-fry the onion for 1 minute. Stir in the rice to absorb the oil. Add the water and yeast extract and bring to the boil. Season to taste, including the saffron and turmeric. Add the sweetcorn and boil for 5 minutes.

Transfer the mixture into a pie dish, Cover with greased greaseproof (waxed) paper and bake in a preheated oven at 200°C/400°F/gas mark 6 for 15 minutes. To serve, oil a dariole mould or small tumbler. Fill it with rice and pack tightly. Turn out on to a plate like a sandcastle. Repeat with the remaining mixture. Serve the rice with Simple Fresh Tomato Sauce and grated cheese.

Risotto Verde

50 ml/2 fl oz/3½ tbsp melted butter
  and oil
1 small onion, chopped
150 g/5 oz/⅔ cup risotto rice
600 ml/1 pt/2½ cups water
1 vegetable stock cube
175 g/6 oz fresh spinach, stalks
  removed and shredded
6 tarragon leaves, chopped
Salt and freshly ground black pepper
50 ml/2 fl oz/3½ tbsp single (light)
  cream
50 g/2 oz/½ cup Pecorino cheese

Heat the butter and oil in a frying pan (skillet) and stir-fry the onion until soft but not brown. Add the rice and stir for 1 minute, then add the water and stock cube. Boil for 15–20 minutes, then add the shredded spinach, tarragon and seasoning. Cook gently for a further 5 minutes. Finally, blend in the cream, cheese and season to taste. The rice should be softer than for pilaf and more creamy.

Indian-style Kedgeree

225 g/8 oz/2 cups cooked Pilaf with
Saffron (see page 137)
15 ml/1 tbsp curry powder
30 ml/2 tbsp desiccated (shredded)
coconut
45 ml/3 tbsp plain yoghurt
4 hard-boiled (hard-cooked) eggs

Mix the pilaf with the curry powder and coconut. Blend in the yoghurt and heat through. Serve hot with sliced hard-boiled eggs.

Split Pea Kedgeree

75 g/3 oz/⅓ cup butter or margarine
1 onion, chopped
225 g/8 oz/1⅓ cups yellow split peas,
soaked for several hours in cold
water
275 g/10 oz/1¼ cups long-grain
brown rice
Pinch of grated nutmeg
Salt and freshly ground black pepper
4 hard-boiled (hard-cooked) eggs,
quartered
150 ml/¼ pt/⅔ cup milk
45 ml/3 tbsp chopped parsley

Melt 50 g/2 oz/¼ cup of the butter or margarine in a large pan. Add the onion and fry (sauté) for 3 minutes, stirring. Add the drained split peas, rice and just enough water to cover. Bring to the boil and cook for about 35 minutes or until the peas and rice are tender and have absorbed all the liquid, adding more boiling water if necessary. Add the seasonings, eggs, the remaining butter or margarine, the milk and most of the parsley. Stir well and simmer for 4 minutes, stirring occasionally. Garnish with the remaining parsley and serve hot.

Pilaf with Chestnuts

225 g/8 oz/2 cups cooked Pilaf with
Saffron (see page 137)
150 g/5 oz/1¼ cups fresh boiled
chestnuts or 1 large can, drained
50 g/2 oz/½ cup Cheddar cheese,
grated

Combine all the ingredients and serve in individual dishes.

Parisian Rice

75 g/3 oz/⅓ cup short-grain pudding
rice
600 ml/1 pint/2½ cups milk, heated
120 ml/4 fl oz/½ cup single (light)
cream
3 egg yolks, beaten
Salt and freshly ground black pepper
Grated nutmeg
100 g/4 oz button mushrooms, sliced
50 g/2 oz/¼ cup butter
Simple Fresh Tomato Sauce (see
page 315)

Place the rice in a deep ovenproof dish and cover with the milk. Bake in a preheated oven at 180°C/350°F/gas mark 4 for 40–50 minutes. Cool completely. In a bowl, mix the cream and egg yolks. Add the cooked rice, season with salt, pepper and nutmeg and add the sliced mushrooms. Butter six small metal dariole moulds and fill them with the mixture. Place in a deep pan half filled with hot water. Bake in a preheated oven at 200°C/400°F/gas mark 6 for 15 minutes. Turn out on to six plates. Serve with Simple Fresh Tomato Sauce spooned over.

Wild Rice Lentil Casserole

225 g/8 oz/1 cup long-grain and wild
  rice mix
100 g/4 oz/⅔ cup green lentils
1 onion, chopped
1 carrot, diced
50 ml/2 fl oz/¼ cup oil and butter
15 ml/1 tbsp tomato purée (paste)
Salt and freshly ground black pepper
5 ml/1 tsp curry powder
Pancakes or Chinese leaves (stem
  lettuce)

Boil the rice and lentils separately for 20 minutes, then drain. Combine the rice and lentils. In a wok or large frying pan (skillet), stir-fry (sauté) the onion and carrot in the oil for 3 minutes. Add the rice and lentils with the tomato purée and all the seasoning. Heat for 5 minutes. Serve as stuffing for cooked pancakes, or spoon on to Chinese leaves.

Cashew Paella

15 ml/1 tbsp olive oil
1 leek, chopped
1 red (bell) pepper, chopped
1 green (bell) pepper, chopped
100 g/4 oz mushrooms, sliced
225 g/8 oz/1 cup long-grain rice
100 g/4 oz/1 cup cashew nuts
600 ml/1 pt/2½ cups vegetable stock
Freshly ground black pepper
Pinch of dried mixed herbs
Salad

Heat the oil and fry (sauté) the vegetables gently for 5 minutes until tender. Add the rice and fry for a further 3 minutes, stirring. Add the nuts, stock and seasoning, bring to the boil and simmer for about 30 minutes until the rice is cooked and most of the water has been absorbed, stirring occasionally. Serve hot with salad.

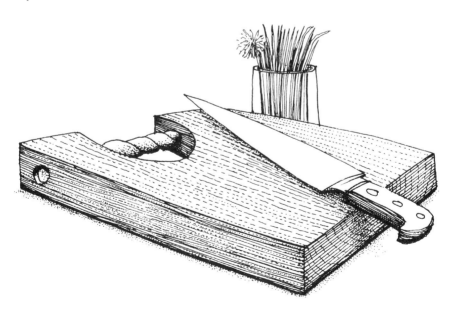

Vegetable Stir-fry with Garlic Rice

SERVES 4

1 aubergine (eggplant), diced
Salt
30 ml/2 tbsp sunflower oil
1 onion, chopped
4 garlic cloves, crushed
1.5 ml/¼ tsp ground cloves
Pinch of dried basil
2.5 ml/½ tsp ground ginger
2 courgettes (zucchini), sliced
1 yellow (bell) pepper, sliced
12 carrots, sliced lengthways
50 g/2 oz/½ cup sweetcorn (corn)
50 g/2 oz mushrooms, sliced
15 ml/1 tbsp tomato purée (paste)
30 ml/2 tbsp soy sauce
225 g/8 oz/1 cup long-grain rice
2.5 ml/½ tsp dried thyme

Sprinkle the aubergine with salt and leave to drain in a colander for 20 minutes to remove the bitterness. Rinse and drain. Heat the oil and fry (sauté) the onion and half the garlic for 3 minutes. Add the aubergine, spices, courgettes, pepper and carrots and stir well. Add the sweetcorn and mushrooms. Stir in the tomato purée and soy sauce. Add just enough water to make a sauce and simmer for about 15 minutes until the vegetables are just tender. Meanwhile, cook the rice in boiling salted water with the remaining garlic and the thyme for the time directed on the packet. Drain well and serve with the stir-fry.

Japanese Risotto

SERVES 4

50 g/2 oz/¼ cup butter or margarine
1 red onion, chopped
225 g/8 oz/1 cup long-grain rice
15 ml/1 tbsp chopped stem ginger
1.5 ml/¼ tsp ground turmeric
Salt and freshly ground black pepper
* or a dash of soy sauce*
600 ml/1 pt/2½ cups hot water
1 red chilli, seeded and sliced
225 g/8 oz firm tofu, cubed
50 g/2 oz/⅓ cup seedless (pitted)
* grapes*
Satsumas or similar fruits, peeled
* and segmented*

Heat the butter or margarine in a saucepan and stir-fry the onion for 2 minutes until soft. Add the rice and ginger and stir to coat well. Add the turmeric, salt and pepper or soy sauce to taste, and the hot water. Bring to the boil and cook gently for 10 minutes. Add the chilli and tofu and continue cooking for a further 10 minutes. Serve on individual plates garnished with grapes and satsumas.

Vegetable Risotto

SERVES 4

1 onion, finely chopped
225 g/8 oz broccoli, cut into tiny
  florets
225 g/8 oz cauliflower, cut into tiny
  florets
2 carrots, sliced
1 red (bell) pepper, diced
100 g/4 oz French (green) beans, cut
  into short lengths
50 g/2 oz/¼ cup butter or margarine
225 g/8 oz/1 cup brown rice
430 g/15½ oz/1 large can chick peas
  (garbanzos)
250 ml/8 fl oz/1 cup dry cider
900 ml/1½ pts/3¾ cups vegetable
  stock
Salt and freshly ground black pepper
5 ml/1 tsp dried mixed herbs
30 ml/2 tbsp chopped parsley

In a large, flameproof casserole (Dutch oven), fry (sauté) the onion, broccoli, cauliflower, carrots, pepper and beans in the butter, stirring, for 3 minutes. Stir in the rice and cook for 1 minute. Add the chick peas, cider, stock, a little salt and a good grinding of pepper and the mixed herbs. Bring to the boil, cover and transfer to a preheated oven at 200°C/400°F/gas mark 6 and cook for 35–40 minutes until the rice and vegetables are tender and the liquid has been absorbed. Sprinkle with parsley and serve.

Baked Eggy Risotto

SERVES 4-6

Prepare as for Vegetable Risotto but omit the chick peas. After 25 minutes of cooking, pour over 3 eggs, beaten with 1 crushed garlic clove and a little salt and pepper. Sprinkle with 30 ml/2 tbsp flaked almonds and return to the oven, uncovered, for 10 minutes until the eggs are set. Serve straight from the dish.

Oven-cooked Corn and Mushroom Pilaf

SERVES 4

1 onion, chopped
1 garlic clove, crushed
25 g/1 oz/2 tbsp butter or margarine
225 g/8 oz/1 cup long-grain rice
600 ml/1 pt/2½ cups vegetable stock
½ bay leaf
100 g/4 oz button mushrooms
200 g/7 oz/1 small can Mexican
  sweetcorn (corn with bell peppers)
Salt and freshly ground black pepper
50 g/2 oz/¼ cup pine nuts
2 tomatoes, sliced
Parsley sprig

In a flameproof casserole (Dutch oven), fry (sauté) the onion and garlic in the butter for 2 minutes, stirring. Add the rice and stir well. Pour on the stock and add the bay leaf, mushrooms and the contents of the can of corn. Season lightly and stir well. Bring to the boil, stir again, then cover and cook in a preheated oven at 200°C/400°F/gas mark 6 for 20 minutes until the rice is tender and has absorbed the liquid. Taste and re-season if necessary. Sprinkle over the pine nuts and fluff up with a fork. Garnish with the sliced tomatoes and a parsley sprig and serve hot.

141

Pasta-based Main Courses

Gnocchi with Fruit and Walnuts

SERVES 4

600 ml/1 pt/2½ cups mixed milk and
water
1 powdered saffron sachet
75 g/3 oz/¾ cup cornmeal
2 egg yolks
1 egg, beaten
Salt and freshly ground black pepper
50 g/2 oz/¼ cup butter
Oil and butter, for shallow-frying
2 apples, cored and sliced
50 g/2 oz/½ cup walnuts
30 ml/2 tbsp seedless (pitted) raisins
75 ml/5 tbsp Madeira

Bring the milk and water to the boil, add the saffron and sprinkle over the cornmeal, stirring. Boil for 6–8 minutes until thickened. Remove from the heat and add the egg yolks, beaten egg, salt, pepper and butter. Pour the hot mixture into a buttered shallow baking tin (pan) and spread it evenly. When cold, turn the mixture on to a clean board. Cut into 4 cm/1½ in oblongs. In a saucepan, heat 15 ml/1 tbsp oil and toss the apple slices, walnuts and raisins for 2 minutes. Add the Madeira and boil for 1 minute. Fry (sauté) the gnocchi in hot oil and butter until golden. Allow four per portion and serve on a plate with the apple, walnuts and raisins in Madeira.

Chinese Noodles and Lychees

SERVES 4

225 g/8 oz thin Chinese egg noodles
50 ml/2 fl oz/3½ tbsp sunflower oil
2 shallots, chopped
1 red (bell) pepper, seeded and diced
2 courgettes (zucchini), sliced
227 g/8 oz/1 small can lychees,
drained and halved
50 g/2 oz cucumber, diced
50 g/2 oz/½ cup blanched almonds,
toasted
120 ml/4 fl oz/½ cup plain yoghurt
Salt and freshly ground black pepper

Cook the noodles according to the packet directions, then drain well. For the sauce, heat the oil in a frying pan (skillet) and stir-fry the shallots and red pepper for 3 minutes. Add the courgettes, lychees, cucumber and almonds and cook for a further 2 minutes. Stir in the yoghurt, heat until warmed through and season to taste with salt and pepper. Divide the noodles between four heated serving plates and pour over the sauce. Serve at once.

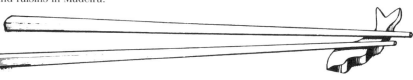

Courgette Pasta

25 g/1 oz/2 tbsp butter or margarine
450 g/1 lb courgettes (zucchini),
  sliced
1 onion, chopped
Pinch of dried tarragon
225 g/8 oz tagliatelle
Salt
300 ml/½ pt/1¼ cups Bechamel Sauce
  (see page 311)
Salt and freshly ground black pepper

Melt the butter or margarine and fry (sauté) the courgettes, onions and tarragon gently until soft. Meanwhile, cook the tagliatelle according to the packet directions. Drain and turn into a serving dish. Spoon the vegetables over the pasta. Season the white sauce with salt and pepper and pour over the dish. Glaze under a hot grill (broiler).

Bean Sprouts and Fennel with Egg Noodles

225 g/8 oz thin Chinese egg noodles
1 fennel bulb, cut into thin strips
45 ml/3 tbsp oil
6 spring onions (scallions),
  diagonally sliced
2 garlic cloves, chopped
2 small pieces fresh root ginger,
  chopped
1 pineapple ring, cut into thin strips
425 g/15 oz/1 large can red kidney
  beans, drained
225 g/8 oz bean sprouts
15 ml/1 tbsp soy sauce
15 ml/1 tbsp white vinegar
15 ml/1 tbsp clear honey
Salt and freshly ground black pepper

Cook the noodles according to the packet directions and drain. Meanwhile, blanch the fennel strips for 2 minutes and drain. In a wok or frying pan (skillet), heat the oil and stir-fry the spring onions for 2 minutes. Add the garlic and ginger and toss for 30 seconds, then add the fennel, noodles, pineapple and red beans. Lastly, add the bean sprouts. Toss. Add the soy sauce, vinegar, honey and salt and pepper. Reheat for 3 minutes. Serve on large plates.

Spaghetti with Lentils, Tomatoes and Herbs

SERVES 4

225 g/8 oz/1⅓ cups green lentils
400 g/14 oz/1 large can tomatoes
600 ml/1 pt/2½ cups vegetable stock
1 onion, chopped
15 ml/1 tbsp chopped oregano
15 ml/1 tbsp chopped marjoram
15 ml/1 tbsp chopped basil
15 ml/1 tbsp chopped parsley
225 g/8 oz spaghetti
Grated Pecorino cheese

Put all the ingredients except the spaghetti and cheese into a large bowl early in the day. Cover and leave for a few hours. Transfer to a saucepan. Bring to the boil, reduce the heat, cover and simmer for about 30 minutes or until the lentils are soft. Meanwhile, cook the spaghetti according to the packet directions. Drain. Divide the spaghetti between four serving plates. Spoon the sauce over and serve with grated Pecorino cheese.

Spaghetti with Piquant Bean Sauce

SERVES 4

350 g/12 oz spaghetti
1 garlic clove, crushed
1 onion, chopped
30 ml/2 tbsp olive oil
15 ml/1 tbsp curry powder
45 ml/3 tbsp smooth peanut butter, preferably wholenut
10 ml/2 tsp tomato purée (paste)
5 ml/1 tsp lemon juice
300 ml/½ pt/1¼ cups vegetable stock
Salt and freshly ground black pepper
225 g/8 oz/2 cups haricot (navy) beans, cooked (see page 10)

Cook the spaghetti according to the packet directions. Drain. Meanwhile, fry (sauté) the garlic and onion in the oil in a pan for 3 minutes, stirring. Add the remaining ingredients, cover and simmer for 7 minutes, stirring occasionally. Add to the spaghetti and toss well. Serve straight away.

Spaghetti Volognaise

15 ml/1 tbsp olive oil
1 garlic clove, crushed
1 onion, chopped
3 celery sticks, chopped
4 carrots, chopped
30 ml/2 tbsp wholemeal flour
400 g/14 oz/1 large can chopped
   tomatoes
300 ml/½ pt/1¼ cups vegetable stock
100 g/4 oz mushrooms, quartered
Salt and freshly ground black pepper
Dash of Worcestershire sauce
2.5 ml/½ tsp dried oregano or
   marjoram
2.5 ml/½ tsp dried basil
225 g/8 oz/2 cups haricot (navy),
   borlotti, red kidney or cannellini
   beans, cooked (see page 10)
350 g/12 oz spaghetti
Cheddar cheese, grated

Heat the oil and fry (sauté) the garlic, onion, celery and carrots for 3 minutes, stirring. Stir in the flour and cook for a further minute. Add the tomatoes, stock mushrooms, seasoning, Worcestershire sauce and herbs and stir well. Bring to the boil, reduce the heat and simmer gently for 10 minutes, stirring occasionally. Add the beans and cook for a further 10 minutes. Meanwhile, cook the spaghetti according to the packet directions. Drain. Serve the Volognaise sauce on a bed of spaghetti with lots of grated Cheddar cheese handed separately.

Egg Pasta Bake

225 g/8 oz ribbon noodles
400 g/14 oz/1 large can chopped
   tomatoes
100 g/4 oz/1 cup Cheddar cheese,
   grated
600 ml/1 pt/2½ cups Bechamel Sauce
   (see page 311)
8 hard-boiled (hard-cooked) eggs
320 g/12 oz/1 large can sweetcorn
   (corn)
5 ml/1 tsp Worcestershire sauce
Salt and freshly ground black pepper
Chopped parsley
3 × 25 g/1 oz packets plain potato
   crisps (chips), lightly crushed
Green salad

Cook the noodles according to the packet directions. Drain. Line the base of a greased, large flat dish with the tomatoes. Cover with the drained noodles. Add the cheese to the white sauce with the eggs, sweetcorn, Worcestershire sauce, salt and pepper and parsley and pour over the tomatoes and noodles. Cook in a preheated oven at 200°C/400°F/gas mark 6 for 40 minutes until well heated through and sprinkle the crisps over the top for the last 5 minutes. Serve with a green salad.

Mixed Bean Pasta Bake

Prepare as for Egg Pasta Bake, but substitute 225 g/8 oz/2 cups cooked mixed dried beans (see page 10) for the hard-boiled (hard-cooked) eggs.

Lentil Lasagne

225 g/8 oz/1⅓ cups red lentils
900 ml/1½ pts/3¾ cups boiling water
400 g/14 oz/1 large can chopped
  tomatoes
30 ml/2 tbsp tomato purée (paste)
30 ml/2 tbsp soy sauce
5 ml/1 tsp chopped thyme
10 ml/2 tsp chopped marjoram
Salt and freshly ground black pepper
30 ml/2 tbsp sunflower oil
1 onion, chopped
1 garlic clove, crushed
100 g/4 oz carrots, chopped
100 g/4 oz celery, chopped
100 g/4 oz/1 cup frozen peas
450 ml/¾ pt/2 cups White Sauce (see
  page 311)
5 ml/1 tsp grated nutmeg
15 ml/1 tbsp grated Pecorino cheese
10 sheets no-need-to-precook lasagne
100 g/4 oz/1 cup Cheddar cheese,
  grated
Sesame seeds
Chopped parsley

Put the lentils in a large pan and pour boiling water over. Bring to the boil, reduce the heat, cover and simmer for 15 minutes until just soft. Drain and add the tomatoes, tomato purée, soy sauce, herbs and seasoning. Fry (sauté) the onion and garlic in the oil for 3 minutes, stirring. Add the carrots, celery and peas and cook for 15 minutes. Stir in the lentils. Flavour the White Sauce with nutmeg and Pecorino cheese. Pour a little of the sauce into a large greased shallow dish. Layer lasagne sheets, the lentil mixture and the white sauce, starting with lasagne and ending with white sauce. Sprinkle with grated Cheddar and sesame seeds and bake in a preheated oven at 190°C/ 375°F/gas mark 5 for 40 minutes. Garnish with chopped parsley.

Fi's Late Vegetable Lasagne

400 g/14 oz/1 large can ratatouille
100 g/4 oz mushrooms, sliced
5 ml/1 tsp dried mixed herbs
6 sheets no-need-to-precook lasagne
175 g/6 oz/1½ cups Cheddar cheese,
  grated
300 ml/½ pt/1¼ cups White Sauce
  (see page 311)

Mix together the ratatouille, mushrooms and herbs. Layer the mixture with the lasagne sheets in a shallow ovenproof dish, ending with a layer of lasagne. Stir most of the cheese into the White Sauce and pour over the top. Sprinkle with the remaining cheese. Bake in a preheated oven at 200°C/400°F/gas mark 6 for 35 minutes.

Cheese, Egg and Tagliatelle Ring

225 g/8 oz tagliatelle
100 g/4 oz/1 cup Cheddar cheese, grated
30 ml/2 tbsp chopped parsley
300 g/12 oz/1 large can sweetcorn (corn)
450 ml/¾ pt/2 cups Bechamel Sauce
  (see page 311)
Salt and freshly ground black pepper
8 hard-boiled (hard-cooked) eggs,
  halved
Paprika
Grated Pecorino cheese

Cook the tagliatelle according to the packet directions. Drain and keep warm. Add the Cheddar cheese, parsley and sweetcorn to the sauce and season with salt and pepper. Heat through. Serve the halved eggs in the middle of a ring of tagliatelle topped with sauce and sprinkled with a little paprika and grated Pecorino to garnish.

Country Ravioli

225 g/8 oz/2 cups strong plain
(bread) flour
2.5 ml/½ tsp salt
1 large egg
35 ml/7 tsp olive oil
100 g/4 oz field mushrooms, finely
chopped
1 small onion, chopped
1 garlic clove, chopped
5 ml/1 tsp tomato purée (paste)
60 ml/4 tbsp chopped parsley
60 ml/4 tbsp chopped basil
15 ml/1 tbsp plain (all-purpose) flour
1 egg, beaten
45 ml/3 tbsp cream cheese
45 ml/3 tbsp Pecorino cheese, grated
Salt and freshly ground black pepper
Ground mace
Semolina (cream of wheat) to
sprinkle
Simple Fresh Tomato Sauce (see
page 315)
Grated cheese

Mix the strong flour and salt in a bowl. Make a hollow in the flour and add the large egg, 15 ml/1 tbsp of the oil and 5 ml/1 tsp water. Mix to a dough and knead on a floured board for 8 minutes. Cover with an inverted bowl and rest for 1 hour. In a wok or large frying pan (skillet) heat the remaining oil and stir-fry the mushrooms, onion and garlic for 3 minutes. Add the tomato purée, parsley, basil, flour and beaten egg, stirring briskly. Remove from the heat and blend in the cream cheese and Pecorino. Season to taste with salt, pepper and mace. To fill the ravioli, roll out the dough on a floured board to a square 3 mm/⅛ in thick, which can be folded in two. On one side of the square, spoon some filling at regular intervals. Fold over the other side of the dough. With a ruler, mark squared lines between each filling. Using a ravioli cutter, separate each square by indenting the cutter into the paste. Sprinkle uncooked semolina over a tray lined with grease-proof (waxed) paper. Place the ravioli on the tray and allow them to dry on the rack above the cooker or in a warm place for 2 hours. To cook, boil in a shallow pan half filled with salted water for 8 minutes. Drain well. Coat with the tomato sauce. (The ravioli will be more tender if marinated in a plain tomato sauce and left overnight to soak up the sauce.) To serve, put the ravioli in individual dishes, four per portion. Sprinkle with grated cheese and bake in a preheated oven at 200°C/400°F/gas mark 6 for 15 minutes.

Spaghettini Romana

225 g/8 oz spaghettini
60 ml/4 tbsp melted butter and oil
100 g/4 oz button mushrooms, sliced
2 garlic cloves, chopped
12 black olives, stoned (pitted)
15 ml/1 tbsp capers
1 green chilli, seeded and sliced
4 large tomatoes, skinned, seeded
and sliced
Salt and freshly ground black pepper
Ground mace
30 ml/2 tbsp mixed chopped parsley
and basil
Grated Pecorino cheese

Boil the spaghettini for 8 minutes until *al dente*. Drain. In a wok, heat the butter and oil and toss the mushrooms, garlic, olives, capers and chilli for 1 minute. Reheat the spaghettini in this mixture for a further minute. Add the tomatoes and toss several times. Add the seasonings to taste. Sprinkle over the herbs, then serve on soup plates with grated Pecorino cheese.

Aubergine Lasagne

SERVES 4

8 sheets lasagne
1 aubergine (eggplant), sliced
  lengthways into four
Oil, for shallow-frying
Seasoned flour
150 g/5 oz spinach, stalks removed,
  chopped
25 g/1 oz/2 tbsp butter
2 garlic cloves, chopped
100 g/4 oz Mozzarella cheese, sliced
Salt and freshly ground black pepper
Grated nutmeg
45 ml/3 tbsp mixed grated Pecorino
  and Cheddar cheese

Place water and salt in a baking tin (pan) and bring it to the boil. Cook the lasagne for 8 minutes. Remove, drain and pat dry on a clean cloth. Remove the sheets with a slicer without breaking them. Sprinkle the aubergine with salt and leave for 30 minutes. Rinse and pat dry. Heat 30 ml/2 tbsp of the oil, dip each aubergine slice in flour, then fry for 1 minute only. Drain on kitchen paper. In the pan, heat a further 30 ml/2 tbsp oil and cook the spinach for 5 minutes. Drain well and press to remove excess moisture. Coat four individual oblong dishes with butter, then sprinkle a little garlic in each. Place one lasagne sheet, then an aubergine slice topped with a slice of Mozzarella cheese, then a layer of spinach on each dish. Season to taste with salt, pepper and grated nutmeg. Cover the spinach with another sheet of pasta, like a sandwich. Brush the top with butter and sprinkle over a mixture of grated Cheddar and Pecorino cheese. Bake in a preheated oven at 200°C/400°F/gas mark 6 for 8 minutes to glaze the top.

Creamy Broad Bean Pasta

SERVES 4

225 g/8 oz/2 cups medium shell pasta
150 g/5 oz/1¼ cups broad (lima)
  beans
60 ml/4 tbsp butter
150 ml/¼ pt/⅔ cup single (light)
  cream
Salt and freshly ground black pepper
Grated nutmeg
30 ml/2 tbsp chopped parsley

Boil the pasta in salted water for 8 minutes. Drain. Boil the broad beans, then remove the outer skins. In a wok or shallow pan, heat the butter and toss the pasta shells and beans for 1 minute. Add the cream, bring to the boil and season to taste, adding grated nutmeg. Sprinkle with parsley and serve.

Pasta with Eggs and Wined Mushrooms

SERVES 4

225 g/8 oz quick-cook wholewheat
  noodles
450 g/1 lb small mushrooms
Salt
175 ml/6 fl oz/¾ cup claret or other
  red wine
50 g/2 oz/¼ cup butter or margarine
20 ml/4 tsp wholemeal flour
4 hard-boiled (hard-cooked) eggs
Chopped parsley

Cook the pasta according to the packet directions, drain and keep warm. Put the mushrooms in a deep frying pan (skillet) with 120 ml/4 fl oz/½ cup of the wine and a little salt. Cover and simmer for 3–4 minutes until they are almost tender. Remove with a draining spoon, then add the remaining wine and the fat to the pan. When the fat has melted, whisk in the flour and stir until the sauce thickens. Return the mushrooms, mix with the sauce, and leave over the lowest possible heat. Shell the hot eggs, holding them in a cloth. Halve them and pile in the centre of a warmed flat platter. Spoon the mushrooms and sauce around them in a ring, and edge the mushroom ring with the pasta. Sprinkle with chopped parsley before serving.

Nutty Pasta

SERVES 4

25 g/1 oz/2 tbsp butter or margarine
1 onion, thinly sliced
225 g/8 oz mushrooms, sliced
175 g/3 oz/¾ cup walnuts, chopped
300 ml/½ pt/1¼ cups soured (dairy
  sour) cream
Pinch of dried tarragon
Freshly ground black pepper
225 g/8 oz tagliatelle or other pasta

Melt the butter or margarine and fry (sauté) the onion and mushrooms for 4 minutes until soft. Add the walnuts, cream and seasonings and heat through, stirring. Meanwhile, cook the tagliatelle according to the packet directions. Drain well. Spoon the pasta on to serving plates and pour over the sauce.

Creamy Corn and Mushroom Tagliatelle

225 g/8 oz tagliatelle
15 g/½ oz/1 tbsp butter or margarine
1 onion, chopped
1 garlic clove, crushed
100 g/4 oz mushrooms, sliced
30 ml/2 tbsp sweetcorn (corn)
150 ml/¼ pt/⅔ cup single (light) cream
Salt and freshly ground black pepper
Pinch of dried mixed herbs
Crusty bread
Green salad

Cook the pasta according to the packet directions. Drain. Meanwhile, melt the butter or margarine and fry (sauté) the onion, garlic and mushrooms for 5 minutes until soft. Stir in the pasta, sweetcorn and cream and heat through. Season to taste with salt, pepper and herbs. Serve with crusty bread and a green salad.

Lasagne Verdi

SERVES 4

45 ml/3 tbsp olive oil
1 red onion, sliced
225 g/8 oz frozen spinach, thawed
Juice of ½ lemon
Grated nutmeg
225 g/8 oz/1 small can chopped
    tomatoes
150 g/5 oz/1¼ cups walnuts, roughly
    chopped
Salt and freshly ground black pepper
6–8 sheets no-need-to-precook
    lasagne verdi
150 ml/¼ pt/⅔ cup plain yoghurt
45 ml/3 tbsp milk or water
150 g/5 oz/1¼ cups Emmental or
    Cheddar cheese, grated

Grease a 1.2 litre/2 pt/5 cup ovenproof pie dish with a little oil or margarine. Heat the olive oil in a frying pan (skillet) and stir-fry the onion for 4 minutes until soft but not brown. Remove from the heat. Season the spinach with lemon juice and nutmeg and spread half in the bottom of the pie dish. Cover with a layer of lasagne followed by a layer of half the tomatoes. Arrange a layer of half the onion on top of the tomatoes in the pie dish, add half the walnuts and season to taste with salt and pepper. Cover with another layer of lasagne, then repeat layers of spinach, lasagne, tomato, onion and walnuts, and finish with a layer of lasagne. Beat the yoghurt with the milk or water and pour over the lasagne. Sprinkle with grated cheese. Bake in a preheated oven at 190°C/375°F/gas mark 5 for 35–40 minutes until golden and bubbling and the lasagne is cooked through.

Sorrento Pasta

15 ml/1 tbsp olive oil
1 onion, chopped
1 garlic clove, crushed
400 g/14 oz/1 large can chopped
  tomatoes
Salt and freshly ground black pepper
Good pinch of caster (superfine)
  sugar
15 ml/1 tbsp tomato purée (paste)
2 sun-dried tomatoes, chopped
400 g/14 oz/1 large can baked beans
5 ml/1 tsp dried basil
50 g/2 oz/1 cup breadcrumbs
50 g/2 oz/½ cup Mozzarella cheese,
  grated

Heat the oil in a saucepan and fry (sauté) the onion and garlic for 2 minutes. Add the tomatoes, a little salt and pepper, the sugar, tomato purée and sundried tomatoes. Bring to the boil and simmer for 5 minutes until pulpy. Stir in the beans and basil and turn into an ovenproof dish. Mix the breadcrumbs and Mozzarella together and sprinkle over. Bake in a preheated oven at 180°C/350°F/gas mark 4 for 30 minutes until golden and crisp on the top.

Mediterranean Spaghettini

30 ml/2 tbsp olive oil
1 bunch of spring onions (scallions),
  chopped
1 garlic clove, crushed
1 red (bell) pepper, sliced
1 green (bell) pepper, sliced
1 yellow (bell) pepper, sliced
30 ml/2 tbsp dry white wine
400 g/14 oz/1 large can chopped
  tomatoes
2 sun-dried tomatoes, chopped
15 ml/1 tbsp sun-dried tomato oil
5 ml/1 tsp clear honey
Salt and freshly ground black pepper
350 g/12 oz spaghettini
A few snipped chives

Heat the oil in a large saucepan and fry (sauté) the spring onions and garlic for 2 minutes. Add the peppers and cook for a further 2 minutes. Add the wine, the canned and sun-dried tomatoes, the tomato oil, honey and a little salt and pepper. Bring to the boil, reduce the heat and simmer for 20 minutes until pulpy and the peppers are tender. Meanwhile, cook the spaghettini according to the packet directions. Drain and return to the saucepan. Add the sauce, toss gently, pile on to warm serving plates and sprinkle with a few snipped chives.

Creamy Rigatoni with Peas and Mushrooms

SERVES 4

50 g/2 oz/¼ cup butter or margarine
350 g/12 oz button mushrooms, sliced
100 g/4 oz/1 cup frozen peas
1 garlic clove, crushed
300 ml/½ pt/1¼ cups soured (dairy sour) cream
45 ml/3 tbsp chopped parsley
Salt and freshly ground black pepper
350 g/12 oz rigatoni

Melt the butter or margarine in a saucepan. Add the mushrooms, peas and garlic and stir well until coated in the fat. Reduce the heat, cover and simmer gently for 10 minutes, stirring occasionally. Stir in the cream and half the parsley. Season with salt and pepper. Heat through. Meanwhile, cook the rigatoni according to the packet directions. Drain and pile on a serving dish. Spoon the sauce over and sprinkle with the remaining parsley before serving.

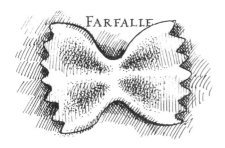

FARFALLE

Japanese Noodles with Tofu

SERVES 4

25 g/1 oz/2 tbsp butter or margarine
175 g/6 oz firm tofu, finely diced
1 bunch of spring onions (scallions), chopped
1 red (bell) pepper, diced
1 green (bell) pepper, diced
15 g/½ oz/2 tbsp cornflour (cornstarch)
250 ml/8 fl oz/1 cup dry white or rice wine
250 ml/8 fl oz/1 cup vegetable stock
2 tomatoes, skinned, seeded and chopped
2 gherkins (cornichons), chopped
350 g/12 oz soba (Japanese buckwheat) noodles
5 ml/1 tsp paprika
2.5 ml/½ tsp curry powder
150 ml/¼ pt/⅔ cup crème fraîche
Salt and freshly ground black pepper

Melt the butter or margarine in a saucepan and fry (sauté) the tofu for 2 minutes, stirring. Reserve a little of the green part of the spring onions for garnish, then add the remainder to the pan with the peppers. Fry (sauté) for 3 minutes, stirring. Remove from the heat and stir in the cornflour. Gradually blend in the wine, then the stock. Add the tomatoes and gherkins. Bring to the boil stirring, and simmer for 10 minutes stirring, occasionally. Meanwhile, cook the noodles according to the packet directions. Drain and return to the saucepan. Stir the paprika and curry powder into the sauce, then blend in the crème fraîche. Season to taste. Add to the noodles, toss and serve garnished with the reserved chopped spring onion tops.

Amalfi Coast Tagliatelle

4 plum tomatoes, skinned, seeded
and chopped
45 ml/3 tbsp capers, chopped
225 g/8 oz/2 cups Mozzarella cheese,
grated
8 basil leaves, chopped
2 eggs, beaten
150 ml/¼ pt/⅔ cup single (light)
cream
350 g/12 oz tagliatelle
Salt and freshly ground black pepper
Basil sprigs

Mix the tomatoes with the capers, cheese, basil, eggs and cream. Cook the tagliatelle according to the packet directions. Drain and return to the saucepan. Add the tomato mixture, toss well and stir over a gentle heat until the cheese has melted and the sauce has thickened. Do not allow to scramble. Serve straight away, garnished with basil sprigs.

Speedy Pasta Layer

225 g/8 oz/2 cups pasta shapes
430 g/15½ oz/1 large can ratatouille
425 g/15 oz/1 large can red kidney
beans, drained
5 ml/1 tsp dried oregano
Freshly ground black pepper
50 g/2 oz/½ cup Cheddar cheese,
grated
50 g/2 oz/1 cup breadcrumbs

Cook the pasta according to the packet directions. Drain. Put a third of the pasta in the base of a 1.5 litre/2½ pt/6 cup ovenproof dish. Spoon half the ratatouille and half the beans over and sprinkle with half the oregano and a little pepper. Add a layer of half the remaining pasta, then the remaining ratatouille and beans and season again. Top with the remaining pasta, then mix the cheese and breadcrumbs together and sprinkle over the top. Bake in a preheated oven at 190°C/375°F/gas mark 5 for about 30 minutes or until piping hot and the top is golden brown.

Noodle Pancakes

150 g/5 oz wholewheat tagliatelle,
broken into short pieces
5 eggs, beaten
Pinch of ground mace
50 g/2 oz/½ cup Pecorino cheese,
grated
Salt and freshly ground black pepper
60 ml/4 tbsp olive oil
175 g/6 oz/1½ cups Mozzarella
cheese, grated
A few torn basil leaves

Cook the tagliatelle according to the packet directions, drain and rinse with hot water. Drain again and return to the saucepan. Mix in the eggs with the mace and cheese and season with salt and pepper. Heat 15 ml/1 tbsp of the oil in a frying pan (skillet) spoon in a quarter of the batter, swirl to coat the base of the pan and fry (sauté) until golden on the base. Turn over to brown the other side. Keep warm while making the remaining pancakes. Sprinkle the pancakes liberally with the Mozzarella, scatter a few basil leaves over and add a good grinding of pepper. Fold in half and flash under a hot grill (broiler) until the cheese melts.

Noodle Pancakes with Tomato and Cheese

1 onion, finely chopped
1 garlic clove, crushed
15 ml/1 tbsp olive oil
400 g/14 oz/1 large can chopped
tomatoes
5 ml/1 tsp dried oregano
15 ml/1 tbsp tomato purée (paste)
Salt and freshly ground black pepper
1 quantity Noodle Pancakes (see left)
100 g/4 oz Mozzarella cheese, sliced

While the pasta is cooking for the pancakes, fry (sauté) the onion and garlic in the oil in a saucepan for 2 minutes, stirring. Add the tomatoes, oregano, tomato purée and a little salt and pepper. Bring to the boil, reduce the heat and simmer for 10 minutes until pulpy. Make the pancakes. Spread the hot tomato sauce over half of each pancake. Top with the slices of cheese, fold over and serve (the cheese will melt in the hot sauce).

Spaghetti with Sweet Garlic and Herb Butter

SERVES 4

350 g/12 oz spaghetti
6 whole garlic cloves, peeled
100 g/4 oz/½ cup unsalted (sweet)
*   butter*
30 ml/2 tbsp chopped parsley
15 ml/1 tbsp chopped sage
15 ml/1 tbsp snipped chives
Salt and freshly ground black pepper
Grated Pecorino cheese

Cook the spaghetti according to the packet directions. Drain and return to the saucepan. Meanwhile, put the garlic in a small saucepan. Cover with plenty of cold water. Bring to the boil and simmer for 5 minutes. Drain, remove from the saucepan and crush. Melt the butter in the same saucepan. Add the crushed garlic and the herbs and season with salt and pepper. Stir until melted, then cook very gently for 2 minutes. Add to the spaghetti, toss gently and pile on to serving plates. Serve sprinkled liberally with grated Pecorino cheese.

Spinach and Ricotta Cannelloni

SERVES 4

225 g/8 oz frozen chopped spinach,
*   just thawed*
100 g/4 oz/½ cup Ricotta cheese
Salt and freshly ground black pepper
1.5 ml/¼ tsp grated nutmeg
12 no-need-to-precook cannelloni
*   tubes*
40 g/1½ oz/⅓ cup plain (all-purpose)
*   flour*
600 ml/1 pt/2½ cups milk
40 g/1½ oz/3 tbsp butter or margarine
1 bay leaf
50 g/2 oz/½ cup Pecorino cheese,
*   grated*
25 g/1 oz/¼ cup wholemeal
*   breadcrumbs*

Mash the spinach with the Ricotta cheese and season with salt, pepper and the nutmeg. Fill the cannelloni tubes with the mixture and place in a single layer in a shallow ovenproof dish. Whisk the flour and milk together in a saucepan until smooth. Add the butter and bay leaf and bring to the boil, whisking all the time. Cook for 2 minutes, stirring with the whisk. Season to taste and remove the bay leaf. Pour the sauce over the cannelloni and sprinkle with the Pecorino cheese and breadcrumbs. Bake in a preheated oven at 200°C/400°F/gas mark 6 for 40 minutes until the cannelloni is tender and the top is golden brown.

Tagliatelle di Napoli

SERVES 4

350 g/12 oz tagliatelle verdi
25 g/1 oz/2 tbsp butter or margarine
1 large Spanish onion, finely
*   chopped*
1 garlic clove, crushed
30 ml/2 tbsp olive oil
450 g/1 lb tomatoes, skinned, seeded
*   and chopped*
5 ml/1 tsp dried basil or oregano
30 ml/2 tbsp dry white wine or water
6 stuffed olives, quartered
Salt and freshly ground black pepper

Cook the tagliatelle according to the packet directions. Drain and toss with the butter or margarine. In a large heavy frying pan (skillet), fry (sauté) the onion and garlic in the oil for 3 minutes. Add the tomatoes, herbs and wine or water and stir for another 3 minutes. Stir in the olives, season with salt and pepper and pour the sauce over the pasta on four warmed serving plates.

Cheese-based Main Courses

Savoury Golden Pudding

320 g/12 oz/1 large can sweetcorn (corn), drained
450 ml/¾ pt/2 cups milk
3 eggs, beaten
30 ml/2 tbsp snipped chives
25 g/1 oz/2 tbsp butter or margarine
Salt and freshly ground black pepper
5 ml/1 tsp made English mustard
50 g/2 oz/½ cup strong Cheddar cheese, grated
Chopped parsley
Crusty bread
Mixed salad

Mix together all the ingredients, except the parsley, bread and salad, and place in a greased ovenproof dish. Bake in a preheated oven at 190°C/375°F/gas mark 5 for about 25–30 minutes until set and golden on top. Sprinkle with chopped parsley and serve with crusty bread and a mixed salad.

Cottage Cheese Loaf

225 g/8 oz/1 cup cottage cheese
50 g/2 oz/½ cup walnuts, chopped
2.5 ml/½ tsp dried oregano
5 ml/1 tsp made English mustard
100 g/4 oz/2 cups wholemeal breadcrumbs
Salt and freshly ground black pepper
2 eggs, beaten
Mixed salad

Mix together all the ingredients except the salad thoroughly. Turn into a greased 450 g/1 lb loaf tin (pan). Bake in a preheated oven at 180°C/350°F/gas mark 4 for 30 minutes or until set. Leave to cool in the tin for 5 minutes, then turn out and serve cut into slices with a mixed salad.

Savoury Sandwich Bake

6 slices bread, spread with a little butter or margarine
Yeast extract
100 g/4 oz/1 cup Cheddar cheese, sliced
3 tomatoes, sliced
3 eggs
300 ml/½ pt/1¼ cups milk
Salt and freshly ground black pepper
Pinch of cayenne
Sesame seeds
Chopped parsley
Everyday Coleslaw (see page 224)

Make up the sandwiches using the bread, yeast extract, cheese and tomatoes and cut into four. Place in the base of a shallow, greased ovenproof dish. Beat together the eggs, milk, salt, pepper and cayenne and pour over the sandwiches. Sprinkle with sesame seeds. Bake in a preheated oven at 190°C/375°F/gas mark 5 for about 40 minutes until set and golden brown. Garnish with chopped parsley and serve with coleslaw.

Cheese Fondue

SERVES 4

300 ml/½ pt/1¼ cups dry white wine
  or dry cider
5 ml/1 tsp lemon juice
450 g/1 lb/4 cups Cheddar cheese,
  grated
15 ml/1 tbsp cornflour (cornstarch)
  mixed with 15 ml/1 tbsp water
25 g/1 oz/2 tbsp butter or margarine
Salt and freshly ground black pepper
Pinch of nutmeg

Place all the ingredients in a large saucepan or metal fondue pot. Cook gently, stirring all the time until the cheese has melted. Taste and re-season if necessary. Pour into fondue pot (if necessary) and take to the table.

Things to dip and dunk: cubes of bread, pineapple cubes, halved raw mushrooms, whole baby sweetcorn (corn), quartered tomatoes, carrot and celery chunks, strips of different coloured (bell) peppers, water chestnuts, bamboo shoots, savoury biscuits, cauliflower or broccoli florets; the list is endless!

Swiss Cheese Fondue

SERVES 4

Prepare as for Cheese Fondue but substitute Emmental (Swiss) cheese for the Cheddar, or use half and half, and add 30 ml/2 tbsp Kirsch to the mixture.

Greek Cheese and Spinach Pie

SERVES 8

600 ml/1 pt/2½ cups milk
75 g/3 oz/½ cup semolina (cream of
  wheat)
100 g/4 oz/1 cup Cheddar cheese,
  grated
100 g/4 oz/½ cup cream cheese
3 eggs, beaten
30 ml/2 tbsp olive oil
100 g/4 oz leaf spinach, washed and
  trimmed
2 garlic cloves, chopped
Salt and freshly ground black pepper
2.5 ml/½ tsp grated nutmeg
45 ml/3 tbsp sunflower oil
12 sheets filo pastry (paste)

In a large, heavy saucepan, bring the milk to the boil and sprinkle over the semolina. Cook for 5 minutes until thick, like porridge. Put the cooked semolina paste into a large mixing bowl. Blend in the cheeses and beaten eggs. Allow the mixture to cool completely. In a shallow pan, heat the olive oil and stir-fry the spinach leaves and garlic for 5 minutes. Remove from the heat and chop the mixture coarsely. Blend it into the cheese mixture. Season to taste, adding the nutmeg. Place six sheets of the pastry as the base in a shallow baking tin (pan), oiled with some of the sunflower oil. Spread the filling over and cover with the remaining six sheets on top of each other, sprinkling the remaining oil over each sheet. With the tip of a knife, mark with a pattern of criss-cross lines. Bake in a preheated oven at 200°C/400°F/gas mark 6 for 30 minutes, then cut along the marked lines.

Brittany Cheesecake

SERVES 4

100 g/4 oz/1 cup plain (all-purpose)
 flour
25 g/1 oz/¼ cup ground almonds
2 eggs, beaten
300 ml/½ pt/1¼ cups mixed milk and
 water
15 ml/1 tbsp chopped parsley
Salt and freshly ground black pepper
Oil
75 g/3 oz/⅓ cup cream cheese,
 softened
175 ml/6 fl oz/¾ cup plain yoghurt
5 ml/1 tsp caraway seeds
2 large tomatoes, sliced
4 lettuce leaves
3 thin slices Emmental (Swiss)
 cheese
150 g/5 oz cucumber, chopped

Place the flour and ground almonds in a bowl. Beat in the eggs and gradually beat in the milk and water. Season with chopped parsley and a pinch of salt. Heat 15 ml/1 tbsp oil in a small omelette pan or frying pan (skillet), measuring about 16 cm/6½ in across. Pour in 75 ml/5 tbsp of the batter mixture. Cook for about 2 minutes until the underside is golden, then turn and cook the other side. Repeat until all the batter has been used, making about eight pancakes. Leave to cool. Beat together the cream cheese, 25 ml/1½ tbsp of the yoghurt and the caraway seeds. Place a pancake on a 20 cm/8 in serving plate and spread with a layer of caraway-flavoured cream cheese. Cover with another pancake and arrange slices of tomato, lettuce leaves and Emmental cheese on top. Add a third pancake and spread with the cream cheese mixture. Repeat the layers until all the ingredients have been used. Press down slightly, using another plate. Mix the remaining yoghurt and the cucumber together and season to taste with salt and pepper. Serve with the gâteau cut into wedges like a cake.

Cheddared Choice

SERVES 4

550 g/1¼ lb frozen mixed vegetables
4 large slices wholemeal bread
1.5 ml/¼ tsp dry mustard powder
1.5 ml/¼ tsp paprika
1.5 ml/¼ tsp salt
15 ml/1 tbsp wholemeal flour
50 g/2 oz/½ cup Cheddar cheese,
 grated
75 ml/5 tbsp water
30 ml/2 tbsp milk
A few drops of Tabasco sauce
2.5 ml/½ tsp lemon juice
50 g/2 oz/¼ cup butter or margarine

Cook the frozen vegetables according to the packet directions. Cut the crusts off the bread and toast both sides lightly. Lay the slices close together in a shallow serving dish. Mix together all the remaining ingredients except the fat in a bowl. Melt the fat in a saucepan. Blend in the ingredients in the bowl, and stir over a moderate heat until the sauce boils and thickens. Drain the vegetables and spread evenly on the toast. Pour the cheese sauce over. Serve at once.

Sesame Cheesecake

60 ml/4 tbsp sunflower oil
1 large onion, sliced
225 g/8 oz/1 cup cream cheese
50 g/2 oz/½ cup blue cheese, mashed
15 ml/1 tbsp flour
3 eggs, separated
Salt and freshly ground black pepper
15 ml/1 tbsp celery seeds
Snipped chives
225 g/8 oz shortcrust pastry (basic
*   pie crust)*
50 g/2 oz/½ cup Cheddar cheese,
*   grated*
30 ml/2 tbsp curry powder
Pinch of sugar
Pinch of salt
30 ml/2 tbsp sesame seeds
Tomato and cucumber slices

Heat the oil in a pan and stir-fry the onion until soft but not brown. Remove from the heat and cool. In a bowl, mash the cream cheese and blue cheese together. Add the onion, flour and the egg yolks. Season with salt, pepper, celery seeds and chives. Oil a 20 cm/8 in loose-bottomed cake tin (pan). Roll out the pastry on a floured board. Sprinkle over the grated cheese and curry powder, rolling the pastry to incorporate the mixture as you dust it with flour. Cut a round of pastry to fit the bottom only of the cake tin. Line the tin with the round of pastry. Knead the remaining pastry into a ball. Roll out to a strip 5 cm/2 in wide. Roll up this band of pastry and unroll it inside the tin, applying it with pressure against the side of the tin – this is the best way to line the side of a cheesecake. Seal to the base by brushing the edge with water. Beat the egg whites in a clean bowl until stiff and add the pinch of salt and sugar. Fold this mixture into the cheese mixture and use to fill the tin. Sprinkle over the sesame seeds. Bake in a preheated oven at 200°C/400°F/gas mark 6 for 30 minutes. Carefully remove from the tin and slip it on to a large round flat dish or plate. Cut into portions and serve hot with tomato and cucumber slices.

Cheese and Mushroom Pudding

40 g/1½ oz/3 tbsp butter or margarine
1 onion, finely chopped
275 g/10 oz button mushrooms,
*   sliced*
100 g/4 oz/2 cups wholemeal
*   breadcrumbs*
2 eggs
300 ml/½ pt/1¼ cups milk
Salt and freshly ground black pepper
2.5 ml/½ tsp grated nutmeg
100 g/4 oz/1 cup Cheddar cheese,
*   grated*

Melt 25 g/1 oz/2 tbsp of the butter or margarine in a pan. Add the onion and mushrooms and fry (sauté), stirring for 3 minutes. Grease a 1.2 litre/2 pt/ 5 cup ovenproof dish with the remaining butter. Add the mushroom mixture with its juice, then stir in the breadcrumbs. Beat the eggs and milk together with a little salt and pepper. Pour into the dish with the nutmeg and half the cheese. Stir well and leave to stand for 15 minutes. Sprinkle with the remaining cheese and bake in a preheated oven at 190°C/ 375°F/gas mark 5 for about 1 hour or until the pudding is risen and set. Serve straight away.

Photograph opposite: **Nut Roast Plait (page 131)**

Swiss Cheese and Tomato Roll

SERVES 4

5 eggs, separated
Salt and freshly ground black pepper
Pinch of cayenne
175 g/6 oz/1½ cups Emmental (Swiss) cheese, grated
25 g/1 oz/¼ cup plain (all-purpose) flour
30 ml/2 tbsp breadcrumbs, toasted
400 g/14 oz/1 large can chopped tomatoes with herbs

Beat the yolks with a little salt and pepper and the cayenne until pale. Beat in 100 g/4 oz/1 cup of the cheese and the flour. Whisk the egg whites until stiff. Fold into the yolk mixture. Grease and line a Swiss roll tin (jelly roll pan) with non-stick baking parchment. Turn the mixture into the tin and bake in a preheated oven at 180°C/350°F/gas mark 4 for 15 minutes until golden and firm to the touch. Put a sheet of non-stick baking parchment on the work surface and sprinkle with the toasted breadcrumbs. Turn the cooked mixture out on to this and remove the cooking paper. Meanwhile, heat the tomatoes, then spread over the surface. Sprinkle with the remaining cheese and roll up, using the paper as a guide. Still using the paper, lift on to the Swiss roll tin. Return to a preheated oven for 5–10 minutes until piping hot and the cheese has melted. Serve sliced.

Photograph opposite: **Vegetable Stir-fry with Garlic Rice (page 140)**

Calzone

SERVES 4

400 g/14 oz/3½ cups plain (all-purpose) flour
15 ml/1 tbsp light brown sugar
Salt and freshly ground black pepper
100 g/4 oz/½ cup butter or margarine
60 ml/4 tbsp olive oil
15 g/½ oz/1 tbsp easy-blend dried yeast
250 ml/8 fl oz/1 cup hot milk
1 onion, chopped
1 garlic clove, crushed
200 g/7 oz frozen chopped spinach, thawed and drained
350 g/12 oz/1½ cups Ricotta cheese
Pinch of cayenne
Pinch of grated nutmeg
4 tomatoes, skinned and chopped
5 ml/1 tsp dried oregano

Mix the flour, sugar and 10 ml/2 tsp salt in a bowl. Add the butter, cut into small pieces, and rub in with the fingertips. Stir in half the oil and the yeast. Mix with the hot milk to form a soft but not sticky dough. Knead gently on a lightly floured surface and wrap in a greased plastic bag while preparing the filling. Fry (sauté) the onion and garlic in the remaining oil for 2 minutes until soft but not brown. Remove from the heat and stir in the remaining ingredients, seasoning well with salt and pepper. Re-knead the dough. Divide into quarters. Roll out each to a circle. Spread the filling over half of each circle, not quite to the edge. Brush the edges with water. Fold over and press the edges well together to seal. Press all round the semi-circles with a floured fork. Transfer to a greased baking sheet. Brush with a little water and bake in a preheated oven at 200°C/400°F/gas mark 6 for about 20 minutes until golden and cooked through. Serve hot.

Cheese and Vegetable Crustie

SERVES 4

175 g/6 oz/1½ cups plain (all-purpose) flour
Salt and freshly ground black pepper
115 g/4½ oz/good ½ cup butter or margarine
75 g/3 oz/⅓ cup mashed potato
2 potatoes, diced
2 carrots, sliced
3 leeks, sliced
200 g/7 oz/1 small can sweetcorn (corn), drained
200 g/7 oz/1 small can chopped tomatoes
100 g/4 oz/1 cup Cheddar cheese, grated
2.5 ml/½ tsp dried mixed herbs
Beaten egg, to glaze

Sift the flour and a pinch of salt into a bowl. Add 100 g/4 oz/½ cup of the butter or margarine and rub in with the fingertips. Work in the mashed potato to form a firm dough. Knead gently on a lightly floured surface and chill for 30 minutes. Melt the remaining butter or margarine in a saucepan. Add the potatoes, carrot and leeks, cover and cook for 10 minutes, stirring occasionally. Stir in the corn and tomatoes, then turn into a 1.5 litre/2½ pt/6 cup pie dish. Stir in the cheese, a little salt and pepper and the herbs. Roll out the pastry to a little larger than the pie dish. Cut a strip off the edge. Brush the edge of the pie dish with water and lay the strip around it. Brush with water again and lay the pastry lid in position. Press the edges well together to seal, trim to fit, then knock up and crimp between finger and thumb. Make leaves out of pastry trimmings and place on top. Make a hole in the centre to allow steam to escape. Brush with beaten egg and bake in a preheated oven at 200°C/400°F/gas mark 6 for 10 minutes then reduce the heat to 180°C/350°F/gas mark 4 and continue cooking for about 40 minutes or until the vegetables are tender.

Leek, Stilton and Walnut Flan

SERVES 4

100 g/4 oz/1 cup walnut halves
175 g/6 oz/1½ cups plain (all-purpose) flour
Salt and freshly ground black pepper
75 g/3 oz/⅓ cup white vegetable fat (shortening)
25 g/1 oz/2 tbsp butter or margarine
4 leeks, sliced
50 g/2 oz/½ cup Stilton cheese, crumbled
150 ml/¼ pt/⅔ cup single (light) cream
2 eggs, beaten
15 ml/1 tbsp chopped parsley

Finely chop half the walnuts and place in a bowl with the flour and a pinch of salt. Add the vegetable fat and rub in with the fingertips. Mix with enough cold water to form a firm dough. Knead gently on a lightly floured surface. Roll out and use to line a 23 cm/9 in flan tin (pie pan). Melt the butter in a saucepan, add the leeks and fry (sauté), stirring, for 10 minutes or until tender. Spread in the pastry case. Roughly chop the remaining walnuts and sprinkle over. Sprinkle on the crumbled cheese. Beat the cream and eggs together with a little salt and pepper and pour into the flan. Sprinkle with the parsley. Set on a baking sheet and bake in a preheated oven at 200°C/400°F/gas mark 6 for about 30 minutes until set and golden.

Curried Cheese and Sweetcorn Grill

SERVES 4

320 g/12 oz/1 large can sweetcorn
(corn), drained
225 g/8 oz/2 cups any pulses, cooked
(see page 10)
450 ml/¾ pt/2 cups Bechamel Sauce
(see page 311)
Salt and freshly ground black pepper
100 g/4 oz/1 cup Cheddar cheese,
grated
2.5 ml/1 tsp curry powder
A few drops of Tabasco sauce
Paprika
Toast triangles
Broccoli

Mix the sweetcorn with the pulses and the sauce in a saucepan. Add a little salt and pepper, half the cheese and the curry powder and Tabasco. Heat through, turn into a flameproof dish and sprinkle with the remaining cheese. Place under a hot grill (broiler) until bubbling and golden brown. Dust with a little paprika. Arrange toast triangles around the edges of the dish and serve with lightly cooked broccoli.

Egg-based Main Courses

Eggy Mexican Tacos

4 taco shells
4 eggs
A knob of butter or margarine
15 ml/1 tbsp milk
Salt and freshly ground black pepper
1 red (bell) pepper, diced
1 small green chilli, seeded and
*   chopped*
Shredded lettuce

Warm the tacos in a preheated oven while preparing the filling. Beat the eggs in a pan. Add the butter and milk. Cook over a gentle heat, stirring all the time, until scrambled but creamy. Do not boil. Season with salt and pepper and stir in the red pepper and chilli. Line the taco shells with shredded lettuce, then fill with the egg mixture. Serve straight away.

Chillied Eggs

40 g/1½ oz/3 tbsp butter or margarine
1 onion, chopped
Pinch of ground ginger
1.5 ml/¼ tsp chilli powder
2.5 ml/½ tsp ground turmeric
30 ml/2 tbsp chopped parsley
8 eggs, beaten
Salt and freshly ground black pepper
100 ml/3½ fl oz/6½ tbsp milk
Hot toast

Melt the butter or margarine in a saucepan. Add the onion and fry (sauté) for 3 minutes, stirring. Add the spices, parsley, eggs and a little salt and pepper. Whisk in the milk and scramble over a gentle heat. Do not boil. Spoon on to hot toast and serve immediately.

Sweet Curried Eggs

25 g/1 oz/2 tbsp butter or margarine
1 onion, chopped
15 ml/1 tbsp plain (all-purpose) flour
15 ml/1 tbsp curry powder
600 ml/1 pt/2½ cups vegetable stock
5 ml/1 tsp sweet pickle
25 g/1 oz creamed coconut
4 hard-boiled (hard-cooked) eggs,
*   halved*
A dash of lemon juice
Salt and freshly ground black pepper
Plain boiled rice

Melt the butter or margarine and fry (sauté) the onion for 3 minutes until soft. Add the flour and curry powder and cook, stirring, for 1–2 minutes. Add the stock and stir until smooth. Simmer for 15 minutes. Add the remaining ingredients except the rice and simmer for a further 3–4 minutes. Serve with plain boiled rice.

164

Roulade Florentine

SERVES 6

30 ml/2 tbsp olive oil
1 onion, chopped
4 mushrooms, chopped
100 g/4 oz leaf spinach, chopped
50 g/2 oz/½ cup cashew nuts,
** chopped**
75 ml/5 tbsp plain yoghurt
Salt and freshly ground black pepper
5 eggs, separated
50 g/2 oz/½ cup Cheddar cheese,
** grated**
30 ml/2 tbsp chopped coriander
** (cilantro) or parsley**
Grated Pecorino cheese
Watercress sprigs

Lightly oil a 23 x 33 cm/9 x 13 in Swiss roll tin (jelly roll pan) and line with greaseproof (waxed) paper. Heat the oil in a frying pan (skillet) and fry (sauté) the onion for 2 minutes without browning. Add the mushrooms, spinach and cashew nuts and cook for 5 minutes. Stir in the yoghurt and boil for 2 minutes. Season to taste with salt and pepper and leave to cool. Place the egg yolks, grated Cheddar, herbs and a pinch of pepper in a bowl and beat together. Place the egg whites in a large bowl with a pinch of salt and whisk until stiff enough to cling to the whisk. Fold carefully into the egg yolk mixture. Pour the roulade mixture into the prepared tin and spread evenly. Smooth the surface with a palette knife. Bake in a preheated oven at 200°C/400°F/gas mark 6 for 10 minutes, then remove from the oven and leave to cool. Place a sheet of greaseproof paper on the work surface and sprinkle with grated Pecorino. Turn the roulade out on to the sheet of paper and peel off the lining paper. Spread the spinach mixture evenly over the roulade and roll up like a Swiss roll, using the sheet of greaseproof paper underneath to help. Lift the whole roulade carefully into a serving dish or cut into slices and serve on individual plates. Garnish with watercress.

Oven Omelette

SERVES 2–4

4 eggs, beaten
250 g/9 oz/good 1 cup cottage cheese
150 ml/¼ pt/⅔ cup milk
Salt and freshly ground black pepper
100 g/4 oz mushrooms, sliced
1 onion, chopped
Pinch of dried mixed herbs

Mix all the ingredients in a bowl. Pour into a well-greased ovenproof dish. Bake in a preheated oven at 200°C/400°F/gas mark 6 for 20 minutes until browned and firm.

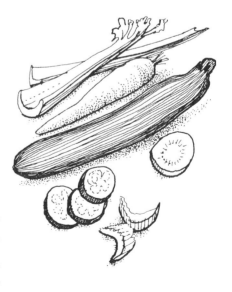

Roasted Eggy Peppers

SERVES 4

2 large red (bell) peppers
30 ml/2 tbsp olive oil
50 g/2 oz/1 cup breadcrumbs
25 g/1 oz/¼ cup ground almonds
15 ml/1 tbsp chopped parsley
15 ml/1 tbsp snipped chives
1 beefsteak tomato, skinned and
  chopped
Salt and freshly ground black pepper
4 eggs
75 g/3 oz/¾ cup Cheddar cheese,
  grated

Halve the peppers and remove the seeds. Cook in boiling salted water for 6 minutes. Drain, rinse with cold water and drain again. Lay in a greased baking tin (pan) and brush all over with some of the oil. Mix together the breadcrumbs, almonds, herbs, tomato and some salt and pepper and spoon into the peppers, making a 'well' in the centre. Break an egg into each and sprinkle with the cheese. Drizzle with the remaining oil and bake in a preheated oven at 180°C/350°F/gas mark 4 for 15–20 minutes or until the eggs are cooked to your liking.

Egg and Potato Nests with Piquant Black Butter

SERVES 4

750 g/1½ lb/3 cups freshly cooked
  mashed potato
100 g/4 oz/½ cup butter
2 slices bread, finely diced
4 eggs
15 ml/1 tbsp chopped parsley
2 gherkins (cornichons), chopped
15 ml/1 tbsp capers, chopped
Freshly ground black pepper
20 ml/4 tsp cider vinegar

Spoon the potato round the edge of 4 greased individual gratin dishes. Flash under a hot grill (broiler) to brown. Meanwhile, melt 25 g/1 oz/2 tbsp of the butter in a frying pan (skillet) and fry (sauté) the bread cubes until crisp and golden. Drain on kitchen paper. Poach the eggs to your liking and transfer to the potato 'nests'. Meanwhile, melt the remaining butter in the wiped-out frying pan and fry until a deep nut brown. Immediately add the parsley, gherkins, capers and a good grinding of pepper and spoon over the eggs. Quickly add the vinegar to the pan, boil to reduce by half and spoon over the eggs. Serve immediately, sprinkled with the croûtons.

Leeks 'n' Eggs

75 g/3 oz/⅓ cup butter or margarine
450 g/1 lb leeks, sliced
15 ml/1 tbsp plain (all-purpose) flour
300 ml/½ pt/1¼ cups vegetable stock
30 ml/2 tbsp chopped sage
90 ml/6 tbsp double (heavy) cream
Salt and freshly ground black pepper
4 hard-boiled (hard-cooked) eggs,
  halved
Toast triangles

Melt the butter or margarine in a saucepan. Add the leeks and cook, stirring, for 3 minutes. Stir in the flour and cook for 1 minute. Gradually blend in the stock and bring to the boil, stirring. Add the sage, cover and simmer gently for 10 minutes, stirring occasionally to prevent sticking. Stir in the cream and season to taste. Lay the eggs in a shallow flameproof dish. Pour the sauce over. Glaze under a hot grill (broiler) and garnish with toast triangles.

South-of-the-border Eggs

75 g/3 oz/⅓ cup butter or margarine
1 bunch of spring onions (scallions),
  chopped
1 green (bell) pepper, chopped
300 g/11 oz/1 large can sweetcorn
  (corn), drained
15 ml/1 tbsp ready-made hot chilli
  salsa
4 eggs
Salt and freshly ground black pepper
60 ml/4 tbsp soured (dairy sour) cream
75 g/3 oz/¾ cup Cheddar cheese, grated

Melt 25 g/1 oz/2 tbsp of the butter or margarine in a large frying pan (skillet). Add the spring onions and green pepper and fry (sauté), stirring, for 3 minutes until softened but not browned. Stir in the corn and chilli salsa and a further 25 g/1 oz/ 2 tbsp of the butter or margarine. Make four 'wells' in the mixture and break an egg into each. Cover and cook for 10 minutes or until the eggs are cooked to your liking. Meanwhile, mix the soured cream and cheese with a little salt and pepper. Spoon over the eggs and place under a hot grill (broiler) until the top is golden and bubbling. Serve straight away.

Spanish Eggs

25 g/1 oz/2 tbsp butter or margarine
2 onions, chopped
4 tomatoes, skinned and chopped
1 garlic clove, crushed
50 g/2 oz/⅓ cup stoned (pitted) green
olives, sliced
15 ml/1 tbsp tomato purée (paste)
8 eggs
50 g/2 oz/½ cup Pecorino cheese,
grated
150 ml/¼ pt/⅔ cup double (heavy)
cream
Salt and freshly ground black pepper
Brown Garlic Bread (see page 325)

Melt the butter or margarine in a saucepan. Add the onions and fry (sauté) for 2 minutes, stirring. Add the tomatoes and garlic and cook for a further 2 minutes. Stir in the olives and tomato purée. Spread in a large shallow ovenproof dish. Make eight small 'wells' in the mixture and break an egg into each. Sprinkle with the cheese, then pour over the cream. Season lightly. Bake in a preheated oven at 180°C/350°F/gas mark 4 for about 15 minutes or until the eggs are cooked to your liking. Serve straight from the dish with lots of garlic bread.

Eggs and Mushrooms with Cucumber Sauce

100 g/4 oz/½ cup butter or margarine
225 g/8 oz button mushrooms
1 cucumber, peeled and chopped
15 ml/1 tbsp plain (all-purpose) flour
150 ml/¼ pt/⅔ cup hot vegetable stock
5 ml/1 tsp dried dill (dill weed)
Salt and freshly ground black pepper
60 ml/4 tbsp double (heavy) cream
4 hard-boiled (hard-cooked) eggs,
sliced
Parsley sprig

Melt half the butter in a saucepan and fry (sauté) the mushrooms for 3 minutes, stirring, until just cooked. Remove from the pan with draining spoon and keep warm. Melt the remaining butter in the wiped-out pan and add the cucumber. Cook, stirring, for 5 minutes. Stir in the flour and cook for 1 minute. Blend in the stock and dill, bring to the boil and simmer for 10 minutes. Season to taste and stir in the cream. Arrange the eggs and mushrooms on a warmed serving dish. Pour the hot sauce over and flash under a hot grill (broiler) to glaze the top. Garnish with a parsley sprig before serving.

Cheese, Egg and Mushroom Pancakes

SERVES 4

1 quantity Basic Pancake Mix (see page 343)
50 g/2 oz/¼ cup butter or margarine
100 g/4 oz button mushrooms, sliced
1 garlic clove, crushed
15 ml/1 tbsp chopped parsley
5 ml/1 tsp dried marjoram
30 ml/2 tbsp soured (dairy sour) cream
2 hard-boiled (hard-cooked) eggs, chopped
Salt and freshly ground black pepper
50 g/2 oz/½ cup Cheddar cheese, grated

Make up the pancakes according to the instructions. Keep warm while preparing the filling. Melt half the butter or margarine in a saucepan and fry (sauté) the mushrooms and garlic, stirring, for about 3 minutes until tender. Stir in the herbs, cream and eggs and season to taste with salt and pepper. Divide the mixture among the pancakes. Roll up and lay in a shallow flameproof dish. Melt the remaining butter and drizzle over, then sprinkle with the cheese. Place under a hot grill (broiler) until the cheese is melted and bubbling and serve straight away.

Turkish Omelette

SERVES 4

1 green (bell) pepper, chopped
1 onion, chopped
60 ml/4 tbsp olive oil
150 g/5 oz cucumber, coarsely chopped
2 tomatoes, coarsely chopped
2.5 ml/½ tsp dried minced (ground) garlic
4 eggs
1.5 ml/¼ tsp salt
Pinch of ground cumin
Pinch of cayenne
60 ml/4 tbsp wholemeal breadcrumbs
30 ml/2 tbsp water

Put the pepper and onion in a 25 cm/ 10 in frying pan (skillet) with the oil. Mix the cucumber and tomatoes with the garlic and keep aside. Fry (sauté) the pepper and onion over a moderate heat for 2 minutes, stirring once or twice. Mix in the cucumber, tomato and garlic and stir-fry for 3 minutes. Beat the eggs in a bowl with the salt, spices, breadcrumbs and water. Stir the egg mixture into the vegetables. Reduce the heat to low, cover the pan with a lid or plate and cook for 5–6 minutes until the eggs are just set. Serve in wedges from the pan.

Egg and Mushroom Pie

900 g/2 lb potatoes
15 g/½ oz/1 tbsp butter or margarine
30 ml/2 tbsp milk
295 g/10½ oz/1 small can condensed
  mushroom soup
4 hard-boiled (hard-cooked) eggs,
  sliced
100 g/4 oz mushrooms, chopped
50 g/2 oz/½ cup Cheddar cheese,
  grated
Salt and freshly ground black pepper
A green vegetable

Boil the potatoes until tender, then drain and mash with the butter or margarine and milk. Heat the soup without allowing it to boil. Stir in the eggs and mushrooms and pour into a casserole dish (Dutch oven). Cover with the mashed potatoes and sprinkle over the grated cheese. Bake in a preheated oven at 200°C/400°F/gas mark 6 for about 15 minutes until the dish is hot and the cheese is browned. Serve with a green vegetable.

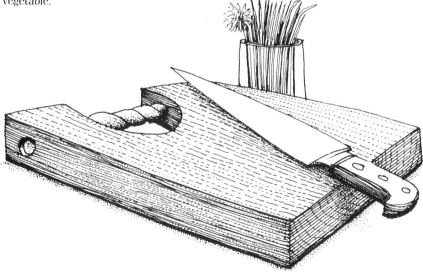

Side Dishes

Fancy something a bit more exciting than plain boiled or steamed veg with your main course? This section is bursting with some of the most tantalising vegetable accompaniments ever! In fact, many of them are mouthwatering enough for a light lunch or supper, if served in slightly larger quantities with some fresh bread. So, whether you want to brighten up vegetarian sausages or turn an everyday nut roast into a dinner party extravaganza, dip into this section for vegetable dishes extraordinaire.

Fried Rice with Hazelnuts

1.2 litres/2 pts/5 cups water
10 ml/2 tsp salt
100 g/4 oz/½ cup long-grain rice
3 eggs
15 ml/1 tbsp plain (all-purpose) flour
90 ml/6 tbsp water
15 ml/1 tbsp chopped parsley
60 ml/4 tbsp sunflower oil
225 g/8 oz/2 cups hazelnuts
25 g/1 oz stem ginger, chopped (from a jar in syrup)
25 g/1 oz candied angelica, chopped
150 g/5 oz/1¼ cups marrowfat peas, cooked
Salt and freshly ground black pepper
Chopped spring onions (scallions)

Bring the water to the boil with the salt and add the rice. Boil for 12 minutes, uncovered. Drain immediately in a colander and run hot or cold water over the rice to wash away the starch. Drain well again. Spread the rice evenly over a large shallow baking tin (pan). Chill overnight. Stir once or twice to allow the rice to dry completely as moisture is evaporated in the fridge. (If you want to serve the cooked rice on the same day, spread the rice on four baking sheets. Roast in a preheated oven at 180°C/350°F/gas mark 4 for 20 minutes, stirring from time to time to bring the moist grains to the top. A little oil can be sprinkled over to avoid sticking on the baking sheet.) To prepare the egg pancakes, beat the eggs in a bowl, then add the flour, water and parsley. In a large pan, heat 15 ml/1 tbsp of the oil and add the egg mixture. Stir a little, cook flat without disturbing, toss on to the other side and cook for 30 seconds more. Turn the pancake on to a pastry board. Roll it up and cut into shreds. In a wok or large saucepan, heat the remaining oil and stir-fry the hazelnuts for 1 minute. Add the ginger and angelica. Combine with the peas and 2 cups of the rice. Season to taste. Mix the rice with the pancake strips and serve in small bowls. Serve the other heated plain fried rice separately. Garnish with spring onions.

Pat's Perfect Rice

Measuring the rice and water in the same jug gives you exactly the right proportions if you use 1 jug of rice to 2 jugs of water. A 1 pint jug takes about 225 g/8 oz rice.

Method 1:
Put the rice, a little salt and pepper, a bay leaf and the water in a large bowl and leave for 1 hour. Heat through in the microwave on high for 4 minutes. Remove the bay leaf and serve.

Method 2:
Place all the ingredients in a saucepan. Cover with a tight-fitting lid. Bring to the boil. Reduce the heat to as low as possible and cook for 25–30 minutes. Remove from the heat. Do not take off the lid. Leave to stand for 5 minutes. Fluff up and serve.

Pecorino Pasta

175 g/6 oz/1½ cups pasta shapes
Salt and freshly ground black pepper
400 g/14 oz/1 large can chopped tomatoes
5 ml/1 tsp dried mixed herbs
15 g/½ oz/1 tbsp butter or margarine
45 ml/3 tbsp grated Pecorino cheese

Cook the pasta in boiling, salted water until just tender. Heat the tomatoes in a pan with the herbs and pepper. Drain the pasta and return it to the hot saucepan. Toss with the butter or margarine. Pour in the tomatoes and season to taste with salt and pepper. Spoon the pasta on to a serving dish and sprinkle with Pecorino cheese.

Pasta Niçoise

SERVES 4

225 g/8 oz/2 cups pasta shapes
5 ml/1 tsp oil
2 garlic cloves, crushed
1 onion, chopped
4 tomatoes, skinned and chopped
15 ml/1 tbsp tomato purée (paste)
2.5 ml/½ tsp dried oregano
2.5 ml/½ tsp dried marjoram
Salt and freshly ground black pepper
A few black olives (optional)

Cook the pasta in boiling salted water until just tender. Drain. Meanwhile, heat the oil and fry (sauté) the garlic and onion for 5 minutes. Stir in the tomatoes, tomato purée and herbs. Add the drained pasta and warm through, stirring. Season with salt and pepper. Garnish with a few olives, if liked, before serving.

FARFALLE

Green Pepper Dhal

SERVES 4

225 g/8 oz/1½ cups split red lentils
600 ml/1 pt/2½ cups vegetable stock
1 small bay leaf
30 ml/2 tbsp sunflower oil
1 onion, chopped
1 green (bell) pepper, chopped
1 garlic clove, crushed
2.5 ml/½ tsp ground cumin
2.5 ml/½ tsp turmeric
2.5 ml/½ tsp chilli powder
*2.5 ml/½ tsp ground coriander
  (cilantro)*
Salt and freshly ground black pepper

Put the lentils in a saucepan with the stock and bay leaf. Bring to the boil, reduce the heat and simmer for 20 minutes until almost tender and most of the liquid has been absorbed. Meanwhile, heat the oil in a separate pan. Add the onion, pepper and garlic and fry (sauté) for 5 minutes until golden and tender. Stir in the spices and fry for a further minute. Add to the cooked lentils and cook for a further 5 minutes, stirring. Season to taste.

Mixed Vegetable Dhal

SERVES 4–6

Prepare as for Green Pepper Dhal but add 1 small cauliflower, cut into florets and blanched in boiling water for 3 minutes, 100 g/4 oz/1 cup peas and 4 tomatoes, cut into wedges, to the onion, pepper and garlic when frying (sautéeing).

Traditional Pease Pudding

SERVES 4

225 g/8 oz/2 cups yellow split peas,
*   soaked for 30 minutes and drained*
50 g/2 oz/¼ cup butter or margarine
2 onions, very finely chopped
1 egg, beaten
Salt and freshly ground white pepper
Pinch of ground mace

Put the peas in a saucepan and cover with cold water. Bring to the boil and simmer until really tender. Drain. Meanwhile, melt the butter or margarine in a flameproof casserole (Dutch oven). Add the onions and fry (sauté), stirring, for 3 minutes until soft but not brown. Remove from the heat and stir in the peas and beaten egg. Season with salt and pepper and the mace and stir well. Press down flat. Cover and bake in a preheated oven for about 30 minutes at 180°C/350°F/gas mark 4 until set. Serve cut into wedges.

Parsley Dumplings

SERVES 4

225 g/8 oz/2 cups self-raising (self-
*   rising) wholemeal flour*
100 g/4 oz/1 cup shredded vegetarian
*   suet*
30 ml/2 tbsp chopped parsley
Good pinch of grated nutmeg
White pepper
2 eggs, beaten
Milk, if needed

Put a large pan of water on to boil. Mix all the dumpling ingredients thoroughly, adding the eggs last to bind the mixture. If necessary add a little milk to make a firm dough. On a floured surface, pat the dough into a block 2.5 cm/1 in thick and cut it into about 30 cubes (this is quicker than rolling it into balls). Drop the cubes, a few at a time, into the boiling water and cook for 5 minutes or until they rise and dance on the surface and are tender and swollen. Remove with a slotted spoon at once, to make room for more cubes, and drain on a tilted plate.

Couscous

175 g/6 oz/1 cup couscous
15 ml/1 tbsp oil
1 red or green (bell) pepper, diced
1 onion, chopped
50 g/2 oz/⅓ cup sultanas (golden raisins)
5 ml/1 tsp lemon juice
Pinch of ground ginger
A dash of soy sauce
Salt and freshly ground black pepper

Put the couscous into a sieve (strainer) and place over a pan of water, making sure the couscous does not touch the water. Bring the water to the boil, then cover and simmer for 20 minutes to steam the couscous until tender. Heat the oil and fry (sauté) the pepper and onion until tender. Add the couscous, sultanas and seasonings and simmer, stirring, for 2 minutes to blend in the flavours. Serve with spiced dishes.

Traditional Polenta

450 ml/¾ pt/2 cups milk
100 g/4 oz/1 cup polenta
50 g/2 oz/¼ cup unsalted (sweet) butter
3 eggs, separated
Salt and freshly ground black pepper
Finely grated Pecorino cheese (optional)

Bring the milk to the boil in a saucepan. Stir in the polenta and cook, stirring, until thickened. Stir in half the butter, then remove from the heat and leave to cool slightly. Beat in the egg yolks and a little salt and pepper. Whisk the egg whites until stiff and fold in with a metal spoon. Turn into a shallow, greased 1.5 litre/2½ pt/ 6 cup ovenproof dish and level the surface. Bake in a preheated oven at 180°C/350°F/gas mark 4 for about 40 minutes until firm and golden. Dot with the remaining butter and sprinkle with a little cheese, if liked. Serve cut into pieces.

Quick Polenta

300 ml /½ pt/1¼ cups warm water
100 g/4 oz/1 cup fine cornmeal
1.5 ml/¼ tsp salt
750 ml/1¼ pt/3 cups hot vegetable
  stock
10 ml/2 tsp olive oil

Blend together until quite smooth the warm water, cornmeal and salt. Bring the hot stock and oil to the boil in a large saucepan. Add the cornmeal mixture slowly, stirring constantly to prevent lumps forming. Boil for 2 minutes, still stirring. Reduce the heat, cover the pan and cook very slowly for 15–20 minutes until the water is all absorbed and no gritty taste remains. Turn into a warmed dish.

Spiced Bulgar and Onions

225 g/8 oz onions, finely chopped
1.5 ml/¼ tsp dried minced (ground)
  garlic
15 ml/1 tbsp oil
75 g/3 oz/½ cup bulgar wheat
1.5 ml/¼ tsp ground coriander
  (cilantro)
1.5 ml/¼ tsp ground cinnamon
450 ml/¾ pt/2 cups vegetable stock
Salt and freshly ground black pepper

Fry (sauté) the onions and garlic in the oil in a saucepan until soft. Remove from the heat. Mix in all the remaining ingredients. Cover the pan and cook gently for 20 minutes or until the stock is all absorbed and the bulgar is soft.

Side-dish Dhal

175 g/6 oz/1 cup red lentils
1 onion, chopped
2 garlic cloves, crushed
15 ml/1 tbsp ground turmeric
15 ml/1 tbsp ground cumin
15 ml/1 tbsp ground coriander
  (cilantro)
10 ml/2 tsp paprika
600 ml/1 pt/2½ cups vegetable stock

Put all the ingredients into a saucepan and bring to the boil. Skim the surface, then simmer for 20–30 minutes until very mushy, stirring frequently to stop it sticking to the bottom of the pan. Add a little more water while cooking if the lentils become too dry.

Quick Vegetable Rice

175 g/6 oz/¾ cup long-grain rice
600 ml/1 pt/2½ cups vegetable stock
75 g/3 oz/¾ cup frozen mixed
  vegetables, thawed

Cook the rice in the stock for 10–15 minutes until almost tender. Add the vegetables and cook for a further 5 minutes. Drain if necessary.

176

Spicy Fried Rice

25 g/1 oz/2 tbsp butter or margarine
1 onion, finely chopped
5 ml/1 tsp ground turmeric
5 ml/1 tsp ground cumin
5 ml/1 tsp ground coriander
  (cilantro)
175 g/6 oz/1½ cups cooked long-grain
  rice

Melt the butter or margarine and fry (sauté) the onion until soft. Add the spices and stir-fry for 2 minutes without allowing the spices to burn. Stir in the rice and stir-fry for 5 minutes until hot.

Lemon Rice

SERVES 4

350 g/12 oz/1½ cups basmati or other
  long-grain rice
750 ml/1¼ pts/3 cups water
1 garlic clove, crushed
10 ml/2 tsp lemon grass or grated
  lemon rind
10 ml/2 tsp ground turmeric
50 g/2 oz creamed coconut, crumbled
Salt and freshly ground black pepper

If you are using basmati rice, soak it in boiling water for 10 minutes, then rinse in cold water several times to remove the starch. Place the rice, water, garlic, lemon grass or lemon rind and turmeric in a saucepan, bring to the boil, reduce the heat, cover and cook very gently for 20 minutes or until just tender and all the liquid has been absorbed. Stir in the coconut and season with salt and pepper. Serve with spicy dishes such as curries or chilli.

Fried Onion Rings

SERVES 4

2 eggs
250 ml/8 fl oz/1 cup milk
3 onions, thickly sliced and separated
  into rings
Wholemeal flour
Celery salt
Freshly ground black pepper
Oil, for shallow-frying

Beat the eggs and milk together in a shallow dish. Add the onion rings and toss well to coat completely. Put about 45 ml/3 tbsp flour in a plastic bag with a little celery salt and pepper. Add a handful of well-drained onion rings and shake until well coated. Shallow-fry in hot oil until golden. Drain on kitchen paper. Keep warm while preparing and cooking the remaining onions in the same way.

Baked Artichoke Cream

SERVES 4

450 g/1 lb Jerusalem artichokes,
  scraped and sliced
Salt and freshly ground black pepper
Good pinch of grated nutmeg
300 ml/½ pt/1¼ cups single (light)
  cream

Cook the artichokes in boiling, salted water for 15 minutes. Drain and arrange in a shallow ovenproof dish. Sprinkle with pepper and nutmeg. Pour the cream over and bake in a preheated oven at 190°C/375°F/gas mark 5 for about 45 minutes until golden on the top.

Baked Parsnip Cream

Prepare as for Baked Artichoke Cream but substitute parsnips for the artichokes.

Scalloped Artichoke Cheese

450 g/1 lb Jerusalem artichokes,
scraped and sliced
50 g/2 oz/¼ cup butter or margarine
300 ml/½ pt/1¼ cups milk
40 g/¾ oz/3 tbsp plain (all-purpose)
flour
Salt and freshly ground black pepper
2.5 ml/½ tsp dried mixed herbs
50 g/2 oz/½ cup Cheddar cheese,
grated
50 g/2 oz/1 cup breadcrumbs

Boil the artichokes in lightly salted water for 15 minutes. Drain. Meanwhile, grease a shallow ovenproof dish with 15 g/½ oz/1 tbsp of the butter. Whisk the milk and flour together in a saucepan. Add the remaining butter and bring to the boil, whisking all the time. Stir in a little salt and pepper and the herbs and cook for 2 minutes, stirring with the whisk. Turn the cooked artichokes into the prepared dish. Pour the sauce over. Mix the cheese and breadcrumbs together and sprinkle over. Bake in a preheated oven at 190°C/375°F/gas mark 5 for about 30 minutes or until golden on the top.

Fragrant Okra and Sweetcorn

40 g/1½ oz/3 tbsp butter
350 g/12 oz okra (ladies' fingers)
100 g/4 oz baby sweetcorn (corn)
cobs
1 garlic clove, crushed
Grated rind of 1 lemon
Grated rind of 1 lime
25 g/1 oz/¼ cup flaked coconut

Melt the butter and add the remaining ingredients except the coconut. Fry (sauté), stirring occasionally, for 8–10 minutes until the vegetables are just cooked. Meanwhile, dry-fry the coconut in a frying pan (skillet) until lightly browned. Turn the vegetables into a serving dish and sprinkle with the toasted coconut before serving.

Fragrant Marrow

Prepare as for Fragrant Okra and Sweetcorn but substitute peeled and diced marrow (squash) for the okra and toasted almonds for the coconut.

Parsnip Bites

450 g/1 lb parsnips, sliced
25 g/1 oz/2 tbsp butter or margarine
15 ml/1 tbsp milk
Salt and freshly ground black pepper
2 eggs, beaten
85 g/3½ oz/1 packet parsley and
thyme stuffing mix
Oil, for deep-frying

Cook the parsnips in boiling, salted water until tender. Drain and return to the saucepan. Mash thoroughly over a gentle heat with the butter or margarine and milk. Season to taste. Remove from the heat and beat in one of the eggs. Leave to cool. Shape into small balls. Roll in the remaining beaten egg, then in the stuffing mix. Deep-fry in hot oil until crisp and golden. Drain on kitchen paper before serving.

Parsnip and Walnut Bites

Prepare as for Parsnip Bites but add 50 g/2 oz/½ cup chopped walnut halves to the parsnips and a handful of crushed cornflakes to the stuffing mix.

Turnips with Piquant Tarragon Sauce

SERVES 4

450 g/1 lb turnips, quartered
50 g/2 oz/¼ cup butter or margarine
15 ml/1 tbsp wholegrain mustard
150 ml/¼ pt/⅔ cup double (heavy)
cream
Salt and freshly ground black pepper
15 ml/1 tbsp chopped tarragon

Cook the turnips in boiling, salted water until tender. Drain. Melt the butter in the same saucepan, stir in the mustard, cream, a little salt and pepper and the tarragon. Return the turnips to the pan and bring to the boil, stirring. Turn into a warm dish and serve.

Autumn Garden Delight

SERVES 4

450 ml/¾ pt/2 cups vegetable stock
4 unripe pears, sliced
1 lemon slice
225 g/8 oz runner beans, sliced
15 ml/1 tbsp white wine vinegar
30 ml/2 tbsp light brown sugar
Sage sprig
Salt and freshly ground black pepper

Put the stock in a saucepan. Add the pears and lemon slice and bring to the boil. Simmer for 10 minutes, then discard the lemon. Add the beans and cook for 10 minutes until just tender. Add the remaining ingredients, seasoning with a little salt and pepper. Cook until the liquid has evaporated. Discard the sage and serve straight away.

Broad Beans with Walnut Sauce

SERVES 4

450 g/1 lb/4 cups fresh shelled or
frozen broad (lima) beans
15 g/½ oz/1 tbsp butter or margarine
15 g/½ oz/2 tbsp wholemeal flour
300 ml/½ pt/1¼ cups vegetable stock
Salt and freshly ground black pepper
50 g/2 oz/½ cup walnuts, chopped

Cook the broad beans in plenty of boiling water until just tender. Drain. Melt the butter or margarine in a pan, add the flour and cook for 1 minute. Gradually blend in the stock, bring to the boil and cook for 2 minutes, stirring. Add salt and pepper to taste and the walnuts and pour over the beans.

Runner Beans with Pecan Sauce

SERVES 4

Prepare as for Broad Beans with Walnut Sauce but substitute sliced runner beans for the broad (lima) beans and chopped pecans for the walnuts.

Runner Beans with Almond Butter

SERVES 4

350 g/12 oz runner beans, sliced
Salt and freshly ground black pepper
50 g/2 oz/¼ cup unsalted (sweet)
  butter
50 g/2 oz/⅓ cup flaked almonds
15 ml/1 tbsp chopped parsley

Cook the beans in boiling, salted water until tender. Drain and turn into a warm serving dish. Meanwhile, melt the butter in a pan. Add the almonds and fry (sauté) until golden. Stir in the parsley and a good grinding of pepper. Pour over the beans and serve straight away.

Runner Beans with Cashew Butter

SERVES 4–6

Prepare as for Runner Beans with Almond Butter but substitute shelled unsalted cashew nuts for the almonds and coriander (cilantro) for the parsley.

Sauced Green Beans and Onions

SERVES 4

450 g/1 lb frozen sliced green beans
Salt and freshly ground black pepper
1 large onion, thinly sliced
45 ml/3 tbsp oil
25 g/1 oz/2 tbsp butter or margarine
30 ml/2 tbsp wholemeal flour
5 ml/1 tsp clear honey
120 ml/4 fl oz/½ cup milk
300 ml/½ pt/1¼ cups plain yoghurt

Cook the beans according to the packet directions. When ready, drain and season well. Spread them evenly in a shallow heatproof serving dish; they should fill about half the depth of the dish. Cover the dish and keep warm. Put the onion in a saucepan with 30 ml/2 tbsp of the oil. Stir-fry for 3–4 minutes until the onion softens and starts to colour. Spread on the beans, reserving any oil in the pan. Cover again, and keep warm. For the sauce, add the remaining oil and all the butter or margarine to the saucepan. Melt over a low heat, then add in turn slowly, the flour, honey and milk, stirring each in thoroughly. Continue stirring until the sauce thickens, then stir in the yoghurt and take the pan off the heat. Season lightly and spoon the sauce over the vegetables. Serve at once.

Greek-style Sauced Green Beans

SERVES 4

Prepare as for Sauced Green Beans and Onions but add a thinly sliced aubergine (eggplant) to the onion when frying (sautéeing) (you may need a little more oil). Top the sauce with 50 g/2 oz/ ½ cup each of grated Cheddar cheese and crumbled Feta cheese. Grill (broil) until the cheese melts and bubbles.

Baked Spiced Carrots

SERVES 4

750 g/1½ lbs carrots, sliced
25 g/1 oz/2 tbsp butter or margarine
Grated rind and juice of 1 orange
Pinch of ground ginger
Pinch of grated nutmeg
Salt and freshly ground black pepper
15 ml/1 tbsp chopped parsley

Put all the ingredients except the parsley in an ovenproof dish. Cover and bake in a preheated oven at 190°C/ 375°F/gas mark 5 for 45 minutes or until just tender. Sprinkle with chopped parsley before serving.

Braised Celery with Walnuts

SERVES 4

1 large celery head
1 small onion, finely chopped
15 g/½ oz/1 tbsp butter or margarine
300 ml/½ pt/1¼ cups vegetable stock
1 bouquet garni sachet
Salt and freshly ground black pepper
50 g/2 oz/½ cup walnut halves
Chopped parsley

Cut the leafy ends and the stump off the celery (reserve for soup). Cut the head into quarters lengthwise. Boil in water for about 20 minutes to soften. Drain. In a flameproof casserole (Dutch oven), fry (sauté) the onion in the butter for 2 minutes, stirring. Add the celery and the remaining ingredients except the parsley. Bring to the boil, cover and simmer for about 45 minutes until the celery is just tender and most of the stock has evaporated. Discard the bouquet garni sachet, sprinkle with parsley and serve straight from the casserole.

Celery and Cabbage Casserole

100 g/4 oz/½ cup butter or margarine
1 small onion, chopped
1 small head celery, sliced
½ small white cabbage, shredded
25 g/1 oz/¼ cup wholemeal flour
300 ml/½ pt/1¼ cups milk
Salt and freshly ground black pepper
25 g/1 oz/½ cup breadcrumbs
25 g/1 oz/¼ cup sunflower seeds or
  chopped peanuts

Melt half the butter or margarine in a pan and fry (sauté) the onion for 3 minutes, stirring. Add the celery and cook for a further 2 minutes. Add the cabbage, cover and continue cooking gently for 5 minutes, stirring occasionally to prevent sticking. Drain, reserving any juice and turn into an ovenproof dish. To make the white sauce, melt 25 g/1 oz/2 tbsp of the remaining butter or margarine in a pan. Stir in the flour and cook for 1 minute. Gradually stir in the milk and reserved cabbage juice, bring to the boil and cook for 2 minutes, stirring, until thickened. Season to taste and pour the sauce over the vegetables. Sprinkle with breadcrumbs and sunflower seeds or peanuts. Dot with the remaining butter or margarine and cook in a preheated oven at 180°C/350°F/gas mark 4 for 20 minutes.

Short-cooked Celery and Carrots

1 vegetable stock cube
150 ml/¼ pt/⅔ cup boiling water
30 ml/2 tbsp dried sliced onions
225 g/8 oz young celery sticks, sliced
3 carrots, sliced
15 g/½ oz/1 tbsp butter or margarine
30 ml/2 tbsp oil
2.5 ml/½ tsp dried oregano
150 ml/¼ pt/⅔ cup plain yoghurt
  (optional)

Crumble the stock cube into the water in a jug. Add the dried sliced onions. Fry (sauté) the celery and carrots for 2 minutes in the butter or margarine and oil. Add the jug of onion stock. Add the oregano. Part-cover the pan, and cook gently for 8 minutes. The celery should be almost tender. Uncover, and cook for 3–4 minutes longer, until the vegetables are tender and the liquid is almost evaporated. Stir in the yoghurt if you using and reheat, but do not boil.

Carrot and Swede Cream

450 g/1 lb mixed carrots and swede
(rutabaga), diced
100 g/4 oz/½ cup quark
15 g/½ oz/1 tbsp butter or margarine
Salt and freshly ground black pepper
Toasted sesame seeds

Boil the vegetables in lightly salted water until just tender. Drain and put with the remaining ingredients, except the sesame seeds, into a food processor or blender. Process for 2 minutes. Reheat and sprinkle with toasted sesame seeds before serving.

Carrot and Parsnip Cream

Prepare as for Carrot and Swede Cream but substitute parsnips for the swede and garnish with caraway seeds instead of toasted sesame seeds.

Herby Glazed Carrots with Cucumber

1 large cucumber, peeled and diced
225 g/8 oz carrots, sliced
15 g/½ oz/1 tbsp butter or margarine
5 ml/1 tsp granulated sugar
Salt and freshly ground black pepper
15 ml/1 tbsp chopped parsley
15 ml/1 tbsp snipped chives

Plunge the cucumber into boiling water. Drain, rinse with cold water and drain again. Put the carrots in a pan with the butter. Cook, stirring, for 1 minute. Add just enough water to cover the carrots. Stir in the sugar and a little salt and pepper. Cover and cook for 10 minutes until tender. Remove the lid, add the cucumber and boil rapidly until all the water has evaporated. Stir in the herbs and serve straight away.

Cheese and Mushroom Fritters

5 ml/1 tsp olive oil
50 g/2 oz mushrooms, sliced
75 g/3 oz/¾ cup Cheddar cheese,
grated
150 ml/¼ pt/⅔ cup Basic Pancake
Mix (see page 343)
Oil, for deep-frying
Salad

Heat the olive oil and fry (sauté) the mushrooms for 2 minutes. Add the mushrooms and cheese to the batter mix. Heat the oil for deep-frying and drop spoonfuls of the mixture separately into the oil to form fritters. Cook in batches if necessary. Fry until golden. Drain well before serving with salad.

Honey and Walnut Glazed Carrots

50 g/2 oz/¼ cup butter or margarine
750 g/1½ lb carrots, quartered
15 ml/1 tbsp clear honey
2.5 ml/½ tsp salt
450 ml/¾ pt/2 cups vegetable stock
50 g/2 oz/½ cup walnut halves,
   roughly chopped

Melt the butter or margarine in a saucepan. Add the carrots, honey and salt. Add just enough stock to part-cover the carrots. Bring to the boil and cook for 15 minutes, stirring occasionally, until the carrots are cooked and the liquid has evaporated. Add the walnuts, toss gently and serve.

Sweet and Sour Carrots and Corn

350 g/12 oz baby carrots
100 g/4 oz baby sweetcorn (corn)
   cobs
45 ml/3 tbsp red wine vinegar
10 ml/2 tsp light brown sugar
25 g/1 oz/2 tbsp butter or margarine
Snipped chives

Put the carrots in a pan with just enough cold water to cover. Bring to the boil and cook for 10 minutes. Add the corn and cook for a further 5 minutes until both vegetables are just tender. Add the remaining ingredients except the chives and boil rapidly until the liquid has evaporated. Stir well and serve garnished with snipped chives.

Spring Peas

1 bunch of spring onions (scallions),
   chopped
25 g/1 oz/2 tbsp butter or margarine
450 g/1 lb/4 cups frozen peas
Salt and freshly ground black pepper

Fry (sauté) the onions in the butter or margarine for 2 minutes, stirring. Add the peas and toss well. Sprinkle with a little salt and pepper. Cover tightly and cook over a gentle heat for 10 minutes, stirring occasionally until the peas are tender and bathed in delicious juices.

Braised Leeks

4 leeks, sliced
40 g/1½ oz/3 tbsp butter or margarine
Good pinch of ground coriander
   (cilantro)
Salt and freshly ground black pepper

Cook the leeks in the butter or margarine in a saucepan over a moderate heat for 3 minutes. Add enough water to part-cover the leeks. Bring to the boil, reduce the heat and cook gently for 4–5 minutes until the leeks are tender. Stir two or three times while cooking. Drain the leeks (keep the cooking liquid for soup), season with coriander and a little salt and pepper and turn into a warmed dish.

Hungarian Baby Beets

SERVES 4

1 onion, thinly sliced
1 eating (dessert) apple, sliced
25 g/1 oz/2 tbsp butter
5 ml/1 tsp light brown sugar
15 ml/1 tbsp white wine vinegar
15 ml/1 tbsp sultanas (golden raisins)
12–16 cooked baby (red) beets
5 ml/1 tsp caraway seeds
Salt and freshly ground black pepper
A little plain yoghurt or soured (dairy sour) cream (optional)

Cook the onion and apple in the butter for 4 minutes, stirring gently. Add the remaining ingredients except the yoghurt and cream and cook gently, stirring occasionally, for 5 minutes. Serve topped with plain yoghurt or soured cream, if liked.

Lemon Cream Chicory

Serves 4

8 chicory heads (Belgian endive)
50 g/2 oz/¼ cup butter or margarine
5 ml/1 tsp caster (superfine) sugar
Grated rind and juice of 1 small lemon
120 ml/4 fl oz/½ cup double (heavy) cream
Salt and freshly ground black pepper
15 ml/1 tbsp chopped parsley

Cut a cone-shaped core out of the base of each head of chicory to remove the bitter part. Melt the butter in a large heavy-based frying pan (skillet). Add the chicory and cook, turning for 1 minute. Sprinkle with the sugar and add the lemon rind and juice. Cover with a lid or foil and cook very gently for about 40 minutes until tender. Transfer the chicory with a draining spoon to a warmed serving dish. Add the cream to the pan juices and boil rapidly for 3–4 minutes until thick and slightly reduced. Season to taste. Spoon over the chicory and sprinkle with parsley.

Creamy Lettuce and Almonds

SERVES 4

1 bunch of spring onions (scallions),
  finely chopped
25 g/1 oz/2 tbsp butter or margarine
1 round lettuce, quartered
150 ml/¼ pt/⅔ cup vegetable stock
1.5 ml/¼ tsp dried mixed herbs
Salt and freshly ground black pepper
10 ml/2 tsp cornflour (cornstarch)
15 ml/1 tbsp water
150 ml/¼ pt/⅔ cup single (light)
  cream
15 ml/1 tbsp toasted, flaked almonds

Fry (sauté) the spring onions in the butter for 2 minutes, stirring. Add the lettuce quarters and turn over in the mixture. Pour on the stock, add the herbs and a little seasoning. Bring to the boil, reduce the heat, cover and simmer very gently for 4 minutes. Transfer the lettuce to a warmed serving dish. Blend the cornflour with the water and stir into the cooking juices. Cook, stirring, for 2 minutes. Blend in the cream and heat through. Taste and re-season if necessary. Pour the sauce over the lettuce and sprinkle with almonds before serving.

Braised Lettuce with Oyster Mushrooms

SERVES 4

1 small onion, finely chopped
100 g/4 oz oyster mushrooms, sliced
15 g/½ oz/1 tbsp butter or margarine
1 iceberg lettuce, quartered
300 ml/½ pt/1¼ cups vegetable stock
Salt and freshly ground black pepper
15 ml/1 tbsp cornflour (cornstarch)
30 ml/2 tbsp water
15 ml/1 tbsp snipped chives

Fry (sauté) the onion and mushrooms in the butter or margarine for 2 minutes, stirring. Cover, reduce the heat and cook gently for 5 minutes until the mushrooms are tender. Add the lettuce quarters and stock and season lightly. Re-cover and cook gently for 8 minutes or until the lettuce is just tender but holds its shape. Transfer the lettuce to a warmed serving dish. Keep warm. Blend the cornflour with the water and stir into the cooking liquid. Bring to the boil and cook, stirring, for 2 minutes until thickened and clear. Taste and re-season if necessary. Spoon over the lettuce, sprinkle with chives and serve.

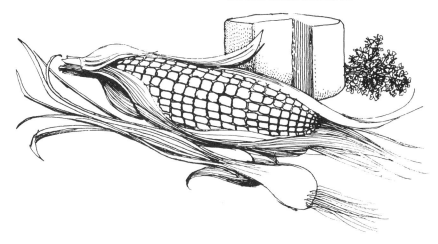

Creamy Cucumber with Dill

1 large cucumber, peeled and thickly
* sliced*
Salt and freshly ground black pepper
300 ml/½ pt/1¼ cups vegetable stock
5 ml/1 tsp dried dill (dill weed)
20 ml/4 tsp cornflour (cornstarch)
150 ml/¼ pt/⅔ cup single (light) cream
5 ml/1 tsp lemon juice

Put the cucumber in a colander. Sprinkle with salt and leave to stand for 15 minutes. Rinse well, then drain. Place in a saucepan with the stock and dill. Bring to the boil and simmer gently for 10 minutes. Remove the cucumber with a draining spoon and place in a flameproof dish. Blend the cornflour with a little of the cream and stir into the pan. Add the remaining cream and cook for 2 minutes, stirring, until thickened. Add the lemon juice and salt and pepper to taste. Pour over the cucumber and glaze under a hot grill (broiler).

Limey Marrow

1 young marrow (squash), peeled
* and diced*
25 g/1 oz/2 tbsp butter or margarine
30 ml/2 tbsp clear honey
Grated rind and juice of 2 limes
5 ml/1 tsp ground cinnamon
2.5 ml/½ tsp grated fresh root ginger
Salt and freshly ground black pepper

Put the marrow in an ovenproof dish. Melt together the remaining ingredients except the salt and pepper in a saucepan. Pour over the marrow and toss gently. Sprinkle with a little salt and pepper and cover with foil. Bake in a preheated oven at 180°C/350°F/gas mark 4 for about 40 minutes or until tender, stirring twice during cooking.

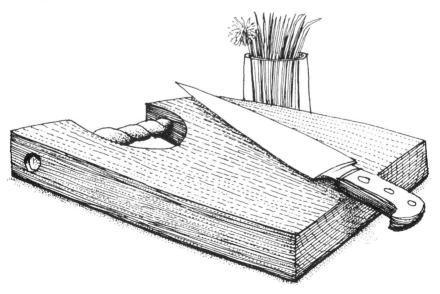

Courgettes with Tarragon

SERVES 4

750 g/1½ lb courgettes (zucchini),
sliced or quartered lengthways
25 g/1 oz/2 tbsp butter or margarine
Salt and freshly ground black pepper
15 ml/1 tbsp chopped tarragon

Put the courgettes into a large pan of boiling water and simmer for 4 minutes. Drain. Add the remaining ingredients, stir well and heat through thoroughly. Serve immediately.

Creamy Lollo Rosso

SERVES 4

1 red onion, finely chopped
1 Lollo Rosso lettuce, quartered
25 g/1 oz/2 tbsp butter or margarine
120 ml/4 fl oz/½ cup vegetable stock
30 ml/2 tbsp red wine
2.5 ml/½ tsp light brown sugar
Freshly ground black pepper
10 ml/2 tsp cornflour (cornstarch)
30 ml/2 tbsp water
150 ml/¼ pt/⅔ cup crème fraîche
15 ml/1 tbsp snipped chives
Paprika

Fry (sauté) the onion and lettuce in the melted butter or margarine for 2 minutes, turning the lettuce over after 1 minute. Add the stock, wine, sugar and a little pepper, cover and simmer for 5 minutes. Lift the lettuce out of the pan and place in a warm dish. Keep warm. Blend the cornflour with the water. Stir into the pan and bring to the boil, stirring until thickened. Simmer for 2 minutes. Stir in the crème fraîche and chives and heat through gently. Pour over the lettuce and dust with paprika before serving.

Corn on the Cob with Butter Sauce

SERVES 4

4 corn cobs
Salt and freshly ground black pepper
30 ml/2 tbsp lemon juice
75 g/3 oz/⅓ cup butter or margarine
25 g/1 oz/¼ cup plain (all-purpose)
flour
300 ml/½ pt/1¼ cups milk
1 egg yolk
Pinch of dried basil

Place the corn in a saucepan and cover with water. Add a pinch of salt and the lemon juice, bring to the boil, then simmer for about 20 minutes until tender. Drain and remove the husks and silks. Meanwhile, melt 25 g/1 oz/2 tbsp of the butter or margarine in a small pan. Stir in the flour, then gradually whisk in the milk. Bring to the boil, whisking continuously, then lower the heat. Add the egg yolk, basil, salt and pepper and the remaining butter or margarine and stir until melted. Pour the sauce over the corn.

Baby Corn in Butter Sauce

SERVES 4

Prepare as for Corn on the Cob with Butter Sauce but substitute 225 g/8 oz baby corn cobs for the large ones and cook for just 3 minutes before adding to the sauce. Use dried tarragon instead of basil to flavour the sauce if liked.

Mushroom Bhaji

175 g/6 oz mushrooms, sliced
1 green (bell) pepper, sliced
1 onion, sliced
2.5 ml/½ tsp salt
10 ml/2 tsp curry powder
5 ml/1 tsp ground turmeric
1.5 ml/¼ tsp chilli powder
30 ml/2 tbsp oil
25 g/1 oz creamed coconut
Plain boiled rice
Curried Cabbage (see page 192)

Mix together the mushrooms, pepper, onion, salt, curry powder, turmeric and chilli powder. Stir well, then leave to marinate for 10 minutes. Heat the oil and fry (sauté) the vegetables and spices for 10 minutes over a low heat, adding a little water and the coconut towards the end of the cooking time. Serve with rice and Curried Cabbage.

Spicy Savoy with Apple

15 ml/1 tbsp sunflower oil
1 onion, chopped
1 Savoy cabbage, shredded
2 eating (dessert) apples, sliced
15 ml/1 tbsp Worcestershire sauce
15 ml/1 tbsp tomato purée (paste)
150 ml/¼ pt/⅔ cup vegetable stock
5 ml/1 tsp ground allspice
2 whole cloves
Salt and freshly ground black pepper

Heat the oil in a large pan. Add the onion and fry (sauté) for 2 minutes. Add the cabbage and apple and toss over a gentle heat until the cabbage begins to soften. Blend the Worcestershire sauce with the tomato purée and stock. Pour over the cabbage and add the spice, cloves and a little salt and pepper. Bring to the boil. Cover with a tight-fitting lid, reduce the heat and simmer for 12–15 minutes or until tender, tossing occasionally. Remove the cloves before serving.

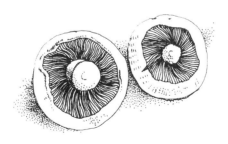

Red Cabbage with Apple and Onion Bake

450 g/1 lb red cabbage, chopped
1 onion, chopped
1 eating (dessert) apple, chopped
Salt and freshly ground black pepper
30 ml/2 tbsp vinegar
25 g/1 oz/2 tbsp butter or margarine
50 g/2 oz/⅓ cup sultanas (golden raisins)

Mix together all the ingredients and place in a large casserole (Dutch oven). Bake in a preheated oven at 160°C/325°F/gas mark 3 for up to 2 hours. Alternatively, cook very gently on top of the stove, stirring occasionally, for about 45 minutes. Add a little water if necessary.

Palermo Cabbage

450 g/1 lb firm-hearted green cabbage, shredded
40 g/1½ oz/3 tbsp butter or margarine
15 ml/1 tbsp clear honey
15 ml/1 tbsp lemon juice
Salt and freshly ground black pepper
60 ml/4 tbsp water
275 g/10 oz tomatoes, quartered

Toss the cabbage in the butter or margarine over a moderate heat for 1 minute. Stir in the honey, lemon juice, a little seasoning and the water. Reduce the heat, cover the pan and simmer for 5 minutes. Add the tomatoes and cook for a further 5 minutes. Stir once or twice during cooking. Serve with any juices in the pan.

Creamed Sprouts with Paprika

450 g/1 lb Brussels sprouts, trimmed and bases slit
150 ml/¼ pt/⅔ cup vegetable stock
10 ml/2 tsp paprika
5 ml/1 tsp tomato purée (paste)
Salt and freshly ground black pepper
25 g/1 oz/2 tbsp butter or margarine
150 ml/¼ pt/⅔ cup crème fraîche

Put all the ingredients, except the crème fraîche, into a pan. Bring to the boil, cover and cook for about 10 minutes, stirring occasionally until the sprouts are tender and the stock has evaporated. Add little more stock or water during cooking if necessary. Stir in the crème fraîche and serve.

Brussels Sprouts with Almonds

450 g/1 lb Brussels sprouts
30 ml/2 tbsp dried sliced onions
100 g/4 oz button mushrooms, sliced
100 g/4 oz cucumber, quartered and sliced
15 g/½ oz/1 tbsp butter or margarine
45 ml/3 tbsp flaked almonds
Lemon juice
Salt and freshly ground black pepper

Cook the sprouts and onions in boiling water for 4 minutes. Add the mushrooms and cucumber and cook for a further 4 minutes. While they cook, melt the fat over a low heat and stir in the almonds until one or two flakes begin to brown. Take the pan off the heat at once, and turn the almonds on to kitchen paper. Drain the vegetables when ready, turn them into a warmed serving dish and toss with a little lemon juice, salt and pepper. Add the almonds, toss again and serve.

Button Sprouts, Chestnuts and New Potatoes

SERVES 4

*225 g/8 oz small, even-sized Brussels
  sprouts, trimmed and bases slit*
30 ml/2 tbsp white vinegar
*225 g/8 oz baby new potatoes,
  scrubbed*
225 g/8 oz button (pearl) onions
100 g/4 oz/½ cup butter
225 g/8 oz small chestnuts, boiled
*Mustard, sesame or caraway seeds
  (optional)*
Salt and freshly ground black pepper
*50 g/2 oz/½ cup grated Pecorino
  cheese*

Wash the sprouts in cold water with
the vinegar. Boil in salted water for 8
minutes. Drain and rinse in very cold
water. Drain finally when they are cold.
Pat dry. Meanwhile, boil the potatoes for
15–18 minutes. Drain. Boil the onions for
4 minutes only. Drain. When ready to
serve, heat the butter in a large pan and
toss the sprouts, onions, potatoes and
chestnuts for 4 minutes. While tossing,
sprinkle with some flavouring seeds if you
wish. Season to taste. Serve on individual
plates and sprinkle with Pecorino cheese.

Broccoli and Button Mushrooms

SERVES 4

60 ml/4 tbsp sunflower oil
225 g/8 oz broccoli florets
12 button (pearl) onions, skinned
*227 g/8 oz/1 small can bamboo
  shoots, drained and cut into thin
  strips*
1 garlic clove, chopped
225 g/8 oz button mushrooms
150 g/5 oz/1¼ cups cashew nuts
*120 ml/4 fl oz/½ cup passata (sieved
  tomatoes)*
15 ml/1 tbsp soy sauce
*1 small piece of fresh root ginger,
  grated*
120 ml/4 fl oz/½ cup water
1 vegetable stock cube
Salt and freshly ground black pepper
2.5 ml/½ tsp sugar or honey
5 ml/1 tsp cornflour (cornstarch)

Heat the oil in a wok or large frying pan
(skillet). Quickly fry (sauté) the vegetables, except the mushrooms, for 3
minutes. Add the garlic, button mushrooms and cashew nuts and stir-fry for 30
seconds. Add the passata, soy sauce, ginger, 75 ml/5 tbsp water and the stock
cube. Boil for 1 minute. Season to taste
with salt, pepper and the sugar or honey.
Blend the cornflour and remaining water,
then add to the mixture, stirring, for a further 4 minutes. Serve hot.

Curried Cabbage

1 cabbage, chopped, thick stalk
  removed
50 g/2 oz/¼ cup butter or margarine
10 ml/2 tsp Chutney (see page 321)
  or use bought
5 ml/1 tsp mild curry powder
15 ml/1 tbsp lemon juice
Salt and freshly ground black pepper
Desiccated (shredded) coconut

Cook the cabbage in boiling, lightly salted water until just tender, but not soggy. Drain. Stir in the remaining ingredients except the coconut. Leave to stand for 5 minutes. Reheat, then turn into a serving dish and garnish with desiccated coconut.

Buttered Greens

450 g/1 lb small heads spring greens
  (spring cabbage)
25 g/1 oz/2 tbsp butter or margarine
30 ml/2 tbsp oil
A few grains each of salt, freshly
  ground black pepper, grated
  nutmeg and light brown sugar

Wash the greens thoroughly and trim off any stems. Bring 2.5 cm/1 in depth of water to the boil in a deep frying pan (skillet) which holds the heads side by side. Add the greens and half the butter or margarine. With two wooden spoons, turn the greens over in the water for 2–3 minutes until the leaves soften (wilt). Cover the pan with a lid, reduce the heat and simmer for 5–7 minutes until the heads are tender. Drain, then press out excess moisture by squeezing the heads in a cloth. Split them lengthways. Heat the oil, remaining fat and seasonings in the dried pan, return the greens and turn them over until well coated. Serve at once.

Photograph opposite: **Chinese Noodles and Lychees (page 142)**

192

Spinach Strata

*2 × 298 g/2 × 10½ oz packets frozen
  cut leaf spinach*
30 ml/2 tbsp dried sliced onions
6–8 slices wholemeal bread
Crunchy peanut butter
Salt and freshly ground black pepper
Grated nutmeg
15 ml/1 tbsp oil

Cook the spinach according to the packet directions but with 30 ml/ 2 tbsp water instead of any fat. While cooking, pour boiling water over the dried onions and leave to soak. Cut the crusts off the bread slices, make two slices into crumbs and reserve. Spread the rest with peanut butter. Use half of them, spread side up, to cover the base of an oiled, oven-to-table round or square baking dish, trimming them to fit. When the spinach is ready, drain it and the onions together. Season with salt, pepper and nutmeg. Spread half evenly in the dish. Cover with the remaining peanut-buttered bread slices, spread side up, then repeat the spinach layer. Melt 30 ml/ 2 tbsp peanut butter with the oil and mix with the breadcrumbs. Scatter them over the dish. Bake in a preheated oven at 190°C/375°F/gas mark 5 until piping hot and the top is golden.

Cheese and Spinach Strata

Prepare as for Spinach Strata, but use 75 g/3 oz/¾ cup grated Cheddar cheese instead of peanut butter. Sprinkle one third over each layer of bread slices and mix the remaining third with the crumbs.

Fruity Cabbage

15 ml/1 tbsp oil
1 cabbage, shredded
1 onion, chopped
1 garlic clove, crushed
1 cooking (tart) apple, chopped
10 ml/2 tsp lemon juice
Salt and freshly ground black pepper

Heat the oil and gently fry (sauté) the cabbage, onion and garlic for about 5 minutes until just soft. Add the apple, lemon juice, salt and pepper, cover and cook over a low heat for 10–15 minutes, stirring occasionally. Serve hot.

Photograph opposite: **Greek Cheese
and Spinach Pie (page 158)**

Fried Aubergines

2 aubergines (eggplants), sliced
Salt
25 g/1 oz/¼ cup plain (all-purpose) flour
1 garlic clove, crushed
Oil, for shallow-frying

Arrange the aubergines in a colander and sprinkle with salt. Leave to stand for 30 minutes. Rinse and dry on kitchen paper. Mix together the flour, a little salt and the garlic. Coat the aubergines in the seasoned flour. Heat the oil and fry (sauté) the aubergines for a few minutes until crisp and brown on both sides. Drain on kitchen paper and serve straight away.

Saucy Peas

175 g/6 oz/1½ cups cooked peas
300 ml/½ pt/1¼ cups Bechamel Sauce
*   (see page 311)*
5 ml/1 tsp sugar
Salt and freshly ground black pepper
5 ml/1 tsp chopped mint (optional)

Add the hot peas to the sauce and seasonings. Heat through. Serve with nut roast or similar dishes.

Broccoli in Tomato Sauce

30 ml/2 tbsp olive oil
1 onion, chopped
25 g/1 oz/¼ cup wholemeal flour
400 g/14 oz/1 large can chopped
*   tomatoes*
Salt and freshly ground black pepper
2.5 ml/½ tsp sugar
750 g/1½ lb broccoli, cut into florets
*   and cooked*
100 g/4 oz/1 cup Cheddar cheese,
*   grated*
A few toasted flaked almonds

Heat the oil and fry (sauté) the onion for 3 minutes until soft. Stir in the flour and cook for 1 minute. Add the tomatoes, salt, pepper and sugar and cover. Bring to the boil, reduce the heat and simmer for 5 minutes, stirring occasionally. Put the broccoli in a greased ovenproof dish, pour the tomato sauce over and sprinkle with grated cheese. Bake in a preheated oven at 190°C/ 375°F/gas mark 5 for 30 minutes or until the topping is golden and bubbling. Sprinkle with almonds and serve.

Peppers and Mushrooms in Tomato Sauce

Prepare as for Broccoli in Tomato Sauce but substitute 1 sliced red and 1 sliced green (bell) pepper and 225 g/8 oz button mushrooms, fried (sautéed) in a little butter or margarine until tender, for the broccoli.

Broccoli with Hazelnut Sauce

SERVES 4

450 g/1 lb broccoli, cut into florets
300 ml/½ pt/1¼ cups vegetable stock
100 g/4 oz/1 cup ground hazelnuts
Pinch of salt
A knob of butter or margarine
10 ml/2 tsp dry white vermouth
A few toasted chopped hazelnuts

Cook the broccoli in the stock until just tender. Drain, reserving the stock. Turn the broccoli into a warmed serving dish and keep warm. Mix the ground hazelnuts with the salt and dot with the fat. Mix in the vermouth and enough hot stock to make a thick sauce of the consistency you want – the hot liquid should melt the fat. Pour the sauce over the broccoli. Flash under a hot grill (broiler) to glaze. Sprinkle with a few toasted chopped hazelnuts before serving.

Cauliflower with Almond Sauce

SERVES 4

Prepare as for Broccoli with Hazelnut Sauce but substitute cauliflower florets for the broccoli and ground almonds for the hazelnuts. Sprinkle with a few toasted flaked almonds instead of chopped hazelnuts.

Polonaise-style Cauliflower

SERVES 4

1 small cauliflower
50 g/2 oz/¼ cup butter or margarine
1 garlic clove, crushed
50 g/2 oz/1 cup breadcrumbs
15 ml/1 tbsp snipped chives
15 ml/1 tbsp chopped parsley
2 hard-boiled (hard-cooked) eggs,
  finely chopped

Trim the cauliflower and cut a deep cross in the stump end. Boil in salted water for about 25 minutes or until just tender. Drain and transfer to a warmed serving dish. Meanwhile, melt the butter or margarine in a saucepan. Fry (sauté) the garlic for 30 seconds until lightly golden but not too brown. Stir in the breadcrumbs and fry until lightly golden. Stir in the remaining ingredients. Sprinkle over the cauliflower and serve.

Cauliflower with Black Bean Sauce

SERVES 4

1 small cauliflower, cut into florets
45 ml/3 tbsp sunflower oil
2 green chillies, seeded and chopped
½ bunch of spring onions (scallions), chopped
1 small red (bell) pepper, chopped
50 g/2 oz/½ cup cooked black beans, mashed
200 ml/7 fl oz/scant 1 cup vegetable stock
15 ml/1 tbsp soy sauce
15 ml/1 tbsp cornflour (cornstarch)

Cook the cauliflower in boiling, salted water until just tender. Drain and transfer to a serving dish. Meanwhile, heat the oil in a saucepan. Add the chillies, spring onions and pepper and fry (sauté) until tender. Stir in the beans and stock and simmer for 2 minutes. Blend the soy sauce and cornflour to a smooth paste. Stir into the sauce and cook, stirring, for 2 minutes until thickened and clear. Spoon over the cauliflower and serve straight away.

Cauliflower Cheese

SERVES 4

1 cauliflower, cut into florets
600 ml/1 pt/2½ cups Bechamel Sauce (see page 311)
Salt and freshly ground black pepper
175 g/6 oz/1½ cups Cheddar cheese, grated
25 g/1 oz/1 cup cornflakes, crushed

Cook the cauliflower in a pan of boiling salted water for 10 minutes, then drain. Make the Bechamel Sauce, season with salt and pepper and stir in the cauliflower. Stir in most of the cheese and pour into an ovenproof dish. Sprinkle with the remaining cheese and the crushed cornflakes. Bake in a preheated oven at 200°C/400°F/gas mark 6 for 20 minutes until cooked through and golden brown.

Blue Cauliflower Cheese

SERVES 4

Prepare as for Cauliflower Cheese but substitute crumbled blue cheese for the Cheddar and crushed bran flakes for the cornflakes.

Tandoori Cauliflower

1 small cauliflower, cut into florets
30 ml/2 tbsp Tandoori spice mix
15 ml/1 tbsp lemon juice
150 ml/¼ pt/⅔ cup plain yoghurt

Cook the cauliflower in boiling, lightly salted water for 5 minutes. Drain and arrange in an ovenproof dish. Mix together the remaining ingredients and pour over the cauliflower. Leave for 1 hour to marinate. Cook in a preheated oven at 200°C/400°F/gas mark 6 for 30 minutes until soft and slightly blackened. Serve with curried dishes.

Cauliflower Fritters

SERVES 4

1 small cauliflower, cut into florets
150 ml/¼ pt/⅔ cup Basic Pancake
  Mix (see page 343)
Oil, for deep-frying

Cook the cauliflower in boiling salted water for about 10 minutes until almost tender. Drain well and dry on kitchen paper. Dip the cauliflower into the batter. Heat the oil and deep-fry the cauliflower until crisp and golden. Drain well on kitchen paper before serving.

Spiced Broccoli Fritters

SERVES 4

Prepare as for Cauliflower Fritters but substitute broccoli florets for the cauliflower and dust with 15 ml/1 tbsp garam masala before coating in batter.

Potato Pudding

SERVES 4

900 g/2 lb potatoes, peeled and
  grated
1 egg, beaten
Salt and freshly ground black pepper

Mix the ingredients together and place in a greased ovenproof dish. Bake in a preheated oven at 180°C/350°F/gas mark 4 for about 1 hour until soft in the centre and crisp on top.

Potch

225 g/8 oz carrots, diced
1 small swede (rutabaga), diced
25 g/1 oz/2 tbsp butter or margarine
Salt and freshly ground black pepper

Cook the carrots and swede in boiling water for about 10 minutes until tender. Drain and mash with the butter or margarine. Season to taste and spoon the mixture into an ovenproof dish. Bake in a preheated oven at 200°C/400°F/gas mark 6 for 10 minutes until a crust forms on the top.

Parsnip Potch

Prepare as for Potch but substitute parsnips for the carrots and add a pinch of nutmeg when seasoning.

Everyday Hash Browns

45 ml/3 tbsp oil
1 onion, chopped
450 g/1 lb potatoes, finely diced
Salt and freshly ground black pepper
Fried eggs

Heat the oil and fry (sauté) the onion over a low heat for 5 minutes until soft. Transfer to a plate. Add the potatoes to the pan and fry for 10–15 minutes until golden on the outside and soft on the inside. Return the onions to the pan, stir and season well with salt and pepper. Cook until warmed through. Serve with fried eggs.

Rose-red Potatoes

45 ml/3 tbsp oil
450 g/1 lb thin-skinned potatoes,
*   scrubbed and cubed*
1 onion, chopped
225 g/8 oz/1 small can chopped
*   tomatoes*
5 ml/1 tsp dried savory or basil
2.5 ml/½ tsp Worcestershire sauce
60 ml/4 tbsp hot water
Salt and freshly ground black pepper

Heat the oil in a deep frying pan (skillet) with a lid. Add the potato cubes and onion and stir over a fairly high heat for 4 minutes until the potatoes begin to brown. Stir in the tomatoes with their juice. Add the savory or basil, Worcestershire sauce and hot water. Season to taste. Cover the pan, reduce the heat and cook gently for 10 minutes or until the potatoes are tender.

Stir-fried Potatoes and Peas with Sage

SERVES 4

30 ml/2 tbsp oil
450 g/1 lb small potatoes, scrubbed
  and sliced
2 shallots, sliced or 6 spring onions
  (scallions), bulbs only, sliced
7.5 ml/1½ tsp cornflour (cornstarch)
Pinch of sugar
250 ml/8 fl oz/1 cup vegetable stock
  or water
2 sage leaves, chopped
225 g/8 oz/2 cups frozen peas
2 tomatoes, sliced (optional)
2 lettuce leaves, shredded (optional)
Salt and freshly ground black pepper

Heat the oil in a frying pan (skillet) with a lid and stir-fry all the sliced vegetables gently for 5 minutes. Stir in the cornflour and sugar and cook for 1 minute. Add the stock or water, sage and peas, cover and cook gently for 10 minutes. Add the tomatoes and lettuce, if using, cover again and cook for 2–3 minutes. Season if necessary.

Bubble and Squeak

SERVES 4

450 g/1 lb/2 cups mashed potato
225 g/8 oz/2 cups cooked Brussels
  sprouts or cabbage, chopped
Salt and freshly ground black pepper
Butter or margarine, for shallow-
  frying

Mix together the potato and greens. Season generously with salt and pepper. Heat a little butter or margarine in a heavy-based frying pan (skillet). Add the vegetable mixture to the pan and press into a pancake shape. Cook until browned on the underside, then turn over and brown the other side or brown the top under the grill (broiler). Serve straight from the pan.

Multi Bubble and Squeak

SERVES 4

Prepare as for Bubble and Squeak, but substitute cooked mixed vegetables for the cabbage or sprouts.

Cheesy Mash

SERVES 4

450 g/1 lb potatoes, diced
30 ml/2 tbsp milk
25 g/1 oz/2 tbsp butter or margarine
Salt and freshly ground black pepper
50 g/2 oz/½ cup Cheddar cheese, grated

Cook the potatoes in boiling salted water until soft. Drain. Mash the potatoes with the remaining ingredients. Turn into a buttered flameproof dish and brown under a hot grill (broiler).

Cheese and Onion Mash

SERVES 4

Prepare as for Cheesy Mash but add 2 sliced onions, fried (sautéed) in a little butter or margarine until soft and golden, with the cheese.

Scalloped Potatoes

SERVES 4

450 g/1 lb potatoes, sliced
1 onion, sliced
100 g/4 oz/1 cup Emmental (Swiss)
  cheese, grated
Salt and freshly ground black pepper
1 egg
150 ml/¼ pt/⅔ cup milk

Grease a shallow ovenproof dish and layer the potatoes, onion and cheese in the dish, seasoning with salt and pepper as you go. Whisk together the egg and milk and pour over the vegetables. Bake in a preheated oven at 180°C/350°F/gas mark 4 for about 1½ hours until tender throughout and browned on top.

Garlicky Scalloped Potatoes

SERVES 4

Prepare as for Scalloped Potatoes but sprinkle 1–2 crushed garlic cloves between the layers.

Tomato Potato

SERVES 4

450 g/1 lb potatoes, cut into chunks
400 g/14 oz/1 large can chopped
  tomatoes
25 g/1 oz/½ cup breadcrumbs
50 g/2 oz/½ cup Cheddar cheese,
  grated

Cook the potatoes in boiling salted water for about 10 minutes until just soft. Drain and arrange in an ovenproof dish. Pour over the tomatoes and bake in a preheated oven at 180°C/350°F/gas mark 4 for 15 minutes. Mix together the breadcrumbs and cheese and sprinkle over the top. Return to the oven or place under a hot grill (broiler) for a few minutes until the cheese is browned and bubbling.

Pizza Potatoes

SERVES 4

Prepare as for Tomato Potato but add 20 g/2 oz/⅓ cup halved, stoned (pitted) black or green olives to the cooked potatoes in the dish and sprinkle 2.5 ml/½ tsp dried oregano over the tomatoes before baking.

Minty New Potatoes and Peas

15 ml/1 tbsp sunflower oil
350 g/12 oz whole small onions,
peeled
750 g/1½ lb new potatoes, scrubbed
350 g/12 oz/3 cups frozen peas
30 ml/2 tbsp plain (all-purpose) flour
600 ml/1 pt/2½ cups vegetable stock
45 ml/3 tbsp chopped mint
Salt and freshly ground black pepper

Heat the oil in a large pan, add the veg-etables and cook for 3 minutes, stir-ring. Sprinkle in the flour, then stir in the stock, mint, salt and pepper. Bring to the boil, then simmer for 20 minutes until the vegetables are tender.

Potato and Apple Delight

100 g/4 oz/½ cup butter
2 shallots, chopped
100 g/4 oz eating (dessert) apples,
cored and sliced into rings
450 g/1 lb small waxy potatoes, sliced
Salt and white pepper
Grated nutmeg
60 ml/4 tbsp clear honey, heated
100 g/4 oz/1 cup flaked almonds,
toasted
Icing (confectioners') sugar

Put 25 g/1 oz/2 tbsp of the butter in the base of four 250 ml/8 fl oz/1 cup pie dishes with 5 ml/1 tsp chopped shallots. Arrange the apple and potato slices in alternate rows. Season with salt, white pepper and nutmeg. Brush the top of each pie with hot honey. Ladle 90 ml/6 tbsp water on to each pie. Bake in a preheated oven at 200°C/400°F/gas mark 6 for 30 minutes. Brush with melted butter and honey from time to time to keep the tops golden. Sprinkle with toasted flaked almonds just before serving and dust the top with icing sugar. Serve with nut roasts or just with salad.

Baked Marrow and Potato Perfection

SERVES 4

1 marrow (squash)
225 g/8 oz waxy potatoes, sliced
50 g/2 oz/¼ cup butter
3 garlic cloves
150 ml/¼ pt/⅔ cup double (heavy)
  cream
Salt and white pepper
Grated nutmeg

Halve the marrow lengthways and cut in two again, making four portions. Scoop out the seeds with a spoon. Scrape the outer skin with a potato peeler. Part-cook for 3 minutes in boiling salted water. Remove, drain and pat dry. Place the marrow pieces in a buttered baking dish. Boil the potato slices for 4 minutes only, so that they retain their texture without breaking. Drain. In a small saucepan, heat the butter and fry (sauté) the garlic for 30 seconds. Pour the garlic butter into the cavity of each marrow case. Arrange the par-boiled potato on each marrow, overlapping the slices. Coat the potatoes with cream. Season with salt, pepper and grated nutmeg. Bake in a preheated oven at 200ºC/400ºF/gas mark 6 for no more than 20 minutes until browned.

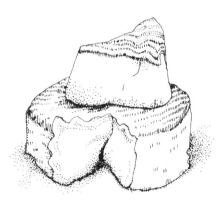

Clapshot

SERVES 4

450 g/1 lb potatoes, sliced
450 g/1 lb swede (rutabaga) or
  turnip, cut into small cubes
1 onion, chopped
50 g/2 oz/¼ cup butter
Salt and white pepper
Snipped chives

Boil the potato, swede or turnip and onion for about 12–15 minutes, removing any scum as it rises. Drain and mash to a fine purée, then pass through a sieve (strainer). Flavour with butter, salt and pepper. Present in individual pie dishes sprinkled with snipped chives.

Stuffed Potatoes with Cream Cheese

SERVES 4

2 large potatoes, 225 g/8 oz each
25 g/1 oz/2 tbsp butter, melted
100 g/4 oz/½ cup cream cheese
60 ml/4 tbsp plain yoghurt
Salt and white pepper
Snipped chives

Wash and scrub the potatoes and wipe dry. Halve lengthways. With the point of a knife, make criss-cross indentations over the cut surfaces to speed the baking. Brush the top with the butter and wrap in foil. Bake in a preheated oven at 200ºC/400ºF/gas mark 6 for 45–60 minutes. When baked, remove the foil and scoop out the hot pulp. Pass it through a sieve (strainer) if possible, otherwise mash it well. In a bowl, blend the hot mashed potato with the cream cheese, yoghurt and seasoning. Spoon the mixture back into the potato skins. Smooth it into a domed shape with a palette knife. Reheat for 5 minutes, then sprinkle the top with chives and serve.

Cabbage and Potato Sog

75 g/3 oz/⅓ cup butter
1 small green cabbage, shredded
4 large potatoes, thinly sliced
10 ml/2 tsp celery seeds
Salt and freshly ground black pepper
250 ml/8 fl oz/1 cup vegetable stock
30 ml/2 tbsp dry sherry

Use some of the butter to grease a flameproof casserole (Dutch oven). Put a layer of cabbage in the bottom, then a layer of potatoes. Dot with some of the remaining butter, sprinkle with a few of the celery seeds and a little salt and pepper. Repeat the layers and seasoning until all the cabbage and potatoes are used. Pour over the stock and sherry. Cover with a lid and simmer on top of the stove for about 1 hour or until the vegetables are tender. Remove the lid and, if necessary, boil rapidly until any excess liquid is evaporated. Flash under a hot grill (broiler) to brown.

American Hash Browns

4 large potatoes, diced
30 ml/2 tbsp sunflower oil
1 large onion, finely chopped
5 ml/1 tsp paprika
Salt and freshly ground black pepper

Cook the potatoes in boiling, salted water for about 5 minutes or until just tender. Drain. Meanwhile, heat the oil in a large frying pan (skillet). Add the onion and fry (sauté), stirring, for 2 minutes. Add the potatoes, paprika and a little salt and pepper. Fry, tossing over a high heat until golden brown and 'falling', adding a little more oil if necessary. Serve hot straight from the pan.

Potato Parcel

A knob of butter or margarine
1 large potato, thinly sliced
30 ml/2 tbsp milk
Salt and freshly ground black pepper

Spread a little of the butter on a 23 cm/9 in square of foil. Overlap the potato slices in layers in the centre of the foil, leaving enough to wrap over round the edges. Dot with the remaining butter. Spoon on the milk and sprinkle with salt and pepper. Draw the foil up over and fold the edges together to seal. Transfer to a baking sheet. Bake in a preheated oven at 190°C/375°F/gas mark 5 for about 1 hour or until the potatoes are tender. Serve straight from the parcel.

Cheesy Potato Parcel

Prepare as for Potato Parcel but add 15–30 ml/1–2 tbsp grated Emmental (Swiss) cheese to the parcel.

Onion Potato Parcel

Prepare as for Potato Parcel but add 2 chopped spring onions (scallions) to the parcel.

Mushroom Potato Parcel

Prepare as for Potato Parcel but add 2–3 sliced button mushrooms to the parcel.

Spiced Baby Roast Potatoes with Mustard Seeds

500 g/1 lb 2 oz/ l pack baby roasting potatoes, scrubbed
45 ml/3 tbsp olive oil
Sea salt
30 ml/2 tbsp black mustard seeds
1 fresh green chilli, seeded and chopped

Put the potatoes in a roasting tin. Toss in the oil and sprinkle with sea salt and the mustard seeds. Roast in a preheated oven at 190°C/375°F/gas mark 5 for about 1½ hours, shaking the pan occasionally, until crisp and golden. Sprinkle over the chopped chilli, toss again, then turn into a warmed serving dish.

Scalloped Potatoes with Onion

750 g/1½ lb potatoes, scrubbed and thinly sliced
45 ml/3 tbsp olive oil
2 onions, thinly sliced
15 ml/1 tbsp chopped parsley

Cook the potatoes in boiling, salted water for 3 minutes. Drain. Heat a third of the oil in a large, deep frying pan (skillet). Add about a third of the onions and potatoes to the pan and cook, turning occasionally, for 1 minute. Push to one side and add a little more oil. Add half the remaining vegetables and cook, turning for 1 minute. Push to the side, add the remaining oil and vegetables. Cook for 1 minute, then stir all together and cook, turning occasionally, for about 10 minutes until golden and cooked through. Turn into a serving dish, sprinkle with parsley and serve.

Hot Potato Salad

1 kg/2¼ lb baby new potatoes, scrubbed
1 onion, finely chopped
10 ml/2 tsp caster (superfine) sugar
30 ml/2 tbsp olive oil
90 ml/6 tbsp water
¼ vegetable stock cube
90 ml/6 tbsp white wine vinegar
Salt and freshly ground black pepper
30 ml/2 tbsp soured (dairy sour) cream
15 ml/1 tbsp snipped chives

Boil the potatoes in lightly salted water until tender. Drain and turn into a warmed serving dish. Meanwhile, fry (sauté) the onion and the sugar in the oil for 10 minutes, stirring, until golden and caramelised. Add the water, stock cube and vinegar to the pan and bring to the boil. Cook for 2 minutes, stirring. Season to taste. Stir in the soured cream and pour over the potatoes. Toss gently, sprinkle with the chives and serve.

Russian Revolution

2 potatoes, diced
2 carrots, diced
1 turnip, diced
100 g/4 oz/1 cup frozen peas
2 eggs
Pinch of mustard powder
Pinch of caster (superfine) sugar
100 g/4 oz/½ cup butter, melted
White wine vinegar
Salt and freshly ground black pepper
A little chopped parsley

Put all the vegetables except the peas in a pan of boiling, lightly salted water and cook for 5 minutes. Add the peas and cook for a further 5 minutes or until the vegetables are tender. Drain. Meanwhile, whisk the eggs in a saucepan with the mustard and sugar. Whisk in the melted butter and cook over a gentle heat, whisking all the time until thickened. Do not boil or the mixture will curdle. Spike with vinegar and seasoning to taste. Add to the vegetables, toss gently and serve hot, garnished with chopped parsley.

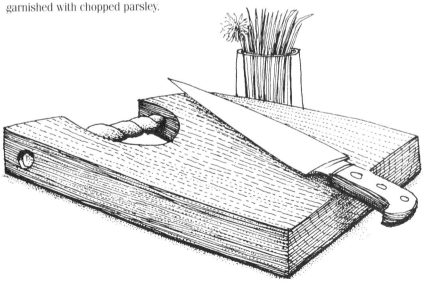

Salads

If you think salad means a few limp leaves and the odd slice of tomato and cucumber, think again. Here are the most exciting, colourful and nutritious creations you've ever tasted!

They don't have to be eaten just on hot summer days: even in the bitterest winter, try serving a light, hot soup followed by one of these stunning salads for a truly memorable meal.

Quantities can be as flexible as you like: add more or less of any ingredient and if you don't have a particular item make a substitute or simply leave it out!

Spinach Mousse, Bean and Egg Salad

450 g/1 lb spinach
30 ml/2 tbsp sunflower or corn oil
1 onion, roughly chopped
15 ml/1 tbsp vegetarian gelatine
20 ml/4 tsp Worcestershire sauce
Salt and freshly ground black pepper
150 ml/¼ pt/⅔ cup Greek-style plain
*   yoghurt*
150 ml/¼ pt/⅔ cup double (heavy)
*   cream*
Mixed salad leaves
425 g/15 oz/1 large can red kidney
*   beans, drained*
1 garlic clove, crushed
15 ml/1 tbsp red wine vinegar
3 hard-boiled (hard-cooked) eggs
4 cherry tomatoes

Wash the spinach thoroughly in several changes of cold water and discard any tough stalks. Heat half the oil in a pan, add the onion and fry (sauté) for 2 minutes until soft but not brown. Add the spinach and cook, stirring, for 1 minute. Reduce the heat, cover and cook gently for 5 minutes until the spinach and onions are tender. Tilt the pan and add the gelatine to the juices. Boil, stirring, for 2 minutes (or according to the packet directions). Cool slightly, then purée in a blender or food processor. Add the Worcestershire sauce and a little salt and pepper. Whip the yoghurt and cream together until peaking. Fold into the purée. Turn into an oiled 1.2 litre/2½ pt/5 cup ring mould and chill until set. Turn out on to a bed of mixed salad leaves. Mix the drained beans with the garlic, the remaining oil and the vinegar. Season to taste. Spoon into the centre of the ring and garnish round the ring with quartered hard-boiled eggs and cherry tomatoes.

Egg and Potato Salad

750 g/1½ lb new potatoes, cut into
*   bite-sized pieces*
2 hard-boiled (hard-cooked) eggs,
*   chopped*
15 ml/1 tbsp chopped parsley
15 ml/1 tbsp mayonnaise
5 ml/1 tsp made English mustard
5 ml/1 tsp wine vinegar
Freshly ground black pepper

Simmer the potatoes in boiling water for about 15 minutes until just cooked but still firm. Drain and leave to cool. Mix together the remaining ingredients and add to the potatoes. Stir together well. Chill before serving. The taste improves if covered and left in the fridge overnight before serving.

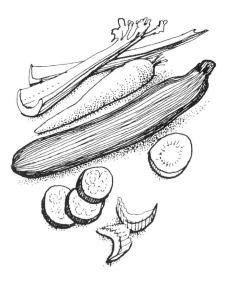

Curried Eggstravaganza

225 g/8 oz/2 cups wholewheat pasta
shells
1 carrot, grated
1 parsnip, grated
½ bunch of spring onions (scallions),
chopped
1 small red (bell) pepper, chopped
¼ cucumber, chopped
40 g/1½ oz/⅓ cup salted peanuts
45 ml/3 tbsp olive oil
15 ml/1 tbsp red wine vinegar
Salt and freshly ground black pepper
4 hard-boiled (hard-cooked) eggs,
halved
60 ml/4 tbsp Greek-style plain yoghurt
15 ml/1 tbsp milk
10 ml/2 tsp curry paste
15 ml/1 tbsp curried fruit chutney
Coriander (cilantro) leaves

Cook the pasta according to the packet directions. Drain, rinse with cold water and drain again. Place in a bowl with the carrot, parsnip, spring onions, pepper, cucumber and peanuts. Toss gently. Drizzle over the olive oil and vinegar and season lightly. Toss gently and arrange on four serving plates. Lay two egg halves on top, cut sides down. Blend together the remaining ingredients except the coriander leaves. Season to taste and spoon over the eggs. Garnish with coriander leaves and serve.

Salade aux Coquillettes

225 g/8 oz/2 cups pasta shells
1 mouli (Japanese white radish),
peeled and cut into5 mm/¼ in
cubes
1 bunch of radishes, sliced
¼ cucumber, cut into5 mm/¼ in cubes
1 garlic clove, chopped
1 tomato, skinned, seeded and
chopped
30 ml/2 tbsp walnut oil
15 ml/1 tbsp wine vinegar
Salt and freshly ground black pepper
8 lettuce leaves or Chinese leaves
(stem lettuce)
4 black olives, stoned (pitted)
2 tangerines, peeled and segmented

Cook the pasta shells in boiling water for 8 minutes. Drain, rinse in cold water until cold, then drain again. Combine the pasta, mouli, radishes and cucumber in a salad bowl. Blend the garlic, tomato, oil and vinegar in a blender or food processor. Add to the salad, season with salt and pepper and toss well. Line individual serving plates with lettuce or Chinese leaves and pile the salad on top. Garnish with olives and tangerine segments.

Vermicelli Salad Nankin-style

225 g/8 oz vermicelli
5 ml/1 tsp grated fresh root ginger
15 ml/1 tbsp soy sauce
75 ml/5 tbsp pineapple juice
30 ml/2 tbsp olive oil
Salt and freshly ground black pepper
1 garlic clove, chopped
100 g/4 oz mushrooms, sliced
100 g/4 oz cooked fresh or canned
  chestnuts
100 g/4 oz bean sprouts
Watercress sprigs

Cook the pasta in boiling salted water for 5 minutes. Drain well. Rinse in cold water until cold and drain again. Place the ginger, soy sauce, pineapple juice, oil, a little seasoning and the garlic in a blender or food processor and blend well. Add to the pasta with the mushrooms, chestnuts and bean sprouts. Pile on to serving plates and garnish with watercress before serving.

Salad Lilloise

4 chicory (Belgian endive) heads
225 g/8 oz spinach or chard leaves,
  shredded
75 g/3 oz button mushrooms, sliced
150 g/5 oz/1¼ cups walnut halves
75 ml/5 tbsp mayonnaise
Grated rind and juice of 1 lemon
30 ml/2 tbsp soured (dairy sour) cream
30 ml/2 tbsp apple purée (apple sauce)

Cut a cone-shaped core out of the base of the chicory. Separate two of the chicory heads into leaves and slice the remaining two. Mix the sliced chicory with the spinach or chard, mushrooms and walnuts. Beat the mayonnaise, lemon rind and juice, cream and apple purée together. Add a third of the dressing to the salad and toss. Serve the salad on individual plates garnished with the chicory leaves. Serve the remaining dressing separately.

Jamaican Citrus Salad

SERVES 2 OR 4

4 lettuce leaves
2 oranges, peel and pith removed
and segmented
1 grapefruit, peel and pith removed
and segmented
75 g/3 oz/¾ cup red kidney beans,
cooked (see page 10)
75 g/3 oz bean sprouts
75 ml/5 tbsp plain yoghurt
Juice of 1 lemon
Salt and freshly ground black pepper

Arrange the lettuce leaves on two or four plates and arrange the fruit segments on top. Sprinkle the beans and bean sprouts all over. Blend the yoghurt with the lemon juice and salt and pepper to taste. Serve with the salad.

Summer Lunch Pudding

SERVES 6

400 g/14 oz/1 large can chopped
tomatoes
2 courgettes (zucchini), grated
2 carrots, grated
1 turnip, grated
1 bunch of spring onions (scallions),
finely chopped
1 red (bell) pepper, finely chopped
15 ml/1 tbsp chopped parsley
8 basil leaves, chopped
Salt and freshly ground black pepper
Good pinch of caster (superfine)
sugar
8 slices bread from a large sliced loaf
45 ml/3 tbsp crème fraîche or quark

Put the tomatoes in a saucepan with all the prepared vegetables and the parsley. Bring to the boil, reduce the heat and simmer uncovered for about 10 minutes until pulpy and the vegetables are tender, stirring occasionally. Stir in the basil and season to taste with salt, pepper and the sugar. Meanwhile, cut the crusts off the bread. Use six of the slices to line a 1.2 litre/2 pt/5 cup pudding basin. Place the basin on a plate (to catch any drips later). Spoon the vegetable mixture into the basin. Lay one of the remaining slices of bread on top, then cut the last slice to fill in the gaps and cover the top completely. Cover with greaseproof (waxed) paper, then place a saucer or small tea plate on top and weigh down with heavy weights or cans. Leave to cool, then chill overnight. When ready to serve, carefully loosen the edge with a round-bladed knife and turn out on to a serving plate. Cut into wedges and spoon a little crème fraîche or quark on each slice.

Cucumber and Walnut Salad

SERVES 4

1 large cucumber, halved and sliced
8 radishes, sliced
1 large green (bell) pepper, sliced
1 spring onion (scallion), chopped
50 g/2 oz/½ cup walnut pieces,
*   roughly chopped*
Thyme sprig, chopped
Chopped parsley
30 ml/2 tbsp soy sauce
7.5 ml/1½ tsp olive oil
7.5 ml/1½ tsp lemon juice
1.5 ml/¼ tsp ground ginger
10 ml/2 tsp clear honey

Place all the salad ingredients and thyme in a salad bowl. Mix all the remaining ingredients in a jug. At the table, toss the salad in about half the dressing. (This dressing keeps for weeks. Make extra, chill it, and use it later to make a sliced raw mushroom salad or for marinating tofu.)

Cooling Summer Salad

SERVES 4–6

225 g/8 oz cherry tomatoes,
*   quartered*
1 cucumber, peeled and cubed
1 honeydew melon
8 basil leaves
45 ml/3 tbsp sunflower oil
15 ml/1 tbsp cider vinegar
Good pinch of chilli powder
Salt and freshly ground black pepper

Put the tomato quarters in a bowl. Add the cucumber. Cut the top off the melon and discard the seeds. Scoop out the flesh with a melon baller, or carefully remove it using a serrated knife, then cut into dice. Add to the bowl. Cut a thin slice off the base of the melon so it stands upright, then place the shell on a serving plate. Tear the basil leaves into pieces and add to the bowl. Pour over the oil and vinegar. Add the chilli powder, a little salt and a good grinding of pepper. Toss gently. Pile back in the melon and serve.

Stuffed Salad Tomatoes

SERVES 4

4 beef tomatoes
4 hard-boiled (hard-cooked) eggs,
  chopped
1 Weetabix, crushed
Salt and freshly ground black pepper
10 ml/2 tsp mayonnaise
15 ml/1 tbsp chopped parsley

Cut a slice off the top of each tomato. Scoop out the seeds into a bowl. Mix the eggs and Weetabix. Season with a little salt and pepper, then fold in the mayonnaise and parsley. Pile back into the tomatoes, replace the lids and chill until ready to serve.

Flageolet and Leek Salad

SERVES 4

2 small leeks, finely shredded
2 × 25 g/2 × 5 oz/2 large cans
  flageolet beans, drained
1 garlic clove, crushed
45 ml/3 tbsp olive oil
15 ml/1 tbsp white wine vinegar
2.5 ml/½ tsp dried mixed herbs
Salt and freshly ground black pepper
15 ml/1 tbsp chopped parsley
30 ml/2 tbsp pumpkin seeds

Put the leeks in a bowl. Rinse the beans under cold running water, then drain well again. Add to the bowl. Whisk the garlic, oil, vinegar, herbs and a little salt and pepper together. Pour over the salad and toss well. Mix the parsley and pumpkin seeds together and scatter over.

Greek-style Broad Beans

SERVES 4

1 large onion, chopped
1 garlic clove, crushed
60 ml/4 tbsp olive oil
450 g/1 lb/4 cups shelled broad
  (lima) beans
400 g/14 oz/1 large can chopped
  tomatoes
150 ml/¼ pt/⅔ cup white wine
1 bouquet garni sachet
Salt and freshly ground black pepper
Chopped coriander (cilantro), to
  garnish

Fry (sauté) the onion and garlic in the oil for 3 minutes, stirring. Add the remaining ingredients except the coriander and bring to the boil. Reduce the heat, cover and simmer gently for 10 minutes until the beans are tender. Remove the beans from the pan with a draining spoon. Boil the sauce rapidly for 5 minutes until well reduced and pulpy. Discard the bouquet garni. Return the beans to the sauce and heat through. Serve straight away sprinkled with the coriander.

Artichoke and Bean Sprout Salad

350 g/12 oz bean sprouts
1 red onion, sliced and separated into rings
400 g/14 oz/1 large can artichoke hearts, drained
430 g/15½ oz/1 large can chick peas (garbanzos), drained
30 ml/2 tbsp olive oil
3 sun-dried tomatoes, chopped
8 black olives, stoned (pitted) and quartered
15 ml/1 tbsp sun-dried tomato oil
15 ml/1 tbsp red wine vinegar
100 g/4 oz/1 cup pasta shapes, cooked
Salt and freshly ground black pepper
30 ml/2 tbsp chopped parsley
Paprika

Put all the ingredients except half the parsley and the paprika in a salad bowl with a little salt and a good grinding of pepper. Toss well. Sprinkle with the remaining parsley and a dusting of paprika.

Toulouse Salad

1 little gem lettuce
1 head of radicchio
100 g/4 oz lamb's tongue lettuce or rocket
100 g/4 oz button mushrooms, sliced
4 baby carrots, scrubbed and thinly sliced
8 radishes, sliced
12 stuffed olives, sliced
½ bunch of spring onions (scallions), diagonally sliced
1 tomato, skinned and roughly chopped
1 small red (bell) pepper, roughly chopped
170g/6 oz/1 small can evaporated milk
5 ml/1 tsp Dijon mustard
1.5 ml/¼ tsp cayenne
Salt and freshly ground black pepper

Tear the salad leaves into pieces and place in a salad bowl. Add the mushrooms, carrots, radishes, olives and spring onions. Put the remaining ingredients and a little salt and pepper in a blender or food processor and run the machine until the mixture is smooth. Just before serving, add to the salad and toss gently. Serve immediately.

Brazil Nut Bounty

SERVES 6

75 g/3 oz/¾ cup pasta shells
75 g/3 oz/¾ cup brazil nuts, coarsely
* chopped*
200 g/7 oz/1 small can Mexican
* sweetcorn (corn with bell peppers)*
1 large green eating (dessert) apple,
* unpeeled and diced*
1 red (bell) pepper, diced
1 garlic clove, crushed
150 ml/¼ pt/⅔ cup crème fraîche
15 ml/1 tbsp lemon juice
Salt and freshly ground black pepper
5 ml/1 tsp caster (superfine) sugar
15 ml/1 tbsp chopped tarragon
Tarragon sprig

Cook the pasta according to the packet directions. Drain, rinse with cold water and drain again. Place in a salad bowl with the nuts, corn, apple and red pepper. Blend together the remaining ingredients except the tarragon and pour over. Toss gently and garnish with a tarragon sprig before serving.

Greek Village Salad

SERVES 4

½ crisp lettuce, shredded
¼ small white cabbage, shredded
2 beef tomatoes, halved and sliced
5 cm/2 in piece cucumber, diced
1 small onion, sliced and separated
* into rings*
100 g/4 oz/1 cup Feta cheese, cubed
* or crumbled*
8 black or green Greek olives
30 ml/2 tbsp olive oil
15 ml/1 tbsp red wine vinegar
5 ml/1 tsp dried oregano
Salt and freshly ground black pepper
Greek bread

Place the lettuce and cabbage in a large, shallow dish and mix well. Scatter the tomatoes, cucumber, onion, cheese and olives over. Drizzle with oil and vinegar. Sprinkle over the oregano and a little salt. Finish with a good grinding of pepper. Serve with lots of Greek bread.

Florence Salad

SERVES 4

½ small white cabbage, shredded
1 small fennel bulb, shredded,
* reserving the green fronds*
30 ml/2 tbsp snipped chives
225 g/8 oz/2 cups Mozzarella cheese,
* cubed*
45 ml/3 tbsp single (light) cream
15 ml/1 tbsp lemon juice
Caster (superfine) sugar
Salt and freshly ground black pepper
4–6 plum tomatoes, sliced

Put the cabbage and fennel in a salad bowl. Add half the chives and the cheese. Whisk the cream and lemon juice together. Sweeten to taste with sugar, then season well with salt and pepper. Pour over the salad and toss well. Arrange the tomatoes in overlapping slices around the edge of the bowl and sprinkle with the remaining chives before serving.

Bosnian Cabbage Salad

SERVES 4–6

1 small white cabbage, finely
shredded or coarsely grated
½ small onion, grated
Salt and freshly ground black pepper
5 ml/1 tsp caster (superfine) sugar
45 ml/3 tbsp olive oil
15 ml/1 tbsp red wine vinegar

Put the cabbage in a wooden salad bowl. Add the onion and mix well. Season with a little salt, lots of pepper and the sugar. Pour over the oil and vinegar and toss well. Taste and add a little more oil or vinegar if necessary. Leave to stand for at least 1 hour before serving.

Crunchy Shreds

SERVES 4

1 large raw beetroot (red beet)
1 large carrot
½ celeriac (celery root)
1 small onion, grated
45 ml/3 tbsp olive oil
15 ml/1 tbsp lemon juice
8 basil leaves, shredded
Salt and freshly ground black pepper

Using the shredder attachment of a food processor, shred the beetroot, carrot and celeriac. Place in a bowl and add the remaining ingredients. Toss well and serve.

In the Pink

SERVES 4

2 cooked beetroot (red beets), diced
1 red onion, sliced and separated
into rings
430 g/15 ½ oz/1 large can red kidney
beans, drained
15 ml/1 tbsp mayonnaise
15 ml/1 tbsp plain yoghurt
Salt and freshly ground black pepper
Lollo rosso leaves

Mix the beetroot with the onion and kidney beans. Blend the mayonnaise and yoghurt together and fold in. Season to taste. Pile on to a bed of lollo rosso leaves and serve.

Chicory and Mandarin Salad

SERVES 6

2 heads chicory (Belgian endive)
300 g/11 oz/1 small can mandarin
*   orange segments in natural juice*
4 celery sticks, chopped
1 bunch of watercress
50 g/2 oz/½ cup blue cheese,
*   crumbled*
150 ml/¼ pt/⅔ cup Mayonnaise (see
*   page 305)*
1 garlic clove, crushed
30 ml/2 tbsp chopped parsley
A little milk (optional)
Freshly ground black pepper

Cut a cone-shaped core out of each chicory head. Cut the leaves into thick slices. Place in a bowl. Drain the mandarins, reserving the juice. Add the fruit to the bowl with the celery. Discard the feathery stalks from the watercress and separate the leaves into small sprigs. Add to the bowl. Mash the cheese with enough of the reserved juice to make a smooth paste. Stir in the mayonnaise and garlic and most of the parsley. Thin to a pouring consistency with a little more juice or milk. Season with pepper. Spoon the salad on to 6 serving plates. Spoon the dressing over, sprinkle with the remaining parsley and serve.

English Country Garden Salad

SERVES 4

1 round lettuce, torn into pieces
4 tomatoes, quartered
5 cm/2 in piece cucumber, peeled
*   and diced*
1 bunch of radishes, trimmed and
*   halved*
50 g/2 oz/½ cup raw shelled peas
2 large carrots, grated
4 hard-boiled (hard-cooked) eggs,
*   quartered*
Vinaigrette Dressing (see page 303)

Arrange the lettuce in a large salad bowl. Scatter over the tomatoes, cucumber, radishes and peas. Put a pile of the grated carrot in the centre and surround with the eggs. Serve with the vinaigrette dressing handed separately.

217

East Meets West Salad

½ head of Chinese leaves (stem
lettuce), shredded
100 g/4 oz button mushrooms, sliced
200 g/7 oz bean sprouts
1 red (bell) pepper, cut into thin
strips
1 red eating (dessert) apple, diced
50 g/2 oz/½ cup walnut halves
45 ml/3 tbsp plain yoghurt
15 ml/1 tbsp light soy sauce
5 ml/1 tsp chopped parsley
5 ml/1 tsp chopped tarragon
5 ml/1 tsp snipped chives
15 ml/1 tbsp walnut oil
Onion salt
Freshly ground black pepper
A little milk

Put the Chinese leaves, mushrooms, bean sprouts, pepper and apple in a bowl. Reserve a few of the walnut halves for garnish and roughly cut up the remainder. Add to the bowl. Blend the yoghurt with the soy sauce, herbs and oil until well blended. Season to taste with the onion salt and pepper. Thin, if necessary, with a little milk to form a fairly runny dressing. Pour over the salad and toss gently. Garnish with the reserved walnuts before serving.

Mediterranean Rustic Salad

1 small crisp lettuce, torn into pieces
4 tomatoes, diced
½ cucumber, skinned and diced
1 small onion, sliced and separated
into rings
12 stoned (pitted) green olives
30 ml/2 tbsp chopped mixed herbs
45 ml/3 tbsp olive oil
15 ml/1 tbsp white wine vinegar
Salt and freshly ground black pepper

Divide the lettuce between four serving plates. Scatter the tomatoes, cucumber, onion and olives over. Sprinkle liberally with the herbs. Drizzle with the oil and vinegar and season with a little salt and a good grinding of pepper.

Italian Rustic Salad

Prepare as for Rustic Mediterranean Salad but omit the onion and top the salad with a drained jar of carrot and celeriac antipasto instead.

Cheese and Corn Crispit

1 small, crisp lettuce, torn into pieces
1 carrot, finely diced
¼ cucumber, diced
4 tomatoes, cut into wedges
200 g/7 oz/1 small can sweetcorn
(corn), drained
100 g/4 oz bean sprouts
1 bunch of radishes, trimmed and
quartered
225 g/8 oz/2 cups Cheddar cheese, diced
150 ml/¼ pt/⅔ cup fromage frais
15 ml/1 tbsp chopped parsley
10 ml/2 tsp chopped chervil
1 garlic clove, crushed
15 ml/1 tbsp olive oil
Salt and freshly ground black pepper
A little milk

Arrange the lettuce on four plates. Mix together the next seven ingredients and pile on the lettuce. Whisk the fromage frais with the herbs, garlic and oil until well blended. Season to taste and thin with a little milk. Drizzle over the salad and serve.

Cottage Cheese and Peach Perfection

1 little gem lettuce, torn into bite-
sized pieces
1 bunch of watercress, trimmed and
separated into small sprigs
2 ripe peaches, skinned and sliced
75 g/3 oz/½ cup seedless (pitless) red
grapes, halved
350 g/12 oz/1½ cups cottage cheese
25 g/1 oz/¼ cup pecan halves,
roughly chopped
50 g/2 oz/½ cup Danish blue cheese,
crumbled
30 ml/2 tbsp mayonnaise
5 ml/1 tsp lemon juice
15 ml/1 tbsp single (light) cream

Arrange the lettuce and watercress on four serving plates. Chop a quarter of the peach slices and reserve with four of the grape halves for garnish. Mix the chopped peaches with the remaining grapes, the cottage cheese and nuts. Pile on to the plates. Beat the blue cheese with the mayonnaise, lemon juice and cream until fairly smooth. Spoon over the salads and garnish with the reserved chopped peach slices and grape halves.

Crunchy Italian Salad

SERVES 4

1 garlic clove, crushed
15 g/½ oz/1 tbsp butter
15 ml/1 tbsp olive oil
2 slices ciabatta bread, cubed
½ head radicchio, torn into pieces
75 g/3 oz young spinach leaves
175 g/6 oz/1½ cups Mozzarella
  cheese, cubed
¼ cucumber, peeled and diced
3 (preferably plum) tomatoes, sliced
½ jar pickled carrot, celeriac and
  pepper antipasto, drained
50 g/2 oz/⅓ cup black olives
45 ml/3 tbsp olive oil
15 ml/1 tbsp red wine vinegar
Salt and freshly ground black pepper

Heat the garlic with the butter and oil in a frying pan (skillet). Add the bread and fry (sauté) until golden brown. Drain on kitchen paper. Arrange the radicchio and spinach leaves attractively in four salad bowls and scatter the cheese, cucumber and tomatoes over. Spoon the antipasto mixture on top and dot with olives. Drizzle with oil, then vinegar and sprinkle with salt and a good grinding of pepper. Scatter the garlic croûtons over and serve.

Scandinavian Potato Salad

SERVES 4

450 g/1 lb new potatoes
150 g/5 oz watercress leaves
4 spring onions (scallions), chopped
2 egg yolks
Salt and freshly ground black pepper
2.5 ml/½ tsp Dijon mustard
45 ml/3 tbsp olive oil
45 ml/3 tbsp soured (dairy sour) cream
Juice of 1 lemon
Mixed salad leaves

Boil the potatoes for 20 minutes. Slice and place in a large bowl. Add the watercress leaves and onions. Place the egg yolks in a bowl with salt and pepper and the mustard. Whisk while adding the oil in a very thin stream until the mixture thickens. Blend in the cream and lemon juice. While still warm, toss the salad gently with this dressing. Divide between four plates on a bed of mixed salad leaves.

Potato Salad from Provence

450 g/1 lb baby new potatoes, boiled
and drained
225 g/8 oz green beans, halved,
cooked and drained
90 ml/6 tbsp olive oil
30 ml/2 tbsp white wine vinegar
1 onion, sliced and separated into
rings
3 tomatoes, quartered
1 green (bell) pepper, sliced into
rings
12 black olives
Salt and freshly ground black pepper
5 ml/1 tsp dried Herbes de Provence
15 ml/1 tbsp chopped parsley

Put the hot potatoes and beans in a
large salad bowl. Add the remaining
ingredients except the parsley. Toss well
and cool to room temperature. Sprinkle
with chopped parsley before serving.

Hot Mushroom Salad

225 g/8 oz field mushrooms, peeled
and sliced
A small thyme sprig
60 ml/4 tbsp olive oil
Salt and freshly ground black pepper
2 garlic cloves, chopped
Small fried bread croûtons
Mixed salad leaves
30 ml/2 tbsp wine vinegar

Fry (sauté) the mushrooms and thyme
in the oil for 1 minute. Season to taste
and add the garlic and croûtons. Toss for
30 seconds, then remove the thyme.
Divide the mushrooms between four
plates on a bed of salad leaves. Drizzle a
little vinegar over the salad mixture just
before serving.

Quick Potato and Mushroom Salad

580 g/1¼ lb/1 large can new potatoes,
drained and halved
4–6 button mushrooms, sliced
15 ml/1 tbsp dill seeds or cumin
seeds
5 ml/1 tsp French mustard
2.5 ml/½ tsp salt
1.5 ml/¼ tsp white pepper
Pinch of white sugar
30 ml/2 tbsp white vinegar or lemon
juice, or half and half
60 ml/4 tbsp olive oil

Put the potatoes and mushrooms in a
bowl and sprinkle with the seeds.
Heat the remaining ingredients to boiling
point in a saucepan and pour over the
vegetables. Toss well, then turn into a
chilled salad bowl. Chill until ready to
serve.

Carrot and Olive Salad

SERVES 4

450 g/1 lb young carrots, coarsely
* grated*
16–20 stuffed olives
45 ml/3 tbsp orange juice
15 ml/1 tbsp lemon juice
150 ml/¼ pt/⅔ cup Tofu Dressing (see
* page 304)*
Chopped parsley

Mix the carrots and olives together. Toss with the orange and lemon juice. Mix in the Tofu Dressing with a fork, blending it in thoroughly. Pile the salad in a dish and garnish with chopped parsley.

Curried Salad

SERVES 4

300 ml/½ pt/1¼ cups vegetable stock
50 ml/2 fl oz/3½ tbsp tomato juice
2 carrots, coarsely chopped
6 large radishes, sliced
1 small green (bell) pepper, diced
1.5–2.5 ml/¼–½ tsp curry powder
6 spring onions (scallions), sliced
7.5 cm/3 in piece cucumber, diced
1 sharp eating (dessert) apple, diced
425 g/15 oz/1 large can flageolet or
* broad (lima) beans, drained*
90 ml/6 tbsp chilled cottage cheese or
* yoghurt*

Heat the vegetable stock and tomato juice in a saucepan. Add the carrots, radishes and pepper at simmering point, sprinkle with curry powder to taste, bring to a slow boil and cook, covered, for 5 minutes. Add the spring onions, reduce the heat slightly and simmer, covered, for another 5 minutes. Add the cucumber, apple and beans and cook, uncovered, for 4 minutes. If the sauce is too thin, boil rapidly to reduce. Serve hot or cold, topped with chilled cottage cheese or yoghurt.

Sweet and Crunchy Salad

SERVES 4

6 large carrots, grated
75 g/3 oz/½ cup raisins
1 red eating (dessert) apple, diced
* and tossed in lemon juice*
1 green eating apple, diced and
* tossed in lemon juice*
100 g/4 oz/1 cup sunflower seeds
15 ml/1 tbsp plain yoghurt
15 ml/1 tbsp clear honey
Salt and freshly ground black pepper
Lettuce leaves

Mix the carrots, raisins, apples and seeds together. Blend the yoghurt with the honey and a little salt and pepper. Add to the mixture and toss gently. Pile on to lettuce leaves and serve.

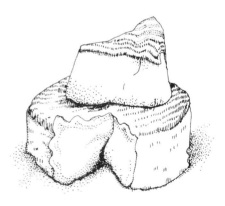

Sweet and Savoury Summer Special

SERVES 4

1 pear, diced
½ Galia or other green-fleshed
   melon, diced
1 courgette (zucchini), diced
1 425 g/15 oz/large can artichoke
   hearts, drained and quartered
15 ml/1 tbsp olive oil
5 ml/1 tsp lemon juice
Salt and freshly ground black pepper
A few crisp lettuce leaves, torn into
   pieces
15 ml/1 tbsp chopped parsley
5 ml/1 tsp chopped thyme
15 ml/1 tbsp toasted flaked almonds

Mix the pear, melon, courgette and artichoke hearts together. Add the oil and lemon juice, a little salt and a good grinding of pepper and toss gently. Pile on to a bed of lettuce and sprinkle with the herbs and almonds.

Waldorf Salad

SERVES 4

4 celery sticks, sliced
1 eating (dessert) apple, diced
2 bananas, sliced
50 g/2 oz/½ cup walnuts, chopped
45 ml/3 tbsp mayonnaise

Place the fruit and nuts in a large bowl and gently mix together. Add the mayonnaise and toss together well. Chill before serving.

Chinese Bean Sprout Salad

SERVES 4

4 pineapple rings, diced
400 g/14 oz/1 large can bean sprouts,
   drained and rinsed
100 g/4 oz firm tofu, diced
1 quantity Sweet and Sour Dressing
   (see page 304)

Mix together the pineapple, bean sprouts and tofu. Pour over the dressing and toss well. Chill before serving.

Grape and Pear Salad

SERVES 4

100 g/4 oz/⅔ cup seedless (pitless)
   grapes
2 pears, diced
100 g/4 oz/1 cup Lancashire cheese,
   cubed
45 ml/3 tbsp grape or apple juice
A dash of soy sauce
15 ml/1 tbsp olive oil

Mix together the fruit and cheese. Mix together the juice, soy sauce and olive oil. Pour over the salad and chill before serving.

Greek Grape and Melon Salad

SERVES 4

Prepare as for Grape and Pear Salad but substitute half a ripe honeydew melon, diced, for the pears and Feta cheese for the Lancashire cheese. Garnish with a few Greek black olives before serving.

Salad Alice

1 head lettuce, torn into pieces
350 g/12 oz/1 large can pineapple
    cubes, drained
1 grapefruit, segmented
50 g/2 oz/½ cup hazelnuts, chopped
45 ml/3 tbsp olive oil
10 ml/2 tsp lemon juice
Salt and freshly ground black pepper

Place the lettuce leaves in a large bowl. Add the fruit and nuts. Mix together the oil and lemon juice and pour over the salad. Season with salt and pepper and toss well.

Frozen Cheese Salad

100 g/4 oz/½ cup cottage cheese
100 ml/3½ fl oz/6½ tbsp evaporated
    milk
10 ml/2 tsp snipped chives
Salt and freshly ground black pepper
Lettuce
Felafels (see Felafels Jerusalem,
    page 224)
Pitta breads

Mix together all the ingredients except the lettuce, Felafels and pittas and press gently into a freezer container. Cover and freeze until firm. Cut into slices and serve with lettuce, Felafels and pitta bread.

Photograph opposite: **Spanish Eggs**
(page 168)

Orange and Cucumber Cheese Salad

225 g/8 oz/1 cup cottage cheese
2 oranges, segmented
½ cucumber, sliced
45 ml/3 tbsp oil
15 ml/1 tbsp lemon juice
Salt and freshly ground black pepper
5 ml/1 tsp orange liqueur

Mix together the cheese, oranges and cucumber. Pile on to plates. Blend the oil, lemon juice, a little seasoning and the liqueur together. Drizzle over and chill before serving.

Everyday Coleslaw

2 large carrots, grated
½ small white cabbage, shredded
½ small onion, grated (optional)
90 ml/6 tbsp olive oil
30 ml/2 tbsp mayonnaise
1.5 ml/¼ tsp made English mustard
Freshly ground black pepper
Lemon juice

Mix together the vegetables. Place all the dressing ingredients, except the lemon juice, in a screw-topped jar and shake well to mix. Add lemon juice to taste. Pour the dressing over the vegetables and mix well.

Fruit and Nut Coleslaw

Prepare as for Everyday Coleslaw but add 75 g/3 oz/¾ cup mixed peanuts and raisins and ½ bunch chopped spring onions (scallions) instead of the grated onion.

Cabbage-pineapple Coleslaw

SERVES 4

½ small firm white or Savoy cabbage
5 or 6 spring onions (scallions),
*   chopped*
227/8 oz/1 small can pineapple in
*   natural juice, drained and diced*
75 g/3 oz/½ cup seedless (pitless)
*   raisins*
150 ml/¼ pt/⅔ cup plain yoghurt
30ml/2 tbsp mayonnaise
Salt and freshly ground black pepper

Mix the cabbage, onions, pineapple and raisins in a salad bowl. Blend the yoghurt and mayonnaise with a little salt and pepper. Pour over and toss well.

Cabbage, Peach and Tofu Slaw

SERVES 4

Prepare as for Cabbage and Pineapple Coleslaw but substitute a can of peach slices, chopped, for the pineapple and Tofu Dressing (see page 304) instead of the yoghurt and mayonnaise.

Waldorf Slaw

SERVES 4

225 g/8 oz white cabbage, shredded
2 celery sticks, chopped
50 g/2 oz/⅓ cup sultanas (golden
*   raisins)*
1 red eating (dessert) apple, diced
50 g/2 oz/½ cup walnuts, chopped
15 ml/1 tbsp snipped chives
Salt and freshly ground black pepper
60 ml/4 tbsp mayonnaise
Sesame seeds

Mix all the ingredients, except the seeds, together well. Turn into a serving bowl. Sprinkle with a generous helping of sesame seeds to garnish and leave to stand for 30 minutes before serving.

Winter Slaw

SERVES 4

½ small red cabbage, shredded
2 cooked beetroot (red beets), diced
50 g/2 oz/⅓ cup raisins
1 red onion, sliced into rings
60 ml/4 tbsp French Dressing (see
*   page 303)*
Chopped parsley

Put the cabbage, beetroot, raisins and onion in a bowl. Add the dressing and toss gently but thoroughly. Sprinkle with chopped parsley and leave to stand for 1 hour before serving, if possible.

Photograph opposite: **Honey and Walnut Glazed Carrots (page 184) and Spicy Savoy with Apple (page 189)**

Fresh Pineapple and Cashew Nut Coleslaw

225 g/8 oz white cabbage, coarsely
grated
2 green apples, diced
2 red apples, diced
4 slices fresh pineapple, diced
60 ml/4 tbsp sunflower oil
30 ml/2 tbsp cider vinegar
30 ml/2 tbsp soft blue cheese,
mashed with a little cream
5 ml/1 tsp salt
Freshly ground black pepper
5 ml/1 tsp caraway seeds
5 ml/1 tsp sugar
15 ml/1 tbsp single (light) or soured
(dairy sour) cream
60 ml/4 tbsp cashew nuts, chopped

Combine the cabbage, apples and pineapple in a large mixing bowl. In a smaller bowl, place the oil, vinegar, cheese, salt and a good grinding of pepper, the caraway seeds and sugar. Add the cream and whisk the mixture well. Toss the coleslaw into this mixture. Serve on four plates. Finally, sprinkle over the chopped cashew nuts.

Chicory and Potato Salad

4 heads chicory (Belgian endive)
Juice of 1 lemon
90 ml/6 tbsp melted butter and oil,
mixed
Salt and freshly ground black pepper
450 g/1 lb new potatoes, boiled and
thinly sliced
30 ml/2 tbsp grated Emmental
(Swiss) cheese
Mixed salad leaves
Mustard and cress
Chopped parsley

Cut a cone-shaped core out of the bases of the chicory. Boil the heads for 12 minutes in salted water to which half the lemon juice has been added. Drain and press out the moisture. Heat half the butter and oil in a pan and shallow-fry the chicory for 3 minutes on each side over a low heat until light brown. Season with salt and pepper. Remove from the pan and drain on kitchen paper. In the same pan, toss the potatoes with more butter and oil until golden. Season to taste. Place the chicory in a shallow flameproof dish and sprinkle over the grated cheese. Brown under the grill (broiler) for 1 minute. Arrange the salad leaves and cress around the edge of four plates. Drizzle lemon juice over the leaves. Add the chicory and sautéed potatoes. Sprinkle with chopped parsley.

Curried Sweetcorn Salad

SERVES 4

2 × 350 g/2 ×12 oz/2 large cans sweetcorn (corn), drained
15 ml/1 tbsp snipped chives
30 ml/2 tbsp mayonnaise
15 ml/1 tbsp lemon juice
30 ml/2 tbsp Chutney (see page 321) or use bought
Salt and freshly ground black pepper
10 ml/2 tsp paprika
15 ml/1 tbsp mild curry powder
15 ml/1 tbsp chopped parsley

Mix together all the ingredients, except the parsley, in a bowl. Garnish with chopped parsley and serve, or chill until required.

Mixed Pulse Salad

SERVES 4

430 g/15½ oz/1 large can chick peas (garbanzos), drained
425 g/15 oz/1 large can red kidney beans, drained
200 g/7 oz/1 small can sweetcorn (corn), drained
45 ml/3 tbsp French Dressing (see page 303)
15 ml/1 tbsp chopped parsley

Mix the chick peas, beans and sweetcorn in a salad bowl. Just before serving, toss with the dressing, coating well, and mix in the parsley.

Mixed Bean Salad

SERVES 4

100 g/4 oz/1 cup red kidney beans, cooked (see page 10)
100 g/4 oz/1 cup butter beans, cooked
100 g/4 oz/1 cup haricot (navy) beans, cooked
225 g/8 oz/2 cups broad (lima) beans, cooked
225 g/8 oz French (green) beans, cut into thirds, cooked
1 small onion, finely chopped
1 garlic clove, crushed
45 ml/3 tbsp olive oil
15 ml/1 tbsp cider vinegar
Salt and freshly ground black pepper
2 hard-boiled (hard-cooked) eggs, quartered

Mix together all the beans in a large salad bowl. Scatter the onion over. Put all the remaining ingredients, except the eggs, in a screw-topped jar and shake well until blended. Pour over the beans and toss well. Arrange quartered eggs attractively in the centre to garnish.

Mushroom and Bean Sprout Salad

SERVES 4

225 g/8 oz mushrooms, thinly sliced
5 ml/1 tbsp Worcestershire sauce
30 ml/2 tbsp soy sauce
Salt and freshly ground black pepper
225 g/8 oz bean sprouts, roughly
  chopped
Good pinch of ground ginger

Put the mushrooms into a large bowl and sprinkle with the Worcestershire sauce, soy sauce, salt and pepper. Leave for 1 hour. Add the bean sprouts, sprinkle with ginger and stir in well.

Sunny Mushroom and Bean Sprout Salad

SERVES 4

Prepare as for Mushroom and Bean Sprout Salad but add a 200 g/7 oz/ 1 small can drained sweetcorn (corn) and 1 small red (bell) pepper, cut into thin rings.

Classic Tomato, Onion and Chive Salad

SERVES 4

2 onions, sliced into rings
Salt and freshly ground black pepper
6 tomatoes, sliced
10 ml/2 tsp snipped chives
5 ml/1 tsp mustard powder
30 ml/2 tbsp olive oil
30 ml/2 tbsp red wine vinegar
Good pinch of caster (superfine)
  sugar

Put the sliced onions on a plate, sprinkle with salt and leave for 30 minutes. Rinse thoroughly and pat dry on kitchen paper. (This process softens the onions and takes away the strong taste.) Place layers of onion and tomato in a flat dish, sprinkle with chives and a good grinding of pepper. Put the remaining ingredients in a screw-topped jar with a pinch of salt. Shake vigorously, then pour over the salad. Leave to stand for 10 minutes before serving.

Watercress, Orange and Onion Salad

1 bunch of watercress
2 oranges
1 small onion, sliced into rings
30 ml/2 tbsp olive oil
5 ml/1 tsp lemon juice
Salt and freshly ground black pepper

Trim any feathery stalks off the watercress. Arrange the leaves attractively in a shallow dish. Grate the rind and squeeze the juice from one of the oranges into a bowl. Remove and discard all the rind and pith from the remaining orange and slice the flesh. Cut each slice in half and arrange attractively over the watercress. Scatter the onion rings on top. Add the oil, lemon juice and a little salt and pepper to the orange rind and juice. Whisk until well blended. Pour over the salad and serve.

Citrus Fruits on Spinach and Bean Sprouts

1 lime
1 lemon
1 tangerine
2 oranges
2 grapefruit
Green lettuce, spinach leaves and a
*   handful of bean sprouts*
150 g/5 oz/scant 1 cup red morello
*   cherries, stoned (pitted)*
45 ml/3 tbsp salted peanuts, coarsely
*   chopped*
45 ml/3 tbsp walnut or peanut oil
Salt and freshly ground black pepper

Peel and remove the skins and pith of each fruit. Cut each fruit into segments, collecting the juice in the same bowl. Wash the spinach leaves and remove the stems. Drain well. Wash and drain the lettuce leaves and bean sprouts. Pat the leaves dry on kitchen paper. Arrange a bed of leaves on four plates. Place the mixture of citrus fruits in the centre with the juice. Decorate with red cherries and sprinkle over the peanuts. Drizzle a little oil over the leaves, then add seasoning.

Royal Salad

225 g/8 oz/2 cups shelled broad (lima) beans
50 g/2 oz/½ cup pistachio nuts
75 ml/5 tbsp single (light) cream
15 ml/1 tbsp Anisette liqueur
Juice of 1 lemon
Salt and freshly ground black pepper
4 Chinese leaves (stem lettuce)
8 large strawberries, sliced

Boil the beans for 7 minutes and drain. Remove the tough skin of each bean to reveal the green inner bean. Scald the pistachio nuts and remove the skin to reveal the green nut. Combine the cream, liqueur and lemon juice in a bowl. Season with salt and pepper and toss the beans and nuts in this dressing. Arrange one large Chinese leaf on each of the four plates. Divide the bean mixture between the leaves and garnish with strawberry slices.

Pickled Cauliflower Salad

1 small cauliflower, separated into florets
12 small gherkins (cornichons)
12 small pickling onions, peeled
150 ml/¼ pt/⅔ cup dry white wine
45 ml/3 tbsp olive oil
75 ml/5 tbsp wine vinegar
30 ml/2 tbsp clear honey
5 ml/1 tsp coriander (cilantro) seeds
5 ml/1 tsp black peppercorns
10 ml/2 tsp salt
5 ml/1 tsp ground turmeric
1 green chilli, seeded and sliced
1 iceberg lettuce, shredded
5 ml/1 tsp celery seeds
4 hard-boiled (hard-cooked) eggs, sliced

Place the cauliflower in a large earthenware bowl or shallow dish. Rub the gherkins with salt. Leave for 30 minutes, then wash off the salt, pat dry and place in the dish with the cauliflower and the onions. In a pan, boil the wine, oil, vinegar, honey, all the seasonings and spices for 3 minutes. Pour the hot mixture over the raw vegetables. Leave to marinate overnight. To serve, arrange a bed of shredded iceberg lettuce on four plates and spoon the pickle mixture on top. Drizzle a little of the pickling mixture over the salad. Garnish each plate with sliced hard-boiled egg.

Cucumber and Mint in Yoghurt Dressing

SERVES 4

1 cucumber, peeled and halved,
*   seeded and sliced*
Salt and white pepper
150 ml/¼ pt/⅔ cup plain Greek-style
*   yoghurt*
2 garlic cloves, chopped
1 small green chilli, seeded and
*   chopped*
8 mint leaves, chopped
4 Chinese leaves (stem lettuce)

Place the cucumber in a large bowl. Sprinkle with 5 ml/1 tsp salt and leave for 15 minutes to remove the excess moisture. Drain well, then rinse off in cold water. Drain well. Pat dry on kitchen paper. Blend together the yoghurt, garlic, chilli and chopped mint. Season to taste. Combine the cucumber and dressing. Arrange one Chinese leaf on each of four plates and fill them with cucumber salad.

Tomato and Cucumber in Brandy Dressing

SERVES 4

2 large beef tomatoes, 100 g/4 oz
*   each, sliced*
1 cucumber, sliced diagonally
8 chicory (Belgian endive) leaves,
*   sliced*
25 g/1 oz/¼ cup blue cheese, mashed
45 ml/3 tbsp walnut or olive oil
Juice of 1 lemon
45 ml/3 tbsp brandy
Salt and freshly ground black pepper
5 ml/1 tsp sugar
8 walnut halves

Arrange the tomato and cucumber slices alternately in rows on four plates. Place the chicory leaves in the centre. Blend the remaining ingredients except the walnuts in a bowl until smooth and creamy. Drizzle over the salad. Garnish with walnuts.

Courgette Pasta Salad in Basil Sauce

SERVES 4

150 g/5 oz/1¼ cups short-cut
*   macaroni*
45 ml/3 tbsp olive oil
1 fennel bulb, cut into small thin
*   strips*
2 courgettes (zucchini), diagonally
*   sliced*
6 basil leaves, chopped
2 garlic cloves, chopped
Salt and freshly ground black pepper
75 ml/5 tbsp single (light) cream
Mixed salad leaves
Juice of 1 lemon

Cook the macaroni according to the packet directions. Drain, rinse with hot water and drain again. Heat the oil in a wok of large frying pan (skillet) and stir-fry the macaroni and fennel for 1 minute. Add the courgettes, basil leaves, garlic and seasoning. Toss for 1 minute. Stir in the cream and reheat for 30 seconds. Arrange assorted salad leaves on four plates. Serve piping hot on the salad leaves. Squeeze the lemon juice over at the last moment.

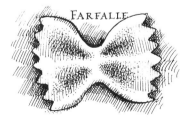

FARFALLE

Avocado and Rice Bean Salad

SERVES 4

100 g/4 oz/1 cup black-eyed beans,
soaked overnight and drained
100 g/4 oz/½ cup long-grain rice
600 ml/1 pt/2½ cups water
Salt and freshly ground black pepper
45 ml/3 tbsp sunflower oil
1 onion, chopped
7.5 ml/1½ tsp curry powder
15 ml/1 tbsp tomato purée (paste)
2 ripe avocados, stoned (pitted) and
sliced
30 ml/2 tbsp mango chutney
4 tomatoes, skinned, seeded and
chopped

Boil the beans in plenty of water for 1½ hours. Drain, rinse with cold water and drain again. Boil the rice in the measured water for 20 minutes, rinse in cold water and drain again. Combine the cooked rice and beans. Season to taste. Heat the oil and stir-fry the onion until soft but not coloured. Add the curry powder and tomato purée and 250 ml/8 fl oz/1 cup water. Boil for 8 minutes, then sieve (strain) or liquidize. Arrange a mound of rice mixture on four plates. Pour curry sauce around. Garnish the top of the rice mixture with avocado slices. Place a spoonful of mango chutney in the centre. Serve the salad with a side plate of chopped tomato pulp.

Simple Pasta Salad

SERVES 4

100 g/4 oz/1 cup pasta shapes
1 garlic clove, crushed
90 ml/6 tbsp olive oil
5 ml/1 tsp tomato purée (paste)
Salt and freshly ground black pepper
Pinch of dried tarragon
15 ml/1 tbsp wine vinegar

Cook the pasta in boiling salted water until just tender. Drain and leave to cool. Put all the remaining ingredients into a screw topped jar and shake well to mix. Pour over the pasta and toss together well. Chill before serving.

Pickled Pasta Salad

SERVES 4

Prepare as for Simple Pasta Salad but add 15 ml/1 tbsp chopped gherkins (cornichons), 25 g/1 oz/2 tbsp sliced stuffed olives and 5 ml/1 tsp capers to the cold pasta.

Bulgar Salad

SERVES 4

225 g/8 oz/2 cups bulgar wheat
1 bunch of spring onions (scallions),
chopped
2 eating (dessert) apples, chopped
75 g/3 oz/¾ cup Feta cheese, cubed
50 g/2 oz/½ cup cashew nuts
10 ml/2 tsp chopped parsley
10 ml/2 tsp chopped tarragon
30 ml/2 tbsp olive oil
15 ml/1 tbsp wine or cider vinegar
15 ml/1 tbsp lemon juice
Freshly ground black pepper
15 ml/1 tbsp chopped mint
1 quantity Yoghurt Dressing (see
page 306)

Soak the bulgar in boiling water for 30 minutes, drain, if necessary and leave to cool. Mix together all the remaining ingredients except the Yoghurt Dressing in a large bowl, then add the dressing and toss together well.

Garlic and Herb Cheesecake with Tomato Salad

SERVES 6

25g/1 oz packet cheese and onion
flavoured potato crisps (chips)
25 g/1 oz/1 cup cornflakes
25 g/1 oz/2 tbsp butter, melted
15 ml/1 tbsp vegetarian geleteine
600 ml/1 pt/2½ cups vegetable stock
100 g/4 oz/½ cup soft cheese with
garlic and herbs
15 ml/1 tbsp chopped parsley
1 egg, separated
150 ml/¼ pt/⅔ cup whipping cream
Pinch of chilli powder
Salt and freshly ground black pepper
Parsley sprig
450 g/1 lb tomatoes, sliced
1 small onion, finely chopped
30 ml/2 tbsp olive oil
15 ml/1 tbsp red wine vinegar
Pinch of caster (superfine) sugar

Oil an 18 cm/7 in round, deep loose-bottomed cake tin (pan). Crush the crisps and cornflakes together and stir in the melted butter. Press into the base of the tin and chill while preparing the filling. Sprinkle the gelatine over 150 ml/¼ pt/⅔ cup of the stock. Bring to the boil and cook for 2 minutes, stirring, until the gelatine is completely dissolved (or follow the packet directions). Stir in the remaining stock and leave until cold but not set. Gradually whisk into the cheese, then stir in the parsley. Chill until on the point of setting, then whisk in the egg yolk. Whip the egg white, then the cream (so you don't have to wash the whisk), until peaking. Fold the cream, then the egg white into the cheese mixture. Season to taste with the chilli powder, salt and pepper. Turn into the prepared tin and chill until set. Remove the tin and place on a serving plate. Garnish with the parsley sprig. Meanwhile, arrange the tomatoes in a dish and sprinkle with the onion. Drizzle over the oil and vinegar, sprinkle with sugar, then a little salt and a good grinding of pepper. Serve with the cheesecake.

Leaf Salad with Tofu

SERVES 4

½ small iceberg lettuce or Chinese
leaves (stem lettuce), shredded
1.5 ml/¼ tsp dried thyme
100 g/4 oz button mushrooms, sliced
50 ml/2 fl oz/3½ tbsp French
Dressing (see page 303)
175 g/6 oz Marinated Tofu, diced
(see page 254)
10 ml/2 tsp chopped parsley

Mix the lettuce with the thyme in a salad bowl. Toss the mushrooms in the dressing in a small bowl. Drain the tofu and place on a plate with the parsley. At serving point, toss the mushrooms and dressing lightly with the lettuce. Fold in the tofu cubes carefully, without breaking them if possible. Sprinkle with the parsley.

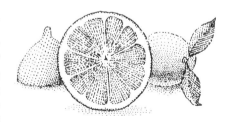

Avocado, Ricotta and Pine Nut Salad

SERVES 4

2 ripe avocados, sliced
Lemon juice
1 red (bell) pepper, chopped
50 g/2 oz/½ cup pine nuts
50 g/2 oz/⅓ cup stuffed olives, sliced
225 g/8 oz/1 cup Ricotta cheese
Salt and freshly ground black pepper
Good pinch of grated nutmeg
Shredded lettuce leaves
15 ml/1 tbsp olive oil
Paprika
Garlic bread

Toss the avocado slices in lemon juice to prevent browning. Mix the pepper, pine nuts and olives with the Ricotta. Season to taste with salt, pepper and the nutmeg. Pile on to a bed of lettuce and arrange the avocado in a starburst pattern round the edge. Drizzle with olive oil and dust with paprika before serving with hot garlic bread.

Swiss Cheese Salad

SERVES 4

175 g/6 oz/1½ cups Emmental (Swiss) cheese, thinly shredded
½ celeriac (celery root), thinly shredded
4 tomatoes, finely diced
50 g/2 oz/⅓ cup stoned (pitted) black olives
15 ml/1 tbsp chopped parsley
Good pinch of caster (superfine) sugar
30 ml/2 tbsp olive oil
10 ml/2 tsp red wine vinegar
Salt and freshly ground black pepper

Mix together the cheese, celeriac, tomatoes and olives. Pile on to plates. Whisk the remaining ingredients together and drizzle over.

Indian Rice Salad

SERVES 4

175 g/6 oz/¾ cup long-grain rice
2.5 ml/½ tsp salt
10 ml/2 tsp ground turmeric
50 g/2 oz/⅓ cup raisins
1 banana, sliced
50 g/2 oz creamed coconut, grated
1 red (bell) pepper, diced
30 ml/2 tbsp sweetcorn (corn)
2.5 ml/½ tsp dried tarragon
A few pineapple chunks

Cook the rice in boiling water with the salt and turmeric for about 15 minutes until tender. Drain, rinse with cold water and drain again. Mix the rice with the remaining ingredients and toss well. Chill before serving.

Sunshine Rice Salad

175 g/6 oz/¾ cup long-grain rice
Salt
5 ml/1 tsp ground turmeric
227 g/8 oz/1 small can pineapple in
    juice
200 g/7 oz/1 small can sweetcorn
    (corn), drained
5 ml/1 tsp dried tarragon
15 ml/1 tbsp lemon juice
5 ml/1 tsp soy sauce
15 ml/1 tbsp olive oil
Salt and freshly ground black pepper

Cook the rice in boiling salted water with the turmeric for about 15 minutes until tender. Drain, rinse with cold water and drain again. Mix together all the remaining ingredients and pour over the cooled rice. Toss together well. Chill before serving.

Colourful Pineapple Rice Salad

75 g/3 oz/¾ cup cooked long-grain
    rice
2 pineapple slices, preferably fresh,
    cubed
4 mushrooms, sliced
75 g/3 oz cucumber, cubed
1 celery stick, sliced
1 green chilli, seeded and sliced
25 g/1 oz/¼ cup peanuts
30 ml/2 tbsp lemon juice
15 ml/1 tbsp peanut (groundnut) oil
Salt and freshly ground black pepper
30 ml/2 tbsp pineapple juice
5 ml/1 tsp grated fresh root ginger
Watercress
Toasted peanuts

Place the rice in a bowl with the pineapple, mushrooms, cucumber, celery, chilli and peanuts. Whisk togther the lemon juice, oil, a little seasoning, the pineapple juice and ginger. Pour over the salad and toss well. Spoon on to four plates and garnish with watercress and a sprinkling of toasted peanuts.

Wild Rice Speciality Salad

4 vegetarian sausages
225 g/8 oz/1 cup wild rice mix (mixed
    long-grain and wild rice)
225 g/8 oz/2 cups shelled fresh peas
    (about 450 g/1 lb unshelled
    weight)
8 dried figs, quartered
1 red (bell) pepper, diced
1 garlic clove, crushed
45 ml/3 tbsp olive oil
15 ml/1 tbsp white wine vinegar
5 ml/1 tsp clear honey
Salt and freshly ground black pepper
2.5 ml/½ tsp Dijon mustard

Cook the sausages according to the packet directions. Leave until cold, then cut into bite-sized pieces. Meanwhile, cook the wild rice mix according to the packet directions. Drain, rinse with cold water and drain again. Place in a bowl with the sausages, peas, figs and red pepper. Whisk the remaining ingredients well together and pour over the salad. Toss well and chill for 1 hour to allow the flavours to develop.

Beany Rice Ring with Tarragon Mushrooms

SERVES 4 or 5

175 g/6 oz/¾ cup brown rice
425 g/15 oz/1 large can mixed pulses, drained
1 small garlic clove, crushed (optional)
30 ml/2 tbsp olive oil
15 ml/1 tbsp lemon juice
Good pinch of caster (superfine) sugar
Salt and freshly ground black pepper
175 g/6 oz button mushrooms
30 ml/2 tbsp water
30 ml/2 tbsp mayonnaise
15 ml/1 tbsp plain yoghurt
15 ml/1 tbsp chopped tarragon
A few tarragon leaves
Lemon twists

Cook the rice according to the packet directions. Drain, rinse with cold water and drain again. Place in a bowl with the pulses and garlic, if using. Drizzle the oil and lemon juice over. Sprinkle on the sugar and season well. Toss thoroughly and turn into a 1.2 litre/2½ pt/5 cup ring mould. Chill while preparing the filling. Place the mushrooms in a saucepan with the water and boil rapidly, stirring, for 2 minutes only. Turn into a bowl and leave to cool. Fold in the mayonnaise, yoghurt and chopped tarragon and season to taste. Turn the rice ring out on to a serving plate. Pile the mushroom mixture in the centre and garnish with tarragon leaves and lemon twists.

Peacock Feather Fan of Carrots and Cucumber

SERVES 4

150 g/5 oz/⅔ cup green lentils
45 ml/3 tbsp olive oil
45 ml/3 tbsp grapefruit juice
2 spring onions (scallions) or shallots, chopped
5 ml/1 tsp clear honey
Salt and freshly ground black pepper
2 large carrots, thinly sliced diagonally
½ cucumber, thinly sliced diagonally
4 hard-boiled (hard-cooked) eggs, thinly sliced
Snipped chives

Boil the lentils for 20 minutes or until tender. Drain. Blend together the oil, grapefruit juice, onions, honey and a little salt and pepper. Toss the lentils in the dressing while still hot. Allow to cool. Blanch the carrots in boiling water for 1 minute. Drain, rinse with cold water and drain again. On four plates arrange a row of carrot, cucumber and eggs to imitate peacock feathers. Spoon the lentils in the centre and sprinkle chives all over.

236

Light Bites

This section has loads of recipes for when you feel like something tasty, but not too filling, that's easy to cook and can be knocked up relatively quickly. They're ideal for any time of day, a leisurely brunch of light, melting Cheese and Mushroom Croissants, perhaps, or the surprise pancake dish, Brittany Eggs, to a simply stunning snack lunch or supper of an out-of-the-ordinary Pizza Quiche or a gorgeous, gooey Courgette Swiss Rarebit.

Choose any recipe to fill your hunger gap in the most sumptuous, tempting way.

Toasted Snackwiches

SERVES 4

12 slices small wholemeal bread, crusts removed
Butter or margarine
90 ml/6 tbsp Green Pea Spread (see page 302)
2 large tomatoes, ends discarded and sliced into 4
90 ml/6 tbsp peanut butter

Spread eight slices of bread with the butter or margarine. Cover four of the spread slices with Green Pea Spread, using 25 ml/1½ tbsp on each. Cover with the second buttered slice, fat side up. Lay two tomato rounds on each slice. Spread the remaining four buttered bread slices with peanut butter. Place them, spread side down, on the tomato. Press lightly with your palm to 'seal' the sandwiches. Cut each sandwich into three equal strips or fingers and stick a cocktail stick (toothpick) through each to hold the bread slices together. Place the strips on a sheet of foil on the grill (broiler) rack. Toast for 1–2 minutes on each side until lightly coloured. Serve three strips per person while still warm.

Cheese and Herb Sandwiches

SERVES 4

Prepare as for Toasted Snackwiches but use soft cheese with garlic and herbs instead of the Green Pea Spread.

Quick 'C' Sandwiches

Here are a few simple sandwich ideas to top up your daily input of vital vitamins and minerals with spreads you can buy. The quantities given are for one sandwich, made with slices from a large wholemeal loaf.

Peanut Butter-Orange Sandwich

Spread one slice of bread with peanut butter. Cover it with two or four thin slices of peeled orange, cut across the segments. Sprinkle very lightly with freshly ground black pepper. Cover with a second slice of bread spread with butter or margarine.

Cheese-Orange Sandwich

Make a sandwich as above but use thinly sliced Mozzarella cheese instead of peanut butter and add a few torn basil leaves.

Cottage-Grapefruit Sandwich

Spread two slices of bread with cottage cheese with chives. Cover one slice with two grapefruit slices, cut across the segments, then into small bits. Top with the second bread slice lightly spread with butter or margarine.

Tomato-Cheese Sandwich

Spread two slices of bread with low-fat soft cheese. Sprinkle one with a little grated onion. Cover with three or four pieces of tomato flesh without the seeds and juice. Grind a little black pepper over them. Top with the second bread slice, lightly spread with butter or margarine.

'Fruit Salad' Sandwich

Spread one slice of bread with cottage cheese with pineapple. Cover it with orange slices cut as above. Top with a second slice of bread spread with a little butter or margarine and coarse-cut orange marmalade.

Christmas Sandwich

Spread two slices of bread thinly with butter or margarine. Spread one thinly with a vegetarian mincemeat (obtainable in health food stores). Top with a slice of mature Cheddar cheese, then the second bread slice lightly spread with butter or margarine.

Cream Cheese and Bean Sprout Open Sandwich

Spread thick slices of white bloomer loaf with cream cheese. Sprinkle with fresh or drained canned beansprouts and a few cold cooked peas. Drizzle with a little French dressing and add a good grinding of black pepper.

German Special Open Sandwich

Lightly butter pumpernickel. Spread thinly with German mustard. Top with a thin slice of Emmental (Swiss) cheese, then a spoonful of drained sauerkraut. Sprinkle with caraway seeds.

Avocado Spicy Open Sandwich

Dip slices of ripe avocado in lemon juice. Lay on a slice of granary bread, thickly spread with cream cheese. Top with a spoonful of spicy tomato salsa and a black olive.

Nutty Cooler Open Sandwich

Mash some chopped walnuts into cream cheese. Spread on a thick slice of wholemeal bread. Grate a little cucumber and squeeze out all the juice. Toss in a splash of vinegar and a good grinding of black pepper. Pile on top and garnish with a walnut half.

Curried Smasher Open Sandwich

Mash canned pease pudding with mango chutney and curry paste to taste. Spoon on to rye crispbread. Arrange halved cucumber slices and onion rings along the top, pressing in gently so they don't fall off. Sprinkle with black mustard seeds and serve straight away.

Cosa Nostra

SERVES 4

2 pizza base mixes
225 g/8 oz/1 small can chopped
*   tomatoes, drained*
50 g/2 oz/½ cup cooked French
*   (green) beans, cut into short*
*   lengths*
½ small red or green (bell) pepper,
*   finely diced*
10 ml/2 tsp capers
60 ml/4 tbsp grated Mozzarella
*   cheese*
5 ml/1 tsp dried oregano
A little olive oil
Passata (sieved tomatoes)
Grated Pecorino cheese

Make up the pizza base mixes and knead gently into 1 ball. Divide the dough into quarters. Roll out each quarter to a 20 cm/8 in round. Divide the tomatoes, beans, pepper, capers, cheese and oregano between the centres of the dough rounds. Brush the edges with water. Draw the dough up over the filling to form parcels. Place sealed sides down on an oiled baking sheet and brush the parcels with oil. Bake in a preheated oven at 200°C/400°F/gas mark 6 for about 20 minutes until golden brown. Transfer to warmed plates and spoon a little hot passata over. Sprinkle with grated Pecorino cheese before serving.

Tiffin Time

SERVES 4

2 naan breads
225 g/8 oz/1 small can pease pudding
10 ml/2 tsp curry paste
30 ml/2 tbsp curried fruit chutney
Lemon juice
Shredded lettuce
Chopped cucumber

Grill (broil) the naans according to the packet directions. Heat the pease pudding in a small pan with the curry paste and chutney. Spread over the warm naans and sprinkle with lemon juice. Add some shredded lettuce and chopped cucumber and fold in halves. Cut each into four wedges and serve in a paper napkin.

Cheese and Tomato Croissants

SERVES 4

4 ready-split croissants
2 tomatoes, thinly sliced
50 g/2 oz/½ cup Mozzarella cheese, grated
8 torn basil leaves

Open the croissants gently. Slide in tomato slices and stuff with cheese. Push in a few torn basil leaves. Grill (broil) until the cheese melts, turning once. Take care not to allow the croissants to burn.

Cheese and Mushroom Croissants

SERVES 4

Prepare as for Cheese and Tomato Croissants but spread the insides with a 215 g/7½ oz/1 small can creamed mushrooms and fill with Cheddar cheese instead of Mozzarella. Grill (broil) as before.

Cheese, Sage and Onion Croissants

SERVES 4

Prepare as for Cheese and Tomato Croissants but add thinly sliced onion, separated into rings, instead of the tomato. Use Cheddar instead of Mozzarella and add a few chopped sage leaves. Grill (broil) as before.

Ploughman's Slices

SERVES 2

2 slices wholemeal bread
Sweet pickle
25 g/1 oz/2 tbsp butter or margarine
50 g/2 oz/½ cup strong Cheddar cheese, grated

Toast the bread on both sides. Spread one side with pickle. Mash the butter and cheese together and pile on top. Grill (broil) until golden and bubbling.

Pizza Slices

SERVES 2

Prepare as for Ploughman's Slices but spread the toast with tomato purée (paste) and sprinkle with a little dried oregano, then add the mashed butter and cheese.

Herby Cheese Slices

SERVES 2

Prepare as for Ploughman's Slices but spread the toast with a little yeast extract and mash in 15 ml/1 tbsp each of chopped parsley and snipped chives with the butter and cheese.

Swiss Cheese Slices

SERVES 2

Prepare as for Ploughman's Slices but spread the toast with a little whole-grain mustard. Use grated Emmental (Swiss) cheese instead of butter and add a dash of Kirsch for an authentic flavour.

Waffle Wonders

SERVES 2

4 potato waffles
4 Cheddar cheese slices
4 eggs
A little oil or butter
Shredded lettuce
Tomato ketchup (catsup)

Grill the waffles according to the packet directions. Top each with a slice of cheese and return to the grill briefly to melt. Meanwhile fry (sauté) the eggs in the oil or butter. Transfer the cheese-topped waffles to serving plates. Top each with some shredded lettuce, then a fried egg. Serve with ketchup if liked.

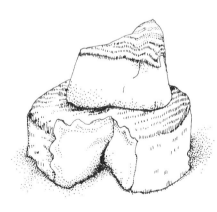

Chilli Bean Potatoes

SERVES 4

4 large even-sized potatoes
Olive oil
Salt
200 g/7 oz/1 small can chopped
  tomatoes
425 g/15 oz/1 large can red kidney
  beans, drained
5 ml/1 tsp chilli powder
5 ml/1 tsp dried oregano
5 ml/1 tsp ground cumin
Salt and freshly ground black pepper
Soured (dairy sour) cream or plain
  yoghurt

Prepare and cook the potatoes as for Cheese and Herb Potatoes (see page 243). Meanwhile, put the tomatoes and drained beans in a saucepan with the chilli powder, oregano and cumin. Bring to the boil, reduce the heat and simmer for 5 minutes. Season to taste. Spoon on to the split and squeezed potatoes. Add a spoonful of soured cream or yoghurt and serve.

Saucy Beanoes

SERVES 4

4 large even-sized potatoes
Olive oil
Salt
400 g/14 oz/1 large can baked beans
20 ml/4 tsp brown table sauce
75 g/3 oz/¾ cup Cheddar cheese,
  grated

Prepare and cook the potatoes as for Cheese and Herb Potatoes (see page 243). Meanwhile, heat the beans in a saucepan. Spoon into the split and squeezed potatoes. Drizzle with the sauce, then top with the cheese. Flash under a hot grill (broiler) until melted and bubbling.

Russian Potatoes

4 large even-sized potatoes
Olive oil
Salt
275 g/10 oz/1 small can diced mixed
* vegetables, drained*
30 ml/2 tbsp mayonnaise
30 ml/2 tbsp salted peanuts
15 ml/1 tbsp chopped parsley
Freshly ground black pepper
Cayenne

Prepare and cook the potatoes as for Cheese and Herb Potatoes (see page 243). Meanwhile, mix the drained vegetables with the mayonnaise, peanuts, parsley and pepper. Mix well. Spoon into the split and squeezed potatoes and sprinkle with cayenne before serving.

Pan Haggerty

25 g/1 oz/2 tbsp butter
1 kg/1¼ lb potatoes, very thinly sliced
450 g/1 lb onions, very thinly sliced
175 g/6 oz/1½ cups Cheddar cheese,
* grated*
Salt and freshly ground black pepper

Spread half the butter over the base and sides of a large frying pan (skillet). Put the potatoes, onions and cheese in layers in the pan, seasoning lightly between each layer. Press down well. Fry (sauté) over a gentle heat for about 15 minutes until the base is crisp and golden. Carefully turn the cake out on to a plate. Melt the remaining butter in the pan, then slide the cake back into the pan, browned side up. Fry gently again for a further 15 minutes or until the cake is cooked through and golden. Serve cut into quarters.

Champ

8 potatoes, cut into even-sized pieces
1 bunch of spring onions (scallions),
* chopped*
400 ml/14 fl oz/1¼ cups milk
Salt and freshly ground black pepper
75 g/3 oz/⅓ cup butter, cut into small
* pieces*
15 ml/1 tbsp sesame seeds, toasted

Cook the potatoes in boiling, salted water until tender. Drain and mash well. Meanwhile, cook the onions in the milk until soft. Stir into the potatoes and mix well. Season to taste. Spoon into four individual hot dishes and make a well in the centre. Divide the butter between the hollows and allow to melt. Sprinkle the toasted seeds around the top of the potato. Eat by taking a little of the potato on a spoon or fork and dipping in the butter.

Cheese and Herb Potatoes

SERVES 4

4 large even-sized potatoes, scrubbed
Olive oil
Salt
100 g/4 oz/1 cup Cheddar cheese,
  grated
25 g/1 oz/2 tbsp butter or margarine,
  softened
15 ml/1 tbsp chopped parsley
15 ml/1 tbsp snipped chives
10 ml/2 tsp chopped thyme or
  tarragon
Freshly ground black pepper

Prick the potatoes all over with a fork. Rub with oil, then salt. Bake in the oven at 190°C/375°F/gas mark 5 for about 1 hour until tender or place on a plate, cover with kitchen paper and microwave for 12–16 minutes, depending on the power of your microwave. Meanwhile, mash the cheese with the butter or margarine, the herbs and a good grinding of pepper. When the potatoes are cooked, transfer to plates and cut a large cross in the top of each. Squeeze gently so the splits open slightly. Top with the cheese mixture and either serve straight away or flash under a hot grill (broiler) to melt completely.

Potatoes with Almond Skordalia

SERVES 4

4 large even-sized potatoes
Olive oil
Salt
175 ml/6 fl oz/¾ cup Aioli (see page
  306)
50 g/2 oz/½ cup ground almonds
30 ml/2 tbsp wholemeal breadcrumbs
10 ml/2 tsp lemon juice
15 ml/1 tbsp chopped parsley
Freshly ground black pepper

Prepare and cook the potatoes as for Cheese and Herb Potatoes. Meanwhile, mix the Aioli with the remaining ingredients, adding pepper to taste. Spoon the cold filling over the hot, squeezed potatoes and serve.

Leek and Apple Packets

SERVES 4

2 leeks, sliced
150 ml/¼ pt/⅔ cup vegetable stock
1 large eating (dessert) apple,
  chopped
2 radishes, chopped (optional)
2 lettuce leaves, shredded
45 ml/3 tbsp cottage cheese
Salt and freshly ground black pepper
2 wholemeal pitta breads

Cook the leeks in the stock until tender. Drain (reserve the stock for soup). Leave to cool. Mix the leeks, apple, radishes and lettuce with the cheese and a little seasoning. Warm the pitta breads, halve crossways and fill with the salad and cheese mixture.

Potato Cakes

Oil, for shallow-frying
1 onion, chopped
225 g/8 oz/1 cup cold mashed potato
5 ml/1 tsp dried mixed herbs
50 g/2 oz/½ cup Cheddar cheese,
*   grated*
Salt and freshly ground black pepper
5 ml/1 tsp paprika
50 g/2 oz/½ cup plain (all-purpose)
*   flour*

Heat 15 ml/1 tbsp of the oil and fry (sauté) the onion over a low heat for 5 minutes. Mix together the onions, potato, herbs, cheese, salt, pepper and paprika. Shape the mixture into flattish cakes and dust with flour. Shallow-fry the cakes in hot oil for about 10 minutes until brown on both sides. Drain on kitchen paper.

Macaroni Cheese

175 g/6 oz/1½ cups quick-cook
*   macaroni*
1 quantity Cheese Sauce (see page
*   311)*
A little extra grated cheese
Sliced tomatoes (optional)

Cook the macaroni according to the packet directions. Meanwhile, make up the cheese sauce. Mix in the drained macaroni and turn into a flameproof dish. Top with a little extra grated cheese and surround with sliced tomatoes, if liked. Grill (broil) until bubbling and golden.

Macaroni and Tomato Cheese

Prepare as for Macaroni Cheese but put half the macaroni cheese in the dish and add a layer of a drained 225 g/8 oz/ 1 small can chopped tomatoes and a sprinkling of dried mixed herbs. Top with the remaining macaroni cheese and continue as above.

Macaroni and Spinach Cheese

Prepare as for Macaroni and Tomato Cheese but substitute a layer of drained, canned chopped spinach for the canned tomatoes and sprinkle with grated nutmeg instead of mixed herbs. Continue as above.

Macaroni and Mushroom Cheese

Prepare as for Macaroni and Tomato Cheese but substitute a layer of drained, canned sliced mushrooms for the tomatoes and sprinkle with dried basil instead of mixed herbs. Continue as above.

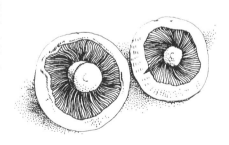

Courgette Swiss Rarebit

SERVES 4

*225 g/8 oz/2 cups Emmental (Swiss)
cheese and mature Cheddar
cheese, grated and mixed*
*150 ml/¼ pt/⅔ cup medium-dry white
wine*
2 garlic cloves, finely chopped
Pinch of cayenne or chilli powder
2 egg yolks
5 ml/1 tsp cornflour (cornstarch)
60 ml/4 tbsp single (light) cream
30 ml/2 tbsp Kirsch
16 slices French bread
2 courgettes (zucchini), thinly sliced
60 ml/4 tbsp grated Pecorino cheese
5 ml/1 tsp paprika
Tomato wedges

In a saucepan, heat the grated cheeses in the white wine with the garlic until melted. Add the cayenne or chilli powder. In a cup, mix the egg yolks, cornflour and cream. Gradually add this mixture to the hot cheese, stirring to blend to a thickish paste. Remove from the heat and add the Kirsch. Allow the mixture to cool completely for easier spreading. Toast the bread and keep hot. Blanch the courgettes for 30 seconds in boiling salted water. Drain and pat dry. Spread the cheese mixture thickly on to the toast. Arrange overlapping slices of courgette on top. Sprinkle over grated Pecorino cheese. When ready to serve, place the rarebit on a baking sheet and heat under the grill (broiler). Sprinkle on the paprika at the last moment. Top with a tomato wedge to garnish.

Cheddary Spaghetti

SERVES 4

175 g/6 oz spaghetti
*100 g/4 oz/1 cup mature Cheddar
cheese, grated*
25 g/1 oz/2 tbsp butter or margarine
Salt and freshly ground black pepper
4 tomatoes, chopped

Cook the spaghetti in boiling salted water until just tender. Drain, then return to the hot saucepan. Add the cheese and butter or margarine and season with salt and pepper. Toss until melted. Throw in the tomatoes, toss once and serve.

Hot Ploughman's

SERVES 4

1 small uncut loaf
225 g/8 oz Cheddar cheese, sliced
Sweet pickle
Tomato wedges

Slice the loaf, but don't cut right through, so that each slice is still attached at the base. Put a slice of cheese and a spoonful of pickle between each slice. Wrap the loaf in foil. Bake in a preheated oven at 220°C/425°F/gas mark 7 for 15–20 minutes. Serve with tomato wedges.

French Cheese Loaf

SERVES 4

1 French stick
225 g/8 oz Brie-type cheese, sliced
3 tomatoes, sliced
5 ml/1 tsp dried Herbes de Provence

Slice the bread, but not right through the base. Lay a piece of cheese and tomato between each slice and sprinkle with herbs. Wrap in foil and bake as for Hot Ploughman's.

Swiss Cheese Pie

225 g/8 oz puff pastry (paste)
175 g/6 oz/1½ cups Emmental (Swiss)
cheese, grated
1 small onion, finely chopped
2 eggs, beaten
300 ml/½ pt/1¼ cups single (light)
cream
2.5 ml/½ tsp freshly grated nutmeg
Salt and freshly ground black pepper

Roll out the pastry and use to line a 20 cm/8 in flan dish (pie pan) on a baking sheet. Prick the base with a fork. Sprinkle with half the cheese and the chopped onion. Beat the eggs and cream together with the seasonings and the remaining cheese. Pour into the dish. Bake in a preheated oven at 200°C/ 400°F/gas mark 6 for about 30 minutes until golden and set.

Soufflé Toasts

4 slices wholemeal bread, lightly
toasted
Butter or margarine
Yeast extract
4 tomatoes, sliced
2 eggs, separated
5 ml/1 tsp made English mustard
50 g/2 oz/½ cup Cheddar cheese, grated
Salt and freshly ground black pepper

Put the toast on a baking sheet. Spread lightly with butter or margarine, then yeast extract. Lay the tomato slices on top. Beat the egg yolks with the mustard and cheese and add a little salt and pepper. Whisk the egg whites until stiff and fold into the cheese mixture with a metal spoon. Pile on top of the tomatoes and bake in a preheated oven at 190°C/

375°F/gas mark 5 for 10-15 minutes until golden and set. Serve immediately.

Cheese and Herb Scotch Eggs

450 g/1 lb/2 cups mashed potato
100 g/4 oz/1 cup Cheddar cheese,
grated
Salt and freshly ground black pepper
A little plain (all-purpose) flour
4 hard-boiled (hard-cooked) eggs,
shelled
1 egg, beaten
85 g/3½ oz/1 packet parsley and
thyme stuffing mix
Oil, for deep-frying

Beat the potatoes with the cheese and season to taste. Dip the shelled eggs in flour, then with floured hands mould a quarter of the potato mixture round each egg to cover completely. Roll gently in beaten egg, then the stuffing mix to coat completely. Deep-fry in hot oil for 4–5 minutes until crisp and golden brown. Drain on kitchen paper and leave to cool.

Pizza Quiche

225 g/8 oz shortcrust pastry (basic
pie crust)
100 g/4 oz/1 cup Cheddar cheese,
grated
3 tomatoes, sliced
5 ml/1 tsp dried oregano
150 ml/¼ pt/⅔ cup milk
2 eggs
Salt and freshly ground black pepper
1 black olive

Roll out the pastry and use to line a 20 cm/8 in flan dish (pie pan), on a baking sheet. Prick the base with a fork, then sprinkle the base with grated cheese. Arrange the tomato slices attractively over. Sprinkle with the oregano. Beat the milk and eggs together with a little salt and pepper. Pour into the flan. Bake in a preheated oven at 200°C/400°F/gas mark 6 for about 35 minutes until set and golden brown. Garnish with an olive in the centre and serve warm.

Asparagus Quiche

Prepare as for Pizza Quiche but omit the tomatoes and arrange a drained 278 g/10 oz/1 small can asparagus spears in a starburst pattern over the cheese before baking. Garnish with a parsley sprig instead of an olive before serving.

Mushroom and Onion Quiche

Prepare as for Pizza Quiche but omit the tomatoes. Cover the cheese with 1 large chopped onion and 75 g/3 oz/1½ cups sliced button mushrooms, both fried (sautéed) in a little butter for 3 minutes first. Use dried mixed herbs instead of oregano. Bake as before.

Corn and Pepper Quiche

Prepare as for Pizza Quiche but omit the tomatoes. Add a 200 g/7 oz/1 small can drained sweetcorn (corn) on top of the cheese and arrange 1 small sliced green or red (bell) pepper around the edge. Use dried or fresh chives instead of oregano. Bake as before.

Tortilla Quiche

Prepare as for Pizza Quiche but omit the tomatoes. Top the cheese with 2 cooked, diced potatoes and a chopped bunch of spring onions (scallions). Use mixed herbs or summer savory instead of oregano. Bake as before.

Sweetcorn Flumbles

90 ml/6 tbsp self-raising (self-rising)
*   wholemeal flour*
5 ml/1 tsp baking powder
2.5 ml/½ tsp onion salt
Freshly ground black pepper
150 ml/¼ pt/⅔ cup plain yoghurt
3 eggs, separated
320 g/11½ oz/1 large can Mexican
*   sweetcorn (corn with bell peppers),*
*   drained*
15 ml/1 tsp snipped chives
5 ml/1 tsp clear honey
Oil, for shallow-frying

Put the flour, baking powder and onion salt in a bowl and mix well. Add a good grinding of pepper. Work in the yoghurt and egg yolks until smooth. Stir in the corn, chives and honey. Whisk the egg whites until stiff and fold them into the mixture with a metal spoon. Heat a little oil in a large frying pan (skillet). Add tablespoonfuls of the batter and fry (sauté) until golden brown underneath. Flip over and brown the other side. Keep warm while cooking the remainder. Serve hot.

Eggy Corn and Banana Waffles

3 eggs
l large banana, thickly sliced
50 g/2 oz/1 cup wholemeal
*   breadcrumbs*
Oil, for shallow-frying
200 g/7 oz/1 small can sweetcorn
*   (corn)*
Salt and freshly ground black pepper
4 waffles, warmed
Parsley sprigs

Beat one of the eggs on a plate. Use to coat the banana slices, then toss the slices in breadcrumbs. Heat enough oil to cover the base of a frying pan (skillet). Fry (sauté) the banana slices until golden. Drain on kitchen paper. Wipe out the pan with kitchen paper and heat a further 15 ml/1 tbsp oil. Beat the remaining eggs with 15 ml/1 tbsp water. Stir in the can of corn and season with salt and pepper. Pour into the hot oil and fry, lifting and stirring until golden brown underneath and just set. Flash under a hot grill (broiler) to brown the top. Cut into four wedges. Place a wedge of corn omelette on top of each waffle and pile a few slices of banana fritter on top. Garnish with parsley and serve.

French Asparagus Soufflé Omelette

3 eggs
Salt and white pepper
2.5 ml/½ tsp lemon juice
4 asparagus tips, fresh cooked or
    canned
30 ml/2 tbsp butter
A little extra butter

Separate two of the eggs. Add the whole egg to the egg yolks and beat well. Season. Whisk the egg whites with the lemon juice until stiff. Fold the meringue into the egg yolk mixture. Heat the asparagus. Heat the butter in a non-stick omelette pan and cook the egg mixture gently over a low heat, without stirring. With a palette knife, lift the omelette to check that it does not get too brown underneath. Cover with a lid and allow to puff up for 30 seconds. At this stage, place the well drained hot asparagus in the middle of the omelette. Fold over. Slip the omelette carefully on to a flat ovenproof dish coated with butter. Bake in a preheated oven at 200°C/400°F/gas mark 6 for 5–8 minutes to allow for more puffing. Serve.

Cheese Soufflé Omelette

SERVES 1

Prepare as for French Asparagus Soufflé Omelette but substitute 50 g/ 2 oz/½ cup grated Cheddar cheese for the hot asparagus tips.

Brittany Eggs

SERVES 4

8 thin pancakes made from ½
    quantity Basic Pancake Mix (see
    page 343)
50 g/2 oz/¼ cup butter, softened
4 eggs

Place the pancakes in a shallow baking tin (pan). Brush with butter. Break an egg on each pancake. Cover with foil and bake in a preheated oven at 220°C/ 425°F/gas mark 7 for 8 minutes or until the eggs are cooked to your liking.

'Blue' Beans with Poached Eggs

SERVES 4

4 eggs
4 lettuce leaves, shredded
30 ml/2 tbsp dried sliced onion
Lemon juice
450 g/1 lb frozen sliced green beans
225 g/8 oz/2 cups soft blue cheese,
    chopped
Wholemeal bread and butter

Poach the eggs to your liking. Meanwhile, put the lettuce in a saucepan with the onion and a little lemon juice and tip in the still-frozen beans. Cook, adding boiling water according to the packet directions but without any fat. Drain the vegetables when ready, and return them to the hot dry pan. Tip in the cheese pieces, and toss or stir for a few moments until the cheese is half-melted. Spread the mixture evenly over four warmed plates and lay a poached egg in the centre of each bed of beans. Serve with wholemeal bread and butter.

Italian-style Frittata

25 g/1 oz/2 tbsp butter or margarine
450 g/1 lb leaf spinach, stalks
*   discarded, washed and dried*
6 eggs, beaten
45 ml/3 tbsp single (light) cream
Salt and freshly ground black pepper
Grated nutmeg
1 garlic clove, chopped
60 ml/4 tbsp olive oil
30 ml/2 tbsp grated Pecorino cheese
*   or semi-soft cheese, cut into small*
*   cubes*
6 walnuts, chopped
Lettuce
Tomatoes
French Dressing (see page 303) or
*   use bought*

In a pan, melt the butter or margarine, add the spinach and cook for 5 minutes. Remove and squeeze out the surplus water to make it as dry as possible. Chop the cooked spinach. Blend the beaten eggs with the spinach, cream and seasoning, including the garlic. In a shallow frying pan (skillet) 20 cm/8 in diameter, heat the oil until smoking. Stir in the egg mixture and scramble a little. Sprinkle with grated Pecorino cheese or the cubes of semi-soft cheese and the walnuts. Cook, without stirring, for 2 minutes, making sure the bottom does not stick to the pan. When the underside is brown, place a cover or large plate over the omelette. Turn the pan upside down to turn the frittata on to a plate. Slide it from the plate back into the pan, adding a little oil. Brown on other side for 1 minute. When ready, the frittata should be soft but set like a sponge cake. Serve on a large, flat plate. Cut into wedges and serve with lettuce, tomatoes and French Dressing.

Shredded Omelette Japanese-style

4 eggs
15 ml/1 tbsp soy sauce
5 ml/1 tsp grated fresh root ginger
Salt and freshly ground black pepper
2.5 ml/½ tsp sugar
Snipped chives
Oil, for shallow-frying
Shredded iceberg lettuce

In a bowl, beat the eggs and add the soy sauce, ginger, salt, pepper, sugar and chives. Heat 5 ml/1 tsp oil in an omelette pan. Pour in 50 ml/2 fl oz/3½ tbsp egg mixture and cook like a pancake for 1 minute, tossing to cook the other side. Slip on to a plate. Continue until you have four omelettes. Put them on top of each other, roll them up and cut into ribbons with a sharp knife. To serve, place shredded lettuce on four plates and top with the egg ribbons.

Poached Eggs Turkish-style

120 ml/4 fl oz/½ cup plain yoghurt
Juice of ½ lemon
1 garlic clove, chopped
25 g/1 oz/2 tbsp butter or margarine
2 eggs

Blend the yoghurt, lemon juice and garlic in a bowl. Leave for 20 minutes, then strain. Place a spoonful of the mixture into two greased ramekin dishes (custard cups) and add an egg to each. Put the dishes in a baking tin (pan) half-filled with water. Cover with foil. Poach in a pre-heated oven at 200°C/400°F/gas mark 6 for 8 minutes. Serve in the same dishes.

Tomato Piperade

SERVES 4

4 large tomatoes, 100 g/4 oz each
30 ml/2 tbsp oil
1 red (bell) pepper, chopped
2 garlic cloves, chopped
3 large eggs, beaten
45 ml/3 tbsp double (heavy) cream
Salt and freshly ground black pepper
30 ml/2 tbsp chopped parsley

Cut the top off each tomato, two-thirds from the top. Keep the slices for lids. Gently squeeze out and discard the seeds, scoop out the pulp and chop. Heat the oil in a saucepan and stir-fry the chopped pepper for 2 minutes, then add the garlic and tomato pulp. Cook for 30 seconds. Blend half the beaten egg with the cream and add to the hot pepper mixture. Scramble for 1 minute, stirring, until smooth and cooked. Remove from the heat. Season and cool. Blend in the remaining beaten egg. Fill the cavity of each tomato with this mixture. Place each tomato in a ramekin dish (custard cup) (this will prevent them from collapsing on baking). Bake in a preheated oven at 200°C/400°F/gas mark 6 for 8 minutes. Replace the raw tomato slice on top of the cooked tomato. Sprinkle parsley on top and serve in the same ramekin dishes.

Chinese Omelette

SERVES 2

4 eggs, beaten
15 ml/1 tbsp soy sauce
Salt and freshly ground black pepper
7.5 ml/1½ tbsp flour
7.5 ml/1½ tbsp Chinese five spice
* powder*
30 ml/2 tbsp oil
1 red (bell) pepper, cut into strips
100 g/4 oz bean sprouts
1 garlic clove, chopped
5 ml/1 tsp grated fresh root ginger
Shredded iceberg lettuce

In a bowl, beat the eggs with the soy sauce, salt and pepper, flour and Chinese spice. In a wok, heat the oil and stir-fry the red pepper and bean sprouts for 2 minutes. Add the garlic and ginger and cook for 30 seconds. Now stir in the beaten eggs, scrambling a little. Cook for 2 minutes, without stirring, then toss or turn over like a pancake to cook the other side. Slip on to a plate and serve on a bed of shredded lettuce.

French Omelette

SERVES 1

2 eggs
1.5 ml/¼ tsp dried marjoram
15 ml/1 tbsp milk
Salt and freshly ground black pepper
Oil, for shallow-frying
½ onion, chopped
50 g/2 oz Brie or Camembert, thinly
*   sliced*

Beat together the eggs, herbs, milk and seasoning. Heat a little oil and lightly fry (sauté) the onion for 2 minutes. Put to one side. Pour the egg mixture into the pan and cook gently until almost set and firm underneath. Sprinkle the onion and cheese over one half of the omelette, fold in half and press lightly. Cook for a further 1–2 minutes.

Spanish-style Omelette

SERVES 4

15 ml/1 tbsp oil
225 g/8 oz cooked potatoes, diced
175 g/6 oz/1½ cups frozen peas
½ red (bell) pepper, diced
225 g/8 oz mushrooms, sliced
25 g/1 oz/2 tbsp butter or margarine
6 eggs
30 ml/2 tbsp water
5 ml/1 tsp dried mixed herbs
Salt and freshly ground black pepper
175 g/6 oz/1½ cups Cheddar cheese,
*   grated*

Heat the oil and fry (sauté) the vegetables for a few minutes until the peas and peppers are softened. Add the butter or margarine. Whisk together the eggs, water and herbs and season with salt and pepper. Add to the pan and keep stirring with a fork to prevent sticking, especially in the middle. When almost set, level the top and sprinkle with cheese. Brown under a hot grill (broiler) for a few minutes. Serve cut into wedges.

Pain Perdu

SERVES 4

4 eggs
Salt and freshly ground black pepper
2.5 ml/½ tsp sugar
8 slices bread, crusts removed
60 ml/4 tbsp oil and melted butter,
*   mixed*
100 g/4 oz fresh strawberries, sliced
Icing (confectioners') sugar

Beat the eggs with the salt, pepper and sugar in a large shallow dish. Dip the bread slices in this mixture. Heat the oil and butter in a large pan. Fry (sauté) the soaked slices, one at a time, for 1 minute on each side until golden. Drain on kitchen paper. Garnish with fresh strawberries and serve dusted with icing sugar.

Eggy Bread

4 eggs
A dash of milk
Salt and freshly ground black pepper
8 slices bread
Oil, for shallow-frying

Break the eggs into a bowl and beat with the milk and salt and pepper. Cut each slice of bread into quarters and dip into the egg mixture until completely coated. Heat the oil and fry (sauté) the soaked bread until browned on both sides. Sprinkle with salt and serve hot.

Cheese and Chive Pancakes

1 quantity Basic Pancake Mix (see
*   page 343)*
225 g/8 oz/1 cup cottage cheese
15 ml/1 tbsp snipped chives
Salt and freshly ground black pepper
15 g/½ oz/1 tbsp butter or margarine

Make the pancakes. Mix together the cheese and chives and season with salt and pepper. Place a few spoonfuls on each pancake and roll up. Arrange them in a shallow ovenproof dish. Dot with butter or margarine. Bake in a preheated oven at 200°C/400°F/gas mark 6 for about 15 minutes until heated through.

Spinach and Ricotta Pancakes

1 quantity Basic Pancake Mix (see
*   page 343)*
225 g/8 oz/1 cup Ricotta cheese
75 g/3 oz frozen spinach, thawed
Salt and freshly ground black pepper
Grated nutmeg
15 g/½ oz/1 tbsp butter or margarine

Make the pancakes. Mix together the cheese and spinach, adding salt, pepper and nutmeg to taste. Place a few spoonfuls on each pancake and roll them up. Arrange them in a shallow ovenproof dish. Dot with butter or margarine. Bake in a preheated oven at 200°C/400°F/gas mark 6 for about 15 minutes until heated through.

Squashed Bean Pancakes

Make the pancakes and fill with Kidney Bean Spread (see page 302), then continue as before.

Cheese and Ratatouille Pancakes

Make the pancakes and fill with a 425 g/15 oz/1 large can ratatouille and slices of Mozzarella cheese, then continue as before.

Marinated Tofu

SERVES 4

283 g/10½ oz/1 block firm tofu
30 ml/2 tbsp soy sauce
45 ml/3 tbsp sherry
15 ml/1 tbsp dark brown sugar
5 ml/1 tsp ground ginger
15 ml/1 tbsp oil
½ garlic clove, crushed
1.5 ml/¼ tsp dry mustard powder

Drain the tofu on a tilted plate while you make the marinade by mixing together all the remaining ingredients. Put the tofu in a container which just holds it and pour the marinade over. Chill for at least 24 hours, longer if possible, turning it over daily to soak both sides.

To grill tofu: Place a block of drained, marinated tofu on a piece of foil in the grill (broiler) pan. Heat the grill while you brush the surface of the tofu with oil. Put it under the grill for 1–2 minutes until it bubbles. Remove the pan from the heat at once, or the tofu will toughen. If you wish, turn the tofu over and grill (broil) the other side as well.

To serve tofu: Cut plain marinated or grilled tofu into slices, or slice a thick block through the centre horizontally, and cut both parts into fingers or small cubes.

Notes:

- For breakfast or to use the tofu as a salad ingredient, marinate it in a single block as above; when it is cut up, the white surfaces will not be flavoured.
- To use cubed tofu for cocktail snacks or in a dish of mixed vegetables, slit the tofu through the centre before marinating it and lay the thin sheets side by side in the marinade; both sides of each small cube will then be flavoured.
- Cubes of grilled, marinated tofu make a good substitute for cheese in a salad.

Hot Desserts

All the desserts in this book are vegetarian orientated. That is, they use lots of nutritious ingredients like fruit, nuts, honey and carob. These hot ones are particularly good on chilly winter days, or after light or cold main courses. And for those of you with a naturally sweet tooth, at least you can tell yourself that eating these puds will actually do you good!

As with other parts of the meal, it is worth making sure you keep a balance. So, if you have had rice in your main course, for instance, avoid a rice-based dessert. Or follow a main course with lots of fruit with a carob, nutty or boozy, creamy dessert.

Spiced Honey Toasts

SERVES 4

4 large square slices wholemeal
  bread
Butter or margarine
1 large banana
75 ml/5 tbsp clear honey
30 ml/2 tbsp water
1.5 ml/¼ tsp ground cinnamon
Good pinch of ground ginger
Pinch of freshly ground black pepper
30 ml/2 tbsp pine nuts

Toast the bread lightly on both sides. Cut off the crusts and spread one side with butter or margarine. Lay on warmed plates, spread side up. Skin and slice the banana and lay the slices on the toasts. Melt the honey, water and spices in a saucepan and pour over the banana slices. Sprinkle with the pine nuts. Serve straight away with knives and forks.

Baked Apple and Cranberry Pudding

SERVES 6

Butter or margarine, for greasing
150 g/5 oz/1¼ cups wholemeal flour
Good pinch of salt
100 g/4 oz/½ cup light brown sugar
4 large eggs, beaten
375 ml/13 fl oz/1½ cups milk or
  single (light) cream, or half milk
  and half cream
350 g/12 oz cranberries
225 g/8 oz apples, sliced
Icing (confectioners') sugar, sifted

Thoroughly grease a 16 cm/6½ in flan tin (pie pan) which is 4 cm/¾ in deep. Place the flour, salt and sugar in a bowl and mix together. Beat the eggs and milk or cream together and add gradually to the flour, beating well to form a smooth batter. Arrange the fruits in the bottom of the tin and pour over the batter. Bake in a preheated oven at 200°C/400°F/gas mark 6 for 45 minutes. Invert on to a dish and cut into wedges. Dust with icing sugar just before serving.

Baked Plum Pudding

SERVES 6

Prepare as for Baked Apple and Cranberry Pudding but substitute 450 g/1 lb plums, halved and stoned (pitted) for the cranberries and apples.

Peach Clafoutie

SERVES 4

420 g/14½ oz/1 large can peach
  slices, drained reserving the juice
1 quantity Basic Pancake Mix (see
  page 343)
25 g/1 oz/¼ cup flaked almonds
Icing (confectioners') sugar, sifted

Arrange the peaches attractively in a greased shallow ovenproof dish. Make up the pancake mix and pour over. Sprinkle with the almonds. Bake in a preheated oven at 200°C/400°F/gas mark 6 for about 30 minutes until risen and golden brown. Dust with sifted icing sugar and serve hot with the juice.

Photograph opposite: **Citrus Fruits on Spinach and Bean Sprouts (page 229)**

Tropical Banana Fritters

SERVES 4

100 g/4 oz/1 cup desiccated
  (shredded) coconut
2 bananas, mashed
75 g/3 oz/⅓ cup light brown sugar
Grated rind of 1 lime
30 ml/2 tbsp dark rum
Good pinch of baking powder
Oil, for deep-frying

Put 25 g/1 oz/¼ cup of the cocount to one side. Mix the remainder with the bananas, sugar, lime rind, rum and baking powder, working well in together. Shape into small balls and roll in the remaining coconut. Deep-fry in hot oil for 3 minutes until golden brown. Drain on kitchen paper and serve hot.

Pancakes with Strawberries and Bananas

SERVES 4

1 quantity Basic Pancake Mix (see
  page 343)
100 g/4 oz strawberries, thinly sliced
2 bananas, thinly sliced
150 ml/4 fl oz/⅔ cup crème fraîche
Icing (confectioners') sugar, sifted

Make the pancakes, mix the strawberries and bananas together and use to fill the pancakes. Roll up. Place two on each of four serving plates. Top with a dollop of crème fraîche and dust with sifted icing sugar. Serve straight away.

Photograph opposite: **Easy Corn and Banana Waffles (page 248)**

Special Mincemeat Pancakes

SERVES 4

1 quantity Basic Pancake Mix (see
  page 343)
15 ml/1 tbsp each raisins, sultanas
  (golden raisins), chopped stoned
  (pitted) dates, grated apple, grated
  lemon rind and juice, glacé
  (candied) cherries and chopped
  mixed nuts.
Thick plain yoghurt

Make the pancakes. Mix all the fruits and nuts together. Spread over the pancakes and roll up. Serve immediately topped with thick plain yoghurt.

Plum, Toffee and Almond Pudding

SERVES 4

50 g/2 oz/¼ cup butter or margarine
225 g/8 oz/1 cup light brown sugar
15 ml/1 tbsp lemon juice
5 thick slices wholemeal bread,
  crusts removed, cut into 2.5 cm/
  1 in squares
450 g/1 lb ripe plums, halved and
  stoned (pitted)
50 g/2 oz/½ cup flaked almonds
Greek-style plain yoghurt

Melt the butter or margarine in a large heavy-based frying pan (skillet). Add the sugar and lemon juice and heat, stirring, until the sugar melts. Add the bread cubes and fold into the toffee to coat completely. Take care not to break up the bread too much. Add the fruit. Cover with foil or a lid and cook gently for about 5 minutes or until the plums are tender. Stir again gently, then sprinkle with almonds and serve with Greek-style yoghurt.

Apple Charlotte

SERVES 4–6

450 g/1 lb cooking (tart) apples,
sliced
Pinch of ground cloves
15 ml/1 tbsp lemon juice
100 g/4 oz/½ cup light brown sugar
8 slices wholemeal bread, crusts
removed
75 g/3 oz/⅓ cup butter or margarine,
melted

Put the apples in a saucepan with the cloves, lemon juice and ¾ of the sugar. Cook gently, stirring occasionally, until the apples are pulpy. Meanwhile, dip some of the bread slices in melted butter or margarine and use to line a 1.2 litre/2 pt/ 5 cup ovenproof dish, trimming and patching to fit. Spoon in the purée. Cut the remaining bread slices into four triangles. Dip in the remaining melted fat and lay attractively over the apple. Sprinkle with the remaining sugar and bake in a preheated oven at 180°C/350°F/gas mark 4 for about 40 minutes until the top is crisp and golden.

Apple, Nut and Raisin Charlotte

SERVES 4-6

Prepare as for Apple Charlotte but use ground cinnamon instead of cloves to flavour the apple and add 25 g/1 oz/¼ cup raisins and 25 g/1 oz/¼ cup chopped almonds to the stewed apple before putting it in the dish.

St Clement's Charlotte

SERVES 4–6

1 orange
450 g/1 lb cooking (tart) apples,
sliced
Grated rind and juice of 1 lemon
100 g/4 oz/½ cup light brown sugar
8 slices wholemeal bread, crusts
removed
75 g/3 oz/⅓ cup butter or margarine,
melted

Grate the rind from the orange, peel off and discard the skin and all pith and chop the segments. Put the apples in a saucepan with the lemon rind and juice and three-quarters of the sugar. Cook gently, stirring occasionally, until the apples are pulpy. Meanwhile, dip some of the bread slices in melted butter or margarine and use to line a 1.2 litre/2 pt/ 5 cup ovenproof dish, trimming and patching to fit. Add the chopped orange and rind to the apple mixture and spoon into the bread-lined dish. Cut the remaining bread slices into four triangles. Dip in the remaining melted fat and lay attractively over the apple. Sprinkle with the remaining sugar and bake in a preheated oven at 180°C/ 350°F/gas mark 4 for about 40 minutes until the top is crisp and golden.

Fruit Pizza

SERVES 4

2 egg yolks
50 g/2 oz/¼ cup caster (superfine)
  sugar
30 ml/2 tbsp plain (all-purpose) flour
30 ml/2 tbsp cornflour (cornstarch)
300 ml/½ pt/1¼ cups milk
A few drops of vanilla essence
  (extract)
1 packet pizza dough mix
Mixed fruits, (e.g. seedless grapes,
  bananas, orange segments, apple
  slices)
45 ml/3 tbsp apricot jam
30 ml/2 tbsp water
Plain yoghurt

Cream the eggs and sugar together until thick and pale. Sift the flour and cornflour together into the bowl and beat in, adding a little cold milk to make a smooth paste. Heat the remaining milk in a saucepan until almost boiling and pour on to the egg mixture, stirring continuously. Reheat, stirring, until the mixture boils. Add the vanilla to taste and cook for a further 2–3 minutes. Cover and leave to cool. Make up the pizza dough as directed on the packet and roll out to a 20 cm/8 in round. Place on a greased baking sheet. Spread the dough round thinly with the custard and bake in a preheated oven at 180°C/350°F/gas mark 4 for 10 minutes. Leave to cool. When cold, decorate with a selection of fruit. Place the apricot jam in a saucepan with the water, heat gently, stirring, until the jam melts, then simmer for 1 minute. Strain and brush over the fruits while still warm. Place the pizza under the grill (broiler) until the fruit starts to colour. Serve hot with yoghurt.

Cheat Fruit Pizza

SERVES 4

Use a ready-made pizza base. Spread with 400 g/14 oz/1 large can of custard and bake as for Fruit Pizza. Top with canned, drained or fresh fruit and continue as left.

Mincemeat Jalousie

SERVES 6–8

225 g/8 oz frozen puff pastry (paste),
  just thawed
225 g/8 oz/½ jar vegetarian
  mincemeat
Grated rind and juice of 1 small
  lemon
Milk
Demerara sugar

Cut the pastry in half. Roll out one half to a rectangle about 25 x 20 cm/10 x 8 in. Transfer to a dampened baking sheet. Roll out the other half to the same size. Fold in half lengthways and make a series of cuts along the folded edge to within 2.5 cm/1 in of the open edges (like making a paper lantern when you were a child). Mix the mincemeat with the lemon rind and juice. Spread over the uncut rectangle to within 2.5 cm/1 in of the edges. Brush the edges with water. Carefully unfold the cut piece of pastry and lay on top. Press the edges well together to seal then knock up the edges all round. Brush with a little milk and sprinkle with demerara sugar. Bake in a preheated oven at 220°C/425°F/gas mark 7 for about 15 minutes until puffy and golden brown. Serve warm.

Crêpes Suzette Extraordinaire

SERVES 4

2 eggs, beaten
150 ml/¼ pt/⅔ cup milk
150 ml/¼ pt/⅔ cup water
100 g/4 oz/1 cup plain (all-purpose)
  flour
5 ml/1 tsp oil
Pinch of salt
Oil, for shallow-frying
50 g/2 oz/¼ cup butter
50 g/2 oz/¼ cup sugar
Pinch of ground cinnamon
Grated rind of ½ and juice of 1
  orange
4 yellow peaches, halved and stoned
  (pitted)
300 g/11 oz/1 small can morello
  cherries, drained and stoned
  (pitted)
50 ml/2 fl oz/3½ tbsp brandy
50 ml/2 fl oz/3½ tbsp cherry brandy

To make the crêpe batter, beat together the eggs, milk and water, blend in the flour and beat until smooth. Add the measured oil and the salt and leave for 30 minutes. Heat a little oil in a non-stick small omelette pan and pour in enough batter to cover the bottom of the pan. Cook until golden on the underside, then toss or turn over and cook the other side. Slide on to a sheet of greaseproof (waxed) paper and leave to cool. Repeat until you have made eight crêpes. When cold, chill until required. When ready to serve, first make a syrup by melting the butter and sugar together in a large frying pan (skillet). Add the cinnamon and orange rind and juice and boil for 4 minutes to form a butterscotch syrup. Dip each crêpe in the butterscotch to warm, then fold into quarters and arrange on a flameproof serving platter or metal dish. Pour over the remaining syrup and surround the crêpes with peaches and cherries. Place over the heat. Pour the brandy over the crêpes and heat until boiling. Ignite and then extinguish the flames with the cherry brandy. Serve each guest with two crêpes, one peach and a spoonful of syrup and cherries.

Jam Jalousie

SERVES 6–8

Prepare as for Mincemeat Jalousie (see page 259) but substitute your favourite flavoured jam for the mincemeat.

Pear and Carob Strudels

SERVES 4

2 ripe pears, chopped
25 g/1 oz/¼ cup carob chips
Pinch of ground cinnamon
4 filo pastry (paste) sheets
20 g/¾ oz/1½ tbsp butter or
  margarine, melted

Mix the pears with the carob chips and cinnamon. Brush the pastry sheets with a little of the melted butter or margarine. Fold in half and brush again. Divide the pear mixture between the sheets of pastry, putting it in the middle of one edge. Fold in the sides, then roll up. Transfer to a lightly greased baking sheet and brush with any remaining butter or margarine. Bake in a preheated oven at 190°C/375°F/gas mark 5 for about 10–15 minutes until golden brown.

Sweet Herb and Raisin Tart

SERVES 4

75 g/3 oz/¾ cup self-raising (self-rising) flour
75 g/3 oz/¾ cup wholemeal self-raising flour
75 g/3 oz/⅓ cup butter or margarine
100 g/4 oz/½ cup low-fat soft cheese
50 g/2 oz/¼ cup light brown sugar
1 egg, beaten
50 g/2 oz/⅓ cup raisins
5 ml/1 tsp chopped mint
5 ml/1 tsp very finely chopped rosemary
Grated rind and juice of 1 lemon

Mix the flours together in a bowl. Add the butter or margarine and rub in with the fingertips until the mixture resembles fine breadcrumbs. Mix with enough cold water to form a firm dough. Knead the pastry (paste) gently on a lightly floured surface. Roll out and use to line an 18 cm/7 in flan dish (pie pan) on a baking sheet. Beat the remaining ingredients together and turn into the pastry-lined dish. Bake in a preheated oven at 220°C/ 425°F/gas mark 7 for about 20 minutes until the pastry is golden and the filling is set. Serve warm.

Extra-special Pecan Pie

SERVES 4–6

350 g/12 oz puff pastry (paste)
150 g/5 oz/1¼ cups pecan halves
75 g/3 oz/⅓ cup butter or margarine
175 g/6 oz/¾ cup light brown sugar
4 eggs, beaten
60 ml/4 tbsp golden (light corn) syrup
30 ml/2 tbsp boiling water
5 ml/1 tsp vanilla essence (extract)

Roll out the pastry and use to line a 20 cm/8 in flan dish (pie) pan on a baking sheet. Reserve 25 g/1 oz/¼ cup of the nuts for decoration and roughly chop the remainder. Cream the butter and sugar until light and fluffy. Beat in the egg a little at a time. Mix the syrup with the boiling water and stir into the mixture with the chopped nuts and vanilla essence. Turn into the pastry-lined dish and bake in a preheated oven at 200°C/ 400°F/gas mark 6 for 15 minutes. Put the reserved pecan halves on top to decorate, reduce the heat to 180°C/350°F/gas mark 4 and continue cooking for about 30 minutes or until the filling is a deep golden brown and set. Serve warm with cream.

Normandy Apple Tart

SERVES 8–10

450 g/1 lb/4 cups self-raising (self-rising) flour
5 ml/1 tsp ground cinnamon
25 g/1 oz/⅙ cup icing (confectioners') sugar
150 g/5 oz/⅔ cup butter
100 g/4 oz/½ cup margarine
3 eggs, beaten
175 g/6 oz/¾ cup granulated sugar
450 g/1 lb Bramley cooking (tart) apples, sliced
45 ml/3 tbsp cornflour (cornstarch)
90 ml/6 tbsp water
Icing sugar, for dusting
Cream or Egg Custard Sauce (see page 319)

Grease a large shallow, oblong baking tin (pan). Sift the flour, cinnamon and icing sugar on to a pastry (paste) board. Rub 50 g/2 oz/¼ cup of the butter and the margarine into the flour mixture. Make a well in the centre and blend in 2 of the beaten eggs and 15–30 ml/1–2 tbsp of water. Mix to a dough and knead lightly. Chill for 1 hour. In a shallow pan, melt the remaining butter with the sugar and cook the apple slices for 5 minutes, stirring well. Blend the cornflour and water and stir into the apple mixture to thicken the juice. Cook for 5 minutes and cool. Divide the pastry into two halves. On a floured board, roll out one half and use to line the base of the greased tin. Prick all over with a fork. Part bake in a preheated oven at 220°C/425°F/gas mark 7 for 8 minutes. Remove from the tin and cool. When cold, spread the apple mixture over the baked pastry leaving an edge around. Brush some of the remaining beaten egg all round. Roll out the remaining pastry to the same size and lay over the top. Press the edges together to seal. Complete the baking of the tart at the same oven temperature for another 8–10 minutes until golden brown. Dust with icing sugar. Serve warm, cut into squares, with cream or Egg Custard Sauce.

Walnut Syrup Pie

SERVES 6

225 g/8 oz shortcrust pastry (basic pie crust)
30 ml/2 tbsp plain (all-purpose) flour
100 g/4 oz/½ cup light brown sugar
3 eggs, beaten
Pinch of salt
100 g/4 oz/½ cup butter, melted
225 g/8 oz/⅔ cup maple syrup and honey, mixed
225 g/8 oz/2 cups walnuts, chopped
6 drops of vanilla essence (extract)

Line a well-oiled 20 cm/8 in flan tin (pie pan) with the pastry. In a bowl, mix the flour and sugar. Add the remaining ingredients and beat thoroughly. Fill the pastry case with the mixture. Bake in a preheated oven at 190°C/375°F/gas mark 5 for the first 10 minutes, then reduce the heat to 180°C/350°F/gas mark 4 for a further 20 minutes until set and golden.

Caramelised Apple and Pear Tart

225 g/8 oz small Bramley (tart)
  apples
225 g/8 oz ripe comice pears
Juice of 1 lemon
100 g/4 oz/½ cup butter or margarine
225 g/8 oz/1 cup granulated sugar
Flour for dusting
225 g/8 oz puff pastry (paste) or
  shortcrust pastry (basic pie crust)
Cream flavoured with Kirsch or
  orange liqueur

Peel, core and halve all the fruits, then
sprinkle with lemon juice. Chill in a
shallow dish. Spread the base of a
20 cm/8 in frying pan (skillet) that can
also be placed in a preheated oven with
the butter or margarine. Sprinkle the
sugar over the fat. Arrange all the fruits in
the pan with the cored cavities upwards.
Dust the pastry board with flour and roll
out the pastry to fit the size of the pan.
Lay over the fruit. Trim the edges with a
knife and remove any surplus pastry. Rest
the tart in a cool place for 30 minutes to
prevent shrinking. Place the pan on top of
the cooker for 8 minutes to caramelize
the bottom of the fruit. Ensure even cooking by lifting the edges of the pastry with
a palette knife. Transfer to a preheated
oven and bake at 220°C/425°F/gas mark
7 for a further 20 minutes. Invert the tart
on to a flat plate while still hot so that the
pastry is underneath the fruit. Serve the
tart piping hot with the flavoured cream.

Carob Pudding with Rum Sauce

100 g/4 oz/1 cup self-raising (self-
  rising) flour
5 ml/1 tsp baking powder
30 ml/2 tbsp carob powder
5 ml/1 tsp vanilla essence (extract)
100 g/4 oz/½ cup soft margarine
150 g/5 oz/⅔ cup caster (superfine)
  sugar
2 eggs
30 ml/2 tbsp hot water
15 ml/1 tbsp cornflour (cornstarch)
300 ml/½ pt/1¼ cups milk
30 ml/2 tbsp rum

Sift the flour, baking powder and carob
into a bowl. Add the vanilla essence,
margarine, 100 g/4 oz/½ cup of the sugar,
the eggs and hot water. Beat well together
until smooth. Grease an 18 cm/7 in
round, deep cake tin (pan) and line the
base with baking parchment. Turn the
mixture into the tin and bake in a
preheated oven at 190°C/375°F/gas mark
5 for about 25 minutes until firm to the
touch. Meanwhile, make the sauce. Blend
the cornflour with a little of the milk in a
saucepan. Stir in the remaining milk and
the remaining sugar. Bring to the boil and
cook for 2 minutes, stirring all the time.
Stir in the rum. Turn the cake out on to a
serving dish and remove the paper. Spoon
some of the sauce over and serve with the
remaining sauce handed separately.

Spiced Carrot and Sultana Pudding

75 g/3 oz/¾ cup plain (all-purpose) flour
75 g/3 oz/¾ cup wholemeal flour
75 g/3 oz/⅓ cup butter or margarine
1 carrot, grated
50 g/2 oz/1 cup wholemeal breadcrumbs
300 ml/½ pt/1¼ cups milk, hot
50 g/2 oz/¼ cup light brown sugar
Grated rind and juice of 1 lemon
25 g/1 oz/⅙ cup sultanas (golden raisins), roughly chopped
10 ml/2 tsp mixed (apple pie) spice
2 eggs, beaten

Mix the flours in a bowl. Add the butter or margarine and rub in with the fingertips until the mixture resembles breadcrumbs. Mix with enough cold water to form a firm dough. Knead gently on a lightly floured surface. Roll out and use to line a 20 cm/8 in pie dish. Beat the remaining ingredients together and turn into the pastry-lined dish. Bake in a preheated oven at 190°C/375°F/gas mark 5 for about 40 minutes until set and golden brown on the top.

Dalmatian Pudding

175 g/6 oz/1½ cups self-raising (self-rising) flour
Pinch of salt
5 ml/1 tsp mixed (apple pie) spice
100 g/4 oz/½ cup caster (superfine) sugar
175 g/6 oz/3 cups fresh breadcrumbs
175 g/6 oz/1½ cups vegetarian suet
225 g/8 oz/1⅓ cups mixed dried fruit (fruit cake mix)
100 g/4 oz/⅔ cup stoned (pitted) dates, chopped
A little milk
Egg Custard Sauce (see page 319)

Sift the flour, salt and spice into a bowl. Stir in the remaining ingredients except the milk and custard. Mix well. Mix with enough milk to form a soft but not sticky dough. Knead gently, then place in a greased 450 g/1 lb loaf tin (pan). Cover with foil, twisting and folding under the rim to secure. Place in a roasting tin (pan) containing 4 cm/1½ in boiling water. Bake in a preheated oven at 200°C/400°F/gas mark 6 for 1¼–1½ hours or until risen and firm to the touch. Serve sliced with Egg Custard Sauce. (It's good served cold sliced and buttered too.)

Hazelnut Queen of Puddings

600 ml/1 pt/2½ cups milk
100 g/4 oz/2 cups wholemeal breadcrumbs
15 g/½ oz/1 tbsp butter or margarine
75 g/3 oz/⅓ cup caster (superfine) sugar
A few drops of vanilla essence (extract)
2 eggs, separated
50 g/2 oz/½ cup hazelnuts, finely chopped or ground
45 ml/3 tbsp raspberry jam

Bring the milk to the boil, remove from the heat and stir in the breadcrumbs, butter or margarine, 25 g/1 oz/2 tbsp of the sugar and the vanilla essence. Cool slightly, beat in the egg yolks then pour into a 1.2 litre/2 pt/5 cup ovenproof dish. Leave to stand for 30 minutes, then bake in a preheated oven at 180°C/350°F/gas mark 4 for 30 minutes or until just set. Whisk the egg whites until stiff. Whisk in half the sugar until peaking, then fold in the remaining sugar and the hazelnuts with a metal spoon. Spread the surface of the crumb mixture with the jam, then pile the nut meringue on top. Return to a preheated oven for 15 minutes or until the top is crisp and golden. Serve warm.

Hot Pear and Orange Soufflés

1 large orange
1 ripe pear
20 g/¾ oz/1½ tbsp butter or margarine
20 g/¾ oz/3 tbsp plain (all-purpose) flour
150 ml/¼ pt/⅔ cup milk
25 g/1 oz/2 tbsp caster (superfine) sugar
2 eggs, separated
A little icing (confectioners') sugar

Grate the rind from the orange, then pare off and discard the skin and cut the flesh into small pieces. Peel, core and dice the pear. Mix together and spoon into four greased ramekin dishes (custard cups) on a baking sheet. Put the butter, flour and milk in a saucepan. Whisk until smooth, then bring to the boil, whisking all the time, until thick and bubbling. Remove from the heat and beat in the sugar, orange rind and egg yolks. Whisk the egg whites until stiff and fold into the mixture with a metal spoon. Spoon on top of the fruit in the ramekins and bake in a preheated oven at 200°C/400°F/gas mark 6 for 15–20 minutes until risen and golden. Quickly sift a little icing sugar over the surfaces and serve immediately.

Pineapple Loaf

350 g/12 oz/3 cups plain (all-
purpose) flour
15 ml/1 tbsp baking powder
2.5 ml/½ tsp bicarbonate of soda
(baking soda)
100 g/4 oz/½ cup light brown sugar
150 g/5 oz/⅔ cup butter or margarine
3 eggs, beaten
30 ml/2 tbsp milk
5 ml/1 tsp ground cinnamon
30 ml/1 tbsp clear honey
4 pineapple rings, roughly chopped

Mix all the ingredients together, than pour into a greased 450 g/1 lb loaf tin. Bake on a low shelf in a preheated oven at 180°C/350°F/gas mark 4 for about 1 hour or until firm. Serve warm or cold.

Peach Loaf

Prepare as for Pineapple Loaf but substitute 227 g/8 oz/1 small can peach halves, drained and roughly chopped, for the pineapple and add 10 ml/2 tsp lemon juice.

Nutty Blackberry and Apple Crumble

450 g/1 lb cooking (tart) apples,
chopped
15 ml/1 tbsp sugar
45 ml/3 tbsp water
175 g/6 oz blackberries
100 g/4 oz/1 cup plain (all-purpose)
flour
Pinch of salt
50 g/2 oz/¼ cup butter or margarine
50 g/2 oz/¼ cup light brown sugar
2.5 ml/½ tsp ground cinnamon
50 g/2 oz/½ cup chopped mixed nuts
Egg Custard Sauce (see page 319)

Put the apples into a saucepan with the sugar and water. Heat gently, stirring occasionally, until the apples have gone pulpy. Remove from the heat and stir in the blackberries. Pour into an ovenproof dish. Mix the flour and salt then rub in the butter or margarine until the mixture resembles breadcrumbs. Stir in the sugar, cinnamon and nuts. Sprinkle over the fruit. Bake in a preheated oven at 190°C/375°F/gas mark 5 for 25 minutes or until crisp and golden on top. Serve with Egg Custard Sauce.

Nutty Apricot Crumble

Prepare as for Nutty Blackberry and Apple Crumble but substitute 750 g/1½ lb fresh apricots, halved and stoned (pitted) for the apples and omit the blackberries. Use chopped almonds instead of mixed nuts.

Simple Rice Pudding

SERVES 4–6

100 g/4 oz/½ cup short-grain rice
1.2 litres/2 pts/5 cups milk
50 g/2 oz/¼ cup sugar
Pinch of grated nutmeg
15 g/½ oz/1 tbsp butter or margarine

Put the rice and half the milk into a saucepan, bring to the boil, then simmer for 20–25 minutes until the milk is nearly all absorbed. Add all the remaining ingredients except the butter or margarine, then pour into a greased ovenproof dish. Dot with the butter or margarine. Bake in a preheated oven at 150°C/300°F/gas mark 2 for about 1½ hours. Serve hot or cold.

Jammy Rice Pudding

SERVES 4–6

Prepare as for Simple Rice Pudding but remove the skin 5 minutes before the end of cooking and spoon 45–60 ml/ 3–4 tbsp jam of your choice warmed with 20 ml/4 tsp water over the surface of the rice and return to a preheated oven to glaze.

Brown Rice and Raisin Pudding

SERVES 4

Prepare as for Simple Rice Pudding but substitute brown short-grain rice for the white rice and simmer for 30 minutes, adding a little more of the milk if necessary. Add 50 g/2 oz/⅓ cup raisins with the remaining ingredients.

Bread, Milk and Honey Pudding

SERVES 4

8 slices wholemeal bread, crusts
*   removed*
25 g/1 oz/2 tbsp butter or margarine
45 ml/3 tbsp clear honey
3 eggs
450 ml/¾ pt/2 cups milk
15 ml/1 tbsp light brown sugar

Spread the bread with butter or margarine and honey, cut into halves and layer in an ovenproof dish. Mix together the eggs, milk and sugar and pour over the bread. Bake in a preheated oven at 180°C/350°F/gas mark 4 for about 40 minutes until firm.

Old-fashioned Bread Pudding

SERVES 4

Prepare as for Bread, Milk and Honey Pudding but substitute sugar for the honey. Add 75 g/3 oz/¾ cup mixed dried fruit (fruit cake mix) between the layers, dusting with 5 ml/1 tsp mixed (apple pie) spice. Use white bread if you prefer.

Candied Fruit Pudding

SERVES 4

Prepare as for Bread, Milk and Honey Pudding but scatter 50 g/2 oz/½ cup chopped candied mixed peel and 50 g/ 2 oz/½ cup chopped glacé (candied) cherries between the bread layers.

Swedish Raisin Sour Cake

SERVES 8

225 g/8 oz shortcrust pastry (basic pie crust)
30 ml/2 tbsp plain (all-purpose) flour
2 eggs, beaten
60 ml/4 tbsp caster (superfine) sugar
250 ml/8 fl oz/1 cup soured (dairy sour) cream
225 g/8 oz/1⅓ cups raisins
60 ml/4 tbsp rum or brandy
2 drops of vanilla essence (extract)
3 drops of lemon essence

Roll out the pastry and use to line an oiled flan tin (pie pan) 23 cm/9 in diameter. In a bowl, mix the flour, eggs, sugar and cream to a batter. Add the raisins, rum or brandy and essences. Fill the pastry case (shell) with the mixture. Bake in a preheated oven at 200°C/400°F/gas mark 6 for 20 minutes. Reduce the heat to 180°C/350°F/gas mark 4 and cook for 5 minutes until baked like a custard. Serve warm.

Fried Chinese Ice Cream

SERVES 4

8 scoops of ice cream
Oil, for deep-frying
90 ml/6 tbsp plain (all-purpose) flour
2 eggs, beaten
50 g/2 oz/1 cup white breadcrumbs
15 ml/1 tbsp desiccated (shredded) coconut
Raspberry or Apricot Coulis (see page 319–20)

On a clean baking sheet lined with greaseproof (waxed) paper, place the scoops of ice cream. Refreeze immediately until really frozen – about 6 hours. Heat the oil in a deep-fryer to 190°C/375°F. Coat each frozen scoop of ice cream all over in flour. Dust the surplus away. Dip in beaten egg, then roll in the breadcrumbs mixed with the coconut, making sure that there is a thick coating of crumbs and coconut. Deep-fry for 30 seconds only – this is very important. Serve immediately with Raspberry or Apricot Coulis.

Apple and Apricot Bites

SERVES 6

*2 large Bramley or other cooking
(tart) apples, peeled, cored and cut
into rings.*
6 fresh apricots, stoned (pitted)
30 ml/2 tbsp flour, for dusting
15 ml/1 tbsp ground cinnamon
*600 ml/1 pt/2½ cups Basic Pancake
Mix (see page 343)*
Oil, for deep-frying
*Caster (superfine) sugar, for
sprinkling*
Apricot Coulis (see page 320)

Coat the apple rings and apricots in a
mixture of flour and cinnamon. Dip
each one in batter and deep-fry in hot oil
for 1–2 minutes until golden brown. Drain
on kitchen paper and sprinkle with caster
sugar. Serve with Apricot Coulis.

Apple and Coconut Pie

SERVES 4

25 g/1 oz/2 tbsp butter or margarine
*750 g/1½ lb eating (dessert) apples,
sliced*
5 ml/1 tsp mixed (apple pie) spice
45 ml/3 tbsp light brown sugar
*100 g/4 oz/⅔ cup dates, stoned
(pitted) and chopped*
1 egg white
*50 g/2 oz/½ cup desiccated (shredded)
coconut*
Crème fraîche

Melt the butter or margarine in a
saucepan. Add the apples, spice and
half the sugar. Cover and cook gently, stirring occasionally, for 5 minutes. Stir in the
dates and place in a greased pie dish.
Whisk the egg white until stiff and add the
remaining sugar and the coconut. Continue whisking until stiff again and spread
the mixture over the fruit using a fork.
Bake for 20 minutes in a preheated oven
at 180°C/350°F/gas mark 4 and serve
warm with crème fraîche.

Carob and Orange Baked Alaska

6 slices carob cake
150 ml/¼ pt/⅔ cup orange juice
3 oranges, peeled and chopped
3 egg whites
75 g/3 oz/⅓ cup caster (superfine) sugar
1 quantity Carob Chip Ice Cream (see page 298)

In a greased, shallow ovenproof glass dish, place the slices of cake and soak with the orange juice. Sprinkle the chopped fruit over the top. Whisk the egg whites until stiff and add the sugar. Continue whisking until stiff again. Pile spoonfuls or scoops of the ice cream on to the fruit and cake base and cover completely with the meringue. Bake in a very hot oven at 240°C/475°F/gas mark 9 for 3–5 minutes until the meringue is just turning golden. Serve immediately.

Caramel and Banana Baked Alaska

Prepare as for Carob and Orange Baked Alaska but substitute a plain ready-cooked sponge flan case (pie shell) for the carob cake. Fill with chopped bananas instead of oranges. Use Caramel Ice Cream (see page 297) instead of Carob Chip and continue as above.

Fruit Temptation

225 g/8 oz mixed fresh fruit, chopped
100 g/4 oz/½ cup cottage cheese
15 ml/1 tbsp clear honey
150 g/5 oz/1¼ cups desiccated (shredded) coconut
25 g/1 oz/¼ cup wholemeal flour
25 g/1 oz/2 tbsp sugar
50 g/2 oz/¼ cup butter or margarine
Thick plain yoghurt

Put the fruit in a greased ovenproof dish. Spread the cottage cheese over and drizzle the honey on top. Mix together the coconut, flour, sugar and melted butter or margarine. Spread over the cottage cheese to cover completely. Bake in a pre-heated oven for 20 minutes at 180°C/350°F/gas mark 4. Stand for 5 minutes before serving with thick yoghurt.

Grilled Dessert Grapefruit

2 grapefruit, halved
60 ml/4 tbsp light brown sugar
30 ml/2 tbsp sweet sherry

Place the grapefruit in 4 flameproof dishes. Separate the segments from the membranes with a serrated knife. Sprinkle each grapefruit half with sugar and sherry. Place under a hot grill (broiler) for 3 minutes until the sugar is sticky.

Pineapple Fritters

150 g/5 oz/1¼ cups plain (all-
*   purpose) flour*
100 g/4 oz/1 cup wholemeal flour
5 ml/1 tsp baking powder
Pinch of salt
300 ml/½ pt/1¼ cups water
16 pineapple rings
Oil, for deep-frying
Maple syrup
Ice cream

Put 100 g/4 oz/1 cup of the plain flour, the wholemeal flour, baking powder and salt into a bowl and make a well in the centre. Gradually pour in the water, whisking to make a smooth paste. Dip the pineapple rings in the remaining flour, then in the batter. Heat the oil and deep-fry the fritters in hot oil until crispy. Serve hot with maple syrup and/or ice cream.

Apple Fritters

Prepare as for Pineapple Fritters but substitute cored, sliced eating (dessert) apples for the pineapple rings.

Pear Fritters

Prepare as for Pineapple Fritters but substitute cored, quartered pears for the pineapple rings.

Banana Fritters

Prepare as for Pineapple Fritters but use halved or quartered bananas and serve with Carob Custard Sauce (see page 319).

Carob Bananas

4 bananas, unpeeled
4 carob squares
Quark

Make a slit in the skin along each banana. Poke a chunk of carob into the slit and close the skin around it. Bake in a preheated oven at 200°C/400°F/gas mark 6 for 10 minutes until the carob has just started to melt. Serve with quark.

Citrus Baked Apples

4 cooking (tart) apples
Orange, Lemon or Lime Curd (see
page 321)
Light brown sugar
Egg Custard Sauce (see page 319)

Remove the cores from the apples and cut a line around the centre of the apples. Stand them in an ovenproof dish. Fill the holes with Orange, Lemon or Lime Curd and sprinkle with a little sugar. Add about 2.5 cm/1 in water to the bottom of the dish. Bake in a preheated oven at 180°C/350°F/gas mark 4 for about 1 hour. Serve hot with Egg Custard Sauce.

Mincemeat Apples

4 cooking (tart) apples
Vegetarian mincemeat
Light brown sugar
Egg Custard Sauce (see page 319)

Remove the cores from the apples and cut a line around the centre of the aples. Stand them in an ovenproof dish. Fill the holes with vegetarian mincemeat and sprinkle with a little sugar. Add about 2.5 cm/1 in water to the bottom of the dish. Bake in a preheated oven at 180°C/350°F/gas mark 4 for about 1 hour. Serve hot with Egg Custard Sauce.

Nutty Apples

Prepare as for Citrus Baked Apples but fill the cavities with chopped walnuts and spoon a little golden (light corn) syrup over each instead of the sugar.

Apple Muesli

2 cooking (tart) apples, chopped
225 g/8 oz blackberries
15 ml/1 tbsp lemon juice
15 ml/1 tbsp light brown sugar
(optional)
150 g/5 oz/1¼ cups muesli

Simmer the fruit in the lemon juice and a little water until soft. Add the sugar, if using (if you prefer a sharper taste leave it out). Place in a flameproof dish and cover with muesli. Sprinkle a little sugar on top, if liked. Place under a low grill (broiler) for 10 minutes until the muesli is golden.

Drunken Pears

15 ml/1 tbsp light brown sugar
5 ml/1 tsp lemon juice
300 ml/½ pt/1¼ cups red wine
4 pears, peeled

Dissolve the sugar and lemon juice in the wine over a gentle heat. Cut a slice off the bottom of the pears so that they stand upright and remove the core from the base, if liked. Stand them in a deep dish and pour over the wine. Cover with foil or a lid. Bake in a preheated oven at 160°C/325°F/gas mark 3 for 30 minutes.

Drunken Apples

Prepare as for Drunken Pears but substitute cider for the wine and peeled red (soft fleshed) eating (dessert) apples for the pears.

Nectarines in Wine

15 ml/1 tbsp light brown sugar
5 ml/1 tsp lemon juice
300 ml/½ pt/1¼ cups white wine
4 nectarines, peeled

Dissolve the sugar and lemon juice in the wine over a gentle heat. Cut a slice off the bottom of the nectarines so that they stand upright, if liked. Stand them in a deep dish and pour over the wine. Cover with foil or a lid. Bake in a preheated oven at 160°C/325°F/gas mark 3 for 30 minutes.

Royal Sabayon

4 egg yolks
2 eggs, beaten
50 g/2 oz/¼ cup caster (superfine)
  sugar
50 ml/2 fl oz/3½ tbsp cognac
25 ml/1 fl oz/1½ tbsp Cointreau
75 ml/5 tbsp sweet white wine
75 ml/5 tbsp orange juice
Grated rind and juice of 1 lime or
  1 lemon
Mint leaves
Strawberries
Kiwi fruit

Place the egg yolks, beaten eggs and sugar in a heatproof bowl and beat for 4 minutes with a balloon whisk. Place the bowl over a saucepan of boiling water and whisk for 5 minutes until the mixture thickens like custard. Gradually whisk in the cognac and the Cointreau. Pour the wine and orange juice into a saucepan with the lime or lemon rind and juice and warm without boiling. Gradually pour into the custard, whisking all the time. Leave the mixture to thicken in the bowl over the heat to prevent curdling. Pour into large balloon glasses to serve. Decorate the glasses with mint leaves, slices of strawberry and kiwi fruit and serve immediately.

Foamy Royal Sabayon

Prepare as for Royal Sabayon but add 2 egg whites, whisked until stiff, and fold into the wine custard before pouring into the glasses. Serve with langues de chat biscuits instead of fruit.

Passion Fruit Soufflés

4 ripe bananas
6 passion fruit
3 egg yolks
90 ml/6 tbsp rum
60 ml/4 tbsp double (heavy) cream,
  lightly whipped
6 egg whites
75 g/3 oz/⅓ cup caster (superfine)
  sugar
45 ml/3 tbsp apricot jam (conserve)
3 small just ripe bananas, sliced

Pass the ripe bananas through a sieve (strainer) or mash very thoroughly to a smooth pulp. Collect the pulp from the passion fruit and mix it with the banana purée. Blend with the egg yolks, half the rum and the cream. In a mixing bowl, beat the egg whites until fairly stiff but not dry. Add the sugar, a little at a time. Mix one-third of this meringue with the banana mixture. Beat thoroughly. Fold in the remaining meringue very lightly. Thoroughly butter six individual oven-proof soufflé dishes 250 ml/8 fl oz/1 cup capacity. Dust with caster sugar inside and place on a baking sheet ready for baking at the last moment. Fill each souf-flé dish to the brim. Mark round the edge with the back of a teaspoon to form a groove, detaching the mixture from the side of each dish. This will help in even rising. Bake in a preheated oven at 200°C/400°F/gas mark 6 for about 20 minutes until well risen. Meanwhile, warm the jam and the remaining rum. Add the sliced bananas. Serve with the soufflés immediately accompanied with the sliced bananas in sauce.

Asti Spumante Sabayon

4 egg yolks
30–45 ml/2–3 tbsp caster (superfine)
  sugar
Juice of ½ lemon
250 ml/8 fl oz/1 cup Asti Spumante
  sparkling wine
30 ml/2 tbsp orange liqueur

Whisk the egg yolks, sugar, lemon juice and half the wine in an electric mixer at full speed for 2 minutes. Bring the remaining wine to the boil in a saucepan. Add it to the frothy mixture, whisking at a slow speed. Add the orange liqueur. Increase the speed and whisk for another 2 minutes. The mixture should be thickish, frothy and more than double its original volume. Serve hot in dessert glasses.

Note: For lasting thickness, place the bowl in a shallow pan half-filled with water just under boiling point and whisk by hand for 3 more minutes to ensure it will thicken. Do not allow the temperature to exceed 78–80°C.

Sherry Sabayon

Prepare as for Asti Spumante Sabayon but substitute medium-dry sherry for the Asti Spumante and omit the liqueur.

Cold Desserts

The lovely thing about cold puddings is that often they can be made well in advance and forgotten about until you are ready to serve them. Others can be thrown together at the last minute. This makes them particularly useful when you're entertaining. They are the best option too after a hot, filling main course.

One little tip about home-made ice cream and other frozen desserts – remember to transfer them from freezer to fridge at the beginning of your meal (unless a recipe specifically states otherwise). That way you can be sure they will be the right consistency for eating – not rock hard.

Brandied Fruit Compôte

SERVES 4

225 g/8 oz/1⅓ cups dried fruit salad
300 ml/½ pt/1¼ cups apple juice
Lemon slice
5 cm/2 in piece cinnamon stick
30 ml/2 tbsp brandy
Quark

Wash the dried fruit salad, place in a saucepan with the apple juice and leave to stand for at least 3 hours. Add the lemon slice and the cinnamon. Bring to the boil, reduce the heat, cover and simmer gently for 30 minutes until the fruits are really tender. Discard the lemon and cinnamon. Leave covered until cold, then stir in the brandy and chill until ready to serve with a bowl of quark handed separately.

Fruity Chocolate Chip Dip

SERVES 4

2 large oranges
1 small carton apricot yoghurt
10 ml/2 tsp orange liqueur (optional)
15 ml/1 tbsp toasted chopped nuts
4 chocolate chip chewy bars

Halve the oranges and carefully remove the flesh with a serrated knife. Cut a tiny slice off the base of each orange shell so it stands upright. Chop the orange flesh, discarding any pith or tough membranes. Place in a bowl and mix in the yoghurt and liqueur, if using. Place the orange shells on four individual plates. Spoon in the fruit and yoghurt mixture. Sprinkle with chopped nuts. Cut the cereal bars into bite-sized pieces and arrange around the base of the oranges. Serve with a cocktail stick (toothpick) to spear the pieces of chewy bar then dip in the fruit and yoghurt, and a teaspoon to eat the remainder.

276

Little Baskets of Fruit

100 g/4 oz/⅔ cup icing
(confectioners') sugar, sifted
100 g/4 oz/1 cup plain (all-purpose)
flour
25 g/1 oz/¼ cup ground almonds
3 egg whites
Pinch of salt
1 mango, halved and stoned (pitted)
Juice of 1 lime
25 g/1 oz/2 tbsp sugar
75 ml/5 tbsp white wine
5 ml/1 tsp cornflour (cornstarch)
75 ml/5 tbsp water
450 g/1 lb assorted fresh fruits (e.g.
sliced bananas, cubed pineapple,
halved strawberries or raspberries,
grapes)
Icing sugar, for dusting
Mint leaves

Line 2 baking sheets with non-stick baking parchment and place four greased 18 cm/7 in flan rings on them. For the biscuit mixture, place the first five ingredients in a bowl and beat together to form a creamy batter. Spoon the batter into the four flan rings and spread evenly. Bake in a preheated oven for 8–9 minutes at 190°C/375°F/gas mark 5 until golden. Remove the cooked biscuits from the rings and baking sheet immediately and, while still hot, place each on top of an inverted small heatproof mixing bowl. Let fall or mould them into a cup shape. Leave to cool until firm. For the sauce, scoop the pulp out of the mango halves and place in a saucepan with the lime juice, sugar and wine. Bring to the boil, then purée in a blender or food processor. Return to the pan. Blend the cornflour (cornstarch) with the water and stir into the mango purée. Cook for 4 minutes, stirring, until thickened. Pour a pool of sauce on to four serving plates. Handling the biscuit baskets very carefully, position one on top of the sauce on each plate. Fill the baskets with mixed fruit and dust with icing sugar. Decorate each with a mint leaf. Serve immediately.

Boozy Brandy Snaps

1 quantity Brandy Snap Horns (see
page 344)
2 oranges
300 ml/½ pt/1¼ cups double (heavy)
or whipping cream
30 ml/2 tbsp brandy
Sugar

Make the brandy snap horns. Leave to cool. Peel the oranges, remove the pith and slice the flesh into rounds. Whip the cream and whisk in the brandy. Sweeten to taste. Pipe or spoon into the horns. Serve on a plate, decorated on the side with a few orange slices.

Strawberry Baskets

1 quantity Brandy Snap Baskets (see
page 344)
Sweetened whipped cream
A few drops of vanilla essence
(extract)
About 16–20 small strawberries

Make the brandy snap baskets. Leave to cool. Fill with sweetened whipped cream flavoured with vanilla, and top with small strawberries.

Fruit Yoghurt

SERVES 4

410 g/14½ oz/1 large can fruit in
*   natural juice*
300 ml/½ pt/1¼ cups plain yoghurt
Clear honey

Drain the fruit, reserving the juice. Chop the fruit, if necessary, and add to the yoghurt with enough juice to make it the consistency you prefer. Spoon into wine goblets. Chill before serving drizzled with a little honey.

Soft Fruit Cheese

SERVES 4

225 g/8 oz soft fruits (e.g.
*   strawberries or raspberries)*
225 g/8 oz/1 cup low-fat soft cheese
15 ml/1 tbsp caster (superfine) sugar
5 ml/1 tsp lemon juice
Crisp biscuits (cookies)

Crush the berries, then stir in the remaining ingredients except the biscuits. Mix with a fork until fairly smooth. Turn into small, shallow dishes and chill before serving with crisp biscuits.

Quark Dessert

SERVES 4

600 ml/1 pt/2½ cups vegetarian fruit-
*   flavoured jelly (jello)*
100 g/4 oz/½ cup quark
Fresh fruits

Make up the jelly and chill until the consistency of egg white. Whisk in the quark and chill until set. Decorate with fresh fruits before serving.

Almost Instant Trifle

SERVES 4

1 Swiss (jelly) roll, sliced
200 g/7 oz/1 small can peach slices
1 packet vegetarian raspberry jelly
*   (jello)*
1 packet Peach Dessert Whip
Milk

Arrange Swiss roll slices in the bottom of a dish. Drain the peaches, reserving the juice, chop the fruit and spoon it over the Swiss roll. Make up the jelly, using the fruit juice instead of some of the water. Pour over the sponge and fruit and chill. Make up the peach whip. Spoon over the trifle and chill before serving.

Ginger Rhubarb Crisp

SERVES 4

225 g/8 oz rhubarb, chopped into
*   small pieces*
25 g/1 oz/2 tbsp light brown sugar
25 g/1 oz/¼ cup plain (all-purpose)
*   flour*
15 ml/1 tbsp water
25 g/1 oz/2 tbsp butter or margarine
6 ginger biscuits (cookies), crushed
Crème fraîche
Extra brown sugar, for sprinkling

Cook the rhubarb in a saucepan with the sugar, flour, water and butter or margarine for about 10 minutes until mushy. Press the crushed biscuits into the bottom of a dish or serving bowls. Chill. Pour the rhubarb on to the biscuits and finish with the crème fraîche and a little sugar. Chill well before serving.

Spiced Apple Crisp

SERVES 4

Prepare as for Ginger Rhubarb Crisp but substitute cooking (tart) apples for the rhubarb and add a good pinch of ground cinnamon to them when cooking.

Fresh Fruit Salad

SERVES 4-6

Add 150 ml/¼ pt/⅔ cup pure orange or apple juice, 5 ml/1 tsp lemon juice and a sprinkling of ground cinnamon to a small can of fruit in natural juice as the base of your salad and fill up with washed, chopped fresh fruit, allowing about 45 ml/ 3 tbsp fruit per person. Leaving on any edible peel gives colour and texture and retains much of the goodness. A scooped-out pineapple or melon shell makes a perfect natural receptacle for fresh fruit salad, or use halved grapefruit or large orange shells for individual helpings.

Ambrosia

SERVES 4-6

Soak 150 g/5 oz/1¼ cups desiccated (shredded) coconut in 120 ml/4 fl oz/ ½ cup water for 30 minutes then drain and add to Fresh Fruit Salad, prepared as above.

Carob and Pear Gâteau

SERVES 4

150 g/5 oz/1¼ cups wholemeal self-raising (self-rising) flour
5 ml/1 tsp baking powder
15 ml/1 tbsp carob powder
175 g/6 oz/¾ cup butter or margarine, softened
175 g/6 oz/¾ cup caster (superfine) sugar
3 eggs
45 ml/3 tbsp milk
30 ml/2 tbsp currants or sultanas (golden raisins)
150 ml/¼ pt/⅔ cup whipped cream or crème fraîche
2 ripe pears, peeled and chopped
Carob chips

Grease two 18 cm/7 in sandwich tins (pans). Beat all the ingredients except the cream, pears and carob in a bowl until well mixed, adding enough milk to give a soft dropping consistency. Spoon the mixture into the prepared tins and bake in a preheated oven at 190°C/375°F/gas mark 5 for about 25 minutes until the centres spring back when pressed. Leave to stand for 5 minutes, then turn out on to a wire rack to cool. Fill with half the cream and the pears. Pipe or spread the remaining cream over and decorate with carob chips. Chill until ready to serve.

Carob and Walnut Liqueur Gâteau

SERVES 4

Prepare as for Carob and Pear Gâteau (see page 279) but substitute chopped walnuts for the currants or sultanas (golden raisins). Omit the pears and use 300 ml/½ pt/1¼ cups whipped cream, flavoured with chocolate or coffee liqueur to taste for the filling and topping, before decorating with carob chips.

Chestnut Gâteau

SERVES 4

225 g/8 oz/2 cups carob chips
30 ml/2 tbsp milk
430 g/15½ oz/1 large can
   unsweetened chestnut purée
100 g/4 oz/1 cup flaked almonds
A dash of rum or sherry
150 ml/¼ pt/⅔ cup whipped cream
Extra carob chips

Put the carob and milk in a pan and heat gently, stirring until the carob melts. Beat in the chestnut purée, flaked almonds and sherry. Spread into an 18 cm/7 in greased, loose-bottomed cake tin (pan). Chill overnight or preferably freeze. Remove from the tin and pipe or spoon whipped cream over the top and sides and decorate with carob chips.

Velvet Vanilla Cheesecake

SERVES 8–10

225 g/8 oz digestive biscuits (Graham crackers), crushed
100 g/4 oz/½ cup butter or margarine
600 g/1¼ lb/2½ cups medium-fat soft cheese
225 g/8 oz/1 cup caster (superfine) sugar
2 eggs
5 ml/1 tsp vanilla essence (extract)
150 ml/¼ pt/⅔ cup crème fraîche

Mix the biscuit crumbs with the butter or margarine and press into the base and half-way up the sides of a greased 20 cm/8 in round, deep, loose-bottomed cake tin. Beat together the remaining ingredients except the crème fraîche until smooth and pour into the prepared tin. Smooth the surface. Bake in a preheated oven at 150°C/300°F/gas mark 2 for about 1 hour or until just set. Switch off the oven but leave the cheesecake in there until cool. Loosen the edge and carefully remove the tin. Spread the crème fraîche attractively on top and chill until ready to serve.

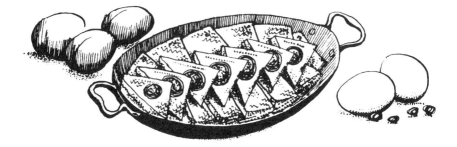

Classic Lemon and Honey Cheesecake

2 eggs, separated
225 g/8 oz/1 cup cottage cheese
225 g/8 oz/1 cup low-fat soft cheese
15 ml/1 tbsp clear honey
5 ml/1 tsp finely grated lemon rind
30 ml/2 tbsp sultanas (golden raisins)
1 x 23 cm/9 in Sweet Crumb Case
(see page 344)
Thinly pared strips of lemon rind

Whisk the egg whites until stiff. Beat together the cheeses, egg yolks, honey, lemon rind and sultanas. Fold the egg whites into the mixture. Pour on to the biscuit base and bake in a preheated oven for 30 minutes at 180°C/350°F/gas mark 4. Cool, then chill. Decorate with strips of thinly pared lemon rind before serving.

Fruit-topped Cheesecake

1 x 23 cm/9 in Sweet Crumb Case
(see page 344)
350 g/12 oz/1½ cups cottage cheese
2 eggs, beaten
50 g/2 oz/¼ cup caster (superfine)
sugar
300 ml/½ pt/1¼ cups soured (dairy
sour) cream
5 ml/1 tsp vanilla essence (extract)
Sliced fresh fruits

Bake the crumb base for 10 minutes in a preheated oven at 180°C/350°F/gas mark 4. Beat together the cottage cheese, eggs, sugar, soured cream and vanilla essence. Pour into the base. Return to a preheated oven for 30–35 minutes until set. Cool, then chill. Decorate with sliced fresh fruits before serving.

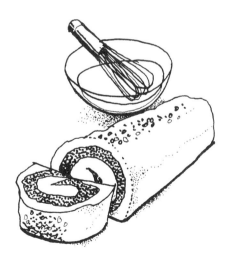

Conil Cherry Cheesecake

SERVES 8

50 g/2 oz/¼ cup unsalted (sweet)
butter
100 g/4 oz digestive biscuits (Graham
crackers), crushed
30 ml/2 tbsp sesame seeds
175 g/6 ozs fresh strawberries,
halved or sliced
225 g/8 oz/1 cup cream cheese
30 ml/2 tbsp Lemon Curd (see page
321)
45 ml/3 tbsp lemon juice
30 ml/2 tbsp caster (superfine) sugar
30 ml/2 tbsp vegetarian gelatine
50 ml/2 fl oz/3½ tbsp water
175 ml/6 fl oz/¾ cup whipping cream
50 g/2 oz Morello cherries, stoned
(pitted)
30 ml/2 tbsp cherry brandy
Toasted flaked almonds

Oil and and line the base and sides of a 20 cm/8 in loose-bottomed cake tin (pan) with a strip of greaseproof (waxed) paper. Melt the butter and mix with the crushed biscuits and sesame seeds. Press the mixture into the bottom of the pre-pared tin. Arrange a row of sliced straw-berries over the biscuit base. The remaining strawberries should be kept to decorate the finished cheesecake. In bowl, blend together the cheese, Lemon Curd, lemon juice and sugar. Dissolve the gelatine in the hot water, bring almost to the boil and add to the cheese mixture. Whip the cream and fold it into the mix-ture. Add the cherries and brandy. Fill the cake tin and chill for 6 hours until set. Before serving, remove the tin and paper and decorate the top with the reserved strawberries. Finish with a sprinkling of toasted flaked almonds.

Luscious Lime Cheesecake

SERVES 6

175 g/6 oz digestive biscuits (Graham
crackers), crushed
75 g/3 oz/⅓ cup butter or margarine,
melted
450 g/1 lb/2 cups cottage cheese
150 g/5 oz/⅔ cup caster (superfine)
sugar
Grated rind of 2 limes
Juice of 1 lime
15 ml/1 tbsp cornflour (cornstarch)
2 eggs

Mix the biscuit crumbs and butter or margarine together and press into the base and half-way up the sides of a lightly greased 18 cm/7 in round, deep loose-bot-tomed cake tin (pan). Put the remaining ingredients in a blender or food processor and run the machine until the mixture is smooth. Spoon into the prepared tin and bake in a preheated oven at 180°C/350°F/gas mark 4 for about 1½ hours until just set. Switch off the oven and leave the cake in there until cool. Loosen the edge, then care-fully remove the tin. Chill until ready to serve.

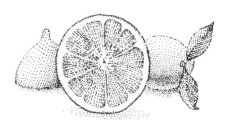

Lemon Tart

*1 x 18 cm/7 in Sweet Crumb Case
(see page 344) or cooked pastry
(paste) case (shell)*
75 g/3 oz/⅓ cup sugar
2 eggs
*Finely grated rind and juice of 1
large lemon*
25 g/1 oz/2 tbsp butter or margarine

Cook the crumb case, if using, in a pre-heated oven at 180°C/350°F/gas mark 4 for 10 minutes. Mix the remaining ingredients together well and pour into the cooked flan case. Bake for 15 minutes. Allow to cool before serving.

Orange Tart

Prepare as for Lemon Tart but use the rind and juice of an orange instead of a lemon.

Lime Tart

Prepare as for Lemon Tart but use the rind and juice of 2 limes instead of a lemon.

Sweet Grapefruit Tart

*225 g/8 oz shortcrust pastry (basic
pie crust)*
4 egg yolks
*50 g/2 oz/¼ cup caster (superfine)
sugar*
Juice of 1 sweet grapefruit
*25 g/1 oz/¼ cup cornflour
(cornstarch)*
30 ml/2 tbsp cold water
2 sweet grapefruit, segmented
Grapefruit marmalade, warmed
Lemon sorbet
Cream

Roll out the pastry on a floured pastry board and use to line a well-greased 23 cm/9 in flan tin (pie pan). Place a piece of crumpled foil on the pastry base and bake blind in a preheated oven at 225°C/425°F/gas mark 7 for 8 minutes. Remove the foil, then bake for a further 5 minutes to dry out. For the filling, whisk the egg yolks and sugar in a metal bowl for 8 minutes. Boil the grapefruit juice in a small saucepan. Blend the cornflour and cold water. Add to the boiling grapefruit juice and cook for 2 minutes. Gradually whisk this hot liquid into the egg mixture. Re-boil the filling for 3–4 minutes until it thickens like a custard. Pour into the flan case (shell) and top with the grapefruit segments. Brush the top with hot, melted grapefruit marmalade. Chill. Serve with lemon sorbet and cream.

Carob and Gooseberry Pie

100 g/4 oz/1 cup plain (all-purpose) flour
45 ml/3 tbsp carob powder
85 g/3½ oz/scant ½ cup butter or margarine
15 ml/1 tbsp caster (superfine) sugar
530 g/18½ oz/l large can gooseberries
1 sachet vegetarian gelatine
150 ml/¼ pt/⅔ cup ready-made custard
A few drops of green food colouring
300 ml/½ pt/1¼ cups double (heavy) cream
A few glacé (candied) cherries, halved
Angelica leaves

Sift the flour and carob powder into a bowl. Add the butter or margarine and rub in with the fingertips until the mixture resembles fine breadcrumbs. Stir in the sugar. Mix with enough cold water to form a soft but not sticky dough. Knead gently on a lightly floured surface. Roll out and use to line a 20 cm/8 in flan dish (pie pan). Prick the base with a fork. Fill with crumpled foil and bake in a preheated oven at 200°C/400°F/gas mark 6 for 20 minutes. Remove the foil and return to the oven for a further 5 minutes to dry out. Remove from the oven and leave to cool. Meanwhile, reserve 45 ml/3 tbsp of the gooseberry syrup, then purée the fruit and remaining juice in a blender or food processor. Sprinkle the gelatine over the reserved syrup and stir until dissolved. Heat until almost boiling, stirring all the time (or according to the packet directions). Stir into the gooseberry purée with the custard and a few drops of food colouring. Chill until on the point of setting, then whip the cream and fold half into the gooseberry mixture. Turn into the cold pastry case and chill until set. Decorate with the remaining whipped cream, halved glacé cherries and angelica leaves.

Reduced Sugar Raspberry Pavlova

3 egg whites
150 g/5 oz/⅔ cup raw cane sugar
5 ml/1 tsp vinegar
1 quantity Cornmeal Custard (see page 320)
150 g/5 oz/1¼ cups raspberries

Dampen a large baking sheet and cover with non-stick baking parchment. Place the egg whites in a large bowl and whisk until stiff. Add the sugar and vinegar and continue whisking until the mixture is very stiff. Spread a circle of meringue on to the baking parchment and pipe or swirl the rest round the outside to make a nest shape. Place in a cool oven, 150°C/300°F/gas mark 2, and immediately turn the heat down to 140°C/275°F/gas mark 1. Cook for 1 hour. Turn off the oven and leave overnight to dry out completely. Peel off the paper. Fill with the cool Cornmeal Custard and top with raspberries.

Strawberry Yoghurt Pavlova

Prepare as for Reduced Sugar Raspberry Pavlova but fill with strawberry Greek-style yoghurt instead of Cornmeal Custard and top with halved strawberries instead of raspberries.

Rhubarb and Banana Yoghurt Fool

450 g/1 lb rhubarb, cut into chunks
15 ml/1 tbsp clear honey
5 ml/1 tsp ground cinnamon
450 g/1 lb ripe bananas, peeled and
 halved
300 ml/½ pt/1¼ cups plain yoghurt
50 g/2 oz/½ cup toasted chopped
 hazelnuts

Put the rhubarb, honey, cinnamon and 45 ml/3 tbsp cold water in a pan and stew gently until the rhubarb is tender. Cool slightly and place in a blender or food processor with the bananas. Run the machine until the mixture is smooth. Leave until cold, then fold in the yoghurt. Turn into individual serving dishes and decorate with the hazelnuts. Chill before serving.

Apple and Banana Yoghurt Fool

Prepare as for Rhubarb and Banana Yoghurt Fool but substitute cooking (tart) apples for the rhubarb and use ground cloves instead of cinnamon for flavouring.

Winter Fruit Fool

225 g/8 oz/1½ cups dried fruit salad
300 ml/½ pt/1¼ cups water
300 ml/½ pt/1¼ cups Cornmeal
 Custard (see page 320)
Chopped toasted hazelnuts

Soak the fruit salad in the water for several hours, then stew until tender. Discard any stones (pits). Purée in a blender or food processor for 2 minutes until smooth and cool. Add the custard and continue to process for a further minute. Chill if liked and serve in tall glasses, decorated with hazelnuts.

Apricot Fool

SERVES 4

*410 g/14½ oz/1 large can apricot
halves, drained reserving the juice*
*450 ml/¾ pt/2 cups Egg Custard
Sauce (see page 319) or use
canned*
150 ml/¼ pt/⅔ cup thick plain yoghurt
*Ratafia Biscuits (see page 343) or
use bought*

Purée the fruit in a blender or food
processor. Fold in the custard, then
fold in the yoghurt to leave a marbled
effect. Spoon into glasses and chill before
serving with Ratafia Biscuits and the juice
handed separately.

Peach Fool

SERVES 4

Prepare as for Apricot Fool but substitute canned peaches for the apricots.
Spike with a little lemon juice if too sweet.

Raspberry Fool

SERVES 4

Prepare as for Apricot Fool but substitute a can of raspberries for the apricots and sieve (strain) after puréeing
before adding to the custard.

Almond Plum Fool

SERVES 4

*410 g/14½ oz/1 large can plums,
drained reserving the juice*
*450 ml/¾ pt/2 cups Egg Custard
Sauce (see page 319) or use
canned*
150 ml/¼ pt/⅔ cup thick plain yoghurt
*Ratafia Biscuits (see page 343) or
use bought*
A few chopped almonds
A few toasted almonds

Remove and discard the stones (pits)
and purée the plums in a blender or
food processor. Fold in the custard, then
fold in the yoghurt and chopped almonds
to leave a marbled effect. Spoon into
glasses and chill. Decorate with toasted
almonds before serving with Ratafia
Biscuits and the juice handed separately.

Carob Slice with Toasted Almonds

175 g/6 oz/1½ cups carob chips
120 ml/4 fl oz/½ cup milk
10 ml/2 tsp vegetarian gelatine
3 eggs, separated
120 ml/4 fl oz/½ cup double (heavy)
　cream
45 ml/3 tbsp caster (superfine) sugar
45 ml/3 tbsp toasted flaked almonds
　Raspberries or poached pear slices
　(optional)

Line a 450 g/1 lb loaf tin (pan) with greaseproof (waxed) paper. Place the carob to melt in a large mixing bowl (preferably stainless steel), over a saucepan of boiling water. Boil the milk and dissolve the gelatine in it. Add the egg yolks to the melted carob. Stir in the hot milk mixture well, then the cream. Whisk the egg whites until stiff. Whisk in the sugar then, when stiff, fold into the carob mixture. Fill the prepared mould and chill for 3 hours or until set. To serve, unmould and cut into thick slices, dipping a knife into boiling water for a neat cut. Place on individual plates and decorate with the almonds. Accompany with fresh raspberries or poached pears, if liked.

Tipsy Savarins

225 g/8 oz/2 cups strong plain
　(bread) flour
50 ml/2 fl oz/3½ tbsp tepid milk
5 ml/1 tsp dried yeast
5 ml/1 tsp icing (confectioners')
　sugar
5 ml/1 tsp plain (all-purpose) flour
2 eggs, beaten
100 g/4 oz/½ cup butter, melted
250 ml/8 fl oz/1 cup water
200 g/7 oz/scant 1 cup sugar
1 tea bag
60 ml/4 tbsp Kirsch
225 g/8 oz black cherries, stoned
　(pitted)
120 ml/4 fl oz/½ cup red wine
5 ml/1 tsp ground cinnamon
5 ml/1 tsp cornflour (cornstarch)
Cream (optional)

Sift the strong flour in a bowl and make a well in the centre. In a cup mix the milk, yeast, icing sugar and plain flour. Pour this into the well of flour and leave to ferment for 15 minutes until it begins to froth. Mix with the beaten eggs to a soft dough. Cover with a cloth or polythene and allow to rise for 1 hour. Knead the butter into the dough until smooth. Allow to rest for 15 minutes. Well oil six small savarin metal-ring moulds and dust with flour. Half-fill each mould with the dough mixture. Allow to prove until double in size. Bake in a preheated oven at 200°C/400°F/gas mark 6 for 15–20 minutes until golden. Unmould and cool on a wire rack. For the syrup, boil the water and all but 25 g/1 oz/2 tbsp of the sugar for 2 minutes. Remove from the heat and add the tea bag. Leave for 8 minutes, then remove the tea bag. Flavour with Kirsch. Pour the hot syrup into a shallow dish. Soak each ring in hot syrup, then carefully transfer to plates. For the filling, boil the cherries, wine, remaining sugar and cinnamon for 2 minutes. Mix the cornflour with a little water and add to the cherries. Cook for 4 minutes to thicken and clear the starch. Fill each ring with cherries. Serve with cream, if liked.

Grape and Apricot Snow

SERVES 4

3 egg whites
450 ml/¾ pt/2 cups apricot yoghurt
225 g/8 oz black grapes, halved and
*   seeded (pitted)*
225 g/8 oz green grapes, halved and
*   seeded*

Whisk the egg whites until stiff and fold into the yoghurt. Layer the yoghurt and most of the grapes into glasses and decorate with the remaining grapes. Chill until required.

Strawberry and Raspberry Snow

SERVES 4

Prepare as for Grape and Apricot Snow but use strawberry yoghurt instead of apricot and raspberries and sliced strawberries for the two types of grapes.

Photograph opposite: **Plum, Toffee and Almond Pudding (page 257)**

Eastern Dream

SERVES 4

12 dates, stoned (pitted) and chopped
2 large bananas, sliced
227 g/8 oz/1 small can pineapple in
*   natural juice, chopped*
Crème fraîche

Mix together the fruits and juice and spoon into glass serving dishes. Top with crème fraîche and serve.

Gourmet Pears

SERVES 4

50 g/2 oz/¼ cup medium-fat soft
*   cheese*
50 g/2 oz/¼ cup cottage cheese with
*   pineapple*
45 ml/3 tbsp sherry
25 g/1 oz/⅙ cup raisins
2 dessert pears, peeled
A few flaked almonds

Beat together both cheeses and 30 ml/2 tbsp of the sherry. Stir in the raisins. Halve the pears, dig out any cores with a teaspoon, and brush all over with the remaining sherry. Arrange on a platter, cut side up. Spoon the cheese mixture on top. Sprinkle with a few flaked almonds. Chill before serving.

Gourmet Pineapple

SERVES 4

For a non-alcoholic dessert, make as for Gourmet Pears but substitute 227 g/8 oz/1 small can pineapple rings in natural juice for the pears. Drain the can before mixing the cheeses, and use the juice instead of sherry.

Sparkling Peaches

2 fresh peaches
Sugar
60 ml/4 tbsp low-fat soft cheese or
  cold cooked brown or white rice
Sparkling white wine, chilled

Dip the peaches in boiling water, skin and halve them and remove the stones (pits). Mix a little sugar into the cheese or rice to taste. Place 15 ml/ 1 tbsp cheese or rice in the bottom of each of four large, stemmed wine glasses. Place a peach half, hollowed side down, on each spoonful of cheese or rice. At serving point, pour enough sparkling wine into each glass to come level with the top of the fruit.

Sparkling Nectarines

Prepare as for Sparkling Peaches but substitute ripe nectarines for the peaches.

Sparkling Strawberries

Prepare as for Sparkling Peaches but substitute 225 g/8 oz halved straw-berries for the peaches and top with sparkling rosé instead of white wine.

Rosy Peaches

300 g/11 oz/1 small can strawberries
  in natural juice, drained, reserving
  the juice
Sugar
2 peaches
60 ml/4 tbsp low-fat soft cheese or
  cold cooked brown or white rice

Mash the strawberries to a purée with a little of the juice. Sweeten the purée to taste. Dip the peaches in boiling water, skin and halve them and remove the stones (pits). Mix a little sugar into the cheese or rice in the bottom of each of four large, stemmed wine glasses. Place a peach half, hollowed side down, on each spoonful of cheese or rice. At serving point, spoon enough of the strawberry purée into each glass to come level with the top of the peach half.

Photograph opposite: **Lime Tart**
(page 283)

Charismatic Fruits

2 small melons, halved, seeded and
    peeled
1 pawpaw, peeled, seeded and sliced
4 kiwi fruit, peeled and sliced
225 g/8 oz fresh lychees or canned,
    drained
225 g/8 oz strawberries, hulled and
    halved
2 bananas, peeled and sliced
4 tangerines, peeled and segmented
Caster (superfine) sugar or honey to
    taste (optional)
Mixed nuts (e.g. pine nuts, walnuts,
    flaked almonds, pistachios)
A large bunch of fresh mint or lemon
    balm leaves
75 ml/5 tbsp Grand Marnier, or
    Cointreau and Kirsch mixed
1 pomegranate
Soured (dairy sour) or whipped
    cream

Place the melon halves on four serving
plates and arrange the other fruits
decoratively on and around the melon. Add
sugar or honey, if necessary. Sprinkle with
nuts and finish with sprigs of mint or lemon
balm leaves. Just before serving, sprinkle
with the liqueur mixture. Cut the
pomegranate in wedges and place one on
each plate, or sprinkle with the seeds only.
Serve with soured or whipped cream.

Apple and Blackcurrant Kissel

3 cooking (tart) apples, sliced
150 g/5 oz/1¼ cups blackcurrants
100 g/4 oz/½ cup sugar
10 ml/2 tsp potato flour
75 ml/5 tbsp water
Pinch of ground cinnamon
150 ml/¼ pt/⅔ cup port
Plain yoghurt or soured (dairy sour)
    cream

Place the apples and blackcurrants in a
saucepan with the sugar, cover and
cook until the apples are soft. Pour the
mixture into a blender or food processor
and blend to a smooth purée. Return to
the saucepan. Blend the potato flour with
the water, stir into the purée and re-boil,
stirring, until thickened. Flavour with a little cinnamon and the wine. Serve cold in
individual glasses or bowls with yoghurt
or soured cream, slightly whipped, if
liked.

Apple and Raspberry Kissel

Prepare as for Apple and Blackcurrant
Kissel but substitute fresh or frozen
raspberries for the blackcurrants and
flavour with 5 ml/1 tsp grated lemon rind
instead of the cinnamon.

Prune Stunner

SERVES 4

*410 g/14½ oz/1 large can prunes in
natural juice*
1 tablet vegetarian orange jelly (jello)
25 g/1 oz/2 tsp butter or margarine
*15 ml/1 tbsp golden (light corn)
syrup*
15 ml/1 tbsp mixed chopped nuts
50 g/2 oz/2 cups bran flakes
Thick plain yoghurt

Drain the prunes, reserving the juice.
Remove the stones (pits) from the
fruit, then sieve or blend to a purée. Make
the juice up to 450 ml/¾ pt/2 cups with
water. Dissolve the jelly tablet in a little of
this, then stir in the remainder with the
fruit purée. Turn into four individual glass
dishes. Chill until set. Melt the butter or
margarine and syrup in a saucepan. Stir
in the nuts and bran flakes. Spread
yoghurt over the set prune mixture and
top with the cereal mixture. Chill again.

Pears in White Wine with Passion Fruit Purée

SERVES 2

*2 large very ripe dessert pears,
peeled, cored and quartered*
4 passion fruit
*300 ml/½ pt/1¼ cups sweet white
wine, such as Graves or Sauterne*
15 ml/1 tbsp clear honey
15 ml/1 tbsp cornflour (cornstarch)
60 ml/4 tbsp water
*Juice of ½ lemon or lime, if
necessary*
*Langues de chats or other biscuits
(cookies) to serve*

Place the pears in two serving glasses
or dishes. Halve the passion fruit and
scoop out the pulp into a small bowl.
Bring the wine and honey to the boil.
Blend the cornflour with the water and
stir into the syrup when boiling. Simmer
for 2 minutes to clear the starch, then add
the passion fruit pulp. Boil for 1 minute
more. Add the lemon or lime juice if not
acid enough. Pour the sauce over the
pears and leave to cool. Serve with
langues de chats or other biscuits.

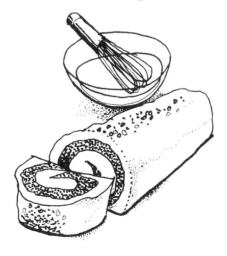

291

Prune Mousse

225 g/8 oz prunes
300 ml/½ pt/1¼ cups cold tea
Thinly pared rind and juice of 1
lemon
15 g/½ oz/1 tbsp vegetarian gelatine
3 eggs, separated
75 ml/3 oz/⅓ cup caster (superfine)
sugar
300 ml/½ pt/1¼ cups double (heavy)
cream
A few toasted whole almonds

Soak the prunes in the tea for several hours or overnight. Place in a saucepan with the lemon rind. Bring to the boil and simmer for 10 minutes until the prunes are really soft. Cool, then remove the stones (pits) and discard the lemon rind. Purée the prunes and juice in a blender or food processor. Make the lemon juice up to 45 ml/3 tbsp with water. Stir in the gelatine until dissolved. Bring almost to the boil, stirring (or according to packet directions). Cool slightly, then stir into the prune purée. Whisk the egg whites until stiff, then the cream until peaking, then the egg yolks with the sugar until thick and pale (so you don't need to wash the beaters in between). Fold the yolk and sugar mixture, then half the cream, and finally the egg whites into the prune purée. Turn into a large glass dish and chill until set. Decorate the top with the remaining whipped cream and a few toasted whole almonds.

Dried Apricot Mousse

Prepare as for Prune Mousse but use dried apricots instead of prunes and soak in half white wine and half apple juice instead of the cold tea.

Apple and Rhubarb Mousse

225 g/8 oz Bramley cooking (tart)
apples, sliced
150 g/6 oz rhubarb, peeled and
chopped
150 g/6 oz/¾ cup granulated sugar
10 ml/2 tsp vegetarian gelatine
150 ml/¼ pt/⅔ cup whipped cream
Ratafia Biscuits (see page 343)

Boil the apple and rhubarb in a cupful of water until soft. Dissolve the sugar and gelatine in this mixture and bring to the boil again. Pass through a sieve (strainer) to obtain a smooth purée or liquidize in a blender. Fold in the whipped cream when the mixture is cold. Spoon into glasses and chill until required. Serve with ratafia biscuits.

Apple and Blackberry Mousse

Prepare as for Apple and Rhubarb Mousse but substitute blackberries for the rhubarb.

St Clement's Mousse

1 tablet lemon vegetarian jelly (jello)
300 g/11 oz/1 small can mandarin
oranges in natural juice, drained,
reserving the juice
15 ml/1 tbsp lemon juice
175 g/6 oz/1 small can evaporated
milk, chilled
Quark
Crystallised (candied) lemon slices
Angelica leaves

Dissolve the jelly in 150 ml/¼ pt/⅔ cup boiling water. Stir in the mandarin orange juice and the lemon juice. Leave until on the point of setting. Whisk the evaporated milk until thick and fluffy. Fold into the jelly mixture and add the fruit. Spoon into glasses and chill until set. Spoon a little quark over and decorate with lemon slices and angelica leaves.

Raspberry Mousse

Prepare as for St Clement's Mousse but use raspberry-flavoured vegetarian jelly (jello) and canned raspberries instead of mandarins. Omit the lemon juice. Decorate with toasted almonds instead of lemon slices and angelica.

Blackcurrant Mousse

Prepare as for St Clement's Mousse but use blackcurrant-flavoured vegetarian jelly (jello) and canned blackcurrants instead of mandarins. Decorate with halved glacé (candied) cherries instead of lemon slices.

Dessert Avocados

10 ml/2 tsp vegetarian gelatine
45 ml/3 tbsp water
2 large, green-skinned avocados
Grated rind and juice of 1 lime
90 ml/6 tbsp icing (confectioners')
sugar
150 ml/¼ pt/⅔ cup double (heavy)
cream
Chopped pistachio nuts

Dissolve the gelatine in the water in a small bowl, then bring almost to the boil by standing in a pan of boiling water for a few minutes (or according to the packet directions). Meanwhile, halve the avocados, remove the stones (pits) and scoop out the flesh. Purée in a blender or food processor with the lime rind and juice and the icing sugar. Add the gelatine and run the machine briefly again. Whip the cream until peaking. Reserve a good spoonful for decoration, then fold the remainder into the avocado purée. Spoon into the shells and chill until set. Decorate with a small spoonful of the reserved whipped cream and some chopped pistachio nuts.

Sherry Syllabub

SERVES 4

300 ml/½ pt/1¼ cups double (heavy)
  cream
60 ml/4 tbsp caster (superfine) sugar
Grated rind and juice of 1 lemon
50 ml/2 fl oz/3½ tbsp medium-dry
  sherry
50 ml/2 fl oz/3½ tbsp Grand Marnier
8 Ratafia Biscuits (see page 343) or
  fresh strawberries

In a bowl, whip the cream until stiff. Blend in the sugar, lemon, sherry and Grand Marnier lightly. Half fill stemmed glasses with this mixture and decorate with Ratafia Biscuits or fresh strawberries when in season.

Cider Syllabub

SERVES 4

Prepare as for Sherry Syllabub but substitute strong cider for the sherry and Calvados for the Grand Marnier and add 15 ml/1 tbsp icing (confectioners') sugar.

Scotch Syllabub

SERVES 4

Prepare as for Sherry Syllabub but substitute whisky for the sherry and Drambuie for the Grand Marnier.

Lovers' Syllabub

SERVES 2

1 passion fruit
15 ml/1 tbsp caster (superfine) sugar
100 g/4 oz/½ cup quark
15 ml/1 tbsp pure orange juice
Lemon juice
1 egg white

Halve the passion fruit. Scoop out the seeds into a sieve (strainer) over a bowl. Rub through the sieve with a wooden spoon (you should get about 15 ml/1 tbsp juice). Stir in the sugar, quark and orange juice. Taste and add a squeeze of lemon juice for sharpness, if necessary. Whisk the egg white until stiff. Fold into the mixture with a metal spoon. Turn into two wine goblets. Chill to allow the mixture to separate into a juicy layer and a fluffy top.

Velvety Peach Melba

SERVES 4

60 ml/4 tbsp low-fat soft cheese
A little caster (superfine) sugar
4 ripe peaches, peeled, halved and
  stoned (pitted)
300 g/11 oz/1 small can raspberries

Sweeten the cheese to taste with a little sugar. Sandwich the peach halves together again with the cheese. Place in glass serving dishes. Drain the raspberries and pass through a sieve (strainer). Add enough of the juice to form a pouring consistency. Pour over the peaches and serve.

Satin Pear Melba

Prepare as for Velvety Peach Melba but substitute large ripe pears for the peaches and cut out the cores with a pointed knife.

Summer Pudding

SERVES 4–6

900 g/2 lb soft fruit (e.g. raspberries, blackberries, blackcurrants)
100–175 g/4–6 oz/½–¾ cup light brown sugar
Pinch of ground cinnamon
8 slices white bread, crusts removed
Egg Custard Sauce (see page 319) or ice cream

Stew the fruit with 100 g/4 oz/½ cup of the sugar and the cinnamon until the fruit is just soft, adding a little more sugar to taste if necessary. Cutting the slices, if necessary, line a large basin with the bread, covering the bottom and sides and reserving a slice for the top. Pour in the fruit and cover with the reserved bread. Press down lightly with a small plate and weigh down with a can. Chill overnight. It is ready to eat when the fruit juice has soaked through the bread. Turn out and serve with Egg Custard Sauce or ice cream.

Golden Pudding

SERVES 4–6

Prepare as for Summer Pudding but substitute a mixture of chopped, stoned (pitted) yellow fruits, such as peaches, nectarines, apricots, mangoes. Omit the cinnamon and add the grated rind of ½ lemon instead.

Autumn Fruit Pudding

SERVES 4

8 slices wholemeal bread
75 g/1½ lb selection of soft fruits (e.g. blackberries, blueberries, raspberries, currants, stoned [pitted] cherries)
30 ml/2 tbsp golden (light corn) syrup or clear honey
120 ml/4 fl oz/½ cup red wine
5 ml/1 tsp vegetarian gelatine
1 small glass of Kirsch
Yoghurt

Line the base and sides of a pudding basin with bread, cutting the slices to fit if necessary. Wash and drain all the fruits. Blend with the syrup or honey and wine and leave the fruits in a colander over a bowl to allow the juices to drip. Fill the lined basin with the fruit mixture. Boil the juice, then add and dissolve the gelatine. Pour this syrup and the Kirsch on to the fruit mixture. Cover with the remaining bread, trimming to fit. Press down lightly with a small plate and weigh down with a can. Chill overnight. Turn out on to a plate and serve with yoghurt.

Strawberry Sorbet

225 g/8 oz fresh strawberries
50 g/2 oz/½ cup icing (confectioners')
sugar
75 g/3 oz/⅓ cup caster (superfine)
sugar
1 egg white
5 ml/1 tsp extra caster sugar
Juice of ½ lemon
45 ml/3 tbsp Grand Marnier

Hull the strawberries and slice. Wash and drain. Retain some slices for decoration and liquidize the remainder with the sugars to a purée. Add 120 ml/4 fl oz/ ½ cup water. Bring to the boil. Meanwhile, in a bowl whisk the egg white with the extra caster sugar. Whisk into the hot purée. Cook for 1 minute. Transfer to a clean bowl and beat the mixture well. Add the lemon juice and liqueur. Oil two metal ice cube trays or a shallow metal dish with greaseproof (waxed) paper and fill them with the mixture. Freeze for 2 hours. If the mixture crystallises, whisk it again and refreeze. The meringue should stabilise the texture. Serve decorated with the reserved strawberries.

Raspberry Sorbet

Prepare as for Strawberry Sorbet but substitute raspberries for the strawberries. Pass the purée through a sieve (strainer) to remove the seeds and flavour with Kirsch instead of Grand Marnier (or omit if preferred).

Blackcurrant Sorbet

Prepare as for Raspberry Sorbet but substitute blackcurrants for the raspberries. Stew them for 5 minutes with the sugar before puréeing.

Raspberry Yoghurt Sorbet

300 g/11 oz/1 small can raspberries
in natural juice
100 g/4 oz/½ cup sugar
2 egg whites
150 ml/¼ pt/⅔ cup plain thick yoghurt
2 kiwi fruit, sliced
2 green eating (dessert) apples, sliced
Kirsch or bottled lime juice to taste

Place the raspberries in a blender or food processor with their juice and blend to a purée. Pass through a sieve (strainer) into a saucepan, add the sugar and boil for 2 minutes. Leave to cool. Whisk the egg whites until stiff and fold into the raspberry purée, then fold in the yoghurt. Pour into a freezer container and freeze for 3 hours. Remove from the freezer and beat the sorbet to break down ice crystals, then refreeze for at least another 3 hours until firm. To serve, scoop the sorbet on to plates and garnish with the kiwi fruit and apple slices. Sprinkle a little Kirsch or lime juice over the fruit.

Strawberry Yoghurt Sorbet

Prepare as for Raspberry Yoghurt Sorbet but substitute canned strawberries for the raspberries and use thick strawberry-flavoured yoghurt instead of plain yoghurt for a more distinctive flavour.

Peanut Brittle Ice Cream

100 g/4 oz/½ cup light brown sugar
100 g/4 oz/½ cup butter
450 ml/¾ pt/ 2 cups milk
2 eggs, beaten
5 ml/1 tsp vanilla essence (extract)
3 thin peanut brittle bars (about
  175 g/6 oz in all)
300 ml/½ pt/1¼ cups double (heavy)
  or whipping cream, whipped
30 ml/2 tbsp lemon juice

Put 25 g/1 oz/2 tbsp of the sugar in a pan and add half the butter. Heat gently until melted, then cook for 2 minutes, stirring. Add 300 ml/½ pt/1¼ cups of the milk and heat, stirring, until the caramel melts into the milk. Whisk in the remaining milk, the eggs and vanilla essence and cook, stirring all the time, over a gentle heat until the custard is thick enough to coat the back of a spoon. Do not allow to boil. Leave to cool completely. Crush the peanut brittle in a plastic bag with a rolling pin. Fold the cream, then the brittle, into the custard. Turn into a fairly shallow container. Freeze for 2 hours or until the mixture is firm around the edges. Whisk with a fork to break up the ice crystals. Return to the freezer and refreeze until firm. Meanwhile, melt the remaining butter and sugar in a saucepan. Add the lemon juice and heat gently until smooth and well blended. Scoop the ice cream into serving dishes and spoon the hot butterscotch sauce over. Serve straight away.

Caramel Ice Cream

100 g/4 oz/½ cup light brown sugar
150 ml/¼ pt/⅔ cup water
25 g/1 oz/2 tbsp butter or margarine
10 ml/2 tsp lemon juice
10 ml/2 tsp arrowroot, blended with a
  little water
400 g/14 oz/1 large can evaporated
  milk, chilled in the fridge
  overnight
2.5 ml/½ tsp vanilla essence (extract)

Put the sugar, water, butter or margarine and lemon juice into a saucepan and heat gently, stirring until melted. Add the blended arrowroot and cook, stirring, until thickened. Cool. Whisk the evaporated milk until thick and creamy and fold into the sauce. Add the vanilla essence. Pour into a container and freeze. Whisk after 1 hour and return to the freezer. Whisk again after another hour and freeze until firm.

297

Carob Chip Ice Cream

SERVES 4

Prepare as for Caramel Ice Cream (see page 297) but fold 30 ml/2 tbsp carob powder and 30 ml/2 tbsp carob chips into the sauce before folding in the whisked evaporated milk.

Carob and Caramel Bombe

SERVES 4

1 quantity Caramel Ice Cream (see page 297)
1 quantity Carob Chip Ice Cream (see above)
Carob chips
Toasted flaked almonds

Make the ice creams. After stirring them for the second time during freezing, use the caramel one to line the base and sides of an ice cream mould or a large pudding basin. Freeze for 30 minutes, then fill the centre with Carob Chip Ice Cream, pressing down firmly. Freeze until firm. To serve, dip the mould into a bowl of very hot water, turn out and decorate with carob chips and toasted flaked almonds.

Boozy Carob Ice Cream

SERVES 4

100 g/4 oz/½ cup butter or margarine
175 g/6 oz/1½ cups carob chips
200 g/7 oz/1¼ cups digestive biscuits (Graham crackers), crushed
3 eggs beaten
30 ml/2 tbsp sweet sherry or coffee liqueur
150 ml/¼ pt/⅔ cup whipped cream
A little extra whipped cream (optional)
Grated nutmeg

Put the butter or margarine and carob in a large pan and heat gently, stirring until melted. Stir in the biscuits, eggs and sherry or liqueur. Leave to cool, then fold in the cream. Put the mixture in a greased mould or pudding basin. Freeze for at least 4 hours before serving. Stand the basin briefly in hot water, loosen the edge with a knife, place a plate on top and invert. Give a shake, if necessary, to loosen, then remove the basin. Pipe a little extra cream, if liked, on top and then sprinkle with a little grated nutmeg. Serve immediately.

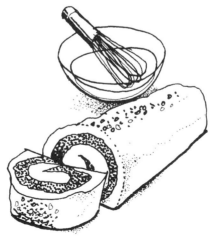

Ice Cream Toppings

Christmas Sauce: 50 g/4 tbsp home-made mincemeat (or a top-quality whole-food brand) melted in the microwave just long enough to be made pourable.

Raspberry Ravish: 225 g/8 oz/2 cups frozen raspberries or other fruit puréed through a sieve (strainer), mixed with a little honey and poured over. Top with crushed meringues.

Pineapple Sauce: Heat 150 ml/¼ pt/⅔ cup pure pineapple juice and 1.5 ml/¼ tsp raw cane syrup in the microwave on high for 2 minutes. Stir in 5 ml/1 tsp arrow-root dissolved in 15 ml/1 tbsp water and heat until thickened. Stir well. Sharpen with lemon juice if necessary.

Bitter Carob Sauce: Dissolve 15 ml/1 tbsp carob powder in 150 ml/¼ pt/⅔ cup black coffee. Add 2.5 ml/½ tsp sugar and heat gently in the microwave. Stir in 5 ml/1 tsp arrowroot dissolved in 15 ml/1 tbsp water and heat until thickened. Stir well.

Hot Orange Sauce: Warm 75 ml/5 tbsp Orange Curd (see page 321). Thin with a little orange juice. Decorate with crys-tallised (candied) orange slices or the thinly pared rind of an orange, blanched, drained and cooled.

Hot Lemon Sauce: Warm 75 ml/5 tbsp Lemon Curd (see page 321). Thin with a little apple juice. Decorate with crys-tallised (candied) lemon slices or thinly pared lemon rind, blanched, drained and cooled.

Nut and Raisin Delight: Chop a 50 g/2 oz/½ cup packet of peanuts and raisins. Put in a saucepan with 60 ml/4 tbsp maple syrup. Heat through. Add a little lemon juice if liked.

Ice Cream Bombes

Ice cream is served all over the world in different flavours. Make up any combinations you like – experiment!

Italian-style

SERVES 6

1 litre/1¾ pts/4¼ cups soft-scoop
  vanilla ice cream
50 g/2 oz/½ cup carob chips
50 g/2 oz/½ cup maraschino cherries,
  chopped
Nuts, carob chips or crystallised
  (candied) fruits (optional)

Put the ice cream in a bowl. Mash in the other ingredients quickly until only just mixed, then press into a very lightly oiled 1 litre/1¾ pt/4¼ cup pudding basin. Cover with foil and freeze. To serve, stand the basin in hot water for 30 seconds. Place a serving plate on top. Hold firmly, invert, give a sharp shake and lift off the basin. Serve immediately, decorated with nuts, carob chips or crystallised fruit, if liked.

Greek-style

SERVES 6

1 litre/1¾ pts/4¼ cups soft-scoop
  vanilla ice cream
50 g/2 oz/½ cup toasted chopped nuts
45 ml/3 tbsp clear honey
15 ml/1 tbsp lemon juice

Prepare as for Italian-style Bombe.

Mexican-style

SERVES 6

2 bananas
15 ml/1 tbsp lemon juice
1 litre/1¾ pts/4¼cups soft-scoop
  vanilla ice cream
25 g/1 oz/2 tbsp crystallised (candied)
  ginger, or 1 piece stem ginger in
  syrup, chopped

Mash the bananas and lemon juice together, then prepare as for Italian-style Bombe.

Caribbean-style

SERVES 6

75 g/3 oz/½ cup raisins
30 ml/2 tbsp rum
1 litre/1¾ pts/4¼ cups soft scoop
  vanilla ice cream

Soak the raisins in the rum for several hours, then prepare as for Italian-style Bombe.

Sauces, Dressings and Spreads

You'll find everything from a basic bechamel sauce to a tangy blue cheese dressing in the next set of pages. They are all designed to add texture and flavour to your meals. Many make delicious dips for parties too. So, if you want to jazz up your salads, vitalize your vegetables, dazzle your desserts or simply spread a little happiness then 'dip' into this section for some clever little extras to send your taste buds reeling!

Kidney Bean Spread

45 ml/15 oz/1 large can red kidney
beans, drained
60 ml/4 tbsp tomato ketchup (catsup)
5 ml/1 tsp chilli powder
Salt and freshly ground black pepper

Mash all the ingredients together. Turn into a small dish and chill. Serve spread on toast or as a dip with vegetable sticks.

Blue Yoghurt Dressing

150 ml/¼ pt/⅔ cup plain yoghurt
15 ml/1 tbsp soft blue cheese
5 ml/1 tsp chopped fresh dill (dill weed)

Mix together all the ingredients and chill before serving.

Raita

150 ml/¼ pt/⅔ cup plain yoghurt
15 ml/1 tbsp chopped mint
1.5 ml/¼ tsp salt
1.5 ml/¼ tsp sugar
5 cm/2 in piece cucumber, finely
chopped
5–10 ml/1–2 tsp milk

Mix together all the ingredients, adding just enough milk to make the mixture creamy but not too runny. Chill before serving.

Bean Spread

100 g/4 oz/1 cup haricot (navy)
beans, cooked (see page 10)
45 ml/3 tbsp plain yoghurt or silken
tofu
Worcestershire sauce

Drain the cooked beans. Grind or process them with the yoghurt or tofu and flavour to taste with a little Worcestershire sauce. Turn into a small pot, cover and store in the fridge.

Green Pea Spread

225 g/8 oz/2 cups cooked fresh or
thawed frozen garden peas
50 g/2 oz/¼ cup low-fat soft cheese
Pinch of grated nutmeg
Salt and freshly ground black pepper
Chopped mint (optional)

Process the peas with the curd cheese, nutmeg and a little salt and pepper. Flavour with chopped mint, if liked.

Red Lentil Spread

225 g/8 oz/1⅓ cups red lentils
50 g/2 oz/½ cup Cheddar cheese, diced
50 g/2 oz/1 cup soft wholemeal
breadcrumbs
50 g/2 oz/¼ cup butter or margarine
A few drops of lemon juice
Pinch of cayenne
Pinch of ground cumin
Salt and freshly ground black pepper
Vegetable fat, melted

Boil the lentils in water until soft. Drain, if necessary, and cool them slightly, then process with the cheese, breadcrumbs and butter or margarine. Work in a few drops of lemon juice, the cayenne and cumin and a little salt and pepper. Taste and adjust the flavourings if necessary. Pack the spread into a bowl, level the top and run a little melted vegetable fat over the top to prevent it drying out. Use within 48 hours or freeze.

Yellow Pea Spread

MAKES 1 POT

Prepare as for Red Lentil Spread but use yellow split peas instead of lentils and soak them for several hours before cooking.

Aubergine Tofu Spread

MAKES 1 POT

1 aubergine (eggplant)
50 g/2 oz/½ cup ground almonds
225 g/8 oz/1 cup silken tofu
Pinch of mixed (apple pie) spice
15 ml/1 tbsp lemon juice
A few drops of onion juice or a
*   squeeze of garlic purée (paste)*

Halve the aubergine lengthways. Grill (broil) it, skin side up, until the flesh is soft. Strip off the skin and chop the flesh into a bowl. Process it with the almonds, tofu and mixed spice. Work in the lemon juice and a few drops of onion juice or the garlic. Put in a pot, cover and chill. Use within 48 hours.

Home-made Peanut Butter

MAKES ABOUT 225 g/8 oz/1 CUP

225 g/8 oz/2 cups roasted peanuts
15 ml/1 tbsp peanut (groundnut) oil
Salt (optional)

Purée the nuts in a blender or food processor until they form a paste, stopping to scrape down the sides every few seconds. Add the oil and blend again. Season with salt, if liked. Store in a screw-topped jar in the fridge.

Cashew Nut Butter

MAKES ABOUT 225 g/8 oz/1 CUP

Prepare as for Peanut Butter but use roasted or plain cashew nuts instead of peanuts.

Hazelnut Butter

MAKES ABOUT 225 g/8 oz/1 CUP

Prepare as for Peanut Butter but use hazelnuts instead of peanuts. Toast them either in a dry frying pan (skillet) or under the grill (broiler), turning frequently until golden brown, before processing.

Vinaigrette Dressing

SERVES 4

90 ml/6 tbsp olive oil
30 ml/2 tbsp wine vinegar
10 ml/2 tsp chopped shallot
5 ml/1 tsp caster (superfine) sugar
15 ml/1 tbsp chopped parsley
Salt and freshly ground black pepper

Shake all the ingredients together in a screw-topped jar. Store in the fridge.

French Dressing

SERVES 4

90 ml/6 tbsp olive oil
30 ml/2 tbsp wine vinegar
10 ml/2 tsp Dijon mustard
Good pinch of caster (superfine)
*   sugar*
Salt and freshly ground black pepper

Shake all the ingredients together in a screw-topped jar. Store in the fridge.

Ginger Dressing

SERVES 4

90 ml/6 tbsp sunflower oil
15 ml/1 tbsp soy sauce
15 ml/1 tbsp lemon juice
1 garlic clove, crushed
2.5 ml/½ tsp grated fresh root ginger

Mix together all the ingredients well. Serve spooned over salad, vegetables or as a dip, especially for Breaded Mushrooms (see page 54).

Chive and Vinegar Dressing

SERVES 4

45 ml/3 tbsp white wine vinegar
90 ml/6 tbsp olive oil
Freshly ground black pepper
15 ml/1 tbsp snipped chives
A dash of lemon juice

Mix together all the ingredients and chill before serving.

Tofu Dressing

SERVES 4

300 ml/½ pt/1¼ cups silken tofu
10 ml/2 tsp Soy Dressing (see right)

Whisk (or purée in a blender) the tofu with the Soy Dressing. For a spicier dressing add more Soy Dressing. You need only half this quantity for the Carrot and Olive Salad (see page 222), but make the full amount as it keeps well in the fridge. Use the rest to dress a coleslaw.

Soy Dressing

SERVES 4

60 ml/4 tbsp soy sauce
15 ml/1 tbsp lemon juice
15 ml/1 tbsp sunflower oil
20 ml/4 tsp clear honey
2.5 ml/½ tsp ground ginger
60 ml/4 tbsp water

Blend all the ingredients together and store in the fridge in a screw-topped jar.

Honeyed Soy Sauce

SERVES 4

60 ml/4 tbsp light soy sauce
15 ml/1 tbsp sunflower oil
15 ml/1 tbsp lime juice
2.5 ml/½ tsp grated fresh root ginger
20 ml/4 tsp clear honey
10 ml/2 tsp medium-dry sherry

Mix together all the ingredients until well blended. Use to dress bean sprouts or as a marinade for tofu or quorn.

Sweet and Sour Dressing

SERVES 4

120 ml/4 fl oz/½ cup pineapple juice
5 ml/1 tsp soy sauce
2.5 ml/½ tsp tomato purée (paste)
Freshly ground black pepper

Mix together all the ingredients and chill before serving. Use as a dressing for salads such as Chinese Bean Sprout Salad (see page 223).

Peanut Dressing

SERVES 4

60 ml/4 tbsp peanut butter
30 ml/2 tbsp olive oil
5 ml/1 tsp lemon juice
5 ml/1 tsp soy sauce
Pinch of dried tarragon

Mix together all the ingredients and chill before serving as a dip or salad dressing.

Hot Yoghurt Dressing

SERVES 4

60 ml/4 tbsp plain yoghurt
Good pinch of chilli powder
Pinch of salt
Pinch of sugar

Mix together all the ingredients and chill before serving. It is especially good with cooked or raw grated carrots.

Mayonnaise

SERVES 8

2 egg yolks
2.5 ml/½ tsp salt
Pinch of white pepper
5 ml/1 tsp Dijon mustard
300 ml/½ pt/1¼ cups lukewarm
*   sunflower oil*
5 ml/1 tsp hot vinegar
Juice of ½ lemon

Place the egg yolks in a bowl with the salt, pepper and mustard. Gradually pour in the warm oil in a thin stream, whisking in one direction only. As the sauce thickens, increase the flow of the oil until all is used. Add the vinegar, then the lemon juice. Store in a screw-topped jar in the fridge.

Pink Dressing

15 ml/1 tbsp tomato ketchup (catsup)
15 ml/1 tbsp Worcestershire sauce
300 ml/½ pt/1¼ cups Mayonnaise (see page 305)

Mix together all the ingredients. Store in a screw-topped jar in the fridge.

Tartare Sauce

5 ml/1 tsp chopped shallots
5 ml/1 tsp chopped capers
5 ml/1 tsp mixed fresh herbs
1 small cocktail gherkin (cornichon)
300 ml/½ pt/1¼ cups Mayonnaise (see page 305)

Mix together all the ingredients. Store in a screw-topped jar in the fridge.

Aioli

3 or 4 garlic cloves, crushed
300 ml/½ pt/1¼ cups Mayonnaise (see page 305)
30 ml/2 tbsp olive oil (optional)

Mix together all the ingredients, adding the olive oil for an authentic taste. Store in a screw-topped jar in the fridge.

Mint Dressing

15 ml/1 tbsp chopped mint or 5 ml/ 1 tsp made mint sauce
300 ml/½ pt/1¼ cups Mayonnaise (see page 305)

Mix together all the ingredients. Store in a screw-topped jar in the fridge.

Plain Salad Cream

300 ml/½ pt/1¼ cups cold White Sauce (see page 311) or Nutty White Sauce (see page 313)
300 ml/½ pt/1¼ cups Mayonnaise (see page 305)
15 ml/1 tbsp vinegar
15 ml/1 tbsp sugar
Salt and freshly ground black pepper

Blend the White Sauce or Nutty White Sauce with the Mayonnaise. Boil the vinegar and sugar together and add to the sauce. Season to taste and store in a screw-topped jar in the fridge.

Yoghurt Dressing

120 ml/4 fl oz/½ cup plain yoghurt
300 ml/½ pt/1¼ cups Mayonnaise (see page 305)
15 ml/1 tbsp sugar

Mix together all the ingredients. Store in a screw-topped jar in the fridge.

Creamier Dressing

SERVES 4

120 ml/4 fl oz/½ cup soured (dairy
    sour) cream or double (heavy)
    cream
600 ml/1 pt/2½ cups Mayonnaise (see
    page 305)
Lemon juice

Mix together the soured or double
cream and the Mayonnaise and add
lemon juice to taste. Store in a screw-
topped jar in the fridge.

Swedish Sauce

SERVES 4

120 ml/4 fl oz/½ cup apple purée
    (apple sauce)
600 ml/1 pt/2½ cups Mayonnaise (see
    page 305)
15 ml/1 tbsp sugar

Mix together the apple purée,
Mayonnaise and sweeten to taste
with sugar. Store in a screw-topped jar in
the fridge.

Blue Cheese Dressing

SERVES 4

25 g/1 oz blue cheese
300 ml/½ pt/1¼ cups Mayonnaise (see
    page 305)
15 ml/1 tbsp chopped parsley
A little milk, if necessary

Mash the cheese thoroughly. Blend in
the Mayonnaise. Add the parsley and
thin with a little milk, if liked. Store in a
screw-topped jar in the fridge.

Blue Cheese Yoghurt Dressing

SERVES 4

25 g/1 oz well-matured blue cheese
150 ml/¼ pt/⅔ cup Mayonnaise (see
    page 305)
150 ml/¼ pt/⅔ cup plain yoghurt
15 ml/1 tbsp snipped chives

Blend together the cheese, Mayonnaise
and yoghurt. Add the chives. Store in
a screw-topped jar in the fridge.

Rosy Dressing

SERVES 4

45 ml/3 tbsp grated beetroot (red
    beet)
300 ml/½ pt/1¼ cups Mayonnaise (see
    page 305)
Lemon juice

Mix together the beetroot and
Mayonnaise and spike with lemon
juice to taste. Store in a screw-topped jar
in the fridge.

Curried Fruit Mayonnaise

SERVES 4

60 ml/4 tbsp Mayonnaise (see page 305)
1 garlic clove, crushed
10 ml/2 tsp curry paste
2.5 ml/½ tsp lemon juice
25 g/1 oz/¼ cup sultanas (golden raisins), chopped
25 g/1 oz/¼ cup dried apricots, chopped

Mix together all the ingredients and chill before serving.

Andes Dressing

SERVES 4

300 ml/½ pt/1¼ cups Mayonnaise (see page 305)
30 ml/2 tbsp tomato purée (paste)
1 canned pimiento cap, finely chopped
Salt and freshly ground black pepper

Mix together all the ingredients and chill until ready to serve.

Verdant Velvet Dressing

SERVES 4

250 ml/8 fl oz/1 cup Mayonnaise (see page 305)
1 garlic clove, crushed
½ bunch of spring onions (scallions), finely chopped
15 ml/1 tbsp chopped tarragon
30 ml/2 tbsp chopped parsley
10 ml/2 tsp lemon juice
120 ml/4 fl oz/½ cup soured (dairy sour) cream
5 ml/1 tsp caster (superfine) sugar
Salt and freshly ground black pepper

Blend all the ingredients together, seasoning to taste with salt and pepper. Taste again and spike with a little more lemon juice, if liked.

Red Square Dressing

SERVES 4

250 ml/8 fl oz/1 cup Mayonnaise (see page 305)
10 ml/2 tsp Worcestershire sauce
30 ml/2 tbsp tomato ketchup (catsup)
5 ml/1 tsp grated fresh root ginger
5 ml/1 tsp grated onion

Mix together all the ingredients and chill for at least 30 minutes to allow the flavours to develop.

Piquant Parisian Dressing

250 ml/8 fl oz/1 cup Mayonnaise (see page 305)
15 ml/1 tbsp Dijon mustard
1 dill pickle, finely chopped
15 ml/1 tbsp chopped stuffed olives
1 firm tomato, seeded and finely chopped
15 ml/1 tbsp snipped chives
1 hard-boiled (hard-cooked) egg, finely chopped
5 ml/1 tsp white wine vinegar
2.5 ml/½ tsp dried dill (dill weed)

Mix together all the ingredients and leave to stand for at least 1 hour before serving.

'It Tastes Like Homemade' Mayonnaise

250 ml/8 oz/1 cup bought mayonnaise
45 ml/3 tbsp olive oil
5 ml/1 tsp lemon juice
Pinch of cayenne
Salt and freshly ground black pepper

Put the mayonnaise in a bowl. Using a balloon whisk, gradually whisk in the oil, whisking well after each little addition until light and well blended. Whisk in the lemon juice and cayenne. Season to taste if necessary.

More-than-a-thousand Island Dressing

250 ml/8 fl oz/1 cup Mayonnaise (see page 305)
1 garlic clove, crushed
5 ml/1 tsp Dijon mustard
1 small red (bell) pepper, finely chopped
15 ml/1 tbsp tomato relish
1 hard-boiled (hard-cooked) egg, finely chopped
5 ml/1 tsp Worcestershire sauce
Salt and freshly ground black pepper

Mix together all the ingredients and chill until ready to serve.

Danish Special

100 g/4 oz/1 cup Danish Blue cheese, crumbled
250 ml/8 fl oz/1 cup soured (dairy sour) cream
5 ml/1 tsp Worcestershire sauce
2.5 ml/½ tsp dried dill (dill weed)
1 dill pickle, finely chopped

Mash the cheese with a fork and gradually work in the cream until fairly smooth. Add the remaining ingredients and chill until ready to serve.

Crunchy Garlic and Lime Dressing

SERVES 4

2 garlic cloves, crushed
2 egg yolks
300 ml/½ pt/1½ cups olive oil
Grated rind and juice of 1 lime
Salt and freshly ground black pepper
30 ml/2 tbsp tiny croûtons

Using a balloon whisk, whisk the garlic and egg yolks together in a bowl. Add a tiny drop of oil and whisk again. Continue in this way until all the oil is absorbed and the mixture is very thick. Alternatively, put the garlic and yolks in a blender and run the machine constantly while pouring on the oil in a thin trickle. Whisk in the lime rind and juice and season to taste. Just before serving, fold in the crunchy croûtons.

Smooth Cheese Dressing

SERVES 4

100 g/4 oz/½ cup low-fat soft cheese
5 ml/1 tsp Dijon mustard
30 ml/2 tbsp olive oil
30 ml/2 tbsp single (light) cream
30 ml/2 tbsp lemon juice
Salt and freshly ground black pepper

Beat the cheese and mustard in a bowl. Gradually beat in the oil, then the cream and lemon juice. Season to taste.

Tangy Yoghurt Dressing

SERVES 4

90 ml/6 tbsp plain yoghurt
45 ml/3 tbsp crème fraiche
2.5 ml/½ tsp Dijon mustard
10 ml/2 tsp lemon juice
Good pinch of cayenne
Salt and freshly ground black pepper

Blend together all the ingredients , season to taste with salt and pepper and chill until ready to serve.

Green Onion and Watercress Dressing

SERVES 4

120 ml/4 fl oz/½ cup Mayonnaise (see page 305)
60 ml/4 tbsp soured (dairy sour) cream
2 spring onion (scallions), finely chopped
1 bunch of watercress, trimmed and finely chopped
10 ml/2 tsp white wine vinegar
Good pinch of caster (superfine) sugar
Good pinch of cayenne
Salt and freshly ground black pepper

Blend the mayonnaise with the cream. Stir in the remaining ingredients, seasoning to taste with salt and pepper. Chill until ready to serve.

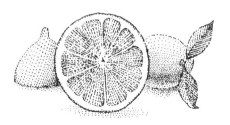

White Sauce

25 g/1 oz/2 tbsp butter or margarine
25 g/1 oz/¼ cup plain (all-purpose)
  flour
Salt and freshly ground white pepper
300 ml/½ pt/1¼ cups milk

Put all the ingredients in a saucepan and whisk until the flour is well blended. Bring to the boil, whisking all the time, and simmer for 2 minutes. Use as required.

Bechamel Sauce

300 ml/½ pt/1¼ cups milk
20 g/¾ oz/3 tbsp plain (all-purpose)
  flour
20 g/¾ oz/1½ tbsp butter or margarine
1 bouquet garni sachet
Salt and freshly ground black pepper

Whisk together the milk and flour in a saucepan until smooth. Add the butter or margarine and the bouquet garni sachet and bring to the boil, whisking all the time. Reduce the heat and simmer for 3 minutes, stirring. Squeeze the bouquet garni against the side of the pan to extract more flavour, then discard. Season to taste with salt and pepper. Use as required.

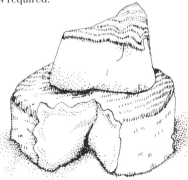

Parsley Sauce

300 ml/½ pt/1¼ cups milk
20 g/¾ oz/3 tbsp plain (all-purpose)
  flour
20 g/¾ oz/3 tbsp butter or margarine
1 bouquet garni sachet
Salt and freshly ground black pepper
30 ml/2 tbsp chopped parsley

Whisk together the milk and flour in a saucepan until smooth. Add the butter or margarine and the bouquet garni sachet and bring to the boil, whisking all the time. Reduce the heat and simmer for 3 minutes, stirring. Squeeze the bouquet garni against the side of the pan to extract more flavour, then discard. Season to taste with salt and pepper and add the parsley. Use as required.

Cheese Sauce

300 ml/½ pt/1¼ cups milk
20 g/¾ oz/3 tbsp plain (all-purpose)
  flour
20 g/¾ oz/1½ tbsp butter or margarine
1 bouquet garni sachet
Salt and freshly ground black pepper
75 g/3 oz/¾ cup Cheddar cheese,
  grated
2.5 ml/½ tsp made English mustard

Whisk together the milk and flour in a saucepan until smooth. Add the butter or margarine and the bouquet garni sachet and bring to the boil, whisking all the time. Reduce the heat and simmer for 3 minutes, stirring. Squeeze the bouquet garni against the side of the pan to extract more flavour, then discard. Season to taste with salt and pepper and add the cheese and mustard. Use as required.

Blue Cheese Sauce

MAKES 300 ML/½ PT/1¼ CUPS

300 ml/½ pt/1¼ cups milk
20 g/¾ oz/3 tbsp plain (all-purpose)
*   flour*
20 g/¾ oz/1½ tbsp butter or margarine
1 bouquet garni sachet
Salt and freshly ground black pepper
75 g/3 oz/¾ cup blue cheese,
*   crumbled*
Lemon juice
15 ml/1 tbsp snipped chives

Whisk together the milk and flour in a saucepan until smooth. Add the butter or margarine and the bouquet garni sachet and bring to the boil, whisking all the time. Reduce the heat and simmer for 3 minutes, stirring. Squeeze the bouquet garni against the side of the pan to extract more flavour, then discard. Season to taste with salt and pepper and add the cheese, a squeeze of lemon juice and the chives. Stir until melted and use as required.

Mushroom Sauce

MAKES 300 ML/½ PT/1¼ CUPS

100 g/4 oz button mushrooms, sliced
A little butter or margarine
300 ml/½ pt/1¼ cups milk
20 g/¾ oz/3 tbsp plain (all-purpose)
*   flour*
20 g/¾ oz/1½ tbsp butter or margarine
1 bouquet garni sachet
Salt and freshly ground black pepper
Worcestershire sauce

Fry (sauté) the mushrooms in a little butter or margarine. Set aside. Whisk together the milk and flour in a saucepan until smooth. Add the measured butter or margarine and the bouquet garni sachet and bring to the boil, whisking all the time. Reduce the heat and simmer for 3 minutes, stirring. Squeeze the bouquet garni against the side of the pan to extract more flavour, then discard. Season to taste with salt and pepper. Add the mushrooms and spike with Worcestershire sauce to taste. Use as required.

French Mustard Sauce

MAKES 300 ML/½ PT/1¼ CUPS

300 ml/½ pt/1¼ cups milk
20 g/¾ oz/3 tbsp plain (all-purpose)
*   flour*
20 g/¾ oz/1½ tbsp butter or margarine
1 bay leaf
Salt and freshly ground black pepper
10 ml/2 tsp cider vinegar
10 ml/2 tsp light brown sugar

Whisk together the milk and flour in a saucepan until smooth. Add the butter or margarine and the bay leaf and bring to the boil, whisking all the time. Reduce the heat and simmer for 3 minutes, stirring. Discard the bay leaf. Season to taste with salt and pepper and add the vinegar and sugar. Use as required.

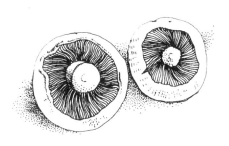

Nutty White Sauce

SERVES 8

100 g/4 oz/1 cup almonds, chopped
600 ml/1 pt/2½ cups water
2.5 ml/½ tsp sugar
Pinch of salt
10 ml/2 tsp cornflour (cornstarch)
60 ml/4 tbsp cold water
Grated nutmeg or ground ginger

Place the almonds in a pan with the water, sugar and salt. Simmer for 10 minutes. Liquidize and strain through a muslin cloth (cheesecloth). Return to the heat and re-boil to thicken the sauce. Blend the cornflour with the cold water and stir into the boiling almond milk. Simmer the sauce for 3 minutes, stirring. Check the seasoning, adding grated nutmeg or ground ginger to taste.

White Mushroom Sauce

SERVES 8

Prepare as for Nutty White Sauce but add 100 g/4 oz/ sliced white mushrooms to the boiling sauce. Simmer for 5 minutes.

Coconut Sauce

SERVES 8

Prepare as for Nutty White Sauce but add 100 g/4 oz/1 cup desiccated (shredded) coconut to the boiling sauce and simmer for 5 minutes.

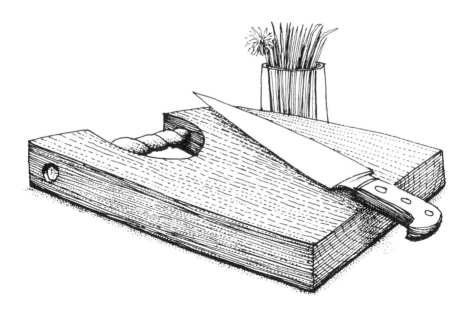

313

Nutty Brown Sauce

60 ml/4 tbsp oil
1 onion, chopped
1 carrot, chopped
100 g/4 oz/1 cup toasted peanuts
10 ml/2 tsp tomato purée (paste)
1 garlic clove, chopped
600 ml/1 pt/2½ cups water
5 ml/1 tsp yeast extract
Small thyme sprig
5 ml/1 tsp cornflour (cornstarch)
45 ml/3 tbsp water
Salt and freshly ground black pepper

Heat the oil in a saucepan and stir-fry the onion, carrot and nuts for 4 minutes. Add the tomato purée and garlic and cook for 1 minute. Stir in the water, yeast extract and thyme. Bring to the boil and simmer for 15 minutes. Sieve (strain) or purée in a blender or food processor. Reheat in a clean saucepan. Blend the cornflour with the water and stir into the pan. Boil for 2 minutes to thicken. Season to taste.

Brown Mushroom Sauce

Prepare as for Nutty Brown Sauce but heat 4 chopped field mushrooms in the boiling sauce for 2 minutes or add sliced, cultivated mushrooms.

Olive Sauce

Prepare as for Nutty Brown Sauce but add 75 g/3 oz/½ cup chopped stoned (pitted) olives to the hot sauce.

Madeira Sauce

Prepare as for Nutty Brown Sauce but add 120 ml/4 fl oz/½ cup Madeira blended with an extra 5 ml/1 tsp cornflour to the boiling sauce.

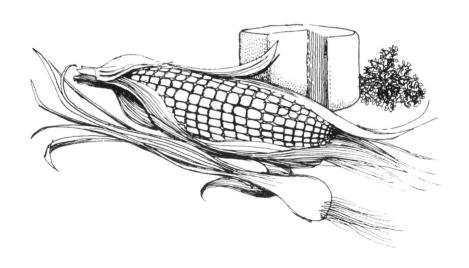

314

Plum Sauce

SERVES 8

*100 g/4 oz/1 cup juicy Victoria
  plums, stoned (pitted)*
15 ml/1 tbsp clear honey
*600 ml/1 pt/2½ cups Nutty Brown
  Sauce (see page 314)*
5 ml/1 tsp mixed (apple pie) spice
1 green chilli, seeded and chopped

Boil the plums and honey for about 5 minutes. Purée in a blender or food processor. Blend this purée into the brown sauce. Flavour with the spice and chopped chilli. Serve with any tofu dish.

Red Bean Sauce

SERVES 8

30 ml/2 tbsp oil
*100 g/4 oz/1 cup red kidney beans,
  cooked (see page 10)*
1 garlic clove, chopped
5 ml/1 tsp yeast extract
15 ml/1 tbsp vinegar
*2.5 ml/½ tsp Chinese five spice
  powder*
*600 ml/1 pt/2½ cups Nutty Brown
  Sauce (see page 314)*
Salt and freshly ground black pepper

Heat the oil in a pan and stir-fry the beans and garlic for 3 minutes. Add the yeast extract, vinegar, spice and brown sauce. Boil for 10 minutes. Pass through a sieve (strainer) or purée in a blender or food processor. If too thick, add either water or Madeira. Season to taste. Serve with any tofu or mushroom dish.

Simple Fresh Tomato Sauce

SERVES 8

60 ml/4 tbsp olive oil
1 onion, chopped
1 garlic clove, chopped
6 tomatoes, coarsely chopped
1 slice red chilli (optional)
600 ml/1 pt/2½ cups water
15 ml/1 tbsp tomato purée (paste)
1 vegetable stock cube
5 ml/1 tsp salt
Sugar
5 ml/1 tsp cornflour (cornstarch)
45 ml/3 tbsp cold water

Heat the oil in a saucepan and stir-fry the vegetables for 4 minutes. Add the water, tomato purée and stock cube and boil for 10 minutes. Season with salt and sugar, pass through a sieve (strainer) or place in a blender or food processor. Reheat to boiling point. Blend the cornflour with the cold water and stir into the hot mixture. Boil for 2 minutes to thicken and clear the starch. Serve with rice or pasta.

Spicy Tomato Sauce

SERVES 4

15 ml/1 tbsp olive oil
1 onion, finely chopped
*400 g/14 oz/1 large can chopped
  tomatoes*
5 ml/1 tsp dried oregano
Pinch of chilli powder
Salt and freshly ground black pepper
A dash of Worcestershire sauce

Heat the oil and fry (sauté) the onion for about 5 minutes until soft. Add the remaining ingredients and simmer for 10 minutes. Serve with Fragrant Dolmas (see page 49), pasta or Basic Nut Roast (see page 133).

Vegetable Gravy

50 g/2 oz/¼ cup butter or margarine
2 onions, finely chopped
15g/½ oz/2 tbsp plain (all-purpose)
  flour
300 ml/½ pt/1¼ cups vegetable stock
5 ml/1 tsp Worcestershire sauce
5 ml/1 tsp yeast extract
Salt and freshly ground black pepper

Melt the butter or margarine in a
saucepan. Add the onions and fry
(sauté) for 5 minutes until golden brown,
stirring all the time. Stir in the flour and
cook for 1 minute. Gradually blend in the
stock and add the flavourings. Bring to
the boil and cook, stirring for 2 minutes
until thickened. Strain, if liked, into a
gravy boat and serve.

Almond Cream Sauce

100 g/4 oz/½ cup quark
100 g/4 oz/1 cup ground almonds
25 g/1 oz/¼ cup Pecorino cheese,
  grated
Good pinch of ground cinnamon
Good pinch of grated nutmeg
150 ml/¼ pt/⅔ cup single (light) or
  half-cream (half-and-half)
45 ml/3 tbsp olive oil
30-75 ml/2-5 tbsp water

Whisk together or purée in a food
processor all the ingredients except
the water. Add enough water to give the
sauce the consistency you want. Taste
and adjust the flavour before pouring the
sauce. Serve with pasta.

Almond Tofu Sauce

If you do not eat dairy foods, use firm tofu
instead of quark, a good pinch of ground
coriander (cilantro) and a little salt
instead of Pecorino cheese, and silken
tofu instead of cream. The sauce will be a
little less thick and a lot less rich.

Lemon Sauce

600 ml/1 pt/2½ cups water
15 ml/1 tbsp sugar
15 ml/1 tbsp clear honey
15 ml/1 tbsp chopped lemon grass
1 vegetable stock cube
2.5 ml/½ tsp ground turmeric
2.5 ml/½ tsp ground ginger
Grated rind and juice of 1 lemon
25 g/1 oz/2 tbsp butter or margarine
15 g/½ oz/2 tbsp flour
2 egg yolks
Salt and freshly ground black pepper

Boil the water with the sugar, honey, lemon grass and stock cube for 5 minutes. Add the turmeric, ginger and lemon rind. Boil for a further 3 minutes. Melt the butter or margarine in a saucepan and add the flour. Cook for 1 minute, stirring, without browning. Whisk into the hot sauce to thicken. Boil for 3 minutes and strain. In a small bowl, mix the egg yolks with a cupful of the sauce. Add it to the remaining sauce. Cook gently for 3 minutes. Lastly add the lemon juice. (If added earlier the sauce would thin down.) Season to taste. Serve with mushroom, potato, tofu or pasta dishes.

Baked Brown Bread Sauce

2 slices wholemeal bread
Milk
1 small onion
2 cloves
2.5 ml/½ tsp grated nutmeg
Salt and freshly ground black pepper

Break up the bread and place in a small ovenproof dish. Pour on enough milk to cover and leave to soak for 5 minutes. Stud the onion with the cloves and push into the middle of the bread. Season the bread with the nutmeg and a little salt and pepper. Top up with a little more milk, then cover with foil and bake in a pre-heated oven (with a nut roast or something similar) at 190°C/375°F/gas mark 5 for about 1 hour. Remove the onion, then beat the sauce with a fork until fairly smooth. Thin with a little more milk, if liked. Turn into a clean serving bowl if necessary and serve.

Cranberry and Port Sauce

225 g/8 oz cranberries
150 ml/¼ pt/⅔ cup water
150 g/5 oz/⅔ cup caster (superfine)
* sugar*
30 ml/2 tbsp port

Put the cranberries and water in a saucepan. Bring to the boil and cook until the cranberries have popped. Stir in the sugar and port and simmer for 4 minutes.

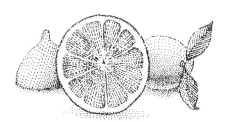

Creamed Spinach Sauce

MAKES ABOUT 450 ML/¾ PT/2 CUPS

450 g/1 lb frozen chopped spinach,
thawed
15 ml/1 tbsp plain (all-purpose) flour
15 g/½ oz/1 tbsp butter or margarine
45 ml/3 tbsp double (heavy) cream
Pinch of grated nutmeg
Salt and freshly ground black pepper

Cook the spinach without any extra water. Stir in the flour and cook for 1 minute. Blend in the butter or margarine and cook for a further minute. Stir in the cream and season with the nutmeg, salt and pepper.

Basic Sweet White Sauce

MAKES 300 ML/½ PT/1¼ CUPS

15 ml/1 tbsp cornflour (cornstarch)
300 ml/½ pt/1¼ cups milk
10 ml/2 tsp caster (superfine) sugar
15 g/½ oz/1 tbsp butter or margarine
A few drops of vanilla essence
(extract)

Blend the cornflour with a little of the milk in a saucepan. Add the remaining milk and the sugar. Bring to the boil and cook for 2 minutes, stirring all the time. Stir in the butter or margarine and the vanilla essence and use as required.

Quick Custard

MAKES 300 ML/½ PT/1¼ CUPS

Prepare as for Basic Sweet White Sauce but whisk in 1 egg yolk with the cornflour and milk.

Foamy Custard

MAKES 300 ML/½ PT/1¼ CUPS

Prepare as for Quick Custard but whisk one egg white until stiff and fold into the made custard.

Sweet Lemon Sauce

MAKES 300 ML/½ PT/1¼ CUPS

Prepare as for Quick Custard but use the grated rind and juice of 1 large lemon, made up to 300 ml/½ pt/1¼ cups with water instead of milk. Sweeten to taste with extra caster (superfine) sugar if necessary. Omit the vanilla flavouring.

Sweet Orange Sauce

MAKES 300 ML/½ PT/1¼ CUPS

Prepare as for Quick Custard but use the grated rind and juice of an orange, made up to 300 ml/½ pt/1¼ cups with pure orange juice instead of milk. Omit the vanilla flavouring.

Sweet Lime Sauce

MAKES 300 ML/½ PT/1¼ CUPS

Prepare as for Quick Custard but use the grated rind and juice of 2 limes, made up to 300 ml/½ pt/1¼ cups with water instead of milk. Sweeten with extra caster (superfine) sugar, if necessary, and add a few drops of green food colouring, if liked. Omit the vanilla flavouring.

Carob Custard Sauce

50 g/2 oz/½ cup carob powder
120 ml/4 fl oz/½ cup water
20 g/¾ oz/1½ tbsp butter or margarine
60 ml/4 tbsp clear honey
1 egg, beaten
5 ml/1 tsp vanilla essence (extract)

Whisk the carob powder and water together in a saucepan until smooth. Bring to the boil, reduce the heat and simmer for 4 minutes. Whisk in the remaining ingredients and cook over a gentle heat until thick and smooth. Serve hot or cold.

Almond Foam

25 g/1 oz/¼ cup ground almonds
300 ml/½ pt/1¼ cups milk
10 ml/2 tsp cornflour (cornstarch)
10 ml/2 tsp caster (superfine) sugar
1 small egg, separated
A few drops of almond essence

Whisk the almonds, milk, cornflour, sugar and egg yolks together in a saucepan. Bring to the boil and cook for 2 minutes, whisking all the time. Remove from the heat. Whisk the egg white until stiff. Fold into the mixture with a metal spoon and flavour with a few drops of almond essence. Serve warm.

Egg Custard Sauce

600 ml/1 pt/2½ cups milk
40 g/1½ oz/3 tbsp sugar
25 g/1 oz/¼ cup cornflour
(cornstarch)
2 egg yolks
45 ml/3 tbsp brandy, rum or Grand Marnier
6 drops of vanilla essence (extract)

Bring the milk to the boil with the sugar. In a cup, mix the cornflour with 45 ml/3 tbsp water. Add the blended cornflour to the boiling milk and stir. Cook for 3 minutes until it thickens slightly. In a small bowl, mix the egg yolks and liqueur. Add about 120 ml/4 fl oz/½ cup of the milk mixture, stirring. Pour the contents back into the thickened sauce. Re-boil for 2 minutes. Flavour with the vanilla essence. Serve hot or cold with any kind of pudding, including ice creams.

Raspberry Coulis

225 g/8 oz fresh or frozen raspberries
75 g/3 oz/⅓ cup caster (superfine) sugar
Juice of ½ lemon

Hull the raspberries, discarding any bad ones. Wash quickly and drain on kitchen paper. Either liquidize all the ingredients to a soft purée or pass them through a nylon sieve (strainer) (never metal as it discolours the fruit). Serve as an accompaniment to ice cream or other frozen desserts.

Apricot Coulis

SERVES 4

450 g/1 lb fresh apricots
150 ml/¼ pt/⅔ cup sweet white wine
or sweet sherry
50 g/2 oz/¼ cup granulated sugar
30 ml/2 tbsp Kirsch or Cointreau

Wash and drain the apricots. Remove the stones (pits). Boil the apricots, wine and sugar for about 4 minutes until soft. Liquidize the mixture to a purée or pass through a nylon sieve (strainer). Lastly add the Kirsch or Cointreau.

Plum Coulis

SERVES 4

Prepare as for Apricot Coulis but substitute ripe plums for the apricots.

Peach Coulis

SERVES 4

Prepare as for Apricot Coulis but substitute 4 large ripe peaches for the apricots.

Nectarine Coulis

SERVES 4

Prepare as for Apricot Coulis but substitute 4 or 5 ripe nectarines for the apricots.

Cornmeal Custard

SERVES 4

15 ml/1 tbsp fine cornmeal
30 ml/2 tbsp sugar
450 ml/¾ pt/2 cups milk
2.5 ml/½ tsp vanilla essence (extract)

Mix the cornmeal and sugar together and make a smooth paste with a little of the milk. Heat the rest of the milk in a saucepan. Pour on to the cornmeal paste, add the vanilla essence and return to the pan. Bring to the boil and simmer for 5 minutes, stirring all the time.

Apple and Cinnamon Spread

MAKES 1 POT

2 large eating (dessert) apples,
chopped
100 g/4 oz/⅔ cup dates, stoned
(pitted) and chopped
2.5 ml/½ tsp ground cinnamon
175 ml/6 fl oz/¾ cup water

Place all the ingredients in a saucepan and cover. Bring to the boil and cook for 15 minutes until soft. Mash with a potato masher, re-cover and cool with the lid still on. Transfer to a sealed container and store in the fridge for up to 1 week.

Photograph opposite: **Teacup Loaf**
(page 329)

Lemon Curd

MAKES ABOUT 450 G/1 LB

2 or 3 lemons
100 g/4 oz/½ cup butter or margarine
225 g/8 oz/1 cup sugar
2 eggs, beaten

Thinly pare the rind from the lemons. Squeeze and strain the juice. Melt the butter or margarine in a bowl over a pan of hot water. Whisk in the sugar, rind, juice and the eggs. Continue cooking over a gentle heat, stirring occasionally, until the mixture thickens and coats the back of a spoon. Strain into clean jars, cover, label and store in a cool, dark place.

Orange Curd

MAKES ABOUT 450 G/1 LB

Prepare as for Lemon Curd but substitute 2 oranges for the lemons.

Lime Curd

MAKES ABOUT 450 G/1 LB

Prepare as for Lemon Curd but substitute 3 or 4 limes for the lemons.

Processor Chutney

MAKES 2.25 KG/5 LB

450 g/1 lb cooking (tart) apples,
* cored and quartered*
450 g/1 lb onions, quartered
450 g/1 lb/2 cups light brown sugar
450 g/1 lb/2⅔ cups sultanas (golden
* raisins)*
450 g/1 lb/2⅔ cups dates, stoned
* (pitted) and chopped*
600 ml/1 pt/2½ cups vinegar
Salt and freshly ground black pepper
2.5 ml/½ tsp cayenne
2.5 ml/½ tsp ground allspice
2.5 ml/½ tsp ground ginger

Place the apples and onions in a food processor and process for 1 minute or until finely chopped. Alternatively, pass through a coarse mincer (grinder). Put all the ingredients into a large bowl, stir well and cover. Leave for 24 hours, stirring occasionally. Bottle and label. Store in a cool, dark place.

Photograph opposite: **Carrot, Orange and Pecan Cake (page 333)**

Breads, Biscuits and Cakes

You could argue that just about all bakery-type recipes are suitable for vegetarians. So why include them in this book? Well, I've chosen recipes that make especially good use of a whole variety of cereals and flours, use lots of nuts and dried fruits, all of which play an important part in a vegetarian diet and are genuinely good and wholesome into the bargain.

In this section there are excellent choices for afternoon tea or for a sweet treat in a lunch box. There are also wonderful accompaniments to soups, starters and main courses, delicious breakfast breads and useful basics like pancake batter, crumb shells and brandy snap baskets.

Yoghurt and Caraway Plait

MAKES 1 LOAF

450 g/1 lb/4 cups strong plain
(bread) flour
5 ml/1 tsp salt
25 g/1 oz/2 tbsp butter or margarine
10 ml/2 tsp easy-blend dried yeast
1 large egg, beaten
150 ml/¼ pt/⅔ cup milk
5 ml/1 tsp clear honey
45 ml/3 tbsp plain yoghurt
5 ml/1 tsp water
15 ml/1 tbsp caraway seeds

Sift the flour and salt into a bowl. Rub in the butter and stir in the yeast. Reserve a teaspoonful of the beaten egg and add the remainder to the flour. Warm the milk with the honey and yoghurt and add to the flour. Mix to form a soft but not sticky dough. Knead gently on a lightly floured surface for several minutes until smooth and elastic. Place in an oiled plastic bag and put in a warm place for about 45 minutes until doubled in bulk. Reknead and cut into three equal pieces. Roll out each piece to a sausage about 30 cm/12 in long. Put side-by-side on the work surface and pinch the three together at one end. Plait them together by passing the right strand over the middle one, then the left one over the new middle one. Continue to the end and pinch the ends together. Transfer to a lightly greased baking sheet. Beat the water with the reserved egg and brush over the surface. Sprinkle with the caraway seeds and leave in the warm for about 20 minutes until well risen again. Bake in a preheated oven at 190°C/375°F/gas mark 5 for about 30–35 minutes until golden and the base sounds hollow when tapped. Cool on a wire rack.

Swiss Christmas Loaf

MAKES 1 LARGE LOAF

150 g/5 oz/⅔ cup soft margarine
3 eggs
Salt and freshly ground black pepper
Grated nutmeg
2.5 ml/½ tsp Dijon mustard
15 ml/1 tbsp chopped parsley
175 g/6 oz/1½ cups Emmental (Swiss)
cheese, grated
100 g/4 oz/1 cup walnuts, chopped
100 g/4 oz/1 cup chopped mixed nuts
275 g/10 oz/2½ cups self-raising (self-
rising) flour
5 ml/1 tsp baking powder
5 ml/1 tsp bicarbonate of soda
(baking soda)
60 ml/4 tbsp milk
60 ml/4 tbsp single (light) cream

Put the margarine in a bowl and beat in the eggs one at a time. Add a good pinch of salt, pepper and nutmeg. Stir in the mustard, parsley, cheese and nuts. Sift the flour and baking powder together. Fold half into the nut mixture. Mix the bicarbonate of soda with the milk. Stir into the nut mixture with half the remaining flour. Work in the remaining flour and the cream. Turn into a greased 900 g/2 lb loaf tin (pan). Level the surface and bake in a preheated oven at 180°C/350°F/gas mark 4 for about 50 minutes or until risen and golden and a skewer inserted in the centre comes out clean. Cool slightly, then serve warm or cold cut into slices and buttered, if liked.

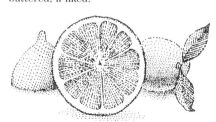

Celery and Cheese Loaf

SERVES 4

275 g/10 oz/2½ cups wholemeal self-
  raising (self-rising) flour
Salt and freshly ground black pepper
50 g/2 oz/¼ cup butter or margarine,
  softened
2 celery sticks, chopped
100 g/4 oz/1 cup Cheddar cheese,
  grated
1 egg, beaten
150 ml/¼ pt/⅔ cup milk

Mix together the flour, salt, pepper, butter or margarine, celery and cheese with a fork. Add the egg and milk and mix to a soft dough. Knead lightly in the bowl with floured hands. Transfer to a greased 450 g/1 lb loaf tin (pan). Bake in a preheated oven at 190°C/375°F/gas mark 5 for 1 hour. Leave in the tin for 5 minutes, then turn out to cool on a wire rack. Serve warm or cold, sliced and buttered.

Cheese and Sun-dried Tomato Loaf

SERVES 4

1 small French stick
100 g/4 oz/½ cup low-fat soft cheese
50 g/2 oz/¼ cup butter or margarine
3 sun-dried tomatoes, chopped
Freshly ground black pepper

Slice the bread, but not right through the base. Mash the cheese and butter or margarine together, work in the tomatoes and season with pepper. Spread between the slices. Wrap in foil and bake in a preheated oven at 200°C/400°F/gas mark 6 for 15 minutes or until the crust feels crispy when squeezed.

Cheese and Olive Loaf

SERVES 4

Prepare as for Cheese and Sun-dried Tomato Loaf but use 50 g/2 oz/⅓ cup chopped stoned (pitted) olives instead of the sun-dried tomatoes and add 2.5 ml/ ½ tsp dried basil.

Herby Baps

SERVES 4

4 brown baps, split into halves
A little butter or margarine
10 ml/2 tsp dried mixed herbs

Spread the baps with a little butter or margarine and sprinkle with the mixed herbs. Place under a hot grill (broiler) for 2 minutes until just browned. Serve with soup or light lunches.

Brown Garlic Bread

SERVES 4

1 brown Vienna loaf
1 garlic clove, crushed or 2.5 ml/
  ½ tsp garlic powder
50 g/2 oz/¼ cup butter or margarine
Salt and freshly ground black pepper
2.5 ml/½ tsp lemon juice

Slice the loaf diagonally into 2 cm/¾ in slices, but not right through the base. Mix the crushed garlic or garlic powder with the butter or margarine, salt, pepper and lemon juice. Spread each slice of bread with the mixture. Reshape the loaf and wrap in foil, sealing the ends firmly. Heat through in a preheated oven at 200°C/400°F/gas mark 6 for 15 minutes. Serve in a long bread basket, still wrapped in the foil to keep it warm.

Brown Herb Bread

SERVES 4

Prepare as for Brown Garlic Bread (see page 325) but substitute 30 ml/2 tbsp chopped mixed herbs for the garlic. Spike with a pinch of cayenne, if liked.

Cheese 'Rolls'

SERVES 4

8 slices wholemeal bread, crusts removed
100 g/4 oz/½ cup butter or margarine, melted
75 g/3 oz/¾ cup Cheddar cheese, grated
Paprika

Flatten each slice of bread by rolling firmly with a rolling pin. Brush each slice with melted butter or margarine, sprinkle with cheese and paprika and roll up. Place on a greased baking sheet and brush with butter or margarine. Bake in a preheated oven at 200°C/400°F/gas mark 6 for 10 minutes, then turn over. Brush with any remaining fat and cook for a further 10 minutes until crisp and golden. Serve hot.

Steamed Chinese Rolls

MAKES 15

Hand-hot water
15 ml/1 tbsp light brown sugar
15 g/½ oz dried yeast
450 g/1 lb plain (all-purpose) flour
5 ml/1 tsp salt
15 ml/1 tbsp melted butter or margarine

Put 150 ml/¼ pt/⅔ cup hand-hot water in a measuring jug. Stir in the sugar until dissolved. Sprinkle over the yeast, stir well and leave in a warm place for 10 minutes until frothy. Sift the flour and salt into a bowl. Make a well in the centre and pour in the yeast mixture and melted butter or margarine. Mix to a soft dough with a little more hand-hot water. Knead well on a lightly floured surface for 5 minutes until smooth and elastic. Return to the floured bowl and cover with clingfilm (plastic wrap). Stand in a warm place for about 45 minutes until doubled in bulk. Knock back and shape into 15 small balls. Place on greaseproof (waxed) paper on a rack and leave in a warm place for 15 minutes until doubled in size. Bring a large roasting tin (pan) of water to the boil. Lay the rack on top and cover with a dome of foil so it doesn't touch any of the rolls. Steam for 15 minutes. Serve warm.

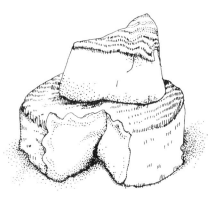

Carob and Orange Morning Rolls

MAKES 12

450 g/1 lb/4 cups strong white
  (bread) flour
5 ml/1 tsp salt
5 ml/1 tsp caster (superfine) sugar
Finely grated rind of 1 orange
15 g/½ oz/1 tbsp margarine
10 ml/2 tsp easy-blend dried yeast
1 egg, beaten
300 ml/½ pt/1¼ cups hand-hot milk
50 g/2 oz/½ cup carob chips
A little flour, for dusting

Mix the flour, salt, sugar and orange rind in a bowl. Rub in the margarine. Stir in the yeast. Reserve a little of the beaten egg for glazing and add the remainder to the flour with enough of the milk to form a firm dough. Knead gently on a lightly floured surface for several minutes until smooth and elastic (or prepare the mixture in a food processor). Place in a greased plastic bag and leave in a warm place for 45 minutes until almost doubled in bulk. Reknead, then knead in the carob chips. Shape into 12 balls and place on a greased baking sheet. Cover and leave in a warm place for 15 minutes until well risen. Brush with the reserved beaten egg and bake in a preheated oven at 220°C/ 425°F/gas mark 7 for 12–15 minutes until golden and the bases sound hollow when tapped. Dust with a little sifted flour and cool on a wire rack.

Irish Potato Cakes

MAKES ABOUT 12

450 g/1 lb/2 cups well-mashed potato
50 g/2 oz/¼ cup soft margarine
50 g/2 oz/½ cup wholemeal flour
Pinch of salt

Beat the mashed potato well, then beat in the margarine, flour and salt. Turn out on to a lightly floured surface and pat out to about 1 cm/½ in thick. Cut into rounds with a plain 7.5 cm/3 in cutter. Prick with a fork and dry-fry in a non-stick frying pan for about 3 minutes on each side until golden brown. Serve hot with butter.

Baked Potato Cakes with Fennel

MAKES ABOUT 12

Prepare as for Irish Potato Cakes but sprinkle the rounds with fennel seeds, pressing them lightly into the surfaces, place on a baking sheet and bake in a preheated oven at 200°C/ 400°F/gas mark 6 for about 20 minutes until lightly golden.

Crustlers

225 g/8 oz/2 cups plain (all-purpose)
flour
Pinch of salt
1.5 ml/¼ tsp baking powder
5 ml/1 tsp poppy seeds
100 g/4 oz/½ cup butter or margarine
1 egg, beaten
A little milk

Sift the flour, salt and baking powder together. Stir in the poppy seeds. Rub in the butter or margarine. Mix with the egg and enough milk to form a firm dough. Knead gently on a lightly floured surface. Pat out to about 2 cm/¾ in thick. Cut into rounds using a 5 cm/2 in cutter. Place on a baking sheet and bake in a preheated oven at 220°C/425°F/gas mark 7 for 10 minutes. With a clean cloth (to protect your hands), carefully pull the rounds apart, lay torn sides up on the baking sheet and continue baking for a further 10 minutes until golden and crispy. Cool on a wire rack and store in an airtight tin for up to 10 days.

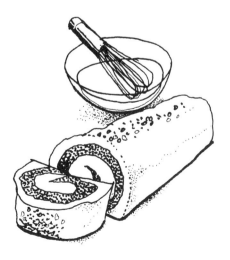

Oat and Rye Cob Loaf

225 g/8 oz/2 cups strong plain
(bread) flour
100 g/4 oz/1 cup rye flour
100 g/4 oz/1 cup fine oatmeal
5 ml/1 tsp salt
20 ml/4 tsp olive oil
10 ml/2 tsp easy-blend dried yeast
10 ml/2 tsp black treacle (molasses)
300 ml/½ pt/1¼ cups hand-hot water
10 ml/2 tsp plain yoghurt or milk
10 ml/2 tsp rolled oats (optional)

Mix the flours, oatmeal and salt together in a bowl. Stir in the oil and yeast. Blend the treacle with the water and add to the bowl. Mix to form a soft but not sticky dough. Knead gently on a lightly floured surface until smooth and elastic. Place in an oiled plastic bag and leave in a warm place for about 45 minutes until almost doubled in bulk. Reknead and shape into a ball. Place on a greased baking sheet. Brush with yoghurt or milk and sprinkle on the rolled oats, if using. Leave in a warm place for about 30 minutes until almost doubled in bulk again. Bake in a preheated oven at 230°C/450°F/gas mark 8 for about 25 minutes until a deep golden brown and the base sounds hollow when tapped. Cool on a wire rack.

Malted Breakfast Bread

175 g/6 oz/1½ cups self-raising (self-rising) flour
7.5 ml/1½ tsp baking powder
2.5 ml/½ tsp bicarbonate of soda (baking soda)
75 g/3 oz/scant ¾ cup muesli
50 g/2 oz/⅓ cup raisins
20 ml/4 tsp black treacle (molasses)
15 ml/1 tbsp golden (light corn) syrup
45 ml/3 tbsp malted milk drink powder or granules
30 ml/2 tbsp sunflower oil
175 ml/6 floz/¾ cup milk

Grease and line a 450 g/1 lb loaf tin (pan) with non-stick baking parchment. Mix the flour, baking powder, bicarbonate of soda, muesli and raisins together in a bowl. Warm the remaining ingredients in a pan, stirring until dissolved. Mix into the dry ingredients. Turn into the tin and bake in a preheated oven at 150°C/300°F/gas mark 2 for about 50 minutes until well risen, golden and just firm. Cool in the tin for 10 minutes, then turn out, remove the paper and leave to cool on a wire rack.

Chocolate Malted Breakfast Bread

Prepare as for Malted Breakfast Bread but use chocolate-flavoured malted milk drink powder or granules instead of plain.

Teacup Loaf

½ teacup butter or margarine
1 teacup sultanas (golden raisins)
½ teacup currants
½ teacup chopped almonds
1 teacup light brown sugar
½ teacup pure orange juice
½ teacup cold tea
2 teacups self-raising (self-rising) wholemeal flour
2.5 ml/½ tsp ground mace

Using a teacup to measure the ingredients (but the same one for all of them so the balance is right), put all the ingredients except the flour and mace in a saucepan. Bring to the boil, stirring until the butter or margarine has melted, then boil for 2 minutes. Leave to cool for 15 minutes. Fold in the flour and mace and turn into a greased 900 g/2 lb loaf tin (pan), base-lined with non-stick baking parchment. Bake in a preheated oven at 180°C/ 350°F/gas mark 4 for about 1¼ hours or until risen, golden and a skewer inserted in the centre comes out clean. Loosen the edges, turn out on to a wire rack, remove the paper and leave to cool.

Fruity Fibre Teacup Loaf

SERVES 6

1 teacup malted All Bran cereal
1 teacup light brown sugar
1 teacup mixed dried fruit (fruit cake
   mix)
1 teacup milk
1 teacup wholemeal self-raising (self-
   rising) flour
Pinch of mixed (apple pie) spice
Pinch of salt
A little extra sugar, for topping

Using the same sized teacup so the balance is right, put the cereal, sugar, mixed fruit and milk in a bowl and soak for 1 hour. Grease a 450 g/1 lb loaf tin (pan). Add the flour, mixed spice and salt to the mixture and combine well. Pour into the tin, sprinkle the top with a little extra sugar and cook in a preheated oven for 1¼ hours at 180°C/350°F/gas mark 4. Remove from the oven, leave in the tin for 5 minutes, then turn out on to a wire rack to cool. Serve sliced and buttered.

Apricot Teacup Loaf

SERVES 6

Prepare as for Fruity Fibre Teacup Loaf but substitute chopped ready-to-eat dried apricots for the mixed fruit, omit the spice and add 15 ml/1 tbsp clear honey.

Belgian Tea Loaf

SERVES 4

1 teacup sultanas (golden raisins) or
   raisins
1 teacup milk
1 teacup light brown sugar
100 g/4 oz/½ cup butter or margarine
1 egg, beaten
2 teacups wholemeal self-raising
   (self-rising) flour
Pinch of ground cinnamon
Pinch of salt
A little sugar for sprinkling

Using the same sized teacup so the balance is right, put the sultanas or raisins, milk, sugar and butter or margarine into a saucepan and bring to the boil, stirring until the fat has melted. Leave to cool slightly. Beat in the egg, flour, spice and salt. Pour into a greased 450 g/1 lb loaf tin, sprinkle with a little more sugar and bake for 1 hour in a preheated oven at 190°C/375°F/gas mark 5. Turn out after 5 minutes on to a wire rack to cool. Serve sliced and buttered.

Banana Tea Bread

SERVES 4–6

100 g/4 oz/½ cup butter or margarine
100 g/4 oz/½ cup light brown sugar
3 bananas, mashed
1 egg
15 ml/1 tbsp clear honey
1.5 ml/¼ tsp ground cinnamon
225 g/8 oz/2 cups self-raising (self-rising) flour
5 ml/1 tsp baking powder
45 ml/3 tbsp milk

Soften the butter or margarine, then beat in the sugar until smooth. Add the bananas, egg, honey and cinnamon. Slowly mix in the flour and baking powder, stirring it well in. Stir in the milk. Spoon into a greased loaf tin (pan) and bake in a preheated oven at 160°C/325°F/gas mark 3 for 1–1½ hours until firm.

Banana and Cherry Bread

SERVES 4–6

Prepare as for Banana Tea Bread but add 50 g/2 oz/½ cup quartered glacé (candied) cherries to the mixture.

Banana and Pecan Bread

SERVES 4–6

Prepare as for Banana Tea Bread but add 50 g/2 oz/½ cup chopped pecans to the mixture and substitute maple syrup for the honey, if liked.

Tropical Teabread

MAKES 1 LOAF

2 limes
50 g/2 oz/¼ cup caster (superfine) sugar
75 ml/5 tbsp water
450 g/1 lb ripe bananas
100 g/4 oz/½ cup soft margarine
175 g/6 oz/¾ cup dark brown sugar
2 eggs, beaten
225 g/8 oz/2 cups wholemeal flour
12.5 ml/2½ tsp baking powder
2.5 ml/½ tsp mixed (apple pie) spice
50 g/2 oz/⅓ cup dates, stoned (pitted) and chopped

Finely grate the rind of ½ a lime and reserve. Thinly pare the remainder and cut into fine shreds. Squeeze the juice. Dissolve the caster sugar in the water. Add the shredded lime rind and boil for 3 minutes. Cool. Mash the bananas with the lime juice thoroughly. Beat in the margarine, sugar and grated lime rind until light and soft. Beat in the eggs. Fold in the flour, baking powder and spice, then the dates. Alternatively, blend the bananas and juice in a food processor. Add the remaining ingredients except the dates and blend until smooth. Fold in the dates. Turn into a greased 900 g/2 lb loaf tin (pan), lined with non-stick baking parchment. Level the surface. Bake in a preheated oven at 180°C/350°F/gas mark 4 for about 1 hour or until risen and golden and a skewer inserted in the centre comes out clean. Cool slightly, then turn out on to a wire rack, remove the paper and leave to cool.

Vitality Scones

MAKES 8

225 g/8 oz plain (all-purpose) flour
10 ml/2 tsp baking powder
15 ml/1 tbsp bran
Pinch of salt
50 g/2 oz/¼ cup margarine
45 ml/3 tbsp clear honey
2 whole dried bananas, chopped
25 g/1 oz/⅙ cup sultanas (golden
  raisins)
1 egg
45 ml/3 tbsp plain yoghurt

Sift the flour and baking powder together. Stir in the bran and salt. Rub in the margarine, then stir in the honey, bananas and sultanas. Beat the egg and yoghurt together. Reserve a spoonful for glazing and mix the remainder into the banana mixture to form a soft but not sticky dough. Pat out to about 2 cm/¾ in thick and cut into 8 rounds using a 6.5 cm/2½ in cutter. Place on a baking sheet and brush with the reserved egg and yoghurt. Bake in a preheated oven at 220°C/425°F/gas mark 7 for about 10 minutes until well risen, golden and the bases sound hollow when tapped. Serve split and buttered.

Cottage Cheese Buns

MAKES 12

100 g/4 oz/½ cup cottage cheese
225 g/8 oz/2 cups self-raising (self-
  rising) flour
1 egg
100 g/4 oz/½ cup sugar
45–60 ml/3–4 tbsp milk

Mix the cheese and flour together. Add the remaining ingredients and mix to a soft dough. Shape into about 12 flattened circles and place on a greased baking sheet. Bake in a preheated oven at 220°C/425°F/gas mark 7 for 10–15 minutes. Serve split and spread with more cottage cheese or butter.

Orange and Carob Chip Cake

SERVES 4

100 g/4 oz/½ cup butter or margarine
100 g/4 oz/½ cup sugar
2 eggs
100 g/4 oz/1 cup wholemeal self-
  raising (self-rising) flour
75 g/3 oz/¾ cup carob chips
50 g/2 oz/½ cup walnuts, chopped
15 ml/1 tbsp fresh orange juice
10 ml/2 tsp finely grated orange rind
Orange Curd (see page 321)

Put the butter or margarine and sugar in a bowl and beat together. Beat in the eggs one at a time. Fold in the flour with the carob chips, walnuts, orange juice and rind and mix well. Turn into two 18 cm/7 in greased sandwich tins (pans) and bake in a preheated oven for 25 minutes at 190°C/375°F/gas mark 5 until risen and the centres spring back when lightly pressed. Turn out on to a wire rack to cool. Sandwich together with Orange Curd.

Carrot Cake

SERVES 4

225 g/8 oz/2 cups self-raising (self-rising) flour
15 ml/1 tbsp baking powder
150 g/5 oz/⅔ cup butter or margarine
100 g/4 oz/½ cup light brown sugar
2 large carrots, grated

Mix the flour and baking powder. Melt the butter or margarine and sugar, then pour into the flour and mix well. Stir in the carrots. Pour into a greased loaf tin (pan). Bake in a preheated oven at 160°C/325°F/gas mark 3 for 1 hour until a skewer inserted into the centre of the cake comes out clean.

Carrot, Orange and Pecan Cake

MAKES 16 SQUARES

225 g/8 oz/1 cup soft margarine
225 g/8 oz/1 cup caster (superfine) sugar
4 eggs, beaten
250 g/9 oz/2¼ cups self-raising (self-rising) flour
5 ml/1 tsp baking powder
Grated rind of 1 orange
350 g/12 oz carrots, grated
75 g/3 oz/¾ cup pecan halves
Juice of ½ orange
350 g/12 oz/2 cups icing (confectioners') sugar, sifted
60 ml/4 tbsp Greek-style plain yoghurt

Beat the margarine, caster sugar, eggs, flour, baking powder and orange rind together until smooth and fluffy. Fold in the carrots. Reserve 15 ml/1 tbsp chopped pecans for decoration and fold the remainder into the cake mixture. Grease and line a 28 × 18 cm/11 × 7 in shallow baking tin (pan) with non-stick baking parchment. Turn the mixture into the prepared tin and smooth the surface. Bake in a preheated oven at 180°C/350°F/gas mark 4 for about 50 minutes or until risen and golden and the centre springs back when lightly pressed. Cool slightly, then turn out on to a wire rack to cool completely. To make the icing, beat the remaining ingredients together until smooth. Spread over the cool cake and decorate with the reserved chopped pecans. Serve cut into squares.

Boiled Fruit Salad Cake

MAKES 1 CAKE

100 g/4 oz/½ cup margarine
175 g/6 oz/¾ cup light brown sugar
120 ml/4 fl oz/½ cup water
75 ml/5 tbsp apple juice
250 g/9 oz/1 small packet dried fruit
salad, chopped, discarding any
stones (pits)
5 ml/1 tsp bicarbonate of soda
(baking soda)
5 ml/1 tsp ground cinnamon
5 ml/1 tsp mixed (apple pie) spice
100 g/4 oz/1 cup self-raising (self-
rising) flour
100 g/4 oz/1 cup wholemeal flour
7.5 ml/1½ tsp baking powder
2 eggs, beaten

Put the margarine in a saucepan with the sugar, water, apple juice, chopped fruit, bicarbonate of soda and the spices. Bring to the boil and boil for 1 minute. Remove from the heat and leave to cool for 5 minutes, stirring occasionally. Mix the flours and baking powder together. Add to the fruit mixture with the beaten eggs. Mix well quickly. Turn into a greased 20 cm/8 in round deep cake tin (pan), lined with non-stick baking parchment. Level the surface and bake in a preheated oven at 180°C/350°F/gas mark 4 for about 1 hour 10 minutes or until a skewer inserted in the centre comes out clean. Cool slightly, then turn out on to a wire rack, remove the paper and leave to cool.

Three Seed Cake

MAKES 1 CAKE

175 g/6 oz/¾ cup butter or margarine
175 g/6 oz/¾ cup caster (superfine)
sugar
3 eggs, beaten
225 g/8 oz/2 cups plain (all-purpose)
flour
10 ml/2 tsp baking powder
5 ml/1 tsp sesame seeds
5 ml/1 tsp caraway seeds
5 ml/1 tsp poppy seeds
60 ml/4 tbsp milk

Beat the butter or margarine and sugar together in a bowl until light and fluffy. Add the eggs a little at a time, beating well after each addition. Sift the flour and baking powder over the surface and sprinkle on the seeds. Fold in lightly but thoroughly with a metal spoon. Add enough milk to form a soft, dropping consistency. Turn into a greased 20 cm/8 in round, deep cake tin (pan), base-lined with non-stick baking parchment. Level the surface. Cook in a preheated oven at 180°C/ 350°F/gas mark 4 for about 1 hour or until firm to the touch. Leave to cool for 10 minutes then turn out on to a wire rack, remove the paper and leave to cool.

Somerset Honey Cake

300 ml/½ pt/1¼ cups medium-sweet
cider
90 ml/6 tbsp clear honey
100 g/4 oz/½ cup soft margarine
100 g/4 oz/½ cup light brown sugar
2 eggs, lightly beaten
175 g/6 oz/1½ cups self raising (self-
rising) flour
100 g/4 oz/1 cup self-raising
wholemeal flour
150 ml/¼ pt/⅔ cup fromage frais

Boil the cider rapidly for 5 minutes until reduced to 150 ml/¼ pt/⅔ cup. Stir in 60 ml/4 tbsp of the honey and leave to cool. Beat the margarine and sugar together until fluffy. Beat in the eggs a little at a time, beating well after each addition. Mix the flours together. Fold a quarter into the cake mixture, then fold in half the cooled cider mixture. Repeat, then fold in the remaining flour. Turn into two greased 20 cm/8 in sandwich tins (pans), base-lined with non-stick baking parchment. Level the surfaces. Bake in a preheated oven at 180°C/350°F/gas mark 4 for 25 minutes until well risen, golden and the centres spring back when pressed lightly with a finger. Turn out and cool on a wire rack. Sandwich together with fromage frais. Warm the remaining honey slightly and brush over the top of the cake.

Somerset Honey and Lemon Cake

Prepare as for Somerset Honey Cake but add the grated rind and juice of a lemon to the cider before boiling and sandwich with a layer of lemon curd and the fromage frais if liked.

Grapefruit Marmalade Crumble Cake

300 g/11 oz/2¾ cups self-raising (self-
rising) flour
175 g/6 oz/¾ cup butter or margarine,
cut into small pieces
200 g/7 oz/scant 1 cup light brown
sugar
75 g/3 oz/¾ cup chopped mixed
candied peel
Grated rind and juice of ½ grapefruit
2 eggs, beaten
30 ml/2 tbsp grapefruit marmalade

Sift the flour into a bowl. Add the margarine and rub in with the fingertips until the mixture resembles fine breadcrumbs. Spoon out about a third of the mixture and reserve. Add 150 g/5 oz/⅔ cup of the sugar to the remaining crumble and mix in. Add the peel, grapefruit juice and beaten eggs and mix well. Turn into a greased and floured 18 cm/7 in loose-bottomed cake tin (pan). Mix the remaining sugar into the reserved crumble with the grapefruit rind. Spread the marmalade lightly over the uncooked cake. Sprinkle with the crumble. Bake in a preheated oven at 190°C/375°F/gas mark 5 for about 1 hour or until a skewer inserted in the centre comes out clean. Cool for 10 minutes, then carefully remove the cake tin and cool on wire rack.

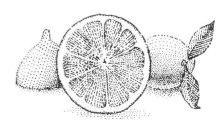

Moist Peach and Almond Cake

225 g/8 oz/1 cup soft margarine
225 g/8 oz/1 cup caster (superfine) sugar
2.5 ml/½ tsp almond essence (extract)
3 eggs
225 g/8 oz/2 cups self-raising (self-rising) flour
100 g/4 oz/1 cup ground almonds
100 g/4 oz/⅔ cup ready-to-eat dried peaches, chopped
15 ml/1 tbsp flaked almonds
15 ml/1 tbsp demerara sugar

Cream the margarine, caster sugar and almond essence until light and fluffy. Beat in the eggs, one at a time, beating well after each addition. Fold in the flour, ground almonds and chopped peaches. Turn into a greased 18 cm/7 in round deep cake tin (pan), lined with baking parchment. Sprinkle the almonds and demerara sugar over the top. Bake in a preheated oven at 150°C/300°F/gas mark 2 for 2½ hours or until shrinking from the sides of the tin and the centre springs back when pressed. Cool for 5 minutes, then turn out and remove the paper.

Crumble Cake

50 g/2 oz/¼ cup butter or margarine
25 g/1 oz/2 tbsp light brown sugar
15 ml/1 tbsp golden (light corn) syrup
15 ml/1 tbsp carob powder
45 ml/3 tbsp sultanas (golden raisins)
A few drops of almond essence (extract)
225 g/8 oz digestive biscuits (Graham crackers), crushed

Put all the ingredients except the biscuits into a large pan and heat gently until the fat and sugar have melted. Add the biscuits and stir well. Press into a greased 18 cm/7 in sandwich tin (pan) and chill overnight. Turn out and cut into small portions as this is very rich.

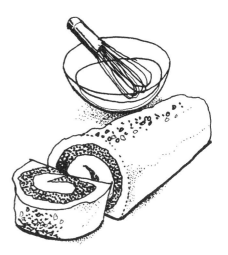

Mincemeat Cake

100 g/4 oz/½ cup butter or margarine
100 g/4 oz/½ cup light brown sugar
3 large eggs
200 g/7 oz/1¾ cups wholemeal self-
  raising (self-rising) flour
350 g/12 oz/1 cup vegetarian
  mincemeat
Pinch of salt
150 ml/¼ pt/⅔ cup milk

Beat the butter or margarine, sugar and eggs together well. Add the flour, mincemeat, salt and milk and continue beating until well blended. Turn into a 20 cm/8 in round cake tin (pan) and bake in a preheated oven at 160°C/325°F/gas mark 3 for 1¼ hours. Leave in the tin for 5 minutes, turn out and cool on a wire rack. Store in an airtight tin.

Swiss Cake

175 g/6 oz/1½ cups unsweetened
  muesli
150 ml/¼ pt/⅔ cup milk
175 g/6 oz/1½ cups wholemeal self-
  raising (self-rising) flour
185 g/6½ oz/good ¾ cup light brown
  sugar
175 g/6 oz/¾ cup butter or margarine
3 eggs, beaten

Place the muesli and milk in a bowl and leave to soak for 30 minutes. Grease an 18 cm/7 in cake tin (pan). Mix together the flour and 175 g/6 oz/¾ cup of the sugar. Rub in the butter or margarine, add the eggs and muesli in milk and beat well. Spoon into the tin and smooth the surface. Sprinkle with the remaining sugar and bake in a preheated oven at 180°C/350°F/gas mark 4 for 1¼ hours, until well

risen and a skewer inserted in the centre comes out clean. Leave in the tin for 5 minutes, then turn out and leave to cool on a wire rack. Store in an airtight tin.

New Year's Eve Cake

100 g/4 oz/½ cup butter or margarine
100 g/4 oz/½ cup caster (superfine)
  sugar
2 large eggs, beaten
75 g/3 oz/¾ cup plain (all-purpose)
  flour, sifted
45 ml/3 tbsp desiccated (shredded)
  coconut
30 ml/2 tbsp rum
2 drops almond essence (extract)
2 drops lemon essence
2 drops vanilla essence

In a bowl, cream the butter and sugar until fluffy. Gradually beat in the eggs, then gently fold in the flour and coconut. Add the rum and flavourings. Oil a 15 cm/ 6 in round, deep cake tin (pan) and line with greaseproof (waxed) paper. Oil again and dust with flour. Fill the tin with the mixture almost to the brim. Level the top. Bake in a preheated oven at 190°C/ 375°F/gas mark 5 for 45–50 minutes until a fine skewer inserted in the centre comes out clean. Invert the tin on to a wire rack and cool. Unmould only when the cake is cold. Leave overnight before serving.

Cornflake Cakes

75 g/3 oz/⅓ cup butter or margarine
75 ml/5 tbsp golden (light corn)
 syrup
45 ml/3 tbsp carob powder
100–175 g/4–6 oz/4–6 cups
 cornflakes

Melt the butter or margarine and syrup in a pan. Stir in the carob powder. Gradually stir in enough cornflakes so that they are coated in the mixture. Put spoonfuls into paper cases (cup cake papers) and leave to cool or eat hot if you can't wait.

Wheatflake Crackle Cakes

25 g/1 oz/2 tbsp butter or margarine
15 ml/1 tbsp golden (light corn)
 syrup
15 ml/1 tbsp carob powder
15 ml/1 tbsp light brown sugar
30 ml/2 tbsp raisins
105 ml/7 tbsp wheatflake breakfast
 cereal, lightly crushed

Put the butter or margarine, syrup, carob powder, sugar and raisins in a large saucepan and heat gently, stirring until the fat and sugar have melted. Add the wheatflakes and coat thoroughly. Put spoonfuls into paper cases (cup cake papers) and chill to set for at least 2 hours. Store in the fridge or in an airtight tin.

Caraway Fingers

175 g/6 oz/1½ cups plain (all-
 purpose) flour
50 g/2 oz/½ cup wholemeal flour
175 g/6 oz/¾ cup butter or margarine,
 cut into small pieces
5 ml/1 tsp caraway seeds
50 g/2 oz/¼ cup caster (superfine)
 sugar

Mix the flours together. Add the butter or margarine and rub in with the fingertips. Knead together to form a ball, then press the mixture into a greased shallow 20 cm/8 in square baking tin (pan). Mix the seeds and sugar together and sprinkle liberally over the surface. Chill for several hours or overnight, then bake in a preheated oven at 180°C/350°F/gas mark 4 for about 20 minutes until just firm but not coloured. Cool in the tin, then cut into fingers.

Cheese and Pecan Sablés

75 g/3 oz/¾ cup plain (all-purpose)
flour
Salt and freshly ground black pepper
75 g/3 oz/⅓ cup butter or margarine
75 g/3 oz/¾ cup Cheddar cheese, grated
25 g/1 oz/¼ cup pecans, chopped
Beaten egg, to glaze

Mix the flour with a pinch of salt and a good grinding of pepper. Rub in the butter, then stir in the cheese and pecans. Knead well to form a firm dough. Roll out to a rectangle about 20 × 10 cm/8 × 4 in. Brush with beaten egg, then cut in half lengthways, then each strip into equal squares, then each square into two triangles. Transfer to a greased baking sheet and bake in a preheated oven at 190°C/ 375°F/gas mark 5 for 10 minutes. Sprinkle with a little salt and serve warm.

Swiss Cheese Palmiers

225 g/8 oz puff pastry (paste)
1 egg, beaten
225 g/8 oz/2 cups Emmental (Swiss)
cheese, grated
5 ml/1 tsp cayenne
Salt and freshly ground black pepper

Roll out the pastry to a large rectangle, about 5 mm/¼ in thick. Brush with the beaten egg. Sprinkle liberally with the cheese and dust with cayenne. Season lightly. Starting at one shorter side, roll up to the centre. Then roll up the opposite side into the centre. Cut the roll into slices and arrange on a dampened baking sheet. Brush with any remaining egg and bake in a preheated oven at 200°C/ 400°F/gas mark 6 for 15 minutes until puffy and golden. Transfer to a wire rack to cool.

Cheese and Herb Palmiers

Prepare as for Swiss Cheese Palmiers but substitute grated Cheddar cheese for the Emmental and sprinkle with 5 ml/ 1 tsp dried mixed herbs and 15 ml/1 tbsp chopped parsley before rolling up.

Cheese and Sesame Palmiers

Prepare as for Swiss Cheese Palmiers but substitute grated Cheddar cheese for the Emmental and sprinkle with 30 ml/ 2 tbsp sesame seeds before rolling up. Sprinkle with a few more seeds before baking.

Blue Cheese Nibbles

75 g/3 oz/¾ cup wholemeal flour
75 g/3 oz/⅓ cup unsalted (sweet)
butter
75 g/3 oz/¾ cup blue cheese, crumbled
1 egg, beaten
45 ml/3 tbsp plain yoghurt or single
(light) cream
30 ml/2 tsp fennel seeds

Put the flour in a bowl. Rub in the butter and stir in the cheese. Mix with enough beaten egg to form a soft but not sticky dough. Knead gently, then wrap and chill for 30 minutes. Roll out thinly on a floured surface and cut into rounds using a 5 cm/2 in plain cutter. Transfer to baking sheets. Brush with yoghurt or cream and sprinkle with fennel seeds. Bake in a preheated oven at 180°C/ 350°F/gas mark 4 for about 12 minutes or until golden brown. Cool slightly, then transfer to a wire rack to cool.

Carob Bar Cookies

MAKES ABOUT 20

50 g/2 oz/¼ cup butter or margarine
50 g/2 oz/¼ cup caster (superfine)
  sugar
1 egg
175 g/6 oz/1½ cups self-raising (self-
  rising) flour
2 carob-coated caramel and nut bars,
  chopped

Melt the butter or margarine in a saucepan. Stir in the sugar, then leave to cool slightly. Add the egg, flour and carob bars and mix to a lumpy dough. Make into about 20 small flat rounds about 4 cm/1½ in across and place on a greased baking sheet. Bake in a pre-heated oven at 190°C/375°F/gas mark 5 for 15–20 minutes. Cool on a wire rack.

Shortbread Biscuits

MAKES 8 or 9

175 g/6 oz/1½ cups self-raising (self-
  rising) flour
Pinch of salt
100 g/4 oz/½ cup butter or margarine
50 g/2 oz/¼ cup caster (superfine)
  sugar

Mix the flour and salt. Rub in the butter or margarine, then the sugar to form a dough. Roll out on a floured surface into a circle or square 1 cm/½ in thick. Place on a greased baking sheet and mark with a knife into wedges or biscuit shapes. Bake in a preheated oven at 220°C/425°F/gas mark 7 for 15–20 minutes until golden. Leave to cool on the baking sheet.

Peanut Shortcake

MAKES 8 TRIANGLES

250 g/9 oz/2¼ cups plain (all-
  purpose) flour
175 g/6 oz/¾ cup butter or margarine
100 g/4 oz/½ cup caster (superfine)
  sugar
50 g/2 oz/½ cup chopped peanuts
45 ml/3 tbsp smooth peanut butter
45 ml/3 tbsp milk

Put the flour in a bowl and rub in the butter or margarine. Stir in the sugar and chopped nuts. Knead until the mixture forms a ball. Press half the mixture in a 20 cm/8 in flan ring set on a baking sheet. Mix the peanut butter and milk together and spread over using the back of a spoon. Roll out the remaining dough on a lightly floured surface to slightly smaller than the ring. Place on top and press out gently with the fingers to fit the ring. Bake in a preheated oven at 190°C/375°F/gas mark 5 for about 40 minutes until lightly golden. Carefully remove the flan ring and mark into 8 wedges with the back of a knife. Leave to cool before cutting.

Oatmeal Shortbread

175 g/6 oz/1½ cups wholemeal flour
50 g/2 oz/¼ cup caster (superfine)
*   sugar*
100 g/4 oz/½ cup butter or margarine
25 g/1 oz/¼ cup medium oatmeal
Pinch of salt

Put all the ingredients into a food processor and process for 1 minute until a ball forms. Tip into a greased 18 cm/7 in sandwich tin (pan) and press down well. Mark into eight portions and prick all over with a fork. Bake in a pre-heated oven for 45 minutes at 160°C/325°F/gas mark 3 until pale golden in colour. Cool in the tin, mark the wedges again, then store in an airtight container.

Carob Chews

50 g/2 oz/¼ cup sugar
30 ml/2 tbsp golden (light corn)
*   syrup or black treacle (molasses)*
75 g/3 oz/⅓ cup butter or margarine
225 g/8 oz/2 cups rolled oats
45 ml/3 tbsp carob powder
5 ml/1 tsp vanilla or almond essence
*   (extract)*
25 g/1 oz/¼ cup walnuts, chopped
50 g/2 oz/⅓ cup sultanas (golden
*   raisins), chopped*

Put the sugar, syrup or molasses and butter or margarine in a large pan and heat gently until the fat and sugar have melted. Stir in the remaining ingredients and mix well. Press into a greased 25 × 16 cm/10 × 6 in shallow tin (pan). Chill to set for at least 3 hours. Cut into 5 cm/2 in squares and serve.

Carob, Almond and Pecan Brownies

50 g/2 oz/½ cup plain (all-purpose)
*   flour*
15 ml/1 tbsp wheatgerm
1.5 ml/¼ tsp baking powder
25 g/1 oz/¼ cup chopped almonds
25 g/1 oz/¼ cup chopped pecan nuts
65 g/2½ oz/scant ⅓ cup butter or
*   margarine*
50 g/2 oz/½ cup carob chips
175 g/6 oz/¾ dark brown sugar
2 eggs, beaten
2.5 ml/½ tsp almond essence (extract)

Mix together the flour, wheatgerm, baking powder and nuts. Melt the butter or margarine with the carob and sugar in a saucepan or microwave, stirring occasionally. Cool slightly, then beat in the eggs and almond essence. Pour into the flour mixture and blend evenly. Turn into a greased 28 × 18 cm/11 × 7 in shallow baking tin (pan). Bake in a pre-heated oven at 180°C/350°F/gas mark 4 for 35 minutes. Cool in the tin, then cut into squares.

Oaty Jewels

150 g/5 oz/⅔ cup margarine
175 g/6 oz/¾ cup light brown sugar
15 ml/1 tbsp golden (light corn)
syrup
225 g/8 oz/2 cups rolled oats
50 g/2 oz/½ cup glacé (candied)
cherries, quartered
50 g/2 oz/½ cup angelica, roughly
chopped
50 g/2 oz/½ cup chopped candied peel
2.5 ml/½ tsp ground cinnamon

Melt the margarine, sugar and syrup in a pan. Stir in the remaining ingredients. Turn into a greased 28 × 18 cm/ 11 × 7 in Swiss roll tin (jelly roll pan). Press down well and bake in a preheated oven at 190°C/375°F/gas mark 5 for about 25 minutes until lightly golden. Cool for 10 minutes, then mark into fingers with a knife. Leave until cold, then remove from the tin.

Walnut Brownies

50 g/2 oz/½ cup wholemeal flour
Pinch of baking powder
1.5 ml/¼ tsp salt
75 g/3 oz/⅓ cup butter or margarine
50 g/2 oz/½ cup carob chips
175 g/6 oz/¾ cup light brown sugar
2 eggs, beaten
2.5 ml/½ tsp vanilla essence (extract)
50 g/2 oz/½ cup walnuts, chopped

Mix together the flour, baking powder and salt. Melt the butter or margarine and carob chips in a bowl over a pan of hot water (or in the microwave). Beat in the sugar, eggs and vanilla essence. Stir into the flour mixture with the walnuts. Turn into a greased 18 × 28 cm/7 × 11 in baking tin (pan). Bake in a preheated oven at 180°C/350°F/gas mark 4 for 35 minutes. Cool in the tin, then cut into squares. Store in an airtight tin.

Flapjacks

100 g/4 oz/½ cup butter or margarine
75 g/3 oz/⅓ cup light brown sugar
60 ml/4 tbsp golden (light corn)
syrup
300 g/11 oz/1¾ cups rolled oats

Melt the butter or margarine, sugar and syrup in a saucepan over a low heat. Stir in the oats until totally covered. Spoon into a greased baking tin (pan) and spread until about 1cm/½ in thick. Bake in a preheated oven at 180°C/350°F/gas mark 4 for about 25 minutes until golden. Leave to cool in the tin, then cut into squares.

Banana Sultana Flapjacks

75 g/3 oz/⅓ cup soft margarine
100 g/4 oz/½ cup light brown sugar
15 ml/1 tbsp golden (light corn)
syrup
1 large ripe banana, mashed
50 g/2 oz/⅓ cup sultanas (golden
raisins)
275 g/10 oz/2½ cups rolled oats

Beat the margarine, sugar and syrup until light and fluffy. Beat in the banana, then stir in the sultanas and oats. Press into a greased 18 × 28 cm/7 × 11 in Swiss roll tin (jelly roll pan). Bake in a preheated oven at 180°C/350°F/gas mark 4 for about 30 minutes until golden brown. Cool slightly, then mark into fingers with the back of a knife. Leave until cold, then cut up and store in an airtight tin.

Ratafia Biscuits

MAKES 16 BISCUITS

100 g/4 oz/½ cup granulated sugar
50 g/2 oz/½ cup ground almonds
7.5 ml/½ tbsp ground rice
1 egg white
25 g/1 oz/¼ cup almonds, split
Apricot jam, boiled (optional)

Well oil and flour a 30 cm/12 in baking sheet. Line with rice paper (as it is edible). In a bowl, blend together the sugar, almonds and ground rice, then beat in the egg white for 2 minutes. Using a 5 mm/¼ in plain tube (tip) and piping bag, pipe the ratafia mixture on to the prepared baking sheet into button-sized biscuits 1 cm/½ in diameter, or in the shape of a pear or cat's tail. Place one split almond on top of each biscuit. Bake in a preheated oven at 190°C/375°F/gas mark 5 for 15 minutes until golden in colour. Sandwich together two biscuits with boiled apricot jam, if liked.

Basic Pancake Mix

MAKES 8

100 g/4 oz/1 cup plain (all-purpose)
    flour
Pinch of salt
300 ml/½ pt/1¼ cups milk
1 egg, beaten
15 ml/1 tbsp butter or margarine,
    melted
Oil, for shallow-frying

Whisk the flour, salt, milk and egg to a smooth batter. Whisk in the melted butter or margarine. Heat a little oil in a frying pan (skillet). Pour in just enough mixture to cover the bottom of the pan and cook until just brown underneath. Toss or turn over and cook the other side. Serve as a sweet with sugar and lemon juice, or a savoury course filled with cottage cheese, cooked vegetables or ratatouille (or see individual recipes).

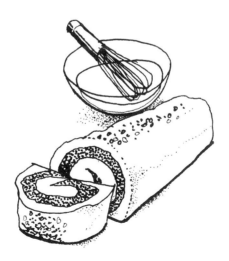

Brandy Snap Horns and Baskets

100 g/4 oz/½ cup butter
100 g/4 oz/½ cup light brown sugar
100 g/4 oz/⅓ cup golden (light corn) syrup
5 ml/1 tsp ground ginger
100 g/4 oz/1 cup plain (all-purpose) flour
5 ml/1 tsp lemon juice
5 ml/1 tsp orange juice

Dampen one or two baking sheets and line with non-stick baking parchment. Place the butter, sugar, syrup and ginger in a saucepan and heat gently until melted. Add the flour and mix well. Stir in the lemon and orange juice. Drop small spoonfuls of the mixture on to baking sheets, allowing plenty of room for expansion between each one. Bake in a preheated oven at 190°C/375°C/gas mark 5 for a few minutes until bubbly and golden. While still hot, remove the rounds from the baking sheets and roll around greased cream horn tins (pans). Leave in place until set, then twist gently to remove and leave to cool. Alternatively, place the hot rounds in greased, fluted bun tins (muffin pans) and leave to set.

Sweet Crumb Case (Shell)

225 g/8 oz digestive biscuits (Graham crackers) or any other plain, wholemeal variety, crushed
75 g/3 oz/⅓ cup butter or margarine, melted
15 ml/1 tbsp golden (light corn) syrup
Pinch of ground ginger

Mix the biscuits into the melted butter or margarine with the syrup and ginger and mix well. Press into two 18 cm/7 in or one 23 cm/9 in greased flan dishes. Chill for 2 hours to set. Fill as desired (see individual recipes).

Drinks and Nibbles

Tempting little savoury and sweet morsels, and delicious drinks to wash them down. All these recipes are ideal for just about any party, from a few friends over for dinner to a slap-up birthday or anniversary celebration.

Herby Bites

225 g/8 oz/1 cup low-fat soft cheese
60 ml/4 tbsp Dry Roasted Peanuts
(see page 350), ground
4 spring onions (scallions), chopped
15 ml/1 tbsp chopped parsley
15 ml/1 tbsp snipped chives
15 ml/1 tbsp chopped tarragon
Salt and freshly ground black pepper

Mix all the ingredients together thoroughly, reserving 30 ml/2 tbsp of the ground peanuts. Form into 2.5 cm/1 in balls and roll in the remaining ground peanuts. Chill before serving.

Panir Dumplings

450 g/1 lb/2 cups cream cheese
3 eggs, beaten
50 g/2 oz/1 cup breadcrumbs
1 small onion, chopped
1 small garlic clove, chopped
15 ml/1 tbsp chopped basil or mint
45 ml/3 tbsp wholemeal flour
Salt and freshly ground black pepper
45 ml/3 tbsp plain yoghurt
5 ml/1 tsp curry powder
50 g/2 oz/½ cup chopped almonds
Oil, for deep-frying
225 g/8 oz/1 small can pineapple
cubes or lychees, drained

In a bowl, combine the cream cheese, two of the beaten eggs, the breadcrumbs, onion, garlic and herbs and blend to a paste. Divide the mixture and roll into small balls. For the coating, season the flour with salt and pepper and beat together the remaining egg, the yoghurt and curry powder. Roll the balls in the seasoned flour, then dip in the egg mixture and finally roll in the almonds. Heat the oil and deep-fry the cheese balls for 1 minute until golden. Drain well on kitchen paper. Serve the cheese balls on cocktail sticks (toothpicks) with a pineapple cube or lychee added to each one.

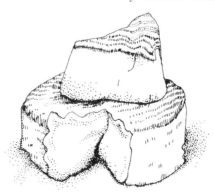

Fried Coconut Cream Delight

SERVES 6

450 ml/¾ pt/2 cups coconut milk or
    water and desiccated coconut (see
    method)
65 g/2½ oz/5 tbsp butter
225 g/8 oz/2 cups plain (all-purpose)
    flour
Salt and freshly ground black pepper
5 ml/1 tsp sugar
4 eggs
4 egg yolks
50 ml/2 fl oz/3½ tbsp white rum
225 g/8 oz/4 cups mixed desiccated
    (shredded) coconut and
    breadcrumbs
Oil, for deep-frying
Lettuce leaves

Either use the coconut milk or boil 600 ml/1 pt/2½ cups water with 75 g/ 3 oz/¾ cup desiccated coconut. Liquidize, then strain. Heat 25 g/1 oz/2 tbsp of the butter in a saucepan, add 30 ml/2 tbsp of the flour and cook, stirring, for 30 seconds. Gradually stir in the coconut milk and simmer until thick. Season with salt, pepper and the sugar. Beat 3 of the whole eggs and 2 of the egg yolks in a bowl. Add to the sauce. Cook for 2 minutes to thicken further. Remove from the heat. Add the rum. Thoroughly grease a shallow baking tin (pan) with butter and oil and pour in the custard mixture. Cool completely, then chill for 30 minutes. Turn on to a clean board and cut into neat squares. Sprinkle the coconut and crumb mixture on to a baking sheet. Place the remaining eggs in another shallow dish and the remaining flour on another plate. First dip each set custard in seasoned flour, then in beaten egg, and finally coat in coconut crumbs. Heat the oil to 190°C/375°F and deep-fry the custard fritters for 30 seconds only until golden. Drain well and serve on a bed of lettuce leaves.

Butter Bean and Rice Cakes

MAKES ABOUT 16

225 g/8 oz/1 small can butter beans,
    drained
125 g/5 oz/1¼ cups cold Pilaf with
    Saffron (see page 137)
2 eggs, beaten
Salt and freshly ground black pepper
90 ml/6 tbsp seasoned flour
Oil, for shallow-frying

Mince (grind) or pound the beans and cooked rice to a paste. Blend the paste with the beaten eggs. Season and divide the mixture into small balls. Flatten into bite-sized cakes and coat in seasoned flour. Heat the oil in a large frying pan (skillet) and fry (sauté) the cakes for 1 minute on each side until golden. Drain on kitchen paper. Serve warm.

Easy Canapés

MAKES 12 CANAPES

Buy ready-made small toasts or baby rice cakes. Cover with any of the savoury spreads (see pages 302–3). Spread neatly, peaking it in the centre. If you have time, sprinkle the spread with finely chopped parsley, sieved hard-boiled (hard-cooked) egg yolk or a sprinkling of paprika, depending on the colour and flavour of the spread.

Cream Cheese Morsels

MAKES 24

450 g/1 lb/2 cups cream cheese
4 eggs, beaten
100 g/4 oz/2 cups breadcrumbs
15 ml/1 tbsp ground almonds
2 garlic cloves, chopped
45 ml/3 tbsp chopped parsley
Salt and freshly ground black pepper
Seasoned flour
100 g/4 oz/1 cup plain (all-purpose)
   flour
600 ml/1 pt/2½ cups milk
Oil, for shallow-frying
Pineapple cubes

In a large mixing bowl, blend the cream cheese, half of the beaten egg, the breadcrumbs, ground almonds, garlic and parsley. Season. Divide the mixture into 24 small balls, using enough seasoned flour to prevent them being sticky. Beat the plain flour and the remaining eggs together, then gradually blend in the milk until smooth. Dip the cheese balls into the batter, draining the surplus batter against the side of the bowl. Shallow-fry in hot oil for 1 minute per batch until golden. Drain on kitchen paper and serve on cocktail sticks (toothpicks) with pineapple cubes.

Potted Stilton Boats

MAKES ABOUT 20

50 g/2 oz/½ cup Stilton cheese,
   crumbled
40 g/1½ oz/3 tbsp butter or
   margarine, softened
Good pinch of ground mace
15 ml/1 tbsp port or medium sherry
Celery sticks

Mash the cheese with the butter. Work in the mace and port or sherry. Spread down the grooves in celery sticks and cut into bite-sized pieces.

Herby Cheese Boats

MAKES ABOUT 20

85 g/3½ oz packet soft cheese with
   garlic and herbs
Celery sticks
30 ml/2 tbsp chopped parsley

Spread the cheese down grooves in celery sticks. Cut into bite-sized pieces, then dip the cheesy sides in chopped parsley.

Cheese and Pineapple Boats

MAKES ABOUT 20

1 small carton cottage cheese with
   pineapple
Celery sticks
Paprika

Spoon the cheese and pineapple down the grooves of celery sticks. Dust liberally with paprika, then cut into bite-sized pieces.

Cheese and Tomato Bites

MAKES ABOUT 12

200 g/7 oz/1 small carton low-fat soft
   cheese
1 individual serving instant tomato
   soup powder
30 ml/2 tbsp grated Pecorino cheese
Toasted mixed nuts

Mash the cheese with the tomato soup powder and Pecorino cheese. Shape into small balls and roll in chopped nuts. Chill until ready to serve.

Cheese and Asparagus Pinwheels

MAKES ABOUT 30

5 slices wholemeal bread, crusts removed
Low-fat soft cheese
5 canned or cooked fresh or frozen asparagus spears

Flatten the bread lightly with a rolling pin (don't squash it flat!). Spread with the cheese. Lay an asparagus spear along one end of each slice, then roll up. Cut into slices and arrange on a plate.

Herb and Bean Pinwheels

MAKES ABOUT 30

Prepare as for Cheese and Asparagus Pinwheels but use garlic and herb cheese instead of plain and canned or cooked fresh or frozen French (green) beans instead of asparagus spears.

Citrus Pinwheels

MAKES ABOUT 30

Prepare as for Cheese and Asparagus Pinwheels but put a line of drained canned mandarin oranges in place of the asparagus spear in each roll.

Mexican Pinwheels

MAKES ABOUT 30

Prepare as for Cheese and Asparagus Pinwheels but use strips of red (bell) pepper instead of asparagus spears and sprinkle lightly with cayenne before rolling up.

Devilled Crunchies

SERVES ABOUT 6

75 g/3 oz/⅓ cup butter or margarine
100 g/4 oz/2 cups Shreddies breakfast cereal
5 ml/1 tsp garlic salt
1.5 ml/¼ tsp chilli powder

Melt the butter or margarine in a roasting tin (pan). Add the cereal and toss until coated. Bake in a preheated oven at 200°C/400°F/gas mark 6 for 8 minutes until crisp and browned. Sprinkle with the garlic salt and chilli powder and toss well. Leave to cool. Store in an airtight container.

Nuts That Bite Back

SERVES 4–6

175 g/6 oz/1½ cups whole blanched almonds
25 g/1 oz/2 tbsp butter or margarine
5 ml/1 tsp chilli powder
5 ml/1 tsp mixed (apple pie) spice
2.5 ml/½ tsp salt

Fry (sauté) the almonds in the butter or margarine until golden brown, tossing all the time. Sprinkle on the spices and salt and mix well. Drain on kitchen paper and leave to cool.

Nut Clusters

SERVES 4

100 g/4 oz/1 cup carob chips
100 g/4 oz/1 cup mixed chopped nuts
25 g/1 oz/⅛ cup raisins, glacé
  (candied) cherries or sultanas
  (golden raisins)

Melt the carob chips in a pan over hot water or in the microwave. Cool slightly and stir in the nuts and raisins. Place teaspoonfuls on to greaseproof (waxed) paper and leave to harden.

Dry Roasted Peanuts or Other Nuts

Put about 45 ml/3 tbsp raw peanuts or other nuts on a piece of kitchen paper in the microwave and spread out in a ring to prevent the middle ones burning. Microwave on high for 3–4 minutes or until golden brown. Cool. Store in a screw-topped jar.

Savoury Dry Roasted Nuts

Prepare as for Dry Roasted Peanuts but microwave on a plate instead of kitchen paper and sprinkle with 30 ml/ 2 tbsp soy sauce for the last 1 minute of cooking time.

Spicy Nuts

Prepare as for Dry Roasted Peanuts but sprinkle with a little sea salt and chilli powder after cooking.

Black and Gold Bites

Ready-to-eat prunes
Stuffed green olives
Ready-to-eat dried apricots
Slivered almonds
Stoned (pitted) black olives

Make a slit in the side of a prune and remove the stone. Push a stuffed olive into the cavity. Cut in half and secure on a cocktail stick (toothpick), cut side up. Make a slit in the side of a dried apricot. Push a slivered almond into the hole in the black olive. Push inside the apricot. Cut in half and spear on cocktail sticks, cut side up.

Savoury Puff Twists

MAKES 60

250 g/9 oz packet frozen puff pastry
  (paste), thawed
15 ml/1 tbsp yeast extract
50 g/2 oz/½ cup Cheddar cheese,
  finely grated
Beaten egg, to glaze

Roll out the pastry on a lightly floured surface to a 30 cm/12 in square. Spread with the yeast extract, then sprinkle with the cheese. Fold in half and flatten lightly with a rolling pin. Brush with beaten egg, then cut into thin strips. Hold each end of a strip and twist it. Place on a dampened baking sheet. Repeat with the remaining strips. Bake in a preheated oven at 200°C/400°F/gas mark 6 for about 10 minutes until puffy and golden brown. Serve warm or cold.

Cheese Straws

MAKES ABOUT 48

100 g/4 oz/1 cup plain (all-purpose)
flour
Good pinch of salt
1.5 ml/¼ tsp cayenne
65 g/2½ oz/scant ⅓ cup butter or
margarine
65 g/2½ oz/scant ¾ cup Cheddar
cheese, grated
1 small egg, beaten

Sift the flour, salt and cayenne into a
bowl. Add the butter or margarine and
rub in with the fingertips. Stir in the
cheese. Mix with enough beaten egg to
form a firm dough. Roll out on a lightly
floured surface to a rectangle about 5
mm/¼ in thick. Cut into thin strips about
7.5 cm/3 in long. Transfer to a greased
baking sheet. If liked, roll out the trimmings and cut into rings using a large and
small cutter. Bake in a preheated oven at
180°C/350°F/gas mark 4 for about 7 minutes until pale golden brown. Cool on a
wire rack. Serve, if liked, in small bundles, held in place with the pastry rings.

Cheese and Sesame Straws

MAKES ABOUT 48

Prepare as for Cheese Straws but add
30 ml/2 tbsp sesame seeds with the
cheese.

Cheese and Caraway Straws

MAKES ABOUT 48

Prepare as for Cheese Straws but add
30 ml/2 tbsp caraway seeds with the
cheese.

Cheese and Poppy Seed Straws

MAKES ABOUT 48

Prepare as for Cheese Straws but add
30 ml/2 tbsp poppy seeds with the
cheese.

Dilly Dallies

MAKES ABOUT 24

6 slices wholemeal bread, crusts
removed
24 slices dill pickle
175 g/6 oz/1½ cups Cheddar cheese,
grated
15 g/½ oz/1 tbsp butter or margarine
2.5 ml/½ tsp dried dill (dill weed)

Toast the bread and cut into quarters.
Place on a baking sheet. Top each
piece of toast with a slice of dill pickle.
Mash the cheese with the butter and dill.
Pile on top of the pickle slices. Bake in a
preheated oven at 220°C/425°F/gas mark
7 for about 5 minutes until golden and
bubbling. Serve hot.

Pizza Bites

MAKES 24

6 slices white or wholemeal bread,
crusts removed
4 tomatoes, each sliced into 6 rounds
50 g/2 oz/½ cup Mozzarella cheese,
grated
5 ml/1 tsp dried oregano

Toast the bread and cut into quarters.
Place on a baking sheet. Lay a slice of
tomato on each, then top with the cheese.
Sprinkle with oregano. Bake in a preheated oven at 220°C/425°F/gas mark 7
for about 5 minutes or until the cheese
has melted and bubbles. Serve straight
away.

Peanut Pop-ins

MAKES ABOUT 20

200 g/7 oz/1 small carton low-fat soft
  cheese
30 ml/2 tbsp crunchy peanut butter
5 ml/1 tbsp brandy (optional)
45 ml/3 tbsp granary breadcrumbs
100 g/4 oz/1 cup salted peanuts,
  finely chopped

Beat the cheese and peanut butter until smooth, adding the brandy, if using. Work in the breadcrumbs. Roll into small balls, then roll in the chopped nuts. Chill until ready to serve.

Savoury Stuffed Cherry Tomatoes

Cut a slice off the tops of cherry tomatoes. Scoop out the seeds with a teaspoon and drain upside-down on kitchen paper. Fill with any of the savoury spreads (see pages 302–3) and garnish as for Easy Canapés (see page 347).

Savoury Stuffed Cucumber

MAKES ABOUT 12

Cut a cucumber into 2.5 cm/1 in lengths. Use a teaspoon to scoop out the seeds but not right through so there is a 'base' to each slice. Dry on kitchen paper, then fill with any of the savoury spreads (see pages 302–3) as for Savoury Stuffed Cherry Tomatoes.

Baby Pittas

Warm baby party pitta breads. Make a small slit in each and fill with any of the savoury spreads (see pages 302–3).

Peanut-stuffed Tomatoes

MAKES ABOUT 30

Prepare the peanut mixture as for Peanut Pop-ins but don't roll into balls or roll in chopped peanuts. Instead, cut the tops off and scoop out the seeds from about 30 cherry tomatoes. Spoon in the peanut mixture and top with the lids.

Sumptuous Cheese Slices

MAKES ABOUT 30

100 g/4 oz/1 cup Danish Blue cheese,
  crumbled
100 g/4 oz/½ cup quark
25 g/1 oz/2 tbsp butter
15 ml/1 tbsp snipped chives
25 g/1 oz/¼ cup green olives, stoned
  (pitted) and chopped
25 g/1 oz/¼ cup black olives, stoned
  and chopped
15 ml/1 tbsp medium-dry sherry
50 g/2 oz/½ cup toasted chopped nuts
1 box round salted crackers

Mash the blue cheese, quark and butter together until well blended. Work in the chives, olives and sherry. Shape into two rolls about 2.5 cm/1 in diameter. Roll in toasted nuts and chill until fairly firm. When ready to serve, cut the rolls into thin slices. Lay on crackers and serve straight away.

Cheese Crunchies

MAKES ABOUT 36

8 slices bread
Butter or margarine
Yeast extract
100 g/4 oz/½ cup cream cheese
50 g/2 oz/2 cups cornflakes, crushed

Make the bread, butter or margarine and yeast extract into sandwiches, then cut into 2.5 cm/1 in cubes. Spread each cube on all sides with cream cheese, then toss in the cornflakes. Serve.

Wheaty Garlic and Herb Crunchies

MAKES ABOUT 36

Prepare as for Cheese Crunchies but use wholemeal bread and garlic and herb cheese instead of plain cream cheese. Toss in crushed bran flakes instead of cornflakes.

Carob-coated Nuts

SERVES 4

Melt 225 g/8 oz/2 cups carob chips and dip whole brazil nuts, walnuts, almonds, peanuts, etc. into it (tweezers or fine tongs help considerably). Transfer to greaseproof (waxed) paper to set.

Stuffed Dates

Remove the stones (pits) from fresh dates and fill with either a whole walnut, almond, a piece of fresh pineapple, mandarin segment or other fresh fruit, or a small piece of freshly made almond paste. These dates are not freezable when stuffed with fresh fruit.

Tomato Juice Zinger

SERVES 6

600 ml/1 pt/2½ cups tomato juice
30 ml/2 tbsp lime or lemon juice
6 fresh basil leaves, torn
5 ml/1 tsp Worcestershire sauce
A few drops of Tabasco sauce
Thinly pared rind of ½ orange
2.5 ml/½ tsp onion salt
Freshly ground black pepper

Mix all the ingredients together and chill for at least 1 hour to allow the flavours to develop. Strain into a jug and serve over ice.

Bloody Maria

SERVES 6

Prepare as for Tomato Juice Zinger but add 6 measures of vodka to the mixture.

Red Devil

SERVES 6

Prepare as for Tomato Juice Zinger but add a seeded fresh green chilli and 6 measures of gin.

Caribbean Cocktail

SERVES 4

2 ripe bananas
30 ml/2 tbsp lemon juice
225 g/8 oz/1 small can pineapple in
*   natural juice*
250 ml/8 fl oz/1 cup orange juice
15 ml/1 tbsp grenadine syrup
Crushed ice

Purée the bananas in a food processor or blender with the lemon juice. Add the pineapple and blend again until smooth. Add the orange juice and grenadine syrup and blend briefly again. Pour over crushed ice and serve.

Caribbean Rum Cocktail

SERVES 4

Prepare as for Caribbean Cocktail but add 4 measures of dark rum with the orange juice.

Tropical Cocktail

SERVES 4

Prepare as for Caribbean Rum Cocktail but add coconut liqueur instead of rum.

Peach and Apple Sling

2 ripe peaches, peeled, stoned (pitted)
  and roughly chopped
10 ml/2 tsp lime juice
120 ml/4 fl oz/½ cup apple juice
1.5 ml/¼ tsp grated fresh root ginger
600 ml/1 pt/2½ cups American ginger
  ale
Crushed ice

Purée the peaches in a blender or food processor with the lime juice. Add the apple juice and root ginger and blend briefly. Add the ginger ale, whizz up again, then quickly pour over crushed ice and serve.

Punchy Peach and Apple Sling

SERVES 4

Prepare as for Peach and Apple Sling but add 4 measures of peach liqueur or brandy to the mixture before adding the ginger ale.

Festive Fizz

SERVES 4

25 g/1 oz/¼ cup blanched almonds
25 g/1 oz/¼ cup walnuts
25 g/1 oz/¼ cup peanuts
30 ml/2 tbsp clear honey
75 ml/5 tbsp whisky
3 ice cubes
Juice of 2 oranges
300 ml/½ pt/1¼ cups ginger ale
4 orange slices
1 kiwi fruit, sliced

Place the nuts, honey, whisky, ice cubes and orange juice in a blender or food processor and blend well. Pour into four glasses and top up with ginger ale. Serve decorated with slices of orange and kiwi fruit.

Muscadet Cassis

SERVES 6

1 bottle Muscadet white wine, chilled
3 ice cubes
4 lime slices
75 ml/5 tbsp blackcurrant syrup
  (Cassis)

Place all the ingredients in a 1.2 litre/ 2 pt/5 cup jug and mix well. Pour into glasses to serve.

Scandinavian Julglogg

SERVES 8

1.5 litres/2½ pts/6 cups red wine
100 g/4 oz/⅔ cup seedless (pitless)
  grapes or raisins
100 g/4 oz/⅓ cup clear honey
15 g/½ oz/2 tbsp cardamom seeds
4 cloves
1 piece of cinnamon stick
Grated rind of 1 lemon
Grated rind of 1 lime
1 litre/1¾ pts/4¼ cups Aquavit

Place the wine, grapes or raisins, honey, cardamom seeds, cloves and cinnamon in a large saucepan and bring to the boil. Remove from the heat and add the lemon and lime rinds and the Aquavit. Just before serving, reheat gently and ignite. Serve in punch cups. If preferred, the spices may be removed with a slotted spoon.

Tequila à la Sancho

SERVES 4

8 ice cubes
60 ml/4 tbsp grenadine syrup
60 ml/4 tbsp banana liqueur
120 ml/4 fl oz/½ cup tequila
60 ml/4 tbsp double (heavy) cream

Place two ice cubes in each of four glasses and add 15 ml/1 tbsp grenadine, followed by 15 ml/1 tbsp banana liqueur and 30 ml/2 tbsp tequila. Top each glass with 15 ml/1 tbsp cream and serve.

Not-so-punchy Tequila

SERVES 6

Make as for Tequila à la Sancho but put all the ingredients in a blender or food processor with 2 large ripe bananas. Blend until smooth. Divide between six tall glasses and top up with chilled ginger ale. Stir well and serve.

Peach and Pineapple Punch

SERVES 14

2 lemons
2 limes
2 oranges
1.75 litres/3 pts/7½ cups water
300 ml/½ pt/1¼ cups heather honey
3 pineapple slices
4 large peaches
1 small bunch of black (purple)
  grapes, seeded
300 ml/½ pt/1¼ cups strong tea
6 cloves
1 piece of cinnamon stick
300 ml/½ pt/1¼ cups brandy or whisky

Pare the rind from one lemon, one lime and one orange, then squeeze the juice from all the lemons, limes and oranges. Reserve the juice and place the rind in a saucepan with the water. Bring to the boil and stir in the honey until dissolved. Simmer for 5 minutes. Remove from the heat and stir in the lemon, lime and orange juices. Add all the remaining ingredients and stir well. Chill for at least 3 hours, then transfer to a large punch bowl to serve.

Raspberry Mulled Wine

150 g/5 oz/1¼ cups raspberries, fresh,
* frozen or drained canned*
75 ml/5 tbsp brandy
1 bottle red Bordeaux wine
1 piece of cinnamon stick
75 g/3 oz/¼ cup clear honey

Place the raspberries in a bowl, add the brandy and leave to soak. (If using canned raspberries, add the juice also.) Place the wine and cinnamon in a saucepan and bring to the boil. Boil for 2 minutes, then add the honey and stir until dissolved. Purée the raspberries and brandy in a blender or food processor, then pass through a sieve (strainer) and add to the wine mixture. Remove the cinnamon and serve the hot mulled wine in punch cups.

Morello Brandy Fizz

SERVES 4

400 g/14 oz/1 large can morello
* cherries, stoned (pitted)*
300 ml/½ pt/1¼ cups carbonated
* mineral water, chilled*
150 ml/¼ pt/⅔ cup brandy
3 ice cubes
4 orange slices

Mix all the ingredients together in a large jug and serve.

Papino with Pawpaw

SERVES 4

600 ml/1 pt/2½ cups cold milk
50 ml/2 fl oz/3½ tbsp lemon sorbet
1 pawpaw, peeled, seeded and sliced
Juice of 1 lime
2 ice cubes
Mint or borage leaves

Place all the ingredients except the herbs in a blender or food processor and blend well. Pour into four tall glasses, decorate with mint or borage leaves and serve at once. Alternatively, reserve slices of pawpaw and lime to decorate.

Grenadine Orangeade

SERVES 4

300 ml/½ pt/1¼ cups orange juice
300 ml/½ pt/1¼ cups ginger ale
50 ml/2 fl oz/3½ tbsp grenadine syrup
1 pomegranate

Place the orange juice in a cocktail shaker or large jug and top up with ginger ale. Add the grenadine syrup and mix well. Cut the pomegranate into thin wedges and add to the drink. Serve straight away.

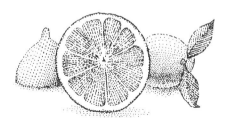

Honeyed Apple Squash

SERVES 4–6

450 g/1 lb apples
Thinly pared rind and juice of 1
*   large lemon*
600 ml/1 pt/2½ cups boiling water
30–45 ml/2–3 tbsp clear honey

Finely chop the apples but do not peel or core. Place in a saucepan with the lemon rind. Add the water, bring to the boil, cook for 1 minute, then remove from the heat, stir well and leave until cold. Squash the fruit down gently with a potato masher or the back of a spoon from time to time. Stir in the lemon juice and sweeten to taste with honey. Strain into a jug. Chill until ready to serve, diluted with still or fizzy water.

Blackberry and Apple Squash

SERVES 4–6

Prepare as for Honeyed Apple Squash but use half apples and half blackberries.

Gooseberry Squash

SERVES 4–6

Prepare as for Honeyed Apple Squash but substitute gooseberries for the apples. Cook them for 2 minutes instead of 1 minute. You may need a little more honey to sweeten the drink.

Raspberry and Mint Crush

SERVES 4

300 g/11 oz/1 small can raspberries
*   in natural juice*
Icing (confectioners') sugar, sifted
15 ml/1 tbsp chopped mint
Crushed ice
Sparkling mineral water

Purée the raspberries and the juice in a blender or food processor with the mint, then pass through a sieve (strainer). Stir in icing sugar to taste and add the mint. Pour over crushed ice, then top up with sparkling mineral water. Stir and serve.

Strawberry and Orange Crush

SERVES 4

Prepare as for Raspberry and Mint Crush but substitute canned strawberries for the raspberries and the grated rind and juice of ½ orange for the mint.
Note: you can use 225 g/8 oz fresh fruit for the canned in these recipes, but stew them in 60 ml/4 tbsp apple juice for 3 minutes before puréeing.

Lemon Barley Water

SERVES 4

50 g/2 oz/good ¼ cup pearl barley
50 g/2 oz/¼ cup light brown sugar
Juice of 2 large lemons, strained

Put the barley into a saucepan, just cover with cold water and bring to the boil. Drain and rinse the barley under cold running water. Return the barley to the saucepan, add 600 ml/1 pt/2½ cups cold water and bring to the boil again. Cover and simmer for 1 hour. Strain the liquid into a jug or basin, stir in the sugar and cool. When the mixture is cold, add the strained lemon juice. Dilute with still or sparkling water to serve. Store in the fridge in a screw-topped bottle.

Orange Cordial

SERVES 4

900 ml/1½ pts/3¾ cups boiling water
225 g/8 oz/1 cup sugar
3 oranges, scrubbed
5 ml/1 tsp citric acid

Pour the boiling water over the sugar in a pan. Heat gently, stirring, until the sugar has completely dissolved. Remove from the heat, squeeze in the juice from the oranges, then chop up the skin and flesh and add these too. Stir in the citric acid. Leave to cool, stirring occasionally. Strain and bottle when completely cold. Store in the fridge for up to 3 weeks.

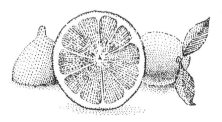

Pineapple and Cranberry Milk Shake

SERVES 4

600 ml/1 pt/2½ cups milk
2 pineapple slices
15 ml/1 tbsp clear honey
50 g/2 oz cranberries
3 ice cubes
Apple and orange slices

Place all the ingredients, except the apple and orange slices, in a blender or food processor and blend for 2 minutes. Pour into four tall glasses, decorate with apple and orange slices and serve at once.

Banana and Rose-hip Whip

SERVES 4

3 ripe bananas
45 ml/3 tbsp rose-hip syrup
750 ml/1¼ pts/3 cups ice-cold milk
Pinch of ground cinnamon

Purée the bananas in a blender or food processor. Add the remaining ingredients and blend until thick and frothy. Pour into glasses and serve immediately.

Carob and Banana Milk Shake

SERVES 1

250 ml/8 fl oz/1 cup ice-cold milk
1 ripe banana
15 ml/1 tbsp carob powder
5 ml/1 tsp clear honey

Put all the ingredients into a blender or liquidizer and run the machine for about 1 minute. Serve with a colourful straw in a tall glass to make the froth last longer.

Mocarob Shake

30 ml/2 tbsp carob powder
15 ml/1 tbsp instant coffee powder
60 ml/4 tbsp boiling water
900ml/1½ pts/3¾cups ice-cold milk
Clear honey
4 scoops vanilla ice cream

Blend the carob and coffee powder together with the boiling water. Whisk in the milk and sweeten to taste with honey. Put a scoop of ice cream in four tumblers and pour the shake over. Serve straight away.

Strawberry Yoghurt Refresher

SERVES 2

100 g/4 oz strawberries, mashed
150 ml/¼ pt/⅔ cup strawberry yoghurt
300 ml/½ pt/1¼ cups ice-cold milk
A little clear honey (optional)

Spoon the mashed strawberries into two tall glasses. Whisk the yoghurt and milk together. Sweeten with honey if liked. Pour over the strawberries and serve.

Raspberry Yoghurt Refresher

SERVES 2

Prepare as for Strawberry Yoghurt Refresher but substitute raspberries and raspberry yoghurt for the strawberries and strawberry yoghurt.

Banana Yoghurt Refresher

SERVES 2

Prepare as for Strawberry Yoghurt Refresher but substitute a large, mashed, ripe banana mixed with 5 ml/ 1 tsp lemon juice for the strawberries and a banana or vanilla yoghurt for the strawberry yoghurt.

Apricot Yoghurt Refresher

SERVES 2

300 g/11 oz/1 small can apricots in natural juice
150 ml/¼ pt/⅔ cup apricot yoghurt
Ice cubes

Finely chop the apricots and place in two glasses. Whisk the yoghurt with the apricot juice and pour over. Add ice cubes before serving.

Ginger Frappé

SERVES 2

300 ml/½ pt/1¼ cups ice-cold milk
150 ml/¼ pt/⅔ cup double (heavy) cream
60 ml/4 tbsp ginger wine
Crushed ice

Put the ingredients except the ice in a blender and run the machine until frothy. Pour over crushed ice and serve immediately.

Malted Honey Frappé

SERVES 2

30 ml/2 tbsp malted drink powder
30 ml/2 tbsp boiling water
150 ml/¼ pt/⅔ cup ice-cold milk
2 scoops vanilla ice cream
Whipped cream
Chopped nuts

Blend the malted drink powder with the water in a blender until smooth. Add the milk and ice cream and blend until thick and frothy. Pour into glasses and top with whipped cream and chopped nuts.

Index

Everyday Eating made more exciting

Foulsham books are available from all good bookshops; or you can telephone Macmillan Direct on 01256 329242 or order on our website www.foulsham.com